T0137817

IFIP Advances in Information and Communication Technology

672

Editor-in-Chief

Kai Rannenberg, Goethe University Frankfurt, Germany

Editorial Board Members

TC 1 – Foundations of Computer Science
   Luís Soares Barbosa⊚, University of Minho, Braga, Portugal

TC 2 – Software: Theory and Practice
   Michael Goedicke, University of Duisburg-Essen, Germany

TC 3 – Education
   Arthur Tatnall⊚, Victoria University, Melbourne, Australia

TC 5 – Information Technology Applications
   Erich J. Neuhold, University of Vienna, Austria

TC 6 – Communication Systems
   Burkhard Stiller, University of Zurich, Zürich, Switzerland

TC 7 – System Modeling and Optimization
   Lukasz Stettner, Institute of Mathematics, Polish Academy of Sciences, Warsaw, Poland

TC 8 – Information Systems
   Jan Pries-Heje, Roskilde University, Denmark

TC 9 – ICT and Society
   David Kreps⊚, National University of Ireland, Galway, Ireland

TC 10 – Computer Systems Technology
   Achim Rettberg, Hamm-Lippstadt University of Applied Sciences, Hamm, Germany

TC 11 – Security and Privacy Protection in Information Processing Systems
   Steven Furnell⊚, Plymouth University, UK

TC 12 – Artificial Intelligence
   Eunika Mercier-Laurent⊚, University of Reims Champagne-Ardenne, Reims, France

TC 13 – Human-Computer Interaction
   Marco Winckler⊚, University of Nice Sophia Antipolis, France

TC 14 – Entertainment Computing
   Rainer Malaka, University of Bremen, Germany

IFIP Advances in Information and Communication Technology

The IFIP AICT series publishes state-of-the-art results in the sciences and technologies of information and communication. The scope of the series includes: foundations of computer science; software theory and practice; education; computer applications in technology; communication systems; systems modeling and optimization; information systems; ICT and society; computer systems technology; security and protection in information processing systems; artificial intelligence; and human-computer interaction.

Edited volumes and proceedings of refereed international conferences in computer science and interdisciplinary fields are featured. These results often precede journal publication and represent the most current research.

The principal aim of the IFIP AICT series is to encourage education and the dissemination and exchange of information about all aspects of computing.

More information about this series at https://link.springer.com/bookseries/6102

Terje Gjøsæter · Jaziar Radianti ·
Yuko Murayama
Editors

Information Technology in Disaster Risk Reduction

7th IFIP WG 5.15 International Conference, ITDRR 2022
Kristiansand, Norway, October 12–14, 2022
Revised Selected Papers

 Springer

Editors
Terje Gjøsæter (iD)
University of Agder
Kristiansand, Norway

Jaziar Radianti (iD)
University of Agder
Kristiansand, Norway

Yuko Murayama (iD)
Tsuda University
Tokyo, Japan

ISSN 1868-4238 ISSN 1868-422X (electronic)
IFIP Advances in Information and Communication Technology
ISBN 978-3-031-34209-7 ISBN 978-3-031-34207-3 (eBook)
https://doi.org/10.1007/978-3-031-34207-3

This Springer imprint is published by the registered company Springer Nature Switzerland AG
The registered company address is: Gewerbestrasse 11, 6330 Cham, Switzerland

Preface

The role of information and communication technology (ICT) in disaster situations is becoming more important than ever in these recent years, especially to mitigate and reduce the risks associated with the effects of disasters. Disaster risk reduction (DRR) is the concept and practice of reducing disaster risks through systematic efforts to analyze and reduce the causal factors of disasters (UNESCO). DRR also has been laid out in the United Nations Sendai Framework for Disaster Risk Reduction 2015–2030, which aims to reduce human loss and affected people in a disaster globally, and to reduce direct economic loss and damage to critical infrastructure and disruption of basic services.

Information and communication technologies offer numerous capabilities that were unimaginable before. The Covid-19 pandemic is a case where society turned to ICT to ensure that mission critical operations required by citizens were sustained, and basic service disruptions could be avoided. Multiple countries should work rapidly together to employ every means to prevent new risks from emerging, to reduce on-going disaster risk, and to manage residual risk. Multi-disciplinary scholars have contributed various methods and empirical and theoretical studies on the role of ICT in disaster risk reduction. For example, they discuss the role of ICT in sustainable disaster management, enabling ICT to support community monitoring of hazard and vulnerability, and governance in a flood context, early warning, mobile alerts, and mobile apps in general, the use of geographical information systems (GIS) and Remote Sensing, and applying data integration and data science from the perspective of disaster risk reduction.

IT and ICT have also been studied as enablers to acquire critical information to achieve a common understanding and situational awareness among the various stakeholders involved in responding to the crisis, and to save lives and property. Modern information and communication technologies can significantly facilitate decision-making processes and thus help to reduce the consequences of disasters.

The Seventh IFIP WG5.15 Conference on Information Technology in Disaster Risk Reduction (ITDRR 2022), held during October 12–14, 2022, at the University of Agder, Kristiansand, Norway. Due to the risk of further outbreaks of the Covid-19 pandemic, ITDRR 2022 was held in hybrid format, with 45 participants: 34 on-site and 11 on-line.

The conference focused on ICT aspects of the challenges in disaster risk reduction. The main topics included areas such as: information analysis for situation awareness, evacuation, rescue, Covid-19 issues, risk assessment, and disaster management.

ITDRR 2022 invited experts, researchers, academicians, and all others who were interested in disseminating their work to attend the conference. The conference established an academic environment that fostered the discussion and exchange of ideas among different levels of academic, research, business, and public communities.

The Program Committee received 33 paper submissions, out of which 23 research papers were finally accepted. The papers have passed through a thorough single-blind review process. First each paper was assigned to three or four PC members through bidding, allowing them to review papers that were close to their main competence, expertise, and interests. Conflicts of interests were marked since the beginning to accommodate PC members that are also authors. Second, the reviewers provided scores and recommendations for acceptance or rejection. Third, the PC chairs reviewed all feedback from the reviewers, and discussed which decision to reach for any borderline papers.

These 7th IFIP WG 5.15 ITDRR proceedings comprise 23 articles, and 8 sections: Strategic disaster risk reduction; situational awareness; telecommunications, sensors, and drones; collaborative emergency management; cybersecurity and privacy; earthquake and climate forecasting; social media analytics; and community resilience.

Eden and Gonzalez's paper is a keynote speaker's article that addresses the challenges for understanding systemic risks in our complex, interconnected world. The authors suggest a novel approach and method for impactful risk assessment through a causal mapping technique that fulfills transparency and relevant requirements in relation to the experts and the power brokers, i.e., those who have power to act.

In the *situational awareness* section, *Polikarpus et al.* conduct a study on Effective Command and the dynamic decision-making assessment methodology as a theoretical framework for SA assessment and implementation of virtual reality software using sixteen different virtual simulations in an organization. *Bu Daher et al.* propose an ontology that enables the integration, data sharing to various involved actors, and updating of flood-related data in real time during a disaster. The authors underpin how the proposed approach improves both the information interoperability and evacuation priority judgement. *Ogbonna et al.* show the importance of universal design principles in designing rescue applications by emphasizing the presence of situational disabilities and accessibility barriers, based on a Nigerian flooding case. *França et al.* applied six awareness criteria to improve the so-called "Drones to Rescue" in a survey conducted among emergency management stakeholders. The authors also specify some suggestions when using drone operations to actually contribute to enhancing the situational awareness.

Under the *telecommunications, sensors, and drones* section, the authors provide examples of innovative technologies that can help to mitigate disasters. *Soshino's* paper discusses the application of fuel cell vehicles to support ICT in Emergency Response. Such a vehicle has embedded functions such as telecommunication and power supply functions and real-time image sharing, as well as the vehicle management applications that were tested. The author concludes that such a fuel cell vehicle is considered a practical solution to support ICT services in emergency management. *Basu et al.* addresses the Covid-19 Sāvdhān platform that exploited the telecom infrastructure to improve the pandemic management in India. This platform allows for SMS dissemination of pandemic-related messages to the geo-targeted population ranging from information about vaccination, quarantine facilities, testing centers, hotspots, lockdown, supplies, and the dynamic of the Covid 19-related regulations. *Fujita and Hatayama* develop an automated model to detect collapsed buildings that can be applied in earthquake scenarios using multiple object tracking (MOT) from aerial videos. The authors point out the failures in previous studies to detect collapsed buildings using the features of debris or damage in terms of discriminating the collapsed and standing buildings that have traditional Japanese features, and success-fully applied the deep learning MOT model. *Seböck et al.* report a study concerning the challenges and success factors for implementing a chemical, biological, radiological, and nuclear (CBRN) City Sensor Network. The project addresses the idea of deploy-ment of sensor networks to achieve early, automatic detection, identification, and protection against attacks with CBRN substances in public enclosed spaces.

Three articles are included under *the collaborative emergency management* section. *Pilemalm et al.* apply a user-centric approach in identifying and designing information systems support for collaborative emergency management, using Norway as a case. The study describes how it moves from needs to requirements to design proposals and covers core elements of the common operational picture needed for shared situational awareness and the artifacts produced through these processes. *Agray and Meesters'* main concern is the increased complexity of crises, requiring more diversity of the actors, which in turn can affect the quality and variety of information systems, pre-senting certain risks during a crisis response. A serious gaming research method highlights the increased cybersecurity risks associated with the use of information technologies during a crisis response and identifies the need for increased awareness, cultural change, and additional capacities to mitigate these risks. *Dokas et al.* discuss the interruption during the construction of the Risk and Resilience Assessment Centre project of Eastern Macedonia and Thrace, due to the plane crash of an Antonov An-12 in Kavala, Greece. This triggered the activation of the center to provide decision support expertise and led to a successful collaboration between researchers and stakeholders. *Ben Amara et al.* address a business continuity robustness assessment approach through sociological indicators. This research work aims to define the pillars of a BCM, propose a BCM robustness assessment grid, and introduce sociological indicators to assess the robustness of the BCM.

The *cybersecurity and privacy* section contains three articles. *Stassen et al.* focus on the dilemma between compliance and pressure, and through a serious game, examine human behavior to improve cybersecurity in natural disasters. The study identifies variables such as time, cognitive load, disruption, coordination, and trust that influence compliance rates. *Andreassen et al.* conduct a study aiming to develop an under-standing of the concept of situational awareness and its function in Managed Security Service Providers (MSSPs) cyber-incident response operations, and to illustrate best practices in security operations teams. The empirical findings are based on best prac-tices adopted by MSSPs operating in Norway. *Barrios et al.* address the privacy by design challenges in the CBRN (Chemical, Biological, Radiological, Nuclear) tech-nologies for preparedness and response, highlighting the management of vulnerable groups' data. The paper discusses issues related to accessibility and consent to enforce privacy rights, and also assesses the integration of privacy-by-design into the devel-oped platform called "Proactive".

Two of the ITDRR articles are about *earthquake and climate forecasting*. *Nasution et al.* suggest a novel approach to representing locations on the earth called Single Value Coordinate System (SVCS), which is applied for a forecasted earthquake to provide the magnitude, location, and time of the earthquake. *Munandar et al.* conduct data analytics concerning climate change using Principal Component Analysis compounded with a Vector Autoregressive Integrated (PC-VARI) model, using several locations in Indonesia as cases.

Two ITDRR papers discuss *social media analytics*. *Rokuse and Uchida* address the challenges of using social media in disasters due to the high volume of data. Machine learning can help classify and extract useful information from tweets, but building models in real time is difficult. Therefore, a model trained on tweets from past disasters was used to extract location mentions from tweets posted during heavy rain disasters in Japan in 2018, 2020, and 2021. Combining data from multiple disasters achieved the best performance, and the model may have achieved generalization performance. Further studies will examine how the model performs with different types of disasters.

Bono et al. raise a popular topic on the use of social media as a source of real-time information that can support crisis response during emergencies. The authors propose a machine-learning-based system that detects the onset of emergency events through the analysis of word mentions on social media which is language-agnostic and can be applied to any language.

Lastly, the ITDRR 2022 authors have contributed from different perspectives in the *community resilience* section. *Matsuno and Matsuura* demonstrate how the use of gamification and serious games using a simulation application can provide knowledge and experience to the users on living in an evacuation shelter. *Gil et al.* propose a strategic approach for food system resiliency from a community-based initiative during the Covid-19 pandemic, using a case study in Medellin, Colombia. The study also identifies change factors considered as a long-term capability to enhance food resilience and to overcome food insecurity. Finally, *Nguyen et al.* provide a comprehensive design of an inventory to gather and manage resilience-related information. Overall, a lot of interesting contributions were provided by ITDRR authors.

The volume editors would like to express their special gratitude to the members of the Program Committee, and to the many reviewers of the papers, for their dedication in helping produce this volume.

ITDRR 2022 selected the following papers for the Best Paper Award and the Best Student Paper Award, based on the review results:

- *The ITDRR 2022 Best Paper Award*: Yasuhiro Soshino, Application of the Fuel Cell Vehicle to Support ICT in Emergency Response
- *The ITDRR 2022 Best Student Paper Award*: Stella Polikarpus, Edna Milena Sarmiento-Márquez, and Tibias Ley, Creation and Use of Virtual Simulations for Measuring Situational Awareness of Incident Commanders

We hope that these awards encourage the awardees and future candidates in their research work and submissions to our future conferences.

March 2023

Jaziar Radianti
Terje Gjøsæter
Yuko Murayama

Organization

Honorary Chairs

Jose J. Gonzalez   University of Agder, Norway
Dimiter Velev   University of National and World Economy, Bulgaria

General Chair

Jaziar Radianti   University of Agder, Norway

Program Committee Chairs

Terje Gjøsæter   University of Agder, Norway
Jaziar Radianti   University of Agder, Norway
Yuko Murayama   Tsuda University, Japan

Publicity Chairs

Bjørn Erik Munkvold   University of Agder, Norway
Plamena Zlateva   Bulgarian Academy of Sciences, Bulgaria
Osamu Uchida   Tokai University, Japan
Benny B. Nasution   Politeknik Negeri Medan, Indonesia

Program Committee

Ahmed A. Aboughonim   University of Agder, Norway
Frederick Benaben   IMT Mines Albi, France
Marcos R. S. Borges   Universidade Federal do Rio de Janeiro, Brazil
Tadeusz Czachorski   Institute of Theoretical and Applied Informatics – PAS, Poland
Ioannis Dokas   Democritus University of Thrace, Greece
Julie Dugdale   Université Grenoble Alpes, France
Terje Gjøsæter   University of Agder, Norway
Igor Grebennik   Kharkiv National University of Radio Electronics, Ukraine
Tim A. Majchrzak   University of Agder, Norway
Rainer Malaka   University of Bremen, Germany
Kenny Meesters   Tilburg University, The Netherlands
Tilo Mentler   Trier University of Applied Sciences, Germany
Bjørn Erik Munkvold   University of Agder, Norway
Yuko Murayama   Tsuda University, Japan
Benny B. Nasution   Politeknik Negeri Medan, Indonesia

Erich Neuhold	University of Vienna, Austria
Sofie Pilemalm	Linköping University, Sweden, University of Agder, Norway
Jaziar Radianti	University of Agder, Norway
Mihoko Sakurai	International University of Japan, Japan
Jun Sasaki	Yamato University, Japan
Hans Jochen Scholl	University of Washington, USA
Walter Seböck	University for Continuing Education Krems, Austria
Devinder Thapa	University of Agder, Norway
A Min Tjoa	TU Wien, Austria
Denis Trcek	University of Ljubljana, Slovenia
Osamu Uchida	Tokai University, Japan
Keisuke Utsu	Tokai University, Japan
Dimiter Velev	University of National and World Economy, Bulgaria
Kayoko Yamamoto	University of Electro-Communications, Japan
Plamena Zlateva	Bulgarian Academy of Sciences, Bulgaria

Reviewer

| Robin Nolte | University of Bremen, Germany |

Local Organizing Committee

Charlotte Nilsen	University of Agder, Norway
Eirik Rustad	University of Agder, Norway
Lucia Castro Herrera	University of Agder, Norway
Sindisiwe Magutshwa	University of Agder, Norway

Contents

Strategic Disaster Risk Reduction

The Strategic Management of Disaster Risk Mitigation 3
  Colin Eden and Jose J. Gonzalez

Situational Awareness

Creation and Use of Virtual Simulations for Measuring Situation
Awareness of Incident Commanders 23
  Stella Polikarpus, Edna Milena Sarmiento-Márquez, and Tobias Ley

Enhancing Interoperability and Inferring Evacuation Priorities in Flood
Disaster Response 39
  Julie Bu Daher, Patricia Stolf, Nathalie Hernandez, and Tom Huygue

Situational Disabilities in Information Systems for Situational Awareness
in Flood Situations in Nigeria 55
  Uchenna Ogbonna, Cristina Paupini, and Terje Gjøsæter

Providing Situational Awareness to Emergency Responders Using Drones 69
  Juliana B. S. França, Jacimar F. Tavares, Angélica F. S. Dias,
  and Marcos R. S. Borges

Telecommunications, Sensors and Drones

Application of the Fuel Cell Vehicle to Support ICT in
Emergency Response 89
  Yasuhiro Soshino

COVID-19 Sāvdhān: Harnessing the Telecom Infrastructure for COVID-19
Management 101
  Saurabh Basu, Suvam Suvabrata Behera, Sandeep Sharma,
  Anugandula Naveen Kumar, Sumit Kumar Jha, Sabyasachi Majumdar,
  Niraj Kant Kushwaha, Arun Yadav, and Pankaj Kumar Dalela

Collapsed Building Detection Using Multiple Object Tracking from Aerial
Videos and Analysis of Effective Filming Techniques of Drones 118
  Shono Fujita and Michinori Hatayama

Challenges and Implementation of CBRN Sensor Networks in Urban Areas . . .   136
  Walter Seböck, Bettina Biron, and Bettina Pospisil

Collaborative Emergency Management

Developing Information Systems for Collaborative Emergency
Management: Requirements Analysis and Prototyping   153
  Sofie Pilemalm, Bjørn Erik Munkvold, and Jaziar Radianti

Shortcomings of Netcentric Operations During the COVID-19 Pandemic   170
  Abir Agray and Kenny Meesters

Work as Imagined vs Work as Done: The Case of an Under Development
Risk and Resilience Research Centre During the Antonov An-12 Crash
Emergency in Greece   185
  *Ioannis M. Dokas, Anastasia K. Paschalidou, Konstantinos Chouvardas,
  Ilias Petrou, Kyriaki Psistaki, Sofia Christoforou, Valkaniotis Sotiris,
  Panagiotis Argyrakis, Apostolos Zeleskidis, Stavroula Charalabidou,
  and Apostolos Vasileiou*

A Business Continuity Robustness Assessment Approach Through
Disruption's Sociological Indicators   197
  *Oussema Ben Amara, Daouda Kamissoko, Ygal Fijalkow,
  and Frederick Benaben*

Cybersecurity and Privacy

Cyber Security Policies in Crisis Response: Exploring the Predicament of
Creating Safe But Workable Systems   215
  Joshua Stassen, Ali Pirannejad, and Kenny Meesters

InCReASE: A Dynamic Framework Towards Enhancing Situational
Awareness in Cyber Incident Response   230
  *Jarl Andreassen, Martin Eileraas, Lucia Castro Herrera,
  and Nadia Saad Noori*

Privacy by Design in CBRN Technologies Targeted to Vulnerable Groups:
The Case of PROACTIVE   244
  *Mariano Martín Zamorano, Natasha Newton, Virginia Bertelli,
  and Laura Petersen*

Earthquake and Climate Forecasting

Transformation of an Esvecees (SVCS) Value to Spherical Coordinates as
the Result of the Earthquake Forecasting Using SLHGN 261
*Benny Benyamin Nasution, Abdul Rahman, M. Rikwan E. S. Manik,
Rina Anugrahwaty, Liwat Tarigan, Rahmat Widia Sembiring,
Indra Siregar, Ermyna Seri, Rina Walmiaty Mardi, Indri Dithisari,
and Marliana Sari*

Data Analytics of Climate Using the PCA-VARI Model Case Study in West
Java, Indonesia. 276
*Devi Munandar, Putri Monika, Ajeng Berliana Salsabila, Afrida Helen,
Atje Setiawan Abdullah, and Budi Nurani Ruchjana*

Social Media Analytics

Location Mention Recognition from Japanese Disaster-Related Tweets 293
Toshihiro Rokuse and Osamu Uchida

Learning Early Detection of Emergencies from Word Usage Patterns
on Social Media. 308
Carlo A. Bono, Mehmet Oğuz Mülâyim, and Barbara Pernici

Community Resilience

Development and Evaluation of a Shelter Simulator Using Gamification 327
Yutaka Matsuno and Mei Matsuura

Strategic Approach to Food System Resiliency from Community-Based
Initiatives During the Covid-19 Pandemic 341
*Juan Camilo Sánchez Gil, Martha Alicia Cadavid Castro,
Luis Alirio López Giraldo, and Guillermo León Moreno Soto*

Web-Based Tool to Facilitate Resilience-Related Information Management. . . . 358
*Hoang Long Nguyen, Salvatore Antonio Marchese, Valentino Gandolfo,
Leonardo Luca Trombetta, Massimo Cristaldi, Uberto Delprato,
and Rajendra Akerkar*

Author Index 375

Strategic Disaster Risk Reduction

The Strategic Management of Disaster Risk Mitigation

Colin Eden[1] and Jose J. Gonzalez[2]([✉])

[1] Strathclyde Business School, United Kingdomand, and Stepchange AS, Glasgow, Norway
`colin.eden@strath.ac.uk`
[2] Centre for Integrated Emergency Management (CIEM), Department for ICT, University of
Agder, and Stepchange AS, Kristiansand, Norway
`josejg@uia.no`

Abstract. Systemic risks are embedded in the complex networks of an increasingly interconnected world. Achieving the Sendai Framework for Disaster Risk Reduction, the Paris Agreement on Climate Change 2015 and the 2030 Agenda for Sustainable Development require that risk mitigation involves not only experts but 'power-brokers' – those with the power to act. Impactful risk assessment and mitigation development requires high levels of ownership of the assessment and mitigation strategies, and so needs to be done fast and involve relatively small amounts of the power-brokers time. This requirement means that the analysis of the risk system will need to be transparent and relevant. We describe a method employing causal mapping with experts and power-brokers stakeholders. These stakeholders interactively undertake a qualitative systemic risk assessment and subsequently develop and agree strategies for risk mitigation explicitly considering (i) the direct purpose of mitigation (the other risks that are likely to be at least partly mitigated – the risks that are directly linked from the mitigated risk), and also (ii) the negative goals that will be mitigated.

Keywords: Systemic risk · Risk systemicity · Risk interdependencies ·
Cascading effects · Risk mitigation · Disaster risk reduction strategies · Sendai
Framework

1 Introduction

1.1 Interconnections Create Systemic Risk

"Systemic risk – risk that is endogenous to, or embedded in, a system that is not itself considered to be a risk and is therefore not generally tracked or managed, but which is understood through systems analysis to have a latent or cumulative risk potential to negatively impact overall system performance when some characteristics of the system change" [1, p. 45]. In particular we note the familiar adage about systems thinking: that the whole is greater than the sum of the parts.

T. Gjøsæter et al. (Eds.): ITDRR 2022, IFIP AICT 672, pp. 3–19, 2023.
https://doi.org/10.1007/978-3-031-34207-3_1

Systemic risk has been explicitly recognised since the 1990's in project risk management [2] and in the context of financial risk [3]. Systemic risk became a hot topic for disaster risk reduction with the Sendai Framework for Disaster Risk Reduction 2015-2030 [4]. While the term "systemic risk" does not appear explicitly in this document intended for politicians, the systemic nature of risks affecting humankind is revealed by numerous wordings in the Sendai Framework. E.g. "underlying disaster risk drivers, such as the consequences of poverty and inequality, climate change and variability, unplanned and rapid urbanization, poor land management and compounding factors such as demographic change, weak institutional arrangements, non-risk-informed policies, lack of regulation and incentives for private disaster risk reduction investment, complex supply chains, limited availability of technology, unsustainable uses of natural resources, declining ecosystems, pandemics and epidemics." [4, §6].

Following the Sendai Framework, the United Nations Office for Disaster Risk Reduction explicated the Sendai Framework thoroughly in terms of systemic risk in its Global Assessment Report on Disaster Risk Reduction (GAR2019) 2019 [1]. (The concept of systemic risk appears 141 times in GAR2019.) The centrality of systemic risk for the Sendai Framework is summarised this way: "The Sendai Framework stipulates that the global community must come to terms with a new understanding of the dynamic nature of systemic risks, new structures to govern risk in complex, adaptive systems and develop new tools for risk-informed decision-making that allows human societies to live in and with uncertainty" [1, p. 36]. The critical importance of systemic risk is characterised by "understanding the systemic nature of risks, and the opportunities afforded by new approaches and new concepts of risk, will be the central challenge of the first half of the twenty-first century" [1, p. 65–66].

Risk in complex societal challenges, and major projects, is systemic. Interconnections create a system of associated risks and outcomes, where the outcomes of risks are risks themselves. Risks are a system where a single risk can cause a plethora of other risks, and, in particular, cause vicious cycles of risks.

The notion of systemic risk is central for disaster risk reduction. There are linkages across three major international agreements, viz. The Sendai Framework Disaster Risk Reduction, the Paris Agreement on Climate Change 2015 and the 2030 Agenda for Sustainable Development. The three agreements recognize that risks increasingly have interdependencies that are responsible for cascading effects within sectors and across multiple sectors, in some cases with global impact [5]. Risk interdependencies imply that risks are causally connected. The systemic risks "are embedded in the complex networks of an increasingly interconnected world. The behaviour of these networks defines quality of life and will shape the dynamic interactions among the Sendai Framework, the 2030 Agenda, the Paris Agreement, New Urban Agenda, and the Agenda for Humanity. Ultimately, the behaviour of these networks determines exposure and vulnerability at all scales." [1, p. 36].

The Guidelines for the Governance of Systemic Risk from the International Risk Governance Center [6] define systemic risk as threats that individual failures, accidents, or disruptions present to a system through the process of "contagion" (i.e., active risks causally affecting and activating other risks). As prominent examples of such threats, the guidelines mention the desertification and collapse of the Aral area, the 2008 financial crisis, fish stocks depletions, pandemics, cyber-security, and global climate change.

Those in the project management field have highlighted the importance of taking account of the ramifications through such a chain of risks, where a single risk can have a greater impact beyond the immediate impacts of a risk [2, 7]. Notably disruption and delay in major projects are consequences of systemic risk [8].

Risk is "a phenomenon that has the potential to deliver substantial harm, whether or not the probability of this harm eventuating is estimable." [9]. But then "harm" is in the eye of the beholder.

In this paper we present two types of risk system: a simple hierarchical system and a potentially much more complex feedback system. The feedback system is more common for societal situations. We consider the properties of these systems and how these properties help in focusing attention when looking to design risk mitigation. We argue that if mitigation is to be successful then it is crucial to not only involve experts but also 'power-brokers' – those with the power to act. In addition, we suggest that this requirement means that risk assessment and mitigation development will need to be done in a manner that provides high levels of ownership of the assessment and mitigation strategies, and so needs to be done fast and involve relatively small amounts of the power-brokers time. This requirement means that the analysis of the risk system will need to be transparent and relevant.

2 Hierarchical Risk Systems

2.1 Hierarchical Risk: An Example

In relatively simple risk systems, the causal interactions create a simple hierarchical system where risks cascade to risk outcomes that are increasingly influenced by several other risks. As the risk cascade unfolds the risks tend to become of greater strategic significance until outcomes are risks to established goals.

Figure 1 shows an example of a personal risk system that maps out potential disaster. It shows a hierarchical risk system related to the purchase of a new sailing yacht by one of the authors. The reason for using this example is that it is simple and yet demonstrates the key aspects of a hierarchical risk system. The system of risks was created to facilitate thinking about how to resolve the 'potential personal disaster' and is the result of a quick 'dump' of risks as they were thought about. The reference numbers show the order in which they were noted. No formalisms were used in creating the risk system, rather the statements in the system derived from thinking "I am risking a disaster because...".

Exploring some of the characteristics of this simple hierarchical risk system (represented by Fig. 1) we note that:

1. Some of nodes in the hierarchy are not obvious risks – but cause risks – they are explanations (e.g., #17 'requirements to be present...'). They need to be explicated because they can be points of possible mitigation actions.

   "It is imperative that our understanding of risk is developed without resorting to reductive measures that isolate and remove from context and ignore systemic charac-teristics. This applies as much to our institutional arrangements for risk governance

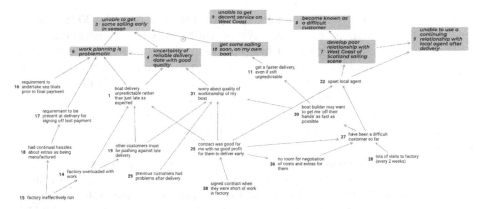

Fig. 1. Hierarchical risk illustrated with a potential personal disaster. Each arrow represents a belief about causality, where A→B implies that A is believed to cause B.

as it does to community organization, research endeavours or policy formulation." [1, p. v]. Context is important.

2. Some risks may be particularly significant because they impact more final risk outcomes (e.g., #25 'contract was good for me…' impacts all outcomes: #3, #9, and #5). The number of final outcomes that a risk impact may indicate an appropriate place to focus mitigation.

3. Adding explanations for risks is often useful and provides useful context and, within the network of risks, may be significant drivers. "However, failure or even intentional ignorance *to capture the role of underlying drivers of systemic risk* will allow small risks to grow into major problems, increasing the opportunity costs of failed interventions and missed opportunities." (Our emphasis) [1, p. 71].

4. Some risks identified are *historical risks* (e.g., #28 'lots of visits…', #29 'previous customers had problems…', #38 'signed contract when they were short of work…'). Traditional risk assessment would likely exclude such risks because although they offer some explanatory content, they are irrelevant since nothing can be done about them. However, although history cannot be changed the impact of that history may be changed, and so mitigation of impact may be possible.

5. The order in which risks are surfaced (#1 'boat delivery unpredictable…' came first) may provide a clue to the most worrying risk. Mitigation of these risks may be a priority for relieving anxiety.

2.2 Implications of Hierarchical Risk SYSTEM for Risk Assessment

A risk assessment that recognises systemicity can usefully show historical impacts where the causality (impact) may be mitigated.

Explanations of causality, including the role of history, are a natural part of explicating a risk system. They provide important context, but more importantly, although not risks, they may be identified as potential intervention points that promote the mitigation of consequential risk.

2.3 The Significance of a 'Negative Goals System'

Inevitably when mapping out risks the final outcomes in a hierarchical system will be expressed as risks – as disastrous outcomes. Negative goals are expressed as such through natural speech. The statements being classified as a goal can be problematic but is based on the notion that the outcome is unquestionably a disaster that must be avoided at all costs, and thus if expressed positively then it would be an unquestioned desired outcome. Given that risk assessment is undertaken in order to develop effective mitigation strategies, then the final outcomes will be outcomes that matter to the organisation – expressions of the goals of the organisation, or more properly expressions of the 'negative goals'. "Goals are aspirational, that is to say they are not statements about what an organisation is but rather what it wants to become" [10, p. 11]. A negative goal is an aspiration to avoid and thus are not simply the final outcomes in a hierarchy. For negative goals the contrasting circumstance would not be expressed as a goal, but the outcome (disaster) itself is of the same status as a goal and must be avoided. (Op. Cit., p. 13.)

In Fig. 1 the negative goals are shown with a grey background (with the exception of the positively expressed goal #10) and represent a *network* of mostly negative goals (as in Fig. 2) – risks that are bad outcomes in their own right and that must be avoided.

A risk register is a document commonly used as a risk management tool. It is a repository for all risks identified and includes additional information about each risk. Risk registers focus on the probability of an event occurring multiplied by the consequence of that event [11]. The idea that the extent of a risk probability multiplied by impact assumes that risk invariably behaves in a linear intuitive fashion and yet, as we will see below, risk can multiply exponentially [12]. A significant danger of risk registers is that "Disaggregation means that there is a danger of inter-related risks like the aforementioned being seen in isolation and 'ticked off' one by one" [13], in other words, the interaction between risks is not acknowledged.

Risk registers often miss the significance of understanding and reaching agreement about why risks matter. Without being explicit and clear about negative goals any analysis of the risk system cannot focus attention on what matters.

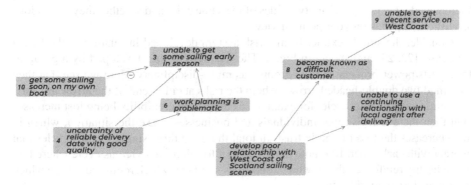

Fig. 2. A negative goals system: a network of interacting goals (Note #10 is a positive goal)

When managers are asked what their goals are then they are typically unlikely to talk about the way in which their behaviour is framed by the avoidance of negative outcomes rather instead they are more likely to believe it is appropriate to focus on positive outcomes. Much management literature argues that "problems are to be formulated against an idealised conception of where the organisation wants to be" [14–17]. And yet, to focus on avoiding disastrous outcomes is a perfectly legitimate activity and one that reflects the reality of organisational life [10], let alone when addressing disasters. Thus, rather than supposing that goals should not only be known but also should be positive, it is appropriate to encourage a legitimacy for expressing negative goals.

2.4 Implications of Acknowledging Negative Goals as a System

Develop an understanding about how many negative goals impact each other, by exploring the negative goals as a system in its own right.

Consider the benefits from mitigation not just in terms of final outcomes but also with respect to other negative goals that are a part of the goals system.

3 Feedback Risk Systems

More complex disaster risk reduction situations typically show as a more complex risk system where the system contains feedback loops [as also noted by, for example, 18, 19]: usually vicious cycles but with some occurrence of virtuous cycles and controlling cycles. Feedback loops show dynamic behaviour – change over time, with for example, vicious cycles showing a situation getting worse over time. Archetypes of feedback are powerfully illustrated in [20], however in risk systems the specifics of the situation matter, and archetypes can be unhelpful. Feedback though is fundamental to understanding social systems [21].

3.1 Vicious/Virtuous and Controlling Feedback Loops

Vicious and virtuous cycles are two sides of the same coin, and whether they are vicious or virtuous depends on your point of view.

Consider the simple extract from a risk system developed in relation to the Covid pandemic [22, 23] and shown in Fig. 3. The risk system was developed by a group of 16 experts/power-brokers and the group was multi-disciplinary. Here we see that they identified two double-headed arrows where the risks at either end of the arrow are parts of a reinforcing vicious cycle: for example, as the risk of credibility being lost increases then then there is a risk that individuals and businesses abuse the situation, which in turn increases the loss of public trust. In total there are three single vicious cycles that interact with each other. But, note there is also a fourth nested vicious cycle where loss of credibility reinforces abuse, which reinforces shortage, which reinforces abuse which reinforces loss of credibility.

Paying attention to nested feedback loops is important because their consideration can pinpoint a key focus for mitigation – in the case above it increases the significance of the chaotic situation.

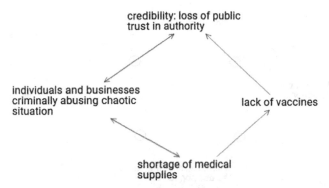

Fig. 3. An example of reinforcing feedback – showing three single vicious cycles (loss of trust causes criminality, and criminality causes loss of trust; shortage causes criminality, and criminality causes shortage; loss of trust causes criminality, criminality causes shortage, shortage causes lack of vaccines, lack of vaccines causes loss of trust) and one nested vicious cycle (loss of trust causes criminality and criminality causes shortage which reinforces criminality which reinforces loss of trust).

However, we also note that from a public 'common good' perspective these are labelled as vicious cycles, but from the perspective of a criminal they are virtuous cycles – they would prefer the situation to become more chaotic.

Within any risk system there will be some 'controlling' (or 'balancing') feedback loops. In this risk situation the risks tend to reduce over time and move to some equilibrium. Figure 4 shows another extract from the Covid pandemic risk model, where increased infection rates caused by non-socially distanced infected interactions increases fear among the population and so reduces the risk of the population breaking quarantine rules. Often balancing loops are unstable, as might be the case in this example. Gradually infection rates drop to a level where fear is no longer of significance, and so the population returns to breaking quarantine rules.

Figures 3 and 4 are, as we stated, extracts from a larger system and in most risk systems there are many vicious cycles and few controlling feedback loops, and they all interact with each other making the risky situation particularly complex. In our Covid model we faced over 5 million feedback loops! Loops originate when causal links form a closed cycle. There is a large number of feedback loops in the Covid risk model because of the high number of causal interconnections among the high number of risks (owing to combinatorial complexity). It is notable that without the availability of powerful software (*Strategyfinder*™) it would not be possible to identify the feedback loops or the risks that are most potent drivers of the feedback loops.

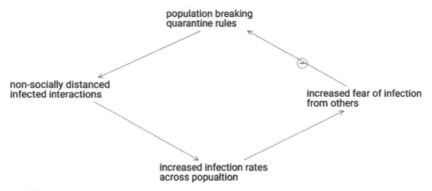

Fig. 4. An example of a controlling or balancing feedback loop, where the minus sign on an arrow represents an increased fear of infection from others decreases the population breaking quarantine rules.

3.2   Feedback from 'Negative Goals'

In discussing hierarchical risk systems we have also suggested that a negative goals system is also hierarchical. However, of course, in complex systems there is also a possibility of feedback that encompasses a negative goal. Figure 5 shows an extract from the Covid risk system where a negative goal related to mental health is a part of a feedback loop and prompts another loop (double-headed).

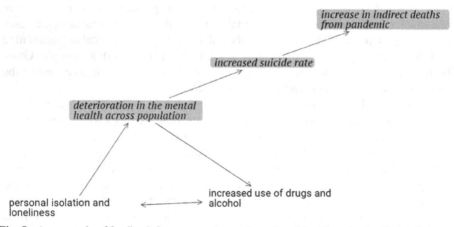

Fig. 5. An example of feedback from a negative goal to other risks. Here the double headed arrow shows a vicious cycle (feedback): increased use of drugs causes personal isolation, and personal isolation causes an increased use of drugs.

3.3 Implications of Acknowledging Feedback

The interactions between risks set up chains of risks, where the resulting consequences can be complex. The interactions between risks, chains of risks, can become self-reinforcing cycles of escalating risks: vicious cycles.

4 Implementing Mitigation – the 'Big Challenge'

4.1 Disaster Risk Reduction Depends upon Power-Brokers

We noted in the introduction that if mitigation is to be successful then it is crucial to not only involve experts but also 'power-brokers' – those with the power to act. A good assessment of the risks and analysis of the risk system is of no use if risk mitigation does not follow. Disaster risk reduction depends upon the people with power, usually across multiple organisations, need to have ownership of the risk mitigation strategies. This requirement means that risk assessment and mitigation development will need to be done in a manner that provides high levels of ownership of both the risk assessment (construction of the risk system network) and development of mitigation strategies. Without such involvement there is a danger that those with the power to act (or ability to influence those with the power) will not believe in the basis for action.

For the development of a reliable map of the risk system we need the involvement of an inter-disciplinary group of 'experts', and yet we also need the involvement of power-brokers/influencers. There is always a trade-off between getting the right participants to add expertise and knowledge and getting those who need strong ownership of the agreed outcomes. Those who need ownership and commitment to the outcomes will be those with the power to act. It is possible that there will be participants in both categories who are not stakeholders – they have no personal stake in the problem or its solutions. Experts might be there simply because they know things that are useful. Powerful players might be there because they can be persuaded to become stakeholders and care about the problem and its solutions.

Getting the right mix of expertise is difficult because often it will only be possible to know what the right expertise is after you have the beginnings of a disaster 'definition' emerging from the first part of developing the risk system.

4.2 Implications of the 'BIG Challenge'

'Fast and furious' risk assessment (construction of the risk system) and development of effective strategies is crucial to ownership and so implementation. Both experts and power-brokers must be involved.

The ability to construct the risk system quickly and directly with the group (whether they be together in the same location or located in their workplace/home) is likely to increase the speed of working. Similarly, the ability to visualise the risk system as a causal map speeds up an appreciation of the nature of the risky situation. Visualisation makes developing strategies that appreciate the systemic nature of the risky situation easier and faster.

5   Analysis of Risk Systems

"The complexity that underlies systemic risk may be sufficiently intricate that quantification and prediction of risk is not easy." [1, p. 43]. Taking account of the dependencies between risks can significantly change the prioritisation of risk factors, as compared to the traditional risk register [24].

Risk registers focus on the probability of an event occurring multiplied by the consequence of that event [11]. Thus, when analysing a risk system, it would make sense to also consider both probability and impact. However, recognising that risks interact systemically must play an important part in risk analysis [25–27].

In a risk system assessing probability and impact is extremely problematic. Probability can be (i) the probability the risk occurs, and/or (ii) the probability that the risk impacts another stated risk: a Bayesian judgement – the probability that if risk occurs then the consequential risk occurs. This issue reflects the issues identified by Ackoff and Emery [28, p. 82–88] where they differentiate strength of belief from intensity of belief and degree of doubt. When asking experts (or managers) for their judgment about probability and impact in a network of causal beliefs we cannot be certain as to what 'definitions' are being used, let alone know how to analytically compute their implications. There is, therefore, a danger that "by reducing risk to a set of numbers, the system of notation can impart an appearance of scientific precision where none exists" [13].

Even if there was clarity about what impact and probability mean in a network, and that clarity could be consistently applied, gathering judgements about impact for an entire network of risks is both time-consuming and laborious [29]. Some authors have argued for a process which begins with assessing the probability and impact of all the individual risks, often using a linguistic scale [see, for example, 30, 31], then immediate dependencies between risks [32]. The strength of these dependencies is also judged using linguistic terms [24, 30, 33]. In a corporate environment we have found that such a process could be undertaken only if completed in under 45 min, beyond this time limit the judgements are hurried and sloppy [8].

Given the need for 'fast and furious' work the analysis must, preferably, be capable of being undertaken with a group in real time. In the first stages of gaining ownership, there needs to be useful ways of analysing a qualitative network of risks. Any such analyses must be transparent and easily understood by those expected to decide on mitigation strategies. Faster and transparent processes involving qualitative modelling lead to a higher probability of engagement and ownership of the risk system developed.

Once ownership has been developed and tentative commitments to strategies for mitigation then there is an opportunity to offer further quantitative exploration of proposed strategies. System dynamics simulation models, such as [34, 35], are an obvious approach for quantitative exploration because they are designed as feedback systems [36, 37] and so the model will be constructed using the qualitative model as the basic structure for the model. The processes of engaging the group involved in developing the qualitative model for estimating parameters used in the simulation model typically forces the group to extend and question their causal assumptions, and this process leads to the refining of strategies agreed during the qualitative strategy development stage using the risk system causal model [38].

5.1 Centrality

Perhaps the easiest measure of significance of a risk, and one that is easily understood, is that of computing the centrality of a risk within the network. However, there are several measures that can be used. The simplest and most easily understood is to consider the number of immediate links into and out of each risk, known as the 'passivity and activity degree' or 'degree centrality' of a risk [39, 40]. This measure considers only the local setting of a risk in the network. Measures that take a greater account of the wider context are closeness and betweenness analyses that derive from social network analysis. Yan and Ding [41] and Lu, et al. [42] provide an interesting exposition on centrality measures. These centralities assist in identifying the 'hubs' in the network that play a role as key passages for risk propagation. Betweenness centrality is a measure of how often a node is a bridge between other nodes. Nodes with high betweenness centrality are often important controllers of power or information. Score increases with the number of shortest paths from each statement to any other statement passing through the statement of interest. The measure identifies that risk that if deleted through effective mitigation *would change the risk situation significantly.* Closeness centrality measures the average distance to the other nodes in the network. A statement with high score has shortest distance to all other statements. Other than 'passivity and activity degree' (counting ins/outs to a risk) these measures are relatively opaque to a group of managers.

5.2 Hierarchical Potency

Consider again the hierarchical risk system in Fig. 1. When a group is asked to identify where they should initially consider mitigation, they do not find it difficult to understand that mitigating some risks is more useful than others, i.e., that some risks impact more 'negative goals' than others. In Fig. 1 risk #25 (a historical statement) impacts every negative goal – it is highly potent. Thus, even though it is a statement about a past action, which has now become a risk, it will be worth considering whether its impact can be changed (the arrows out) by, for example, changing perceptions.

Those risks that impact the maximum number of negative goals are primary candidates for mitigation and may provide the highest level of robustness [43]. Needless to say, they are only candidates and sound judgment may override these suggestions.

5.3 Feedback Potency

As we have noted, feedback loops are crucial to risk mitigation. Mitigating the dynamics derived from a vicious cycle will be more important than hierarchical potency simply because it unfolds over time. When vicious cycles interact with one another they will produce a complex dynamic. Thus, finding which risk, if mitigated, would close down the most vicious cycles is a crucial demand on analysis. Consider the nested vicious cycles shown in Fig. 6 (another extract from the Covid risk system [22, 23]): there are 12 vicious cycles (5 of which nested). Risks #147 (distrust of vaccination) and #26 (credibility) are in 11 of the 12 vicious cycles and so mitigation of either of these risks would close down the most vicious cycles. Mitigating both risks closes down all vicious cycles.

Thus, unless sound judgement suggests otherwise, then focusing attention developing strategies to mitigate the risks would be appropriate.

Similarly, analysis also reveals that if a strategy could be developed that destroys the causal link from #147 (distrust) to #26 (credibility) then this would have the greatest impact on the risk system shown in Fig. 6.

Risk #147 and #26 are in 11 loops (and in all the five nested loops) and so are most potent. The link from 147 > 26 is the potent link.

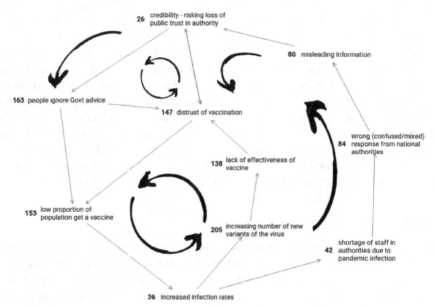

Fig. 6. Extract from the Covid risk system showing five of the twelve vicious cycles. Examples of those not shown are long loop paths such as: 26 > 163 > 153.36 > 205 > 138 > 147 > 26 and 26 > 147 > 153 > 36 > 42 > 84 > 80 > 26.

5.4   Implications of Acknowledging the Issues in the Analysis of a Risk System

Use analyses that most easily understood by those who (i) need to understand the properties of the risk system, and (ii) have the power to mitigate.

Potency analysis, and particularly the potency of both risks and causal links in a feedback system, focuses attention on those risks that are likely to have the greatest impact on disaster reduction.

6 Mitigation and Implementation

We have shown that identifying centrality, potency of risks and potency of causal links can provide a basis for effective strategy development. In managing a risk system there is a danger in not recognising that most organisations (and multi-organisations) never have enough resources to combat all risks. Thus, the development of mitigation strategies must focus initially on those that can most significantly reduce the potential for disaster – the most potent risks. Risks and causal links that are a focus for strategy development need to not only be impactful and potentially mitigate the risk, but also practical.

The two dimensions of impact and practicality will need to be evaluated for the portfolio of proposed strategies. Those strategies that are both impactful and practical will be the most likely strategies to be agreed. However, within a group there will often be disagreement – a lack of consensus – and this disagreement will often be the basis of fruitful discussion that leads to refinement of the strategy through a sort of Delphi process [44, 45]. Sometimes some strategies are seen as highly impactful but not practical, and this leads the group to consider ways in which the strategy can become more practical. Similarly, highly practical mitigation strategies may be refined so that they become more impactful.

Shortage of Health Care Workers in Hospitals

Agreed Strategies, their Purpose, and Implementation Teams

Establish high-level infection protection (PPE) for healthcare and emergency workers
In order to: Directly avoid shortage of Health Care Workers in Hospitals, and Control local outbreaks in hospitals, and so avoid having exhausted health care workers and so reduce possibility of low productivity of working health care staff because o shortage of staff
Implementation Team: Chief physician at short-term nursing home, Hospital contingency planner

Priority of vaccination for health care workers
In order to: Directly avoid shortage of Health Care Workers in Hospitals, and Avoid local outbreaks of virus in nursing homes, and in hospitals Avoid delays in ordinary medical education
Implementation Team: Crisis manager Kristiansand Municipality, Physician specialist in public health

Fig. 7. An extract from an agreed strategy document: a part of strategy agreements for managing the negative goal of 'shortage of healthcare workers'.

We argued earlier that one important benefit of disaster reduction through considering systemic risk is that the risk system makes explicit the purpose of risk mitigation – the causal links out from a risk. This means that when moving from strategy development to implementation there is clarity about (i) the direct purpose of mitigation (the other risks that are likely to be at least partly mitigated – the risks that are directly linked from the mitigated risk), and also (ii) the negative goals that will be mitigated.

Implementation depends on someone (power-broker) taking responsibility for ensuring the strategy is implemented. This person may not act but will be responsible for ensuring action is taken.

Thus, implementation that is effective becomes more likely because purpose is clear and also because responsibility for implementation is clear. Figure 7 shows an extract from the Covid risk system work [22]. The extract shows how the risk system map converts to a 'normal' document that shows strategy, purpose, responsibility.

7 Conclusions

In this paper an approach to systemic risk mitigation is proposed involving not only experts but 'power-brokers' – those with the power to act. Impactful risk assessment and mitigation development requires high levels of ownership of the assessment and mitigation strategies, and so needs to be done fast and involve relatively small amounts of the power-brokers time. This requirement means that the analysis of the risk system will need to be transparent and relevant. There is ample additional evidence from model building with stakeholders (Group Model Building [46, 47]) that working with groups directly facilitates team learning [48] and organizational intervention [49], and that it affects the stakeholders attitudes and behaviours [50].

Taking a holistic view of the impact of risks and the interdependencies between risks across different disciplines highlights the need for trans-disciplinary approach to risk assessment and developing risk mitigation strategies [8, p. 49–50].

In order to meet most of the implications identified in this paper the use of specially design software can be particularly helpful. The software needs to be capable of:

- Quickly pulling together the expertise of a range of experts and power-brokers.
- Showing the expertise about risks and causality as a causal map.
- Visualising the risk system as a 'transitional object' and 'boundary object' [51–54, 55, 56] so that the 'whole can be more than the sum of the parts', where the interaction of expertise creates new insights.
- Analysis of the risk system can be undertaken in real-time directly with the group, and the analysis must be transparent.
- Permitting group members to work together from their own locations and so construct the risk system and develop effective strategies with all able to both contribute and see the developing map.
- Enabling group members to make judgements about both impact and practicality of potential strategies, and so develop agreements with a reasonable degree of consensus.

Our approach to meeting this requirement has been to encourage and advise on the development of such a software platform: *Strategyfinder*™. The platform manages all of the requirements above and works through a browser, rather than requiring any download of software to the local computer (most organisations are extremely hesitant to allow downloads).

References

1. United Nations Office for Disaster Risk Reduction (UNDRR): Global Assessment Report on Disaster Risk Reduction (Fifth Edition). United Nations (2019)

2. Williams, T.M., Ackermann, F., Eden, C.: Project Risk: systemicity, cause mapping and a scenario approach. In: Kahkonen, K., Artto, K.A. (Eds.), Managing Risks in Projects, pp. 343–352. E&FN Spon, London (1997)
3. Schwarz, S.L.: Systemic risk. Georgetown Law J. **97**, 193–249 (2008)
4. UN world conference on disaster risk reduction: Sendai Framework for Disaster Risk Reduction 2015-2030 (2015). http://www.wcdrr.org/uploads/Sendai_Framework_for_Dis aster_Risk_Reduction_2015-2030.pdf. Accessed 25 July 2022
5. Handmer, J., Stevance, A.-S., Rickards, L., Nalau, J.: Policy brief: achieving risk reduction across Sendai, Paris and the SDGs (2019). https://council.science/wp-content/uploads/ 2019/05/ISC_Achieving-Risk-Reduction-Across-Sendai-Paris-and-the-SDGs_May-2019. pdf. Accessed 20 July 2022
6. International Risk Governance Center (IRGC): Guidelines for the Governance of Systemic Risks. International Risk Governance Center (IRGC), Lausanne (2018). https://doi.org/10. 5075/epfl-irgc-257279
7. Williams, T.: The Nature of risk in complex projects. Proj. Manag. J. **48**, 55–66 (2017)
8. Ackermann, F., Eden, C., Williams, T., Howick, S.: Systemic risk assessment: a case study. J. Oper. Res. Soc. **58**, 39–51 (2007)
9. Lupton, D.: Risk, 2nd edn. Routledge, London (2013)
10. Eden, C., Ackermann, F.: Problem structuring: on the nature of, and reaching agreement about, goals. EURO J. Decis. Process. **1**, 7–28 (2013)
11. Adams, J.: Risk. Routledge, London (1995)
12. Masuch, M.: Vicious Circles in Organizations. Adm. Sci. Q. **30**, 14–33 (1985)
13. Drummond, H.: MIS and illusions of control: an analysis of the risks of risk management. J. Inf. Technol. **26**, 263 (2011)
14. Kepner, C.H., Tregoe, B.B.: The Rational Manager: A Systematic Approach to Problem Solving and Decision Making. McGraw Hill, New York (1965)
15. Ackoff, R.L.: Redesigning the Future: A Systems Approach to Societal Problems. Wiley, New York (1974)
16. Ozbekhan, H.: Thoughts on the emerging methodology of planning. Fields within Fields **10**(Winter), 63–80 (1974)
17. Checkland, P.: Systems Thinking. Systems Practice. Wiley, Chichester (1981)
18. Cavallo, A., Ireland, V.: Preparing for complex interdependent risks: a system of systems approach to building disaster resilience. Int. J. Disaster Risk Reduction **9**, 181–193 (2014)
19. Bloomfield, K., Williams, T., Bovis, C., Merali, Y.: Systemic risk in major public contracts. Int. J. Forecast. **35**, 667–676 (2019)
20. Senge, P.M.: The Fifth Discipline: The Art and Practice of The Learning Organization. Doubleday, New York (1990)
21. Richardson, G.: Feedback Thought in Social Science and Systems Theory. University of Pennsylvania Press, Philadelphia (1991)
22. Gonzalez, J.J., et al.: Elicitation, analysis and mitigation of systemic pandemic risks. In: Adrot, A, Grace, R., Moore, K., Zobel, C.W. (Eds.) 18th International Conference on Information Systems for Crisis Response and Management. Blacksburg, ISCRAM, Virginia, pp. 581–596 (2021)
23. Gonzalez, J.J., Eden, C.: Insights from the COVID-19 pandemic for systemic risk assessment and management. In: Sasaki, J., Murayama, Y., Velev, D., Zlateva, P. (eds.) ITDRR 2021. IAICT, vol. 638, pp. 121–138. Springer, Cham (2022). https://doi.org/10.1007/978-3-031-04170-9_9
24. Jamshidi, A., Ait-kadi, D., Ruiz, A., Rebaiaia, M.L.: Dynamics risk assessment of complex systems using FCM. Int. J. Prod. Res. **56**, 1070–1088 (2018)
25. Ren, H.: Risk lifecycle and risk relationships on construction projects. Int. J. Project Manage. **12**, 68–74 (1994)

26. Kwan, T.W., Leung, H. K.: A risk management methodology for project risk dependencies. IEEE Trans. Softw. Eng. (2014)
27. Zhang, Y.: Selecting risk response strategies considering project risk interdependence. Int. J. Project Manage. **34**, 819–830 (2016)
28. Ackoff, R.L., Emery, F.: On Purposeful Systems. Tavistock, London (1972)
29. Marchwicka, E., Kuchta, D.: Modified optimization model for selecting project risk response strategies. Oper. Res. Decis. **27**(2), 77–90 (2017)
30. Wirba, E.N., Tah, J.H.M., Howes, R.: Risk interdependencies and natural language computations. Eng. Constr. Archit. Manag. **3**, 251–269 (1996)
31. Fang, C., Marle, F.: A simulation-based risk network model for decision support in project risk management. Decis. Support Syst. **52**, 635–644 (2012)
32. Fang, C., Marle, F., Zio, E., Bocquet, J.C.: Network theory-based analysis of risk interactions in large engineering projects. Reliab. Eng. Syst. Saf. **106**, 1–10 (2012)
33. Aloini, D., Dulmin, R., Mininno, V.: Risk assessment in ERP projects. Inf. Syst. **37**, 183–199 (2012)
34. Rich, E., Gonzalez, J.J., Qian, Y., Sveen, F.O., Radianti, J., Hillen, S.: Emergent vulnerabilities in integrated operations: a proactive simulation study of economic risk. Int. J. Crit. Infrastr. Prot. **2**, 110–123 (2009)
35. Qian, Y., Fang, Y., Gonzalez, J.J.: Managing information security risks during new technology adoption. Comput. Secur. **31**, 859–869 (2012)
36. Sterman, J.D.: Business Dynamics. Systems Thinking and Modeling for a Complex World. McGraw-Hill Education, Columbus, OH, USA (2000)
37. Mani, K.E., Cavana, R.Y.: Systems Thinking, System Dynamics. Managing Change and Complexity. Prentice Hall, New Zealand (2001)
38. Howick, S., Eden, C.: Supporting strategic conversations: the significance of a quantitative model building process. J. Oper. Res. Soc. **62**, 868–878 (2011)
39. Harary, F., Norman, R., Cartwright, D.: Structural Models: An Introduction to the Theory of Directed Graphs. Wiley, New York (1965)
40. Hage, P., Harary, F.: Eccentricity and centrality in networks. Soc. Netw. **17**, 57–63 (1995)
41. Yan, E., Ding, Y.: Applying centrality measures to impact analysis: a coauthorship network analysis. J. Am. Soc. Inform. Sci. Technol. **60**, 2107–2118 (2009)
42. Lu, L., Chen, D., Ren, X.-L., Zhang, Q.-M., Zhang, Y.-C., Zhou, T.: Vital nodes identification in complex networks. Phys. Rep. **650**, 1–63 (2016)
43. Rosenhead, J.: Planning under uncertainty: II. A methodology for robustness analysis. J. Oper. Res. Soc. **31**, 331–342 (1980)
44. Dalkey, N., Helmer, O.: An experimental application of the Delphi method to the use of experts. Manage. Sci. **9**, 458–467 (1963)
45. Rowe, G., Wright, G.: The Delphi technique as a forecasting tool: issues and analysis. Int. J. Forecast. **15**, 353–375 (1999)
46. Vennix, J.: Group Model Building: Facilitating Team Learning Using System Dynamics. Wiley, Chichester (1996)
47. Rouwette, E.A.J.A., Vennix, J.A.M.: System dynamics and organizational interventions. Syst. Res. Behav. Sci. **23**, 451–466 (2006)
48. Rouwette, E.A.J.A.: Modeling as persuasion: the impact of group model building on attitudes and behavior. Syst. Dyn. Rev. **27**, 1–21 (2010)
49. Ackermann, F., Howick, S., Quigley, J., Walls, L., Houghton, T.: Systemic risk elicitation: using causal maps to engage stakeholders and build a comprehensive view of risks. Eur. J. Oper. Res. **238**, 290–299 (2014)
50. Solarz, J.K., Waliszewski, K.: Holistic framework for COVID-19 pandemic as systemic risk. Eur. Res. Stud. J. **XXIII**, 340–351 (2020)

51. Carlile, P.R.: A pragmatic view of knowledge and boundaries: boundary objects in new product development. Organ. Sci. **13**, 442–455 (2002)
52. Black, L.J., Andersen, D.F.: Using visual representations as boundary objects to resolve conflict in collaborative model-building approaches. Syst. Res. Behav. Sci. **29**, 194–208 (2012)
53. Luna-Reyes, L.F., Black, L.J., Ran, W., Andersen, D.L., Jarman, H., Richardson, G.P., et al.: Modeling and simulation as boundary objects to facilitate interdisciplinary research. Syst. Res. Behav. Sci. **36**, 494–513 (2018)
54. Eden, C.: Behavioral considerations in group support. In: Kilgour, D.M., Eden, C. (Eds.) Handbook of Group Decision and Negotiation, pp. 777–792. Springer, Cham (2021). https://doi.org/10.1007/978-3-030-49629-6_34

Situational Awareness

Creation and Use of Virtual Simulations for Measuring Situation Awareness of Incident Commanders

Stella Polikarpus[1]([⊠]) [iD], Edna Milena Sarmiento-Márquez[2] [iD], and Tobias Ley[2] [iD]

[1] Estonian Academy of Security Sciences, Tallinn, Estonia
stella.polikarpus@sisekaitse.ee
[2] Tallinn University, Tallinn, Estonia

Abstract. Training and measurement of situation awareness (SA) in a dynamic decision-making context is a complex task and depends on personal factors as well as time, space, and situation. Therefore, to measure first-level incident commanders' SA several authentic and immersive virtual simulations of rescue incidents should be used. In this paper, we report on Effective Command and the dynamic decision-making assessment methodology as a theoretical framework for SA assessment and implementation of virtual reality software using sixteen different virtual simulations in an organization. First, we report four aspects needed to be implemented for virtual simulation-based assessment of SA. Next, we analysed the differences between three SA ascending levels: perception, comprehension, and prediction that might be influenced by the scenario storyline. According to prior research, we would expect the difficulty of the three SA levels to be in ascending order and we evaluated that by analysing N = 665 assessment results. We confirmed such an ascending order for most scenarios, and we also identified these scenarios for which this assumption was not met. Finally, we discuss the possibilities of analysing the scenario-based SA level differences in the future when assessing SA with more automated measures. We argue that by improving the assessment of SA, we can foster the training possibilities for incident commanders' dynamic decision-making.

Keywords: Situation Awareness (SA) · Effective Command (EC) · Virtual simulations · The Collaborative Authoring Process Model (CAPM)

1 Introduction

Rescue incident commanders need good situation awareness in a dynamic decision-making context such as fires and traffic accidents or leaks of chemicals to assess hazards and risks for humans and environment. So far it is unrealistic to measure their situational awareness in real time when they need to act in fast developing high risk situations like emergencies are. Despite the difficulties of training and assessing rescue incident commanders situation awareness is hard task for a trainers [1], it seems to be possible to do

© IFIP International Federation for Information Processing 2023
Published by Springer Nature Switzerland AG 2023
T. Gjøsæter et al. (Eds.): ITDRR 2022, IFIP AICT 672, pp. 23–38, 2023.
https://doi.org/10.1007/978-3-031-34207-3_2

with help of virtual simulations using virtual reality technology [2]. Virtual simulations could be co-authored by trainers themselves using the *Collaborative Authoring Process Model* (CAPM), that gives step-by-step guide on how to do it in a training organization context [1]. In The Estonian Academy of Security Sciences the Effective Command behavioural marker framework is used to assess rescue incident commanders situational awareness [3]. The framework, "focuses on five key behaviours: situational awareness, decision-making, objective setting, action behaviours and review" [4, pp. 225–226], and it is created on bases of SPAR dynamic decision-making model, meaning Situation Awareness, Plan, Action and Review [5].

The term *Situation Awareness* (SA) is common but it might mean different things to different people [6, 7]. In this study we refer to Endsley [8, p. 65], who defines SA as a person´s "perception of the elements in the environment within a volume of time and space, comprehension of their meaning, and the projection of their status in the near future". From the definition, it becomes clear that SA levels are: SA level 1 perception (SA1); SA level 2 comprehension (SA2) and SA level 3 prediction (SA3) [9]. Endsley's definition is used as the basis to report the three levels of SA measurement, using Effective Command framework [4] in The Estonian Academy of Security Sciences [3]. It is suggested that improvements in SA2 comprehension and SA3 prediction areas would greatly impact the outcomes of dynamic decision-making assessments using virtual simulations [4]. This suggestion implies that virtual simulation-based training and assessment of rescue incident commanders' SA virtual simulations are needed to train dynamic decision-making in a safe environment without harmful consequences. We define *virtual simulations*, for this paper, as a scenario presented to the learner using software and hardware to create a virtual environment for dynamically changing emergencies. *Dynamic decision-making* could be defined "as making a series of interdependent decisions in an environment that changes over time due to the consequences of the taken decisions or due to autonomous changes in the environment" [10, p. 284]. The research on how to create these virtual simulations for rescue incident commanders' dynamic decision-making training is rather episodic and only a few articles address this issue [1, 11].

Unfortunately, from named research about creation of virtual simulations, it is not clear what are the SA level (resulting from SA assessment) when using CAPM [1] for virtual simulation scenario creation and Effective Command framework (used for simulation implementation) [4]. SA is assessed as part of the dynamic decision-making model Situation Awareness, Plan, Action and Review - SPAR in Effective Command methodology [4, 5]. We do not know how the situation, or in other words emergency type including its dynamic situational elements (like fire, leak, traffic, victims) [1], influences the rescue incident commanders SA assessment results. There are several elements observed by assessors during simulation phase, there is a multitude of possible decisions and interactions done by incident commanders, which bring virtual simulation into a different state each time. Without knowledge about dynamic situational elements, the automated feedback to commanders' SA levels cannot be adjusted to different rescue incidents.

To the best of our knowledge, there is no research focusing on the construction of virtual simulation scenarios, except studies about CAPM. Rather, earlier research has focused on measuring the SA and its different levels [8, 12] disregarding the scenarios used for it. In this article we focus on one SA assessment method Effective Command behavioural marking framework [4]. We **aim** to find out if scenarios influence the SA assessment results on different levels of SA. That being said, we address the following research question:

"What are the differences in the levels of SA of rescue incident commanders assessed through different virtual simulation scenarios created using CAPM?"

This paper is organised as follows: In section two we describe earlier work and the research context. In section three we explain the methods and implemented aspects. Next, we present the results by explaining the evidence supporting the use of Effective Command framework, XVR On-Scene virtual reality software and CAPM with 16 virtual simulation scenarios to assess rescue incident commanders' SA levels in Estonia. Section five discusses the possibility to reuse the already existing assessment scenarios for the FireFront tool and the Quantitative Analysis of Situation Awareness (QASA) method in future developments, with the automating purpose of the assessments of SA based on different levels and multiple scenarios. The final section describes the limitations of the study and proposes future work directions.

2   Challenges in Measuring Situation Awareness

SA is a key factor in managing emergency incidents [5] and it depends on the context and personal factors [13]. As described before, the general SA levels are SA1 perception; SA2 comprehension and SA3 prediction [9]. For rescue incident commanders´ SA1–perception is about his/her ability to collect information by asking the specific question, from the right person, at the right time, and doing 360 degrees recognition of the situation effectively. SA2 – comprehension is about the commanders' ability to collect information into a coherent operational picture. And lastly SA3 – prediction is about being able to prognose what is going to happen next in a dynamically developing rescue incident if resources are applied to stop the spread of hazards and mitigate the risks. Comprehension and prediction levels are very important for the effective use of limited resources in a timely manner.

Simulation based measurements of SA are commonly used [8] as it is almost impossible to measure SA real time when the first level incident commander has to act in fast developing high risk situations, like emergencies. In some jobs, like pilots [14], drivers [15] or teams in gas drilling industry [16], individuals work in a predetermined space (cockpit, car or drilling platform). On the contrary, rescue incident commanders need to work in any space, weather, with hundreds of tools and uncountable situations. Incident commanders are the first ones to respond to emergencies like traffic accidents, fires, or incidents with hazardous materials. They need a good level of SA for safe and fast decision making but have very limited time in a novel space to create their perception of the elements in an emergency environment like a fire or spread of hazardous materials, the health status of victims etc. For SA2 these named examples of dynamic situation elements must be put together to have an operational picture with the comprehension of their meaning. Finally, the projection of their status in the near future is needed for a dynamic decision making. Therefore, virtual simulations are useful for assessing first level rescue incident commanders´ SA [3] and enhancing the training of dynamic decision-making.

"The direct measurement of SA provides a great insight into how operators piece together the vast array of available information to form a coherent operational picture" [9, p. 17]. There are several methods to measure SA. Examples include the SART – situational awareness rating technique, the SAGAT – situation awareness global assessment technique, the SPAM - Situation Present Assessment Method [14], and the QASA - Quantitative Analysis of Situation Awareness method [12] that is used in the FireFront tool [17]. Effective Command methodology assesses key behavioural markers through criteria for dynamic decision-making [4]. Three levels of SA are assessed by two assessors, using virtual reality, based on observations of the dynamic phase of incident response and after action discussion with the trainee [3]. From earlier research there is an understanding that Effective Command methodology allows to measure different SA levels [3, 18], especially SA3 prediction, because the virtual scenario is changed dynamically by the assessors, based on the incident commander's SA1 data gathering on scene. The Effective Command methodology to measure incident commanders' SA is highly mental workload demanding for assessors. The field would benefit from automating some of the actions taken by assessors in a timely manner.

It is claimed that scenario storyline and dynamic situational elements like victims, fire, leak and traffic play an important role in SA assessments [1]. Similarly for pilots, elements like altitude, mission timing and aircraft manoeuvres play an important role in SA [13]. Endsley has divided these elements to measure different SA levels of pilots [13], but we have no information that such work has been done, so far, for rescue incident commanders' SA measurement. Therefore, the data from incident commanders' SA levels, connected to different rescue incidents, and dynamic situational elements used in virtual simulations, is essential to develop automatized SA measuring methods.

3   Methods

Approach and Procedure
To develop virtual simulation scenarios and implement SA assessments of rescue incident commanders, we need to consider four main aspects:

(1) Theoretical model to assess SA – we used Effective Command behavioural marking framework [4].
(2) Platform – we used virtual reality software XVR On-Scene [19] and Effective Command web-based database [20].
(3) Process model to create virtual simulations – we used The Collaborative Authoring Process Model (CAPM) [1].
(4) Assessors – we selected only assessors who are certified to use the Effective Command methodology [21].

In The Estonian Academy of Security Sciences, we use data from year 2016 Effective Command behavioural marker framework [4, 21]. Effective Command methodology is based on dynamic decision-making model SPAR, it is based on research about incident commanders decision-making processes in urban fires [5]. The Effective Command methodology five key-behaviours assessment starts with three levels of SA is circular, meaning that the incident commander updates his/her SA throughout the response phase of an emergency. Therefore, the virtual simulations need to be adoptable to incident commanders' information collection. There are different decision-making strategies defined, like recognition primed, value-based, procedural that incident commanders' use in the first stage of response [5]. Based on the initial SA, the commander creates a plan to execute actions with a clear goal in mind, to save lives and property, by only taking calculated risks to firefighters. He/she needs to review the emergency response (maintaining the SA) and his/her plan to check if the plan is still feasible to execute with the resources at scene and the current development of the situation. Because the SPAR model is a spiral, the review phase plays an important part to keep SA constantly updated.

The second aspect: platforms to create virtual simulations for rescue incident commanders can be different. Nevertheless, to train all three levels of SA, XVR On-Scene virtual reality software has been selected to create virtual simulations [2] and execute the Effective Command criteria based assessments of SA levels. Effective Command methodology web-based platform has eight subsections plus section for written feedback translated and adjusted to the Estonian context [21]. To assess SA using Effective Command methodology three subsections for each SA level needs to be considered as – SA1 perception, SA2 comprehension, and SA3 prediction. All subsections are measured with nine assessment criteria, based on a five-point coloured scale by two assessors [3]. Each section was evaluated on a scale from 20 to 100 points with a threshold above 55,5 points. The score below 55,5 points is considered as fail [4]. The SA assessments of working incident commanders in Estonia and recordings, in the form of SA formal assessment results into Effective Command database, are done systematically and periodically by certified assessors [3, 21].

Thirdly, there is a five steps process model that explains how to build these virtual simulations for Effective Command methodology implementation, The Collaborative Authoring Process Model for Virtual Simulation Scenarios - CAPM [1]. First, the incident commander's virtual simulation scenario map needs to be written to communicate the emergency type, main storyline, dilemmas for decision-making etc. The map is used to find a co-author as well as for contracting the virtual simulations build. The second step is scenario authoring, where the storyline is further developed in a document called "the scenario's user manual", then an XVR On-Scene file is created using the organisational virtual scenario building guidelines. Third, virtual simulations scenario technical testing appears between four Effective Command assessors. The virtual simulation is played through by an expert, who has not seen it before, to test how authentic and immersive the virtual simulation is. Fourth, the virtual scenario needs to be finalized based on improvements suggested in step three. Finally, "the modelling of the threshold playthrough" is to all Effective Command assessors in an organization to learn to use the virtual simulation and to make sure that the incident, in the form of virtual simulation, is presented similarly to all incident commanders. The implementation of CAPM [1] allows different scenarios to be used by assessors in a systematic way and in controlled conditions. This process model has already been adopted for the FireFront tool [11] and the Quantitative Analysis of Situation Awareness (QASA) method as well [12]. The Effective Command methodology implementation analyses in in The Estonian Academy of Security Sciences showed that in 2018 only seven different scenarios were used, 14 scenarios in 2019, and 17 in 2020 [21]. The researchers suggested that using the CAPM allows a stable scenario creation and use for dynamic decision-making assessments [21].

The fourth aspect to implement virtual simulations-based SA assessments in an organization is to train and certify assessors. The assessors will carry out the assessments in a way that they adopt the scenario based on incident commander local recourses and change the virtual simulations-based on commander's information collection, decisions, and actions. Assessors are selected among people who have first level incident command work experience and are trained based on the curriculum where the Effective Command methodology and XVR On-Scene are thought [21]. Training the assessors in an organization is important to avoid assessment biases. The assessors are the ones who need to be able to adopt the scenario storyline to provide context to the commander being measured on all three levels of SA. Once the dynamic phase is played through in virtual simulation, they discuss the dynamic decision-making phase and give quantitative and qualitative feedback to the case on Effective Command platform [4].

Data Collection

We want to find out whether the created virtual simulation, using CAPM, influence the SA assessment results on different levels. To use Effective Command methodology in the Estonian Academy of Security Sciences, two assessors per each incident commander are needed, and it takes around 90 min to play one scenario [3, 21]. In Estonia, the results from a working first level incident commanders' assessment were downloaded from Effective Command platform [20] on 1st July 2022. The details of assessment methodology and assessors training can be found in earlier work [3, 21]. Year 2016 and 2017, or any data having typing errors or missing data, were removed. All scenario codes being marked by assessors to the database as "Incident No", which had less than ten assessment results were deleted as well. We ended up with data from 665 individual assessments in January 2018 to July 2022.

Database download was done directly to MS Excel file. All qualitative feedback was erased as well with columns not relevant to this study like name of the assessor. Prework with data was registered on a table where each rescue incident commanders' assessment results were in one row. The titles for columns are to be found in the first row of data table. First column was named as "name" and second column "personnel No" of person being assessed. Followed by incident number where the scenario codes were retrieved. The fourth column was date of the assessment, the fifth was the name of the assessor who filled the certificate. Columns six to fourteen were the scores of the person assessed (Perception_(SA1); Comprehension_(SA2); Prediction_(SA3); Decision Making; Plan; Communication; Command; Review).

In The Estonian Academy of Security Sciences, first level incident commanders have been assessed from year 2016, however the CAPM was implemented in year 2018. During the time January 2018 to July 2022, 665 assessments were carried out, using sixteen different virtual scenarios which were created using CAPM. Effective Command behavioural markers assessment results (mean scores) are presented on Fig. 1 next section. There have been 21 different certified assessors logged in to fulfil the certificate, the leading assessor did 224 assessments, and four assessors did two or less assessments.

We remind the reader that assessors always worked in pairs [21] and thereby only one assessor logs into Effective Command platform to complete the certificate.

Data Analysis Method

We used MS Excel to extract descriptive statistics like mean scores, standard deviation, etc. We also used it to assess the normality of the data, and to perform single factor ANOVA analyses and post-hoc T-tests. For scenario-based analyses, the filter function was used, in column Incident No, allowing us to see how many times same virtual simulation has been used to assess different rescue incident commanders' SA levels.

4   Results

All eight subsection scores of the Effective Command could be, theoretically, between 20 and 100 points. In Fig. 1 we have calculated the mean scores for each subsection over all 665 assessments. The lowest result from the eight behaviours (see Fig. 1) is *review* (M = 63,9; SD = 7,4), followed by *SA 3* with highest standard deviation (M = 64,3; SD = 8,1), followed by means score for *communicational* skills 64,6 (SD = 7,5). In ascending position, 4th is *decision-making* skills (marked decision, M = 65,2; SD = 8), 5th is *command and control* skill (M = 65,6; SD = 7,6), and 6th is *plan* (M = 65,7; SD = 7,5), while the higher two are *SA1* with means score 67,0 and SD = 7,2 and *SA2* (M = 66,3; SD = 7,6).

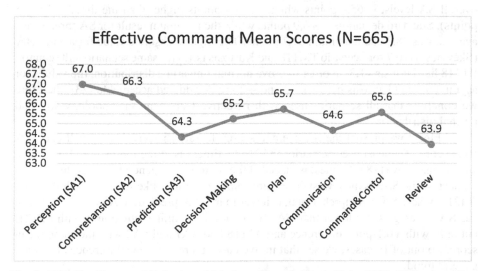

Fig. 1. Effective Command Behavioural Markers Mean Scores in Years 2018–2022 when First Level Rescue Incident Commanders were Assessed.

All eight behavioural markers mean scores for all 16 scenarios, as well standard deviation (SD) and minimum and maximum results, range, and absolute value for asymmetry (Skewness) and Kurtosis are given in Table 1. It turns out that the decision-making has the highest negative Kurtosis (-0,7) meaning the distribution is platykurtic (relatively thin and light tails, tends to be flatter than normal) [22]. However, all behaviour' scores can be seen with normal distribution as the Kurtosis and Skewness are ± 2 [23].

Table 1. Effective Command Behavioural Marking Framework Assessment Results Descriptive Statistics (N = 665).

Measurement	SA1	SA2	SA3	Decision	Plan	Communication	Command	Review
Mean	67,0	66,3	64,3	65,2	65,7	64,6	65,6	63,9
Standard Deviation	7,2	7,6	8,1	8,0	7,5	7,5	7,6	7,4
Kurtosis	– 0,5	0,1	– 0,3	– 0,7	0,1	– 0,6	– 0,4	0,0
Skewness	– 0,3	– 0,3	0,0	0,0	– 0,3	0,2	0,1	0,1
Range	44	55	48	46	51	45	51	51
Minimum	42	31	40	40	35	37	40	33
Maximum	86	86	88	86	86	82	91	84
Total	665	665	665	665	665	665	665	665

Next, we checked if all 16 scenarios results had a normal distribution when SA level mean scores are used. In Table 2, the mean score for all virtual simulations, and overall SA levels, is 65,9 points which is 10,4 points higher than the threshold (55,5 points). Standard deviation was 6,9 points while the minimum result for SA three levels average was 38,3 and maximum 81,7 points. The highest absolute value for asymmetry (Skewness) is 0,7 for Scenario TM118 and Kurtosis is 1.3 for same scenario and scenario RT118 has kurtosis –1.3. In order to prove normal univariate distribution, the values for asymmetry and Kurtosis between –2 and +2 are considered acceptable [23], therefore we conclude that all scenarios used with Effective Command methodology still had normal distribution.

In Fig. 2 we present the SA average scores for all 16 scenarios as well each SA level score. The least used scenario AT121 (15 times) is at the top of Fig. 2 and most used scenario AS118 (78 times) is placed at the bottom. The general trend is that SA1 is highest, while SA3 is the lowest. There are some exceptions like scenario with the code JM218, where SA2: comprehension, is lower than SA3: prediction. AS120 and TM118 has SA2 average score lower than SA1, perception. A similar situation is with SP121, but only with a 0,1-point difference and AT118 had SA1 and SA2 with the same mean score. So out of 16 cases, we see that in five cases there are some differences from the general trend.

To understand the differences between SA levels based on the different scenarios, we performed a single factor (one way) ANOVA. Based on earlier research [3] we hypothesized that if all 665 assessment results are considered, there is a statistically significant difference between SA levels. Results indicate that there is a statistically significant difference between SA levels scores ($F = 21,9$ $p = \; < 0,001$). In Table 3 the post hoc T-test results are presented. The overall trend is that SA1 is highest, SA3 is lowest, and SA2 in between. SA level perception and prediction (Cohen's d = 0,41) as

Table 2. Estonian First Level Incident Commanders Effective Command Situation Awareness Formal Assessment Results in Years 2018–2022 based on CAPM Virtual Simulations.

No	Scenario code	Used (n)	Mean SA score	SD	Skewness	Kurtosis	Min	Max
1	AS118	78	65,7	6,3	– 0,2	– 0,3	50,7	81,7
2	AT118	62	65,2	6,6	0,1	– 0,8	52,0	80,0
3	RT118	60	64,8	8,0	0,1	– 1,3	51,7	79,0
4	LK118	57	65,7	6,4	– 0,3	– 0,4	50,3	77,7
5	JM118	56	66,2	6,2	– 0,2	– 0,8	52,0	77,3
6	TM118	56	65,6	8,4	– 0,7	1,3	38,3	80,3
7	SP121	48	64,7	5,3	– 0,5	– 0,5	51,3	72,3
8	TR218	48	64,2	6,9	0,3	– 0,6	52,7	79,0
9	AT119	41	68,9	4,8	0,0	– 0,3	58,7	80,0
10	AS120	30	67,8	7,6	0,0	– 1,2	54,7	81,7
11	TM218	28	68,6	6,9	0,1	– 1,0	55,7	80,7
12	JM218	25	62,8	6,0	0,3	– 1,0	55,0	74,3
13	TM318	24	68,0	6,4	– 0,6	– 0,2	53,7	78,3
14	JM121	21	66,0	7,0	– 0,4	– 1,2	53,7	75,7
15	TM220	16	65,0	6,9	– 0,3	0,8	49,3	78,3
16	AT121	15	69,0	8,0	– 0,5	– 0,6	55,0	81,3
	Total	665	65,9	6,9	– 0,2	– 0,3	38,3	81,7

well comprehension and prediction (Cohen's d = 0,39) means differences has a small effect but perception and comprehension (Cohen's d = 0,11) has a trivial effect [24].

Table 3. Post-hoc Paired Sample T-Test Results for Situation Awareness Levels Using All CAPM Scenarios Data

SA level	SA level	t	df	p	Cohen's d
Perception -	Comprehension	2,75	664	0,006	0,11
Perception -	Prediction	10,51	664	<,001	0,41
Comprehension -	Prediction	9,95	664	<,001	0,39

As from Fig. 2, we identified some differences in the order of SA levels mean scores. We also did single factor ANOVA for each scenario. Two cases, AS118 (F = 7,67; $p <$ 0,001) and AT119 (F = 4,02; $p = 0,02$) the differences between SA levels are statistically important. It is important to note that these two scenarios are not the scenarios that did not follow the overall trend of SA level scores.

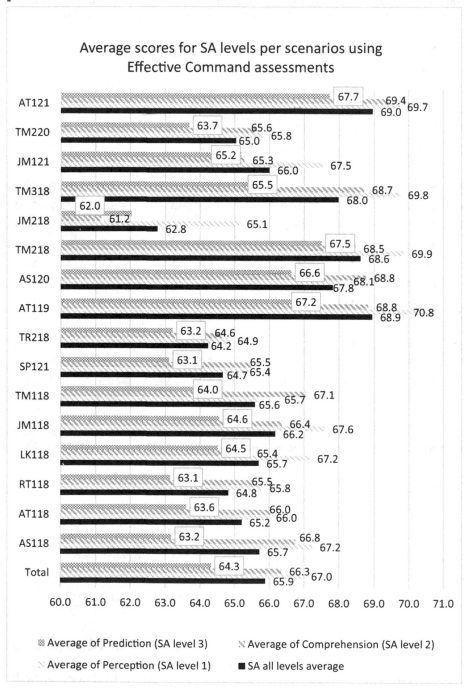

Fig. 2. CAPM Scenarios Situation Awareness Levels Mean Scores when Effective Command Methodology is Used (n = 665)

Therefore, we can say that Effective Command SA assessment methodology generally allows us to understand whether the three SA levels, as mean scores, are in a descending sequence. Despite the exceptional scenarios (AT118, SP121, TM118, AS120, JM218), that did not produce statistically significant differences.

To find out why some scenarios mean scores did not follow the SA levels descending rule, we counted how many individual cases did not follow the logical sequence of level scores. Table 4 presents the results of the individual SA levels' assessment order or if there is no difference between levels scores.

Table 4. Comparison of Individuals Situation Awareness Levels Order

SA level	Individual scores (n)	Comment to order of SA level scores
SA1 = SA2	133	no difference in SA levels scores
SA1 > SA2	298	expected order
SA1 < SA2	234	not expected order
SA2 = SA3	155	no difference in SA levels scores
SA2 > SA3	358	expected order
SA2 < SA3	152	not expected order
SA1 = SA3	126	no difference in SA levels scores
SA1 > SA3	373	expected order
SA1 < SA3	166	not expected order

In Table 4 we observe that all SA levels there are more individuals whose SA levels were in the expected order. We expected SA1 to have higher score than SA2 and SA2 have higher score than SA3. There was no difference between SA1 and SA2 20% of cases, 23% between SA2 and SA3 and 19% between SA1 and SA3. However, in 234 cases there was not expected meaning SA2 comprehension score being higher than SA1 perception score. In 152 cases SA2 was lower than SA3 and 166 cases SA1 was lower than SA3.

5   Discussion

We found 665 assessments in The Estonian Academy of Security Sciences, made by 21 assessors working in pairs from the years 2018 to July 2022. We assessed eight dynamic decision-making behaviours using Effective Command methodology, and the two lowest scores are review and SA3 (Table 1). Both, review and SA3 behaviours are connected to individual information mechanisms that are connected to abilities, experiences, and training [13]. Therefore, there is a need for more possibilities to train and assess SA in a dynamic decision-making context for rescue incident commanders. Furthermore, all dynamic decision-making behaviours had a normal distribution (Table 1), allowing us to conclude that data collected in the training organisation using virtual simulations, has good potential to be used for learning analytics and further statistical analyses.

In our research, we asked what the differences in the levels of SA of rescue incident commanders are if being assessed through different CAPM virtual simulation scenarios. The general trend is that SA1 scores are highest and SA3 are lowest while SA2 in the middle. The same order is found earlier [3] even if not scenarios used to assess SA were created using CAPM. All mean scores are over threshold SA1 perception 67,0, SA2 comprehension 66,3 and SA3 prediction 64,3 points. There is a statistically significant difference between the SA level scores (see Table 3) and rescue incident commanders score higher in SA1 compared to SA3. However, the effect size is small (also Table 3) indicating that adding more people to be assessed using the same virtual simulation, even small differences in SA levels means might become statistically important.

Effective Command methodology together with implementation of CAPM has allowed to assess whether all SA levels and scenario mean scores are in a descending order. The results showed that SA1 has in general higher scores as, from a cognitive point of view, it is easier to collect the information (SA1) than organizing it into a coherent operational picture (SA2). It is even harder to predict the future of the situation in emergency events (SA3) while being under great stress to save lives and property. In other words Endsley states: "the three levels of SA represent ascending levels of SA" [25, p. 8] and therefore the drop of scores in SA levels is well explained with the theoretical model chosen to assess SA.

There are 16 different scenarios constructed adopting CAPM, with the most used scenario having been solved 78 times (see Table 2). The results from this study confirm that the scenario storylines affect SA scores. Similarly to earlier research we suggest applying a systematic approach to author virtual simulations for training and assessing SA in dynamic decision-making contexts [1]. A systematic approach using CAPM will help to clarify the effect of different variables in measuring SA.

Furthermore, to detect how the personal factors influence to SA levels, more individual SA assessments with different virtual simulations need to be carried out. SA depends on space and situation and these dynamical situation elements for different SA levels need to be considered while training and assessing rescue incident commanders' SA levels. In order to find a way to measure SA using fewer human resources, a larger automation is needed. The FireFront is a fully automated way to measure SA and FireFront tool [17], it also allows to distinguish actual SA and perceived SA as well as situation understanding if CAPM is used to create the scenarios for it [11]. The FireFront tool considers time and individual factors while using Quantitative Analysis of Situation Awareness (QASA) measuring method [12]. Earlier research measuring SA using QASA suggested that firefighters maintained a level of confidence in their own SA across two virtual scenarios that were used, but that confidence is unrelated to their actual SA [26]. We agree with authors as they write "In particular, it would be valuable to know whether the actual SA, in any particular situation, is influenced by the resting perceived SA" [26, p. 1481]. But to determine what a rescue incident commander needs to solve very different kinds of incidents to reduce the influence of the virtual simulation storylines (emergency/incident type) on the SA measurement.

6   Limitations and Future Work

As the scenario-based analyses (see Fig. 2) showed that the scenario storyline might be accountable for differences in commanders' SA levels, further research is needed. This interesting finding – virtual simulations influence to the SA levels scores - needs to be further explored as in most research cases SA is measured just using one or two virtual simulations [12, 26]. The analysis of individual SA levels (see Table 4) showed that SA does depend on individual factors. Perhaps not all virtual simulations can pick up the SA levels well. Scenario based differences might be explained with timeline and order of presenting the dynamic situation elements like fire, victims, traffic etc. Therefore, future work should focus on this issue.

Furthermore, future research could focus on identifying the role that individual differences play in SA when the same virtual simulation is used for all incident commanders in Estonia, also by using statements asking about how different situational elements are clearly divided between SA levels. This study can be considered as a departure point to explore the factors affecting SA levels and finding strategies to improve the systematization of SA assessment as well as training dynamic decision-making.

Future work using the CAPM for scenario creation and XVR On-Scene after training output files and Effective Command database could be analysed to improve the learning analytics for virtual simulations-based training and assessment. Therefore, key factors that play a role for each SA level (dynamic situation elements like victims, fire, traffic etc.) while working incident commanders respond to virtually simulated emergencies should be identified from automated analyses of XVR On-Scene after action files to each incident type. This information could be used to automatically propose statements for Quantitative Analysis of Situation Awareness - QASA method and FireFront tool. Proposed work could support assessors and trainers as well to provide even more immersive training of dynamic decision-making using the Effective Command methodology.

The main limitation of the study is that even if the statistically significant order of SA levels was identified, the small differences in SA level mean scores do not play a practical role for incident commander overall SA (also the effect size is small or trivial). As SA assessment is such a complex task, it is very hard to detect if this difference results from personal factors or time, space, or situation (which in the context of virtual simulations-based training is called scenario storyline or incident type). Therefore, the future SA research effort should focus on providing more training possibilities including automated feedback, delivering virtual simulations for incident commanders.

This study did not consider individual differences or additional cognitive aspects related to the participants and future research can also address this matter. In addition to this, only quantitative data was used, a qualitative approach could explain what differences virtual simulations storylines have for SA levels.

7   Conclusion

This study presented the benefits of a strategy to use systematic approach for virtual simulations scenario creation process to automatize in future the SA measuring. It highlighted the experiences and systematic approach in The Estonian Academy of Security

Sciences while laboursome assessment SA levels (665 times with 16 scenarios). With laboursome we mean that two certified assessors assess each rescue incident commander separately while adopting the virtual simulations. As virtual simulations are used with Effective Command the valuable information about SA that is depending on time, space, situation, and personal factors could be better recorded. Therefore, it is feasible to automate some of the work of assessors and to make learning analytics based on scenarios to improve the SA training possibilities with automated feedback in the future.

In this study we showed how using virtual simulations and Effective Command methodology as an assessment method for SA could be used to the different SA method: Quantitative Analysis of Situation Awareness (QASA). Four aspects: SA measurement theoretical framework, platforms, CAPM and assessors are needed to successfully implement the virtual simulations-based dynamic decision-making training in an organization. We conclude that future research on incident commanders' SA measurement topic using virtual simulations to assess different SA levels, is still very much needed. More research is required mainly for two practical reasons. First, to provide more individual and fully automated ways for incident commanders to train their SA in different incident types and to measure their actual and perceived SA. Second, to support assessors work during use of CAPM and the dynamic phase of Effective Command methodology using XVR On-Scene software.

We encourage the scientific community to further develop the virtual simulation platforms with automated learning analytics. We suggest trainers to use CAPM to create the scenarios for virtual simulations based dynamic decision-making training and assessment.

Acknowledgements. We would like to thank the Estonian Rescue Board and The Estonian Academy of Security Sciences for continues funding of rescue incidents training and SA assessments. We struggle to express our profound thankfulness for all the work of the assessors doing the assessments as well building new assessment scenarios using CAPM. Thank you, Katherine Lamb's, for your yearly efforts in training and certifying assessors.

References

1. Polikarpus, S., Ley, T.: Collaborative authoring of virtual simulation scenarios for assessing situational awareness. In: Proceedings of the 18th ISCRAM Conference, pp. 229–237 (2021). http://idl.iscram.org/files/stellapolikarpus/2021/2328_StellaPolikarpus_etal2021.pdf
2. Polikarpus, S., Bøhm, M., Ley, T.: Training incident commander's situational awareness—a discussion of how simulation software facilitate learning. In: Väljataga, T., Laanpere, M. (Eds.) Digital Turn in Schools—Research, Policy, Practice. Lecture Notes in Educational Technology, pp. 219–234. Springer, Singapore (2019). https://doi.org/10.1007/978-981-13-7361-9_15
3. Polikarpus, S., Ley, T., Poom-Valickis, K.: Developing the situational awareness of incident commanders: evaluating a training programme using a virtual simulation. In: Proceedings of the Estonian Academy of Sciences, vol. 19, pp. 195–226 (2020). https://digiriiul.sisekaitse.ee/bitstream/handle/123456789/2595/Proceedings_2020_WEB.PDF?sequence=5&isAllowed=y

4. Lamb, K., Farrow, M., Olymbios, C., Launder, D., Greatbatch, I.: Systematic incident command training and organisational competence. Int. J. Emerg. Serv. **10**(2), 222–234 (Jun.2021). https://doi.org/10.1108/IJES-05-2020-0029

5. Launder, D., Perry, C.: A study identifying factors influencing decision making in dynamic emergencies like urban fire and rescue settings. Int. J. Emerg. Serv. **3**(2), 144–161 (Oct.2014). https://doi.org/10.1108/IJES-06-2013-0016

6. Jones, D.G.: A practical perspective on the utility of situation awareness. J. Cogn. Eng. Decis. Mak. **9**(1), 98–100 (Mar.2015). https://doi.org/10.1177/1555343414554804

7. Jenkins, D.P.D., Walker, G.H.D., Stanton, N.A.P.: What really is going on? situation awareness literature review. In: Distributed Situation Awareness: Theory, Measurement and Application to Teamwork, no. 2009, Ashgate Publishing Ltd., pp. 7–34 (2009)

8. Endsley, M.R.: Measurement of situation awareness in dynamic systems. Hum. Factors J. Hum. Factors Ergon. Soc. **37**(1), 65–84 (Mar.1995). https://doi.org/10.1518/001872095779 049499

9. Endsley, M.R.: Theoretical underpinnings of situation awareness: a critical review. In: Endsley, M.R., Garland, D.J. (Eds.) Situation Awareness Analysis and Measurement. Lawrence Erlbaum Associates Publishers (2000)

10. Donovan, S.J., Güss, C.D., Naslund, D.: Improving dynamic decision making through training and self-reflection. Judgm. Decis. Mak. **10**(4), 284–295 (2015). Accessed 07 June 2020. http://eds.b.ebscohost.com.ezproxy.tlu.ee/eds/pdfviewer/pdfviewer?vid=0&sid= 84c5805a-a737-4197-873e-ab8edd1d60de%2540pdc-v-sessmgr03

11. Polikarpus, S., et al.: Authoring virtual simulations to measure situation awareness and understanding. In: ISCRAM 2022 Conference Proceedings – 19th International Conference on Information Systems for Crisis Response and Management, pp. 428–433 (2022). https://idl. iscram.org/files/stellapolikarpus/2022/2430_StellaPolikarpus_etal2022.pdf

12. Edgar, G., et al.: Quantitative Analysis of Situation Awareness (QASA): modelling and measuring situation awareness using signal detection theory. Ergonomics **61**(6), 762–777 (Jun.2018). https://doi.org/10.1080/00140139.2017.1420238

13. Endsley, M.R.: Toward a theory of situation awareness in dynamic systems. Hum. Factors J. Hum. Factors Ergon. Soc. **37**(1), 32–64 (Mar.1995). https://doi.org/10.1518/001872095779 049543

14. Dalinger, I., Smurov, M., Sukhikh, N., Tsybova, E.: Pilot's situational awareness and methods of its assessment. Indian J. Sci. Technol. **9**(46), (Dec.2016). https://doi.org/10.17485/ijst/ 2016/v9i46/107534

15. Gugliotta, A., et al.: Are situation awareness and decision-making in driving totally conscious processes? Results of a hazard prediction task. Transp. Res. Part F Traffic Psychol. Behav. **44**, 168–179 (2017). https://doi.org/10.1016/j.trf.2016.11.005

16. Crichton, M.T.: Improving team effectiveness using tactical decision games. Saf. Sci. **47**(3), 330–336 (2009). https://doi.org/10.1016/j.ssci.2008.07.036

17. Thoelen, F., et al.: FireFront: a new tool to support training in Fireground situation awareness, situation understanding and Bias. Int. Fire Prof. **34**, 34–39 (2020)

18. Polikarpus, S., Danilas, K.: Olukorrateadlikkuse, olukorramõistmise ja kallutatuse mõõtmine siseturvalisuse valdkonnas. *Turvalisuskompass* **2**(1), pp. 89–107 (2022). https://digiriiul.sis ekaitse.ee/bitstream/handle/123456789/2876/Turvalisuskompass2022-1.pdf?sequence=6& isAllowed=y

19. XVR Simulation: XVR Virtual Reality training software for safety and security (2022). http:// www.xvrsim.com/. Accessed 29 March 2022

20. Effective Command: Effective Command. Effective Command (2022). https://www.effective command.org/. Accessed 29 March 2022

21. Polikarpus, S., Danilas, K.: Eesti päästemeeskonna juhtide visiõppepõhise hindamise rakendamine ja tulemused. *Turvalisuskompass* **1**, 204 (2021). https://digiriiul.sisekaitse.ee/handle/123456789/2844
22. A. Field: Discovering Statistics Using SPSS, 3rd edn. SAGE Publications Inc. (2009)
23. George, D., Mallery, M.: SPSS for Windows Step by Step: A Simple Guide and Reference, 17.0 updat. Pearson, Boston (2010)
24. Goss-Sampson, M.A.: Statistical analysis in JASP a guide for Students (2020)
25. Endsley, M.R.: Situation awareness misconceptions and misunderstandings. J. Cogn. Eng. Decis. Mak. **9**(1), 4–32 (Mar.2015). https://doi.org/10.1177/1555343415572631
26. Graham, E., Catherwood, D., Sallis, G., Brookes, D., Medley, A.: 'I always know what's going on'. Assessing the relationship between perceived and actual situation awareness across different scenarios. World Acad. Sci. Eng. Technol. **6**(11), 1433–1434 (2012)

Enhancing Interoperability and Inferring Evacuation Priorities in Flood Disaster Response

Julie Bu Daher[1](✉) , Patricia Stolf[2] , Nathalie Hernandez[2] ,
and Tom Huygue[1]

[1] IRIT, Université de Toulouse, CNRS, Toulouse INP, UT3, Toulouse, France
`julie.bu-daher@irit.fr`
[2] IRIT, Université de Toulouse, CNRS, Toulouse INP, UT3, UT2, Toulouse, France
`{patricia.stolf,nathalie.hernandez}@irit.fr`

Abstract. Disaster management is a crucial process that aims at limiting the consequences of a natural disaster. Disaster-related data, that are heterogeneous and multi-source, should be shared among different actors involved in the management process to enhance the interoperability. In addition, they can be used for inferring new information that helps in decision making. The evacuation process of flood victims during a flood disaster is critical and should be simple, rapid and efficient to ensure the victims' safety. In this paper, we present an ontology that allows integrating and sharing flood-related data to various involved actors and updating these data in real time throughout the flood. Furthermore, we propose using the ontology to infer new information representing evacuation priorities of places impacted by the flood using semantic reasoning to assist in the disaster management process. The evaluation results show that it is efficient for enhancing information interoperability as well as for inferring evacuation priorities.

Keywords: Disaster management · Semantic web · Flood ontology · Reasoning

1 Introduction

Natural disasters, such as floods, are adverse events resulting from earth's natural processes. They could lead to severe consequences including threatening people's lives, disruption of their normal life and other physical damages in properties, infrastructures and economy. From here comes the need for a disaster management process to limit its consequences. Disaster-related data can be provided from various data sources, and they are usually stored individually. Various actors are involved in the disaster management process; therefore, interoperability problems are common in such situations. The interoperability is defined as the ability of systems to provide services to and accept services from other systems and make them operate effectively [16], and its absence impacts the disaster management process and could adversely affect disaster response

© IFIP International Federation for Information Processing 2023
Published by Springer Nature Switzerland AG 2023
T. Gjøsæter et al. (Eds.): ITDRR 2022, IFIP AICT 672, pp. 39–54, 2023.
https://doi.org/10.1007/978-3-031-34207-3_3

efforts [3]. The problem thus lies in the lack of formalized and structured knowledge, the proper sharing and propagation of this knowledge among different parties involved in the flood management process and thus in a delayed decision making.

The success of the disaster management process is interpreted as "getting the right resources to the right place at the right time; to provide the right information to the right people to make the right decisions at the right level and the right time" [16]. Disaster management is defined as a lifecycle of four phases: mitigation, preparedness, response and recovery [4]. The safety of the population during a disaster is the most important concern; therefore, the evacuation process of victims in the disaster response phase should immediately take place. This process is handled by domain experts, that are the firefighters responsible for taking actions concerning the evacuation. It is a critical process that must respect constraints of efficiency, simplicity and rapidness to ensure the population's safety.

This work is conducted in the frame of "ANR inondations" e-flooding[1]. This project focuses on the mitigation and response phases where it aims at integrating several disciplinary expertises to prevent flash floods and to experiment the effects of decision making on two timescales: short-term and long-term. The short-term timescale aims at optimizing the disaster management process during the disaster, while the long-term timescale aims at improving the territories' resilience for risk prevention from five years to ten years after the disaster. Our work lies in the short-term timescale of the project where we propose assisting in the flood disaster response phase. The objective of our work is two-fold. First, we aim at proposing a solution to the interoperability problem through managing flood-related data and sharing them among different actors involved in the management process. Second, we aim at assisting the experts in decision making concerning victims' evacuation through proposing evacuation priorities to the demand points in a flooded area. We define a demand point as a place that can be impacted by a flood and thus needs to be evacuated if it contains population.

Heterogeneous multi-source data can be structured by considering ontologies. An ontology is defined as a formal, explicit specification of a shared conceptualization [14]. It allows a structuring and a logical representation of knowledge through defining concepts and relations among concepts thus defining a shared vocabulary. Ontology-driven systems have gained popularity as they enable semantic interoperability, flexibility, and reasoning support [12]. Using the concepts and relations of the ontology, we can form a knowledge graph by integrating the data. Ontology-based approaches have been proposed in the domain of natural disasters for information management and sharing among different actors involved in the flood management process as well as for inferring new information. In this work, we propose an ontology that allows managing and sharing information to enhance the interoperability. Using this ontology, we then aim at assisting the firefighters responsible for the evacuation process in taking decisions through proposing evacuation priorities to all demand points in the

---

[1] https://anr.fr/Projet-ANR-17-CE39-0011.

flooded area. The paper is organized as follows. Section 2 discusses the related work in the domain of flood disasters. Section 3 discusses our proposed approach. Enhancing the interoperability is discussed in Sect. 4 and inferring evacuation priorities is discussed in Sect. 5. The evaluation of our approach is presented in Sect. 6 and the conclusion and the future work are discussed in Sect. 7.

2   Related Work

Ontologies have been widely proposed in the literature in various domains including the domain of flood disasters. We distinguish two objectives of the use of ontologies in this domain: information management and sharing as well as reasoning to infer new information. In this section, we discuss the related work for these two objectives.

2.1   Ontologies for Information Management and Sharing

Ontology-based approaches have been proposed in the domain of flood disasters for managing and sharing the information among different actors involved in the disaster management process. In [5], they build an ontology for integrating flood-related data to ensure the coordination of response activities among different agencies involved in the management process and to provide up-to-date information facilitating the decision making by the management committee chairman. Another ontology is proposed by [11] for integrating local knowledge in the flood management process; they define local knowledge as the knowledge comprising preferences of stakeholders and decision makers. These preferences are expressed by describing the data through their proposed ontology. They define concepts describing events and their properties such as "hazard" and "vulnerability", and they define other concepts describing population, material infrastructure and elements at risk. In [6], they present their ontology that is built to enhance the information sharing among different actors handled by different systems in organizations. They manage static data that don't change during the flood as well as dynamic data that evolve throughout the flood. They describe static data through concepts including "area", "flood event" and "flood evacuation" and dynamic data through concepts representing coordination and production acts concerning the disaster. A flood ontology is proposed by [17] for solving the problems of data inaccuracy or unavailability among different agencies. They aim at building an ontology for each agency and integrating them in a global ontology to allow information sharing among different agencies. The ontology of evacuation centers include concepts describing general data about victims and evacuation centers.

2.2   Ontology-Based Approaches for Inferring New Information

Some ontology-based approaches in the literature are proposed for inferring new information from the flood-related data. A flood ontology built by [11] (previously presented) is used in a risk assessment framework to detect flood risks as follows. A user chooses an event type and defines its intensity. The framework then identifies the intensity parameters suitable for this event and infers elements at risk susceptible to this event through matching susceptibility functions against the event using "isSusceptiblityTo" relation that links each susceptibility function to the respective event types. Another ontology is proposed by [7] to capture dynamically evolving phenomena for understanding the dynamic spatio-temporal behaviour of a flood disaster. They then discuss a reasoning approach relying on the ontology to infer new information representing image regions based on their temporal interval relations using SWRL rules[2], that are reasoning rules used to infer new information from a knowledge graph. In [15], they present their hydrological sensor web ontology that integrates heterogeneous sensor data during a natural disaster. They use concepts describing sensors and observations, and they integrate concepts describing temporal and geospatial data. They then present a reasoning approach to infer flood phases from the water precipitation level and observation data.

We notice from the presented approaches that ontologies are commonly used for integrating and sharing flood-related data among the actors involved in the flood management process, while some approaches propose reasoning to infer new information using the ontology. Some ontologies define concepts describing victim's evacuation such as flood, victim as well as evacuation areas, resources and centers [6,17]; however, these concepts are not exploited for inferring new information that assists in the evacuation process.

3   Approach Presentation

As previously discussed, the aim of our proposed work is enhancing the interoperability among actors involved in the disaster management process as well as assisting in the evacuation process of flood victims. Our proposed approach is presented in Fig. 1 and is detailed as follows. We first propose an ontology that formally defines concepts and relations describing the flood-related data. We then rely on the ontology to form our knowledge graph that integrates all the data, and it is updated regularly with evolving data. This knowledge graph can be shared among actors involved in the flood management process so that each actor can access the needed data at the right times. We use this knowledge graph further in a reasoning approach in order to infer new information representing evacuation priorities to all demand points in the study area for the sake of helping firefighters in taking rapid and efficient decisions concerning the evacuation process of flood victims.

3.1   Data Description

Our study area concerns the Pyrénées flood that occurred in June 2013 in Bagnères-de-Luchon, south-western France. It was a torrential flood particularly destructive and dangerous to the population, and it lead to many destructive

---

[2] https://www.w3.org/Submission/SWRL/.

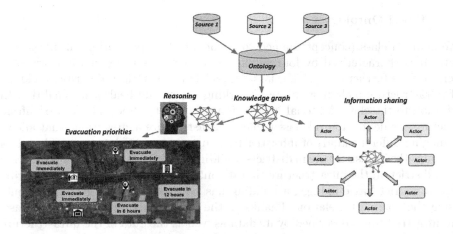

Fig. 1. Our proposed approach

consequences including damaged houses and farms, cut roads and flooded camp-sites. 240 people were evacuated from the areas impacted by this flood.

The flood-related data of our study area are provided from various data sources. These sources include institutional databases used in disaster management including BD TOPO[3] and GeoSirene[4] providing data about hazards, vulnerability, damage and resilience. Certain data sources provide data about geographical locations of roads, buildings and companies in France. Other sources include sensors providing data about water levels and flows, a hydrological model computing the flood generation, a hydraulic model for flood propagation as well as sources providing data about resilience corresponding to some actions taken from the past, socio-economic data, population data as well as danger and vulnerability indices of the flood calculated by domain experts. The vulnerability index measures a demand point's vulnerability, and it is calculated using topographic and social data like population density, building quality and socio-economic conditions. The danger index measures the danger level of a demand point, and it is calculated using water's level and speed obtained from a hydraulic model. These data are classified as static or dynamic data. Static data include number of floors and geographic locations, while dynamic data include water levels and population in a demand point.

4   Enhancing Interoperability

To handle the problem of interoperability among different involved actors in the disaster management process, we have proposed, in a previous work [1], a flood ontology that formally describes and thus provides semantics to the flood-related data.

---

[3] https://www.data.gouv.fr/en/datasets/bd-topo-r/.
[4] https://data.laregion.fr/explore/dataset/base-sirene-v3-ss/.

4.1   Flood Ontology

We define a class (concept) named "demand point" representing an infrastructure. It is characterized by four subclasses that represent evacuation priorities defined for a further usage. The class "Material infrastructure" describes all kinds of infrastructure including habitats, working places and healthcare facilities. In addition to the class "Material infrastructure" that describes all kinds of infrastructure, we define a novel class named "Infrastructure aggregation" that allows managing different kinds of infrastructure in an aggregated manner. This class regroups the infrastructure in districts, buildings and floors. We can thus describe for a district all the infrastructure that it contains. For example, we can describe that a district has buildings, a building has floors, and a floor has apartments using the "has part" relation. Thanks to the "Infrastructure aggregation" class, an infrastructure is described by its data as well as the data of the infrastructure that contains it. It can be useful when the data about a specific infrastructure are unavailable or uncertain; in this case, this infrastructure can be described by the data of the infrastructure containing it.

The class "population" describes the population in an infrastructure including fragile and non-fragile population. This class is reused from [11] with adding some details. "Fragile population" describes elderly, children, and persons with disabilities, reduced mobility or illnesses who should be given a high evacuation priority when a flood occurs. Non-fragile population thus represents all persons that are non-fragile. The relation "is in" defines that a population type is in an infrastructure (or infrastructure aggregation).

In addition to the classes, we define object and data properties. The object properties represent the relations that link classes, and they are divided into static and dynamic object properties. The static object properties represent relations between classes describing static data such as the "contains" relation that links an infrastructure or an infrastructure aggregation to a population. The data properties represent properties describing the classes, and they are divided into static and dynamic data properties. The static data properties include a building's vulnerability index and number of floors, while the dynamic data properties include danger index, submersion height, flood duration, number of population and if a demand point is inhabited.

Our ontology contains 41 classes, 6 object properties and 23 data properties. It is represented as RDF triples[5] and is available online[6] . A visualization of the ontology classes is presented in Fig. 2 where the rectangles represent the classes of the ontology and the arrows represent the relations between classes.

4.2   Knowledge Graph

We have built our knowledge graph that integrates the heterogeneous flood-related data based on the concepts, relations and properties of our proposed ontology [1]. It contains all data instances represented in RDF format. The static

---

[5] https://www.w3.org/TR/rdf11-primer/#section-triple.

[6] https://www.irit.fr/recherches/MELODI/ontologies/i-Nondations.owl.

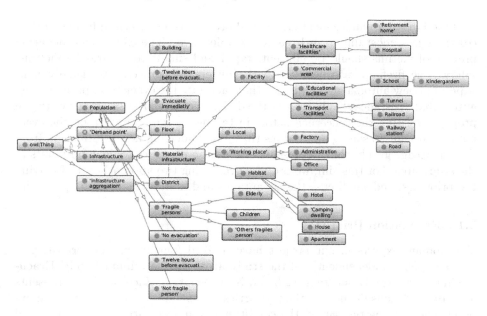

Fig. 2. Visualization of our flood ontology concepts

data are first integrated and transformed into RDF triples that are added to the ontology triples. The dynamic data are then integrated, transformed into RDF triples, updated in real-time throughout the flood and added to the ontology and static data triples. The RDF transformation of static and dynamic data are performed using "rdflib" library in python environment that maps data according to the concepts and relations of the ontology[7].

The knowledge graph is shared among all the actors involved in the management process to enhance the information interoperability and ensure that each actor can access the needed data at the right time. In order to facilitate the data access by the actors of the management process, the knowledge graph can be represented in GQIS[8], a cross-platform desktop geographic information system application that supports viewing, editing, and analyzing geospatial data. The actors can choose the data to visualize to better understand the flood event and take the relevant decisions.

5   Inferring Evacuation Priorities

In addition to the information sharing and enhancing interoperability, the knowledge graph can be used to infer new information that does not exist in the knowledge graph thus enriching it. The enriched knowledge graph can then be shared so that the actors use the new information to take more efficient decisions.

---

[7] https://rdflib.readthedocs.io/.

[8] https://qgis.org/en/site/.

Flood disaster management is a critical process as it concerns limiting adverse consequences, most importantly saving people's lives. Therefore, the evacuation process of victims should be efficient, rapid and simple to ensure the victims' safety. The firefighters concerned in the evacuation process are usually non-experts in new automated techniques that facilitate the evacuation process. Any automated assistance should respect the delicacy of this process. In our work, we propose assisting the concerned actors in taking decisions concerning the evacuation through reasoning approaches that allow inferring new information from the knowledge graph which represents evacuation priorities to demand points in the study area. For this aim, we propose evaluating two approaches for inferring the priorities, and we discuss the advantages and limitations of each approach.

5.1   Evacuation Priorities

The domain experts in our project have defined four evacuation priorities of demand points independently of the study area: Evacuate immediately, Evacuate in 6 h (hours), Evacuate in 12 h and No evacuation. Each priority represents a set of conditions defined on the properties of demand points, and the demand point whose properties satisfy the conditions of an evacuation priority is typed with this priority. The properties used for defining the evacuation priorities represent static and dynamic data properties defined in the ontology to describe demand points including danger and vulnerability indices, flood duration, number of floors, submersion height, housing type and if the demand point is inhabitable. The conditions of priorities are defined in an exclusive manner to avoid any conflicting cases; in addition, they consider all possible properties' values describing demand points. The conditions defining the priority "Evacuate in 12 h" are displayed in Fig. 3.

```
Conditions of the priority "Evacuate in 12h":
    danger_index > 0 && danger_index < 50
    && duration_of_flooding >= 12 && number_of_floors >=1
    && submersion_height > 0.0 && submersion_height <= 1.0
    && vulnerability_index < 50.0 && is_habitated = true
```

Fig. 3. Conditions defining the evacuation priority "Evacuate in 12 h"

5.2   Reasoning Approaches for Inferring Evacuation Priorities

We evaluate two reasoning approaches to infer the evacuation priorities of demand points in our study area. The first approach is reasoning using SPARQL queries, and the second approach is reasoning using SHACL rules.

Inferring Evacuation Priorities Using SPARQL Queries
SPARQL is an RDF query language that can be used to query and retrieve data. SPARQL queries[9] are usually used to query knowledge graphs in order to

---

[9] https://www.w3.org/TR/rdf-sparql-query/.

extract information [15]; however, they can also be used for reasoning over the knowledge graph to infer new information. We propose using SPARQL queries to infer the evacuation priorities of demand points from the knowledge graph containing the flood-related data.

The first step of this approach consists of storing the knowledge graph in a triplestore, also named RDF store, that is a purpose-built database for the storage and retrieval of triples through semantic queries. We have chosen "Virtuoso" triplestore for storing knowledge graphs as it is proved to be efficient in storing a big number of triples in a relatively short time. The results of a benchmark show that Virtuoso can load 1 billion RDF triples in 27 min while other triplestores take hours to load them including BigData, BigOwlim and TDB[10].

We define SPARQL insert and delete queries defining the conditions of each evacuation priority, and we execute the queries on the knowledge graph stored in Virtuoso. The queries allow inferring a new triple for each demand point representing the demand point typed with an evacuation priority based on its properties. The SPARQL query defining the priority "Evacuate in 12 h" is displayed in Fig. 4.

```
prefix owl:<http://www.w3.org/2002/07/owl#>
prefix rdf:<http://www.w3.org/1999/02/22-rdf-syntax-ns#>
prefix ont:<https://www.irit.fr/recherches/MELODI/ontologies/i-Nondations.html#>
DELETE{?x rdf:type ont:12h_before_evacuation; rdf:type ont:6h_before_evacuation;
rdf:type ont:No_evacuation; rdf:type ont:Evacuate_immediatly.}
INSERT{?x rdf:type ont:12h_before_evacuation}
WHERE{?x rdf:type ont:Demand_point ; ont:submersion_height ?a;
ont:vulnerability_index ?b;
ont:danger_index ?c; ont:number_of_floors ?d ; ont:is_habitated ?e; ont:contains ?f;
ont:duration_of_flooding ?g
FILTER(?a > "0.0"^^xsd:double && ?a <= "1.0"^^xsd:double
    && ?b < "50.0"^^xsd:double && ?c > "0"^^xsd:integer && ?c < 50"^^xsd:integer
    && ?d >= "1"^^xsd:integer && ?e = true && ?g >= "12"^^xsd:integer)}
```

Fig. 4. SPARQL query defining the priority "Evacuate in 12 h"

Inferring Evacuation Priorities Using SHACL Rules

Rules are frequently used for reasoning over knowledge graphs to infer new information. Various kinds of rules are used in disaster management including as SWRL rules [8]. In this approach, we propose using SHACL rules to infer evacuation priorities to the demand points in our study area. SHACL (Shapes Constraint Language)[11] is a World Wide Web Consortium (W3C) standard language that defines RDF vocabulary to describe shapes where shapes are collections of constraints that apply to a set of nodes. A SHACL rule[12] is a recent kind of rules

---

[10] http://wbsg.informatik.uni-mannheim.de/bizer/berlinsparqlbenchmark/results/ V7/#exploreVirtuoso.

[11] https://www.w3.org/TR/shacl/.

[12] https://www.w3.org/TR/shacl-af/.

having advantages over other kinds, and it has not been used in this domain yet. A SHACL rule is identified through a unique Internationalized Resource Identifier (IRI) in contrary to other rules. It can also be activated or deactivated upon user's needs where a deactivated rule is ignored by the rules engine. In addition, an execution order of the rules can be defined. In our approach, we use SPARQL rules, a kind of SHACL rules written in SPARQL notation, to infer the evacuation priorities of demand points. The rules are defined in a shape file containing node shapes that represent classes describing the evacuation priorities as well as the used properties. The SPARQL rule representing the priority "Evacuate in 12 h" is displayed in Fig. 5. The rules are executed on the knowledge graph to infer new triples each consisting of a demand point typed with an evacuation priority according to its properties. The knowledge graph is enriched by adding the inferred triples to it, and it is then shared among different actors.

```
sh:rule [
rdf:type sh:SPARQLRule ;
sh:prefixes ns1: ;
sh:construct """
PREFIX ns1:    <https://www.irit.fr/recherches/MELODI/ontologies/i-Nondations.html#>
CONSTRUCT
{   ?this ns1:priority ?priority.}
WHERE{
    $this ns1:danger_index ?danger_index.
    $this ns1:duration_of_flooding ?duration_of_flooding.
    $this ns1:number_of_floors ?number_of_floors.
    $this ns1:submersion_height ?submersion_height.
    $this ns1:vulnerability_index ?vulnerability_index.
    $this ns1:is_habitated ?is_habitated.
FILTER
    (?danger_index > 0 && ?danger_index < 50
    && ?duration_of_flooding >= 12 && ?number_of_floors >=1
    && ?submersion_height > 0.0 && ?submersion_height <= 1.0
    && ?vulnerability_index < 50.0 && ?is_habitated = true).
    BIND ("12h_before_evacuation" AS ?priority).
    }""" ;
    sh:condition ns1:12h_before_evacuation ;];
```

Fig. 5. SHACL rule defining the priority "Evacuate in 12 h"

6 Approach Evaluation

In this section, we first discuss the evaluation of our ontology; then, we discuss the evaluation of the reasoning approaches for inferring the evacuation priorities.

6.1 Ontology Evaluation

In the frame of our project, we have conducted regular interviews with the domain experts in order to get their feedback concerning the ontology vocabulary. The experts' feedback indicate that the concepts describing the infrastructures are sufficient as they include all the possible kinds of infrastructures that can be found in a flooded area. In addition, the concept defining the infrastructure aggregation is important as it solves the problem of missing or unavailable data. Concerning the concepts describing the population with its different categories, they indicate that they are consistent, and the relations between the population and the infrastructure are important as they allow to identify fragile persons in an infrastructure in order to prioritize their evacuation. The concepts and data properties describing the demand points were found to be adequate, and they cover all the properties used for defining the evacuation priorities. The concepts describing the four evacuation priorities are found to be important when used for planning the evacuation and inferring priorities of demand points.

According to the domain experts' feedback and as the ontology is further used to infer evacuation priorities of demand points, it is useful to add concepts describing human and vehicle resources needed for evacuating flood victims in order to allow an efficient resource management.

6.2   Experimental Evaluation of Reasoning Approaches

In this section, we discuss the experimental evaluations conducted to evaluate the two reasoning approaches for inferring the evacuation priorities of demand points. First, we analyze the impact of the variation of the number of knowledge graph instances on the complexity of the two reasoning approaches, and then we evaluate the complexity of the evacuation priorities.

All the conducted experiments run in 4h and 1min on 8 CPUs Core i7-1185G7, and draw 0.28 kWh. Based in France, this has a carbon footprint of 11.01 g CO_2e, which is equivalent to 0.01 tree-months (calculated using greenalgorithms.org v2.1 [9]).

Variation of the Number of Demand Points

Evacuation priorities are inferred to the demand points in the study area; therefore, the number of instances of demand points determines the number of evacuation priorities to be inferred, and it represents the number of times that the conditions of each evacuation priority should be tested in order to infer a priority for a demand point. In this experiment, we aim at analyzing the impact of the variation of the number of instances describing the demand points in the knowledge graph on the complexity of the two reasoning approaches for inferring the evacuation priorities in terms of execution time.

We have 15,078 demand points in our study area. A demand point is described by different instances and relations representing its properties. All the instances are represented in the form of RDF triples where the knowledge graph of our study area contains a total number of 472,594 triples. In order to analyze the impact of the variation of the number of instances, we evaluate the execution time of the reasoning processes with decreasing percentages of demand points in the knowledge graph from 75% to 25% of the total number of demand points. Table 1 displays the number of demand points for each decreasing percentage. Figure 6 shows the execution timesof the two reasoning approaches with decreasing percentages of demand points in the knowledge graph. We recall that the two approaches are reasoning using SPARQL insert and delete queries and using SHACL rules.

We notice from these results that the execution time decreases with decreasing percentages of demand points in the knowledge graph using the two reasoning approaches. It takes significantly less time to infer the priorities using SHACL rules (12.86 s for 100% of demand points) than using SPARQL queries (80.62 s) which makes it a more efficient approach. The SPARQL approach requires the knowledge graph's loading on the triplestore which takes from 3 to 4.5 s depending on its size, while the chosen SHACL implementation is independent of a triplestore.

Our proposed approach of inferring evacuation priorities is a critical approach that should be applied on real use cases of flood disasters; therefore, it should be a reactive approach that helps the firefighters in taking their decisions. Our data represents a real flood disaster case; these results thus prove that the two reasoning approaches are reactive in real use cases while the SHACL approach being more efficient than the SPARQL approach in terms of time. Furthermore, our approach is efficient for our study area which represents a relatively large area of $52.80 \, \text{km}^2$ containing 15,078 demand points and 2,384 inhabitants (2015). The results of decreasing percentages of demand points prove that the reasoning approaches are reactive for varying numbers of demand points and thus for different flood areas.

Table 1. Percentage of demand points in KG

% of demand points in KG	Number of evacuation priorities
100%	15,078
75%	11,308
50%	7,539
25%	3,769

Evaluation of Priorities' Complexity

We define the complexity of an evacuation priority as the complexity of the reasoning process in terms of time upon executing this priority on the knowledge graph. The number of conditions defining a priority impacts its complexity. We define the worst case scenario of an evacuation priority, representing its highest complexity, as the case where all its conditions must be tested for each demand point. It is useful to the actors involved in the evacuation process to know the complexity of an evacuation priority as it allows them to estimate the complexity of inferring evacuation priorities in any flood condition.

The four evacuation priorities are defined by different numbers of conditions. Table 2 shows the number of conditions defining each priority. We evaluate the

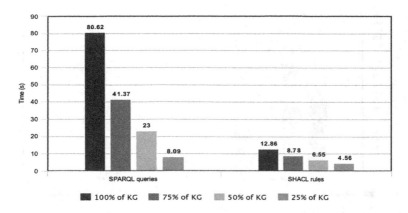

Fig. 6. Execution times (s) of inferring priorities using SPARQL queries and SHACL rules with decreasing percentages of demand points

Table 2. Number of conditions constituting evacuation priorities

Evacuation priority	Number of conditions
Evacuate in 12 h	8
Evacuate in 6 h	16
Evacuate immediately	18
No evacuation	27

complexity of each evacuation priority using the two reasoning approaches for inferring the priorities of demand points.

In order to evaluate the complexity of the evacuation priorities in terms of execution time, there should be an equivalent number of demand points typed with each evacuation priority. This is not the case in our study area as different numbers of demand points are typed with each priority; therefore, we choose to evaluate the complexity using a synthetically generated knowledge graph that satisfies the above condition with considering the worst case scenario. This knowledge graph contains 16,000 demand points; each 4,000 demand points are typed by one evacuation priority, that is their properties satisfy the conditions of this priority. This knowledge graph is generated by generating data representing the demand points with their corresponding properties and transforming these data into RDF triples using the ontology. The RDF triples constituting the knowledge graph are generated using JENA Java library[13].

Figure 7 presents the experimental results in terms of execution time (in seconds) for each evacuation priority using the two approaches for inferring the priorities from the synthetic knowledge graph.

We notice from the results that the execution time increases as the number of conditions defining each priority increases in both approaches (refer to Table

---

[13] https://jena.apache.org/.

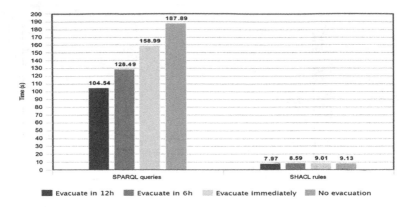

Fig. 7. Execution times (s) of evacuation priorities on the synthetic knowledge graph

2 for the number of conditions defining each priority). This confirms that the number of conditions defining an evacuation priority impacts its complexity. In addition, inferring the priorities using SHACL rules takes less time than using SPARQL queries for all evacuation priorities.

Although the execution time increases with increasing complexity of evacuation priorities, this increase remains reasonable. According to the domain experts, the results show that the reasoning approaches are efficient to be used in different possible scenarios of flood disasters for inferring the evacuation priorities of demand points while the SHACL approach remains more efficient than the SPARQL approach in terms of time.

6.3   Discussion

Inferring evacuation priorities of demand points using SHACL rules is proved to be more efficient than using SPARQL queries as it allows inferring the priorities in a shorter time for different flood disaster scenarios. In addition, the complexity of the evacuation priorities as well as the increase in the number of priorities has a lower impact on the SHACL approach than on the SPARQL approach.

The delicacy of the evacuation process requires proposing solutions that are not only efficient and rapid but also simple to assist in facilitating it. The inferred evacuation priorities of demand points can be accessed and visualized graphically in QGIS where we can view each demand point of the study area typed with an evacuation priority according to its properties that can also be visualized, such as the water level. In addition, these inferred priorities of demand points can be used in an algorithm of vehicle routing that optimizes the routing of the various vehicles used for the evacuation of flood victims [2]. The domain experts indicate that this would assist in the disaster response phase by optimizing the routes of the evacuation vehicles with the help of the priorities of different demand points; in addition, it would help in the preparedness phase through simulations conducted by the concerned actors to enhance the evacuation process.

SPARQL queries defining the evacuation priorities can be integrated in a tool where a natural language query written by the user about an evacuation priority can be transformed into a SPARQL query using existing approaches of query transformations [10, 13]. SHACL rules are based on SPARQL query language; therefore, natural queries can be transformed to rules and then integrated in a tool used by the users to infer information. In addition, integrating SHACL rules in a tool would allow users to choose whether to activate or deactivate rules as well as to set an execution order of different rules based upon their needs.

7   Conclusion and Future Work

In this paper, we have discussed our proposed solutions for enhancing the interoperability in the case of a flood disaster as well as for inferring evacuation priorities to demand points in a flooded area in order to assist in the evacuation process. We have proposed an ontology and a knowledge graph that allow managing and integrating the flood-related data and sharing them among different actors involved in the flood management process [1]. The feedback of the experts has showed that this solution enhances the interoperability. Furthermore, we have discussed two reasoning approaches for inferring evacuation priorities of demand points in our study area, reasoning using SPARQL queries and using SHACL rules. The experimental results have proved that the two reasoning approaches can be used for inferring the priorities while the SHACL approach is more efficient as it allows inferring the priorities in a shorter time thus assisting the involved actors in taking rapid and efficient decisions.

As a future work, we first aim at industrially expressing this work through an interface that integrates SHACL Rules and allows transforming users' natural language queries to rules for the purpose of inferring new information. We also aim at relying on the ontology to infer new information concerning the management of the human and vehicle resources needed for the evacuation process. In addition to inferring new information that assists in the disaster response phase, we aim at inferring new information to improve a past disaster's experience. We thus aim at proposing a learning approach that allows learning from a past disaster's data and adjusting the values of the properties that define the conditions of evacuation priorities.

Acknowledgments. This work has been funded by the ANR (https://anr.fr/) in the context of the project "i-Nondations" (e-Flooding), ANR-17-CE39-0011.

References

1. Bu Daher, J., Huygue, T., Stolf, P., Hernandez, N.: An ontology and a reasoning approach for evacuation in flood disaster response. In: 17th International Conference on Knowledge Management 2022. University of North Texas (UNT) Digital Library (2022)

2. Dubois, F., Renaud-Goud, P., Stolf, P.: Capacitated vehicle routing problem under deadlines: an application to flooding crisis. IEEE Access **10**, 45629–45642 (2022). https://doi.org/10.1109/ACCESS.2022.3170446
3. Elmhadhbi, L., Karray, M.H., Archimède, B.: A modular ontology for semantically enhanced interoperability in operational disaster response. In: 16th International Conference on Information Systems for Crisis Response and Management-ISCRAM 2019, pp. 1021–1029 (2019)
4. Franke, J.: Coordination of distributed activities in dynamic situations. The case of inter-organizational crisis management. Ph.D. thesis, Université Henri Poincaré-Nancy I (2011)
5. Katuk, N., Ku-Mahamud, K.R., Norwawi, N., Deris, S.: Web-based support system for flood response operation in Malaysia. Disaster Prev. Manag. Int. J. **18**(3), 327–337 (2009)
6. Khantong, S., Sharif, M.N.A., Mahmood, A.K.: An ontology for sharing and managing information in disaster response: an illustrative case study of flood evacuation. Int. Rev. Appl. Sci. Eng. (2020)
7. Kurte, K.R., Durbha, S.S., King, R.L., Younan, N.H., Potnis, A.V.: A spatio-temporal ontological model for flood disaster monitoring. In: 2017 IEEE International Geoscience and Remote Sensing Symposium (IGARSS), pp. 5213–5216. IEEE (2017)
8. Kurte, K.R., Durbha, S.S., King, R.L., Younan, N.H., Vatsavai, R.: Semantics-enabled framework for spatial image information mining of linked earth observation data. IEEE J. Sel. Top. Appl. Earth Obs. Remote Sens. **10**(1), 29–44 (2016)
9. Lannelongue, L., Grealey, J., Inouye, M.: Green algorithms: quantifying the carbon footprint of computation. Adv. Sci. **8**(12), 2100707 (2021)
10. Ochieng, P.: PAROT: translating natural language to SPARQL. Expert Syst. Appl. X **5**, 100024 (2020)
11. Scheuer, S., Haase, D., Meyer, V.: Towards a flood risk assessment ontology-knowledge integration into a multi-criteria risk assessment approach. Comput. Environ. Urban Syst. **37**, 82–94 (2013)
12. Schulz, S., Martínez-Costa, C.: How ontologies can improve semantic interoperability in health care. In: Riaño, D., Lenz, R., Miksch, S., Peleg, M., Reichert, M., ten Teije, A. (eds.) KR4HC/ProHealth -2013. LNCS (LNAI), vol. 8268, pp. 1–10. Springer, Cham (2013). https://doi.org/10.1007/978-3-319-03916-9_1
13. Shaik, S., Kanakam, P., Hussain, S.M., Suryanarayana, D.: Transforming natural language query to SPARQL for semantic information retrieval. Int. J. Eng. Trends Technol. **7**, 347–350 (2016)
14. Studer, R., Benjamins, V.R., Fensel, D.: Knowledge engineering: principles and methods. Data Knowl. Eng. **25**(1–2), 161–197 (1998)
15. Wang, C., Chen, N., Wang, W., Chen, Z.: A hydrological sensor web ontology based on the SSN ontology: a case study for a flood. ISPRS Int. J. Geo Inf. **7**(1), 2 (2018)
16. Xu, W., Zlatanova, S.: Ontologies for disaster management response. In: Li, J., Zlatanova, S., Fabbri, A.G. (eds.) Geomatics Solutions for Disaster Management. LNGC, pp. 185–200. Springer, Heidelberg (2007). https://doi.org/10.1007/978-3-540-72108-6_13
17. Yahya, H., Ramli, R.: Ontology for evacuation center in flood management domain. In: 2020 8th International Conference on Information Technology and Multimedia (ICIMU), pp. 288–291. IEEE (2020)

Situational Disabilities in Information Systems for Situational Awareness in Flood Situations in Nigeria

Uchenna Ogbonna[1], Cristina Paupini[1] (iD), and Terje Gjøsæter[1,2(✉)] (iD)

[1] Department of Computer Science, Oslo Metropolitan University, Oslo, Norway
cristpa@oslomet.no, terjeg@uia.no
[2] Centre for Integrated Emergency Management, University of Agder, Kristiansand, Norway

Abstract. Floods are one of the major natural disasters that contribute to the high disaster death rate in the global south, especially in Nigeria. This requires an effort of collaboration from all stakeholders in designing, building, deploying, and maintaining inclusive disaster management systems. This effort can hardly be achieved without the application of universal design principles in designing rescue applications. In this research, we have studied situational disabilities and their effect on situational awareness based on the data collected from victims in Nigeria through a questionnaire with 56 respondents and 5 follow-up interviews. The research work contributed to identifying situational disabilities and their corresponding accessibility barriers based on difficulty experiences collected from the research participants in Nigeria.

Keywords: Universal Design · Universally Designed Rescue Applications · Inclusive Disaster Management Systems · ICT for Situational Awareness

1 Introduction

Natural Disasters have always affected humans. It remains a fact that we are living in a world where different kinds of severe natural disasters occur and impact the socio-economic sphere of the affected areas [1]. Information Communication Technology (ICT) artifacts are essential in emergency management [2], and their accessibility and usability in a disastrous situation through the application of universal design principles has become a scientific discussion topic [3–8].

Universal Design principles are applied in many areas to ensure that products and services are usable for the broadest possible diversity of users [9]. However, there is still room for improvement when it comes to Emergency Management in flood scenarios to mitigate situational disabilities that might hinder situational awareness [10, 11]. Floods are among the most common natural disasters, with 30–50 million people affected each year [12]. In Nigeria, flood accounts for the most frequently occurring natural hazards, with great consequences on life and property [13]. The causes of floods are both natural

T. Gjøsæter et al. (Eds.): ITDRR 2022, IFIP AICT 672, pp. 55–68, 2023.
https://doi.org/10.1007/978-3-031-34207-3_4

and anthropogenic and in the last decades, for instance, many states and cities have witnessed unusual and devastating floods [13].

Research work has shown that individuals in a disaster situation are often unable to access information through the use of technologies in their environment as a consequence of situational factors [10]. Situational awareness is an important factor for effective decision-making, especially when it comes to crisis management [14]. In the context of this paper, situational awareness is defined as the ability to be aware of one's surroundings and identify potential hazards or dangers [15]. Individuals in natural disasters can experience state of shock, trauma, or being unable to move to safety or use available technology to seek help due to the dangerous conditions all around them. In these cases, the individual is said to be situationally disabled. Situational disability is a term used to describe the disability-like difficulties that people face when they are affected by situational factors. In a disaster situation, these factors can make it difficult for them to be aware of what's happening around them or to plan the appropriate action to take [10]. Examples include impaired vision in fogged environments, limited mobility in flooded areas, and hearing impairments in noisy areas. These types of disabilities can pose challenges when carrying out certain tasks or navigating spaces. Individuals might not be able to utilize available means like ICT emergency services, warning announcements, and evacuation plans for evacuation or seeking safety in time. Mitigating situational disabilities in the use of ICT devices provides an opportunity to create a more inclusive emergency management system that benefits all users. This work aims at providing an in-depth systematic understanding of the possible situational disabilities experienced by individuals in flood situations, which hinders situational awareness. It also highlights high-impact scenarios where a universal design approach can be used to enhance situational awareness.

We will examine the ways various factors trigger situational disability and its impact on situational awareness in flood emergency situations in Nigeria through gathered data from flood victims. The core objective of this research work is to identify situational disabilities in a flood situation and study their effect on situational awareness through answering the following research questions.

RQ1: What are the situational disabilities at play in a flood scenario?

RQ2: What are the effects of situational disabilities on situational awareness in a flood scenario?

The rest of the paper is organized as follows. Section 2 reviews existing related research works in the research domain. Section 3 focuses on the methodology of the research work. Section 4 deals with the analysis and results of the study. The discussion is covered in Sect. 5. Conclusion and future works are included in Sect. 6.

2 Background

2.1 Flood-Related Disaster Situations

According to the global survey conducted by the UN published on 10 October 2013, the top hazards or disaster risks faced by survey respondents were floods, with 54% of all hazardous occurrences [16]. Developing countries are more prone to disasters or hazards due to challenges like poverty, lack of resources, lack of educational opportunities, poor infrastructure, lack of trained manpower, lack of awareness and knowledge of disaster and mental health [16]. Research has shown that flooding is the most severe and prevalent adverse event and has serious implications for sustainable development [17].

While the world is currently facing the COVID-19 pandemic, disasters such as flooding are still occurring, but limited attention is being paid. The United Nations 2030 agenda for sustainable development calls for a global partnership in addressing these problems. Intending to highlight areas of possible partnership on disaster-risk reduction, Nigeria like most sub-Saharan African nations is prone to perennial flooding and advocates for national cooperation in managing flood risks. Empirical research on the effects of disaster on people, though sparse, confirms that individuals with disabilities are at higher risk of death [18] and injury [19]. The impacts of floods are catastrophic and most times very difficult to forecast with precision and can subsequently leave people uninformed and subject to surprise amid their daily activities [20]. A study by Olajuyigbe (2012) has shown that the major floods in Nigeria are river floods, coastal floods, and urban floods [21]. Among these, river flooding is the most destructive.

The study by Ruin, Creutin [22] has described Flash floods as high-impact, occasionally catastrophic events that result from the intersection of hydro meteorological extremes and society at small space–time scales, generally on the order of hours. It is further stated that flash floods are much localized in space and time, they are very difficult to forecast with precision and can subsequently jeopardize situational awareness. A study by Jonkman and Kelman [23] has shown that the type of flood and especially its space-time dynamics affect the level of harm suffered. According to the study, different types of floods have different impact levels as shown by their different mortality rates. The difference between these two kinds of floods does not just contribute to the magnitude and type of harm they cause but also plays a role in the emergence of vulnerabilities that do not occur with other flooding phenomena such as general flooding [23]. Studies have also shown that extreme flooding events could trap people in their cars or outside. They mostly happen during rush hours when commuters are on the road [24]. On the other hand, large hydrological scales typically cause building damage and prevent individuals from taking action [24].

2.2 Inclusive Disaster Management

The Sendai Framework For Disaster Risk Reduction [1] emphasizes that disaster risk reduction and risk-aware development are instruments to slow the hazard-perpetuating wheel of disaster exposure like a flood. The infusion of disability-related terms and concepts such as accessibility, inclusion, and universal design throughout the SFDRR document was significant. These concepts, which have their origin in disability studies, are used in the SFDRR document to refer to the needs of all in disaster, not only people with disabilities. Additionally, the Disability Inclusive Disaster Risk Reduction (DIDRR) commits to ensuring that people with disabilities have the same opportunity to access emergency preparedness information, participate in emergency preparedness programs in their community, and be included as a valuable stakeholders in all phases (preparedness, response, and recovery) of local community disaster risk reduction [25].

Disaster risk management involves information-driven activities and tasks [26]. ICT has been seen to have played a major role in community disaster resilience plans, and in particular in supporting people with disabilities and other vulnerable groups [27]. Universal Design guidelines can play a great role in DIDRR Initiative in creating ICT for emergency management that can be used by everyone with or without adaptation in many cases such as in flood emergencies. ICT systems and tools should be developed to be more accessible and usable among a wide range of diversified users to the greatest extent possible. A prerequisite for this type of product development process would be giving attention to diversity among users so that the needs of all types of people may be considered in its conception.

From the perspective of Universal Design, research shows that universal design in ICT and Emergency Management context might not only be important for people with disabilities but also to a wide range of stakeholders who may also be affected by situational disabilities caused by social and environmental barriers that can occur during emergencies [10, 11]. Introducing a universal design approach will make it more likely to develop an effective and efficient system, one which supports decision making while at the same time mitigating situational disability. It becomes even more necessary when dealing with complex systems- ones where there is always lots of information changing rapidly, or hard to obtain [15].

2.3 Situational Disabilities in Flood Scenarios

Situational disabilities can include difficulties in obtaining information, making decisions, or taking action. Situational disability can be caused by the physical environment, communication breakdowns, or psychological factors such as stress or fear [28]. Understanding situational disability in flood situations is the first step towards mitigating it and enhancing situational awareness in difficult situations with more ease in the future. Situational disabilities can range from reduced vision to no vision at all in low light environments or blackouts, limited mobility in crowded areas and blocked hearing in noisy areas, etc. These types of disabilities can pose challenges for people when carrying out certain tasks or navigating spaces. Recent studies by Gjøsæter, Radianti [10] have identified that in many cases, especially in disaster situations, people can suffer from a situational disabilities and environmental barriers.

To fully understand the impact of flood disaster and its effects on emergency management, Gjøsæter, Radianti [11] established frameworks that are crucial to analyze the interaction between different stakeholders and tools in different scenarios of a flood and development of such tools to mitigate a situational disability. The role of various stakeholders in a flood scenario differs in needs, methods of interaction with ICT technologies, and environmental challenges, while they all need to attain Situational Awareness. We see stakeholders in form of first responders who are first on the scene, local members of the general public who might be victims affected by a flood, and control room personnel who are in control of observation, recording, and interpretation of data for decision making, and decision makers responsible for allocation of resources, logistics, government agencies and NGOs who are responsible for pre-post-disaster analysis, offering knowledgeable expertise and allocation of resources.

2.4 Situational Awareness

Situational awareness (SA) originated in military research during World War I and has become one of the key factors in contemporary disaster management [29]. SA can be defined as the cognizance of entities in the environment, understanding of their meaning, and the projection of their status in near future [15]. Endsley [30] has shown that several disastrous incidents were caused by a lack of adequate perception, comprehension, and projection of an action. She further argued that overcoming the challenge of acquisition and understanding information that comes through data is important and can make the difference between success and failure in many situations. Situational awareness is crucial in disaster scenarios and is often difficult to come by due to the challenges in coherently obtaining the necessary information and organizing it.

The fundamental point of gaining situational awareness is familiarity with elements in the environment, as well as understanding what those elements mean [31]. In other words, when people grasp the information they receive and understand its significance- they have gained situational awareness [32]. Situational awareness (SA) is critical to mobilizing a rapid, efficient, and effective response to disasters.

By assessing SA on an individual level [15], in what might be one of her most cited papers, defines SA as the perception of elements in an environment within a volume of time and space. In essence, Endsley claims that SA can only exist if it reflects what has been processed before by an individual since this leads to more understanding of how to respond to new information about a given challenge or event. Furthermore, an individual assessment study by Klein, Calderwood [33] has shown that Short-term and long-term memory are necessary for the speed at which our brain processes information. The basic mechanisms that constitute SA are short-term sensory memory, perception, working memory, and long-term memories which are based on a mental model of SA. This is known, as described by Doyle and Ford [34], to play a vital role in determining what is going on with any given situation - they provide context to what we perceive by defining *"the purpose of a system as well as its functioning"*. This definition gives insight into why the psychological aspect of SA is so important: it's because mental models form such an integral part of understanding anything. The activity theory model by Doyle and Ford [34] represents another way to examine SA. This approach combines consciousness with diverse "in-world" activities and subscribes to a process perspective of SA, arguing that the extent to which information-processing methods are involved in achieving SA is dependent on the nature of the task and goals of an individual.

2.5 ICT-Supported Situational Awareness

Recent disasters and crises have shone a spotlight on the role that Information and Communication Technologies (ICT) can play in gaining situational awareness by connecting people to relevant information, people to rescue workers and resources, and people to people in the immediate aftermath and recovery communication is one of the most important aspects of emergency management [35].

In a case of emergency, communications can be affected in interaction and conversation quality due to connection and noise coming from the background [36], this can have a negative impact on the speech and audio output. Visual distortion can ensue from fog hindering visibility or wetness on the individual palms which in turn can prevent or limit simple mobile device operational gestures. Cold and stiffness of joints limiting simple motoric movements to carry out operations.

On the other hand evidence from a variety of sources indicates that wearable and mobile technologies can lead to distraction and accidents in both the general population and emergency responders [37]. The contradictory nature of wearable and mobile information technologies most times comes with the increased multiple streams of information and the associated reduction of attention to those sources of information due to stress and anxiety [38].

It can be challenging and complicated to maintain sufficient SA levels in an emergency. Gjøsæter et al. [10] examined Endsley's SA-Demons [15] and their relationship with situational disabilities that can arise in a disaster situation and make it more difficult to establish SA by increasing the chance of human error due to usability or accessibility barriers present in the technology.

In large-scale operations such as disaster management, many different parties work collaboratively. In emergency situations, most communication is bound to happen via ICT since agencies may be located over a large geographical area. This means that those who use these types of forms of ICT for their communications receive less information than in face-to-face discussions because implicit or nonverbal cues like body language and environmental stimuli are left out from these events [39].

2.6 Digital Disaster Management: The Case of Nigeria

Nigeria has experienced shocking disasters in recent years, which led to the establishment of the National Emergency Management Agency (NEMA) in March 1999, with the single objective of coordinating disaster management activities in the country. Given the huge impact of natural disasters on society, comprehensive national disaster risk management strategies have been adopted by NEMA in the form of the National Disaster Response Plan (NDRP). NDRP was created for the purpose of processing, structuring, and coordinating an effective response plan for disasters in Nigeria.

Nigeria is one of the countries combating this menace of disaster and has adopted and encouraged the usage of ICT in its NDRP objectives and private partnerships to protect lives and properties among its citizens. This has given rise to a few of many common ICT emergency response platforms that have found their usage in the recent flood disaster that has been witnessed in the country. The advancement of ICT in Nigeria has over the years played an important component in disaster risk management in Nigeria [40]. These ICT tools have been utilized by NEMA and other emergency agencies in all stages of the disaster management cycle.

3 Research Design and Data Collection

In this research work, we have followed a mixture of qualitative and quantitative research methodology in the collection and analysis of the research data [41].

An online survey was conducted among victims of flood in Nigeria. Questionnaires were sent out through email. This study adopts an online questionnaire methodology using SurveyMonkey as an accessible questionnaire tool to accommodate a more diversified groups of participants.

Qualitative interviews were conducted among the victims and individuals who have experienced flooding in Nigeria. This was made possible by NEMA (The Nigerian National Emergency Management Agency). Consent forms for interviews were drawn for participants who consented to be contacted by phone for an oral interview.

The questionnaire was designed based on essential disaster management functionalities through questions about difficulties participants may have experienced in performing a task with an ICT device in a flood emergency scenario. Scales were set to ascertain the level of accessibility of using ICT devices in a flood situation. This task covers visual, audio, speech, cognition, and mobility abilities. The research has been conducted in accordance with the research ethics guidelines stated in "Ethical Guidelines for Research at Oslo Metropolitan University" and "The Nigerian National Code of Research Ethics".

An online survey and interviews were conducted among the victims and individuals who have experienced flooding, this was made possible by NEMA (the Nigerian National Emergency Management Agency). The participants were selected according to NEMA Flood emergency records from different backgrounds, economic classes, literacy levels, demography, and age. questionnaires were sent out through emails. Consent forms for interviews were drawn for participants who consented to be contacted by phone call for an oral semi-structured interview.

We designed an online questionnaire building on the Short Set on Functioning (WG-SS) from the Washington Group on Disability Statistics that provides questions on functioning and activity limitations for use e.g. in national censuses and surveys. WG-SS builds on a bio-psychosocial model of disability that sees disability as a result of the interaction between a person's capabilities and environmental barriers. Our questionnaire is comprised of thirteen functionality questions in consideration of visual, hearing, speech, mobility, and cognition abilities. The questionnaire starts by explaining in detail what is meant by situational disability for each of the functionality variables in order to clarify the terminology to the participants. The survey participants were given a single answer questionnaire with a likert scale of: *no difficulty*; *Some difficulty*; *A lot of difficulties*; *Cannot do at all*; and in addition the options *Refuse to answer*; *Don't know* were provided. From the total of 100 flood victims that received the questionnaire, 56 participants responded.

The information received from the 56 respondents was coded using a set of relevant categories for further quantitative analysis. Later, the data is analyzed according to the research questions of this work. We have considered the Web Content Accessibility Guidelines (WCAG) 2.0 when we analyze the data. This is because of the rational benchmark provided by the accessibility principles that help us to quantify experienced accessibility barriers due to situational disabilities in a better and more scientific way. We have also conducted semi-structured recorded interviews with 5 participants for qualitative thematic analysis and interpretation of users' experience in a flood situation and to identify situational barriers of the victims of flood disaster.

In thematic analysis, the first step always involves a careful understanding of the data at hand. Since the data was recorded in an audio mode in this research, data transcription is therefore needed to have a full grasp of the whole audio transcripts in text mode. The Data transcript requires multiple revisions over time to be able to understand and deduce the kind of themes involved in the transcript. We took the recommendation of taking notes at this stage as it can be used in the next stage of deeper analysis to have a better understanding of the research analysis [42].

The participants were all Nigerians and they spoke English; however, some accents were not correctly transcribed Into English. This affects the literal meaning of some sentences, but with careful listening to the audio recording repeatedly during data in this stage of data familiarization, these data errors were corrected thereby enhancing unbiasedness in the data. The texts of all the participants were then read to understand how this data answers the research questions and a basic form of codes were generated.

We then generated codes and searched for themes. The validity of these themes is then determined to see if they connect with data and research questions as suggested in Braun & Clarke (2006). The steps in the evaluation process are to first identify themes or groupings of ideas and opinions throughout the texts. We then refined specific themes into topics that reflect those particular ideas and opinions. Third, we determined whether our arguments pertain to certain concepts across all texts- so-called "generalizations." The final step is making interpretations of what has been found through evaluating each text individually while also comparing them between themselves.

4 Analysis and Results

In this Section, we will present the analysis part of the research work to identify accessibility barriers resulting from situational disability and how this barrier affects situational awareness. The analysis includes both quantitative and qualitative approaches to address the research questions of this study.

4.1 Analysis

This research involved analyzing 15 quotes selected for relevance from the interview text and dividing them into five themes. During this process, related quotes were grouped to form a theme. This was done by how relevant each theme seemed to be when answering the research questions. After grouping all of the themes, some edits had to be made because it became clear that a few quotes did not fit well within its corresponding theme; this was mainly due to understanding what they meant after revisiting their original transcripts and finding out where they belonged to each topic being studied differently afterward as an attempt at verifying how much a specific quote contributes towards addressing our data-oriented question. Repeated rounds of generating codes for groups and including different revisions have proven fruitful as we are now able not only to classify our data but also to answer more specific questions about the research work.

The responses and opinions were analyzed thematically to shape the pattern of the responses [43]. As a result, 12 codes from the interview text were identified and later divided into three themes presented in Table 1.

Table 1. Themes and Codes.

Themes	Codes/Quotes from Interviews
Situational Barriers to ICT usage	Visual difficulties Cognitive Difficulties mobility difficulties hearing difficulties speech difficulties
Effects of barriers on situational awareness	Poor danger identification Poor decision making Poor location-awareness Poor communication
ICT design barriers	Internet issues Device issues System design issues

Participants were asked questions about the situational difficulties they encountered using an ICT device in a flood situation. Responses were affirmative on several difficulties experienced. *Participant 1* responded that: "It was hard to even use my phone at that moment even though I had so much need for it, but it was not easy to see through the phone because of haze from vapor. When I wanted to call my mother, I tried so hard to wipe the phone screen but there was still water on my hands, so it was difficult seeing anything through my phone." This indicates visual difficulties as well as explaining how it can lead to communication difficulties. *Participant 2* responded that: "I experienced a bit of communication difficulty, I was a bit loss of words, and even though I tried and succeeded to put out a call the person I was calling seem not to hear me quite clearly when I spoke. I had to more effort into raising my voice practically I was like shouting on phone to be heard." *Participant 4* similarly stated that: "Even though I tried using my phone often, but I was not able to concentrate or do any task I was used to even to simply search for a phone contact was not so easy. It is somehow difficult, and a lot of echoes were heard from the background and breakings in the conversation, strange noises were obstructing the signals, and the network signal was so much interfering. I was so tensed up that I wasn't able to hear properly because I was struggling to get to safety." These responses highlight issues of poor communication stemming both from cognitive difficulties as well as auditory ones. *Participant 3* also pointed out that: "I was unable to make a call or anything on my phone, my hand was so numb with cold. I had to jump off the car and rush to the pharmacy to get some gloves to keep my hand warm. As I was not able to hold the phone with my hand, I was unable to make a call with my phone. I was so helpless and disturbed by the scenario. I was very close to having a nervous breakdown. I thought to myself, what if I am in a situation where I am unable to make a call with my phone? What if I am unable to reach anyone?" Here we see the effects of the situation on mobility and dexterity, as well as the psychological pressure and stress of the situation that leads to cognitive difficulties, further supported by *Participant 5* who responded that: "It was raining heavily at the same time it was very hard to say anything as we were both overcome with shock to even hear what was around even to think more of hearing anything with a phone. I was extremely scared; I did not know what would happen next and I was very scared of what would happen to me again."

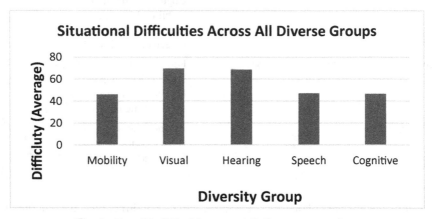

Fig. 1. Situation difficulties across all diverse groups chart.

4.2   Results

The main purpose of the evaluation is to identify situational disabilities and their level of impact on situational awareness. As a result, we analyze the situational difficulties that the respondents experienced based on the level of difficulties across all diverse groups and display the average difficulty rating (as a percentage from 0 to 100%) through the chart in Fig. 1.

However, if we want to answer which diversity group experienced more difficulties (accessibility barriers) or any form of difficulty, we get the result depicted in Fig. 2 (difficulty rating shown as a percentage from 0 to 100%).

If we analyze the mobility barriers that the research participants experienced in a flood situation based on the operability accessibility principle, we get the result summarized in Fig. 3.

We analyzed experienced situational disabilities in consideration of operability because of the direct correlation between mobility and the following issues:

- Performing input tasks without a keyboard is often required in a flood situation.
- Performing tasks with enough time.
- Performing simple navigation techniques to find contents that are critical in a flood situation.

We summarize the result of our thematic analysis based on the responses of interviewees in consideration of the thematic codes in Table 1 and see that situational disabilities can lead to difficulties in mobility, hearing, sight, cognition, and speech. This can have significant effects on situational awareness, and can lead to poor danger identification, poor decision making, poor communication and poor location awareness [10, 11].

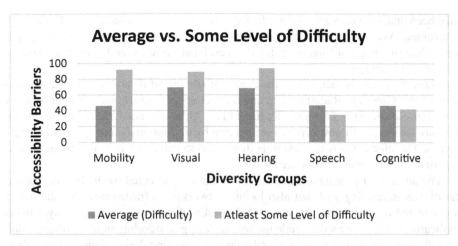

Fig. 2. Average vs. Some level of difficulty comparison chart

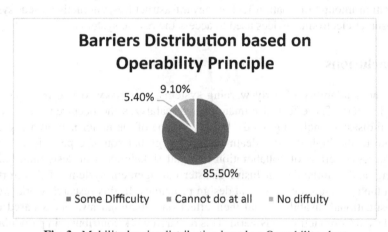

Fig. 3. Mobility barrier distribution based on Operability chart

5   Discussion

We see that people may experience accessibility barriers that are highly related to mobility and hearing. This is because of the environmental change [24] and the stressful psychological condition [28] that resulted from the flood situation. The results depicted in Fig. 1, indicate that people may encounter a serious number of visual accessibility barriers because of the situational disability created by the flood. The consequence of it is that an individual interacting with an ICT device in a stressful or dangerous condition and finds it hard to perceive and understand their surroundings situation will be hindered from the overall process of rescuing and response management. This implies that rescue applications should provide interaction with alternative channels including auditory and gestures. Situational disabilities reported that were related to mobility and speech implies that users who were interacting with an ICT device at the time of the flood might have been unable to interact with the device as the channel from the user to the device is interrupted. As a consequence, the need for alternative interaction channels/devices that triangulate the usage of fingers, tactile devices, hand gestures, and speech recognition systems is paramount.

These findings also align with the theory of situational disabilities in disaster situations from Gjøsæter, Radianti [10], and their effects on situational awareness which is further elaborated in Gjøsæter, Radianti [11]. Although these effects are intuitively obvious, they are until now primarily supported by discussions with experts and practitioners. Therefore, this is the first time they are systematically validated by users with experience from a real disaster scenario.

The attainment of situational awareness is not only affected by the ICT device that the user is interacting with but also by the networking infrastructure that the device is connected to, and the design pattern followed to develop the interactive systems or applications. This shows the challenge we are facing to develop an accessible product through universal design principles and reduce the existing digital divide, especially in Nigeria and other Sub-Saharan African countries. The challenge requires the inclusive orchestration among Information Technology infrastructures, interactive rescue systems, and consumer electronic devices used to access the rescue systems.

6 Conclusions

Despite the availability of early warning systems, it is risky to live in an area with natural disasters. The effect of climate change catalyzes the occurrence and severity of natural disasters including floods. Floods are one of the major natural disasters that contribute to the high disaster death rate in the global south, especially in Nigeria. This requires an effort of collaboration from all stakeholders in designing, building, deploying, and maintaining inclusive disaster management systems. This effort must build on the application of universal design principles. In this research work, we have studied situational disabilities and their effect on situational awareness based on the data collected from victims in Nigeria. This research work contributes in particular with the identification of situational disabilities and their corresponding accessibility barriers based on difficulty experiences collected from the research participants. We also note that these findings are in line with the described effects of situational disabilities in disasters [10, 11].

References

1. UNISDR. Sendai Framework for Disaster Risk Reduction 2015–2030: Building the Resilience of Nations and Communities to Disasters (2015)
2. Palen, L., Liu, S.B.: Citizen communications in crisis: anticipating a future of ICT-supported public participation. In: Proceedings of the SIGCHI Conference on Human Factors in Computing Systems (2007)
3. Radianti, J., Gjøsæter, T., Chen, W.: Universal design of information sharing tools for disaster risk reduction. In: Murayama, Y., Velev, D., Zlateva, P. (eds.) Information Technology in Disaster Risk Reduction. ITDRR 2017. IFIP Advances in Information and Communication Technology, vol. 516. Springer, Cham (2019). https://doi.org/10.1007/978-3-030-18293-9_8

4. Gjøsæter, T., Radianti, J., Chen. W.: Universal design of ICT for emergency management - a systematic literature review and research agenda. In: International Conference on Universal Access in Human-Computer Interaction. Springer, Las Vegas (2018)
5. Gjøsæter, T., Radianti, J.: Evaluating accessibility and usability of an experimental situational awareness room. In: Di Bucchianico, G. (ed.) AHFE 2018. AISC, vol. 776, pp. 216–228. Springer, Cham (2019). https://doi.org/10.1007/978-3-319-94622-1_21
6. Anthony Giannoumis, G., Gjøsæter, T., Radianti, J., Paupini, C.: Universally designed beacon-assisted indoor navigation for emergency evacuations. In: Murayama, Y., Velev, D., Zlateva, P. (eds.) Information Technology in Disaster Risk Reduction. ITDRR 2018. IFIP Advances in Information and Communication Technology, vol. 550. Springer, Cham (2019). https://doi.org/10.1007/978-3-030-32169-7_9
7. Tunold, S., Radianti, J., Gjøsæter, T., Chen, W.: Perceivability of map information for disaster situations for people with low vision. In: Antona, M., Stephanidis, C. (eds.) HCII 2019. LNCS, vol. 11572, pp. 342–352. Springer, Cham (2019). https://doi.org/10.1007/978-3-030-23560-4_25
8. Gjøsæter, T., Radianti, J., Chen, W.: Universal design of ICT for emergency management from stakeholders' perspective. Inf. Syst. Front. **23**(5), 1213–1225 (2020). https://doi.org/10.1007/s10796-020-10084-7
9. Røssvoll, T.H., Fuglerud, K.S.: Best practice for efficient development of inclusive ICT. In: Stephanidis, C., Antona, M. (eds.) Universal Access in Human-Computer Interaction. Design Methods, Tools, and Interaction Techniques for Inclusion. UAHCI 2013. Lecture Notes in Computer Science, vol. 8009. Springer, Berlin, Heidelberg (2013). https://doi.org/10.1007/978-3-642-39188-0_11
10. Gjøsæter, T., Radianti, J., Chen, W.: Understanding situational disabilities and situational awareness in disasters. In: Franco, Z., González, J.J., Canós, J.H. (eds.) 16th International Conference on Information Systems for Crisis Response and Management (ISCRAM 2019) (2019)
11. Gjøsæter, T., Radianti, J., Chen, W.: Towards situational disability-aware universally designed information support systems for enhanced situational awareness. In: 17th International Conference on Information Systems for Crisis Response and Management (ISCRAM 2020) (2020)
12. Platform, U.G.S.I., Number of People Directly Affected by Disaster (Per 100,000) (2020)
13. Magami, I., Yahaya, S., Mohammed, K.: Causes and consequences of flooding in Nigeria: a review. Biol. Environ. Sci. J. Tropics **11**(2), 154–162 (2014)
14. Stanton, N.A., Chambers, P.R., Piggott, J.: Situational awareness and safety. Saf. Sci. **39**(3), 189–204 (2001)
15. Endsley, M.R.: Designing for situation awareness in complex systems. In: Proceedings of the Second International Workshop on Symbiosis of Humans, Artifacts and Environment (2001)
16. UNISDR, Living with Disability and Disasters (2014)
17. Pauver, B., Twigg, J., Sagramola, S.: Migrants, Refugees, Asylum Seekers: Inclusion in Disaster Preparedness and Response. Council of Europe, Lisbon (2016)
18. Aldrich, N., Benson, W.F.: Peer reviewed: disaster preparedness and the chronic disease needs of vulnerable older adults. Preventing Chronic Dis. **5**(1) (2008)
19. Alexander, D., Gaillard, J., Wisner, B.: Disability and disaster. Routledge Handbook Hazards Disaster Risk Reduc. **1**, 413–423 (2012)
20. Shrestha, M.S., Takara, K.: Impacts of floods in South Asia. J. South Asia Disaster Study **1**(1), 85–106 (2008)
21. Olajuyigbe, A., Rotowa, O., Durojaye, E.: An assessment of flood hazard in Nigeria: the case of mile 12 Lagos. Mediterr. J. Soc. Sci. **3**(2), 367 (2012)
22. Ruin, I., et al.: Human vulnerability to flash floods: addressing physical exposure and behavioural questions. Flood Risk Manag. Res. Pract. 1005–1012 (2009)

23. Jonkman, S.N., Kelman, I.: An analysis of the causes and circumstances of flood disaster deaths. Disasters **29**(1), 75–97 (2005)
24. Ruin, I., et al.: Human exposure to flash floods–Relation between flood parameters and human vulnerability during a storm of September 2002 in Southern France. J. Hydrol. **361**(1–2), 199–213 (2008)
25. Gartrell, A., et al.: Disaster experiences of women with disabilities: Barriers and opportunities for disability inclusive disaster risk reduction in Cambodia. Glob. Environ. Chang. **64**, 102134 (2020)
26. Bennett, D., Baker, P., Mitchell, H.: New 9 media and accessible emergency communications. Disability and Social Media: Global Perspectives, p. 119 (2016)
27. Alexander, D.: Disability and disaster: an overview. Disabil. Disaster 15–29 (2015)
28. Ono, M., Devilly, G.J., Shum, D.H.: A meta-analytic review of overgeneral memory: the role of trauma history, mood, and the presence of posttraumatic stress disorder. Psychol. Trauma Theory Res. Pract. Policy **8**(2), 157 (2016)
29. Hagen, K.: Resilience, response, recovery and ethnicity in post disaster processes. SPC Applied Geoscience and Technology, Suva (2013). http://gsd.spc.int/sopac/docs/KimHagenPaper/. Accessed 26 January 2019
30. Endsley, M.R.: Measurement of situation awareness in dynamic systems. Hum. Factors **37**(1), 65–84 (1995)
31. Endsley, M.R., Rodgers, M.D.: Situation awareness information requirements analysis for EN route air traffic control. In: Proceedings of the Human Factors and Ergonomics Society Annual Meeting. Sage Publications Sage, Los Angeles (1994)
32. Mendonça, D., Jefferson, T., Harrald, J.: Collaborative adhocracies and mix-and-match technologies in emergency management. Commun. ACM **50**(3), 44–49 (2007)
33. Klein, G.A., Calderwood, R., Macgregor, D.: Critical decision method for eliciting knowledge. IEEE Trans. Syst. Man Cybern. **19**(3), 462–472 (1989)
34. Doyle, J.K., Ford, D.N.: Mental models concepts for system dynamics research. Sys. Dyn. Rev. J. Syst. Dyn. Soc. **14**(1), 3–29 (1998)
35. Vieweg, S., et al.: Microblogging during two natural hazards events: what twitter may contribute to situational awareness. In: Proceedings of the SIGCHI Conference on Human Factors in Computing Systems (2010)
36. Misra, S., et al.: The iPhone effect: the quality of in-person social interactions in the presence of mobile devices. Environ. Behav. **48**(2), 275–298 (2016)
37. Yager, C., et al.: Emergency vehicle operator on-board device distractions. Texas A&M Transp. Inst. Tech. Rep. **2015**, 1–50 (2015)
38. Lindsay, P.H., Norman, D.A.: Human Information Processing: An Introduction to Psychology. Academic Press (2013)
39. Sonnenwald, D.H., Maglaughlin, K.L., Whitton, M.C.: Designing to support situation awareness across distances: an example from a scientific collaboratory. Inf. Process. Manage. **40**(6), 989–1011 (2004)
40. Abimbola, A.F., et al.: Evaluating the influence of resident agencies' participation in flood management via social media, in Nigeria. Pertanika J. Soc. Sci. Human. **28**(4), 2765–2785 (2020)
41. Ogbonna, U.: Mitigating situational disabilities in information systems for situational awareness in flood situation with universal design (Master thesis), in Oslo Metropolitan University (2022)
42. Dey, I.: Qualitative Data Analysis: A User Friendly Guide for Social Scientists. Routledge (2003)
43. Braun, V.: and V. Clarke, Thematic analysis (2012)

Providing Situational Awareness to Emergency Responders Using Drones

Juliana B. S. França[1]([⊠]), Jacimar F. Tavares[2], Angélica F. S. Dias[3],
and Marcos R. S. Borges[4]

[1] IC/UFRJ, Federal University of Rio de Janeiro, PPGE/UFRRJ, Federal Rural University of
Rio de Janeiro, Rio de Janeiro, Brazil
julianabsf@ic.ufrj.br

[2] Programa de Pós Graduação em Informática, Departamento de Ciência da Computação,
Instituto de Matemática, Universidade Federal do Rio de Janeiro, Rio de Janeiro, Brazil

[3] Inst. Tércio Pacitti/NCE (UFRJ), Federal University of Rio de Janeiro, Rio de Janeiro, Brazil
angelica@nce.ufrj.br

[4] Programa de Pós Graduação em Informática, Universidade Federal do Rio de Janeiro, Rio de
Janeiro, Brazil
mborges@ppgi.ufrj.br

Abstract. Crises and incidents are threatening conditions that require urgent
action. In emergencies, the lack of relevant information can affect and increase the
risks of the crisis scenarios. In this context, response time is crucial for responding to the needs of affected individuals and environments. This study presents an
analysis of six awareness criteria applied in emergency response and how these
criteria could improve the technological and collaborative solution supported by
drones, called "Drones to the Rescue". This research aims to understand how
awareness criteria are considered in real emergency response and how incorporating those into the solution would improve it. To evaluate the potential improvement, we carried out a survey with experts from the Firefight Department, Civil
Defense, Military Police, and Armed Forces from the states of Rio de Janeiro and
Minas Gerais – Brazil. This research concludes that awareness criteria bring new
possibilities and provide new alternatives in emergency response situations.

Keywords: Emergency · Information System · Collaborative Systems ·
Decision-making · Drones

1 Introduction

In recent disasters, we have observed the need for increasingly intelligent systems to
support emergency response [1]. Initiatives that make computational results and their
processing closer to human reasoning have been stimulated and carried out. The need
for these systems has been shown, given the increasing volume of data that need to be
processed, originated by popular content produced on the internet and by the knowledge
of specialists; expert systems that demand more and more accuracy in their results;

T. Gjøsæter et al. (Eds.): ITDRR 2022, IFIP AICT 672, pp. 69–85, 2023.
https://doi.org/10.1007/978-3-031-34207-3_5

decision support systems in complex domains that increasingly need results sensitive to human reasoning and its awareness, and transparency introduced in government systems [2–4].

Lindell [13] report that the concept of emergency concerns harmful events of low intensity; those that cause a limited amount of damage to property or individuals. The response to these events, given their small scale, is the responsibility of the fire department, police department, or medical institution. The term emergence may also refer to the imminence of the occurrence of a particular harmful event; such as the forecast of a hurricane in the next 48 h. The urgency of this situation calls for swift and timely action. Broadly, an emergency is an unexpected event that threatens people, communities, property, or business continuity. Emergency, therefore, requires immediate action, efforts, and resources to minimize or even nullify adverse consequences.

According to França [4], in a world where information is completely spread by the world wide web, we can know very fast, in a general way, about emergencies that happen on the other side of the world. Every situation like this has a great impact on society, so there is a need to interpret the signals that are generated and happen imperceptibly. In this way, the response teams, in emergencies, should be able to act immediately and effectively immediately after being called. Response time, therefore, is critical for controlling the adverse situation [2]. However, response actions can become confusing due to the lack of reliable and integrated information about the emergency scenario. Thus, the coordination of actions loses efficiency as the lack of information and its fragmentation contribute to the inefficient allocation of the resources involved. Complementarily, Vivacqua and Borges [5] state that there is often a lack of information regarding the region around an emergency.

Some authors present [6, 7], in a superficial way, the lack of awareness of sensitive systems to support emergency response. The lack of aerial vision of the site and its surroundings brings limitations to the agents responsible for the response. Often the scenario encountered in these situations presents several risk factors, both for the team responsible for the response and for people who need some support in this environment. In addition, response times associated with effective actions are vitally important in reducing or even eliminating existing risks.

According to [19] designing for awareness is fundamentally about finding ways to convey the sense of collaboration into interdependent activities. Designing an awareness technological solution is a way to provide a common frame of reference, taking into account the importance of often creating a common ground for the users. [20] extend the definition of awareness bringing a statement that joins the system, collaboration, and feelings concepts. For these authors, collaborative systems implement awareness mechanisms in their functionalities and allow an action or effect that enables the understanding through sensations, intelligence, or intuition. Awareness has always been associated with systems, but not with protagonism. Awareness has been treated peripherally for a long time. However, it changed when technological systems migrated to the internet, being called web systems. In this case, the systems started to be supported by awareness and gained more space and prominence with users, markets and new processes such as data analysis, which, in this work, can be seen, in the proposed solution, as an integral part of the technology that works on the use of drones.

In this scenario, the opportunity to apply a solution involving drones was envisioned, aiming to support decision-making in emergency environments by obtaining and communicating useful information to the response teams through awareness solutions. Drones, also known as unmanned aerial vehicles (UAVs), are machines that are gaining popularity and are currently widely used. They can be standalone, remotely controlled, or equipped with cameras; allowing real-time recording and viewing. Until recent years, UAVs use was directly associated with military use, particularly armed attacks [2]. However, researchers, enthusiasts, and other users have contributed to the use of this equipment exceeding military employment and that's why a regulation needs to be discussed [8, 9].

This research aims to support emergency response by raising awareness of a technological solution. The focus is on investigating six awareness criteria and how they can be introduced into a drone technology solution to support decision makers in responding to emergencies. To reach this result, a survey was launched for specialists in emergency response from the Army, Civil Defense and Fire Department. Despite the fact that several corporations were reached by the survey, it is not possible to conclude exactly the number of professionals who received it (much in favor of the means by which it was disseminated: social networks and sending via e-mail to groups). In this sense, we had feedback and direct participation from 30 experts, from which it was possible to collect relevant data. The main objective of this research is to understand how awareness criteria are considered in responding to real emergencies and how these criteria can improve the Drones to the Rescue solution. [10, 11].

This paper is structured into four sections. Section one introduces the main goal of this paper, section two presents the backgrounds related to emergency, disasters, and crisis, besides emergency management, drones, and awareness. Section three present and discuss the technological solution Drones to the Rescue. The following one provides information about research design, methodology, and discusses the results achieved. And to finalize, section four presents and discusses the limitations of this research and highlights the next steps.

2 Background

2.1 Emergency, Disaster and Crisis

The society can undoubtedly be considered as a living complex system and from an organizational perspective are born in a certain place and have their structural dynamics, where it is possible to distinguish two independent structures: the organization itself and its environment [12]. The authors emphasize that the modifications are triggered by the disturbing agent but determined by the structure of the disturbed system. Consequently, the environment and the organization in observation act as mutual sources of disturbances and trigger mutual changes of state. However, the routine of human life may lead us to believe that nothing other than usual will happen. Surprisingly, this apparent normality may suddenly change with one or more traumatic events. These events give rise to dramatic situations capable of transforming the previous state of harmony into a troubled environment, where scenarios of disorder and chaos are presented. This dramatic and potentially traumatic environmental transformation introduces the concept of emergency. An emergency or crisis is a threat condition that requires urgent action.

The concept of disaster is associated with sudden and severe natural disasters such as droughts, forest fires, earthquakes, hurricanes, windstorms, or volcanic eruptions that end up causing damage and harm to the environment, individuals, and property. But the definition of a disaster involves much more than the mere occurrence of these events and is the result of a phenomenon, which may be natural, caused by man or arising from the relationship between them. The phenomenon itself is called an adverse event, and this is the cause of the disaster. Disaster can also be understood as a sudden, a progressive natural or a man-made event that severely affects the community, manifesting the total or partial disruption or destruction of the social system or livelihoods. As a result, the disaster imposes an allocation of resources beyond the normal scope of a jurisdiction or segment of government to address it through exceptional measures or to restore the normality of that community [13].

Responding to a disaster or emergency is enhanced by the actions envisaged in the preparation phase. Relief actions are performed during the response and, finally, the reconstruction phase begins. During the reconstruction, lessons learned feedback the prevention actions envisaged in the preparation phase to refine these preventive measures. Prevention is the first phase and covers actions aimed at preventing disasters or reducing the impact of the consequences. Preparedness is the second phase of disaster management and includes actions to increase the responsiveness of individuals and organizations so that they can act more effectively. The answer is the third phase in emergency and disaster management. It covers the set of actions taken to help and assist the affected parts (people, animals, environment, properties, etc.), reducing damage and losses, to ensure the functioning of the main systems that make up the community infrastructure. Vivacqua and Borges [5] state that this is the most complex and also the most studied phase of all. These authors also report that this phase presents as characteristics unpredictability, high speed of events, a high number of people involved, little time for decision making, unavailability of resources, uncertainty about the situation, and stress on those involved. Reconstruction is the fourth and final phase and encompasses actions for the recovery of the affected parts, such as rebuilding a community, allowing the restoration of the normal state.

2.2 Emergency Management

Over time, individuals and communities have always tried to find a way to deal with disasters. However, organized and systematic attempts at disaster management are relatively recent. As such, the range of situations that could involve emergency management or the emergency management system is extensive. This reinforces the premise that emergency management is a complex and fundamental process for the safety of everyone's daily life and should make daily decisions and not just critical moments [14].

Emergency management encompasses the entire planning and intervention process aimed at minimizing the impact caused by extreme events, as well as the implementation of response and recovery actions to mitigate the social, economic, and environmental consequences that impact the community. It is a multidisciplinary, progressive process, both reactive and preventive. It covers several areas of knowledge such as risk management, leadership, and collaboration [14]; [8].

Vivacqua and Borges [5] affirm the existence of four factors that underline the importance of emergency management: (i) public awareness of risks, emergencies and disasters has increased as the cost of disasters has increased dramatically in recent years; (ii) companies understand that disasters can disrupt their operations and even cause bankruptcy. (iii) there is rapid population growth in high-risk areas. This increases the potential for damage caused by a potential disaster; (iv) Emergency management is increasingly requiring specialized training. In fact, to respond quickly to complex incidents, managers must make coordination decisions in a short time; which leads to restrictions on the ability to analyze issues related to the coordination [15].

2.3 Drones

Drone, also called UAV - Unmanned Aerial Vehicle is a globally recognized English term for a remotely controlled unmanned aircraft. It can be used, for example, for surveillance, delivery, or leisure. This generic term may refer to various vehicles, such as airplanes, helicopters, multi-engines, or any other type of vehicle capable of flying and meeting the above characteristics. The drone may be of various sizes and its ability to fly autonomously may vary, may be completely autonomous, or may depend on human interaction during a flight [8].

Indeed, aerial imaging technology associated with coordinated autonomous flight can quickly reshape disaster response capabilities. Drones are already used around the world in disaster response, such as earthquakes, hurricanes, landslides, floods, and are involved in other stages of the emergency life cycle. This equipment is much more used in the trauma response phase than in other emergency phases; however, it is observed that they are still underused. There are many possibilities of applications, among them, in the emergency context, it is relevant to mention: (i) recognition and mapping, (ii) structural integrity analysis, (iii) temporary delivery of groceries and parts of the infrastructure, (iv) detection and fire extinguishing, (v) fire response in high-rise buildings, (vi) chemical, biological, radiological, nuclear or explosive events, (vii) search and rescue operations, and (viii) risk assessments and logistic support [15].

In fact this equipment is very versatile and offers benefits yet to be explored, among them it is worth mentioning: (i) reduction of exposure of risk response agents; (ii) increased effectiveness of response agents; (iii) clear vision at low altitudes difficult to achieve by manned aircraft; (iv) portability and few requirements to put them into action; and (v) great value for money [16, 17, 25]; [18].

2.4 Awareness

According to [21, 22]; [23] awareness involves cognitive aspects related to the ability of human beings to perform tasks and reason them using their natural ability. Having in hand the information from the awareness achieved, it is also possible to trace the work context between those involved and make the coordination of actions feasible, aiming to transform the communication and work efforts into cooperation between those involved. Different individuals have different skills, knowledge, and contribute with different awareness characteristics to the task. Taking into account different individuals, who work together, it is possible to make their analyses complementary, conflicting, or converging. It brings diversity to the results, improving it.

Awareness has different elements that enable the analysis of a context. Gerosa [22] defend the contextualization of actions and those involved, allowing everyone to situate themselves and obtain an understanding of the whole. To achieve this common under-standing, the authors suggest some questions, as follows in the 5W1H structure: (1) who performed a certain action? (2) what was done? (3) where was the action taken? (4) when was the action taken? (5) why was the action done? (6) how was the action carried out? In addition to the 5W1H structure, the authors suggest other contextualization questions in order to strengthen the awareness development, as:

- What is the common goal of those involved?
- What is the role of each involved in the context?
- What can be done by others?
- How to proceed in a given scenario?
- What is the impact of the actions implemented?
- How far can I go in my participation?
- Who is around and acting in the actions performed?
- Which locations are being considered?
- What is the source of the problems being discussed?
- How important is the action?
- What relationships exist between those involved?
- What is being analyzed?
- Who did what in past actions (authorship)?

Other aspects being defended by researchers of the emergency response field and awareness to contextualize an action are the tools and resources able to represent the scenario analyzed and the discussions conducted during a real emergency [10]. These artifacts can be physical things such as paper and maps, or even technological systems or electronic devices [24].

Awareness brings to collaborative technological solutions a common ground, and a real understanding of what is being presented. In the next sections, a technological solution based on drones will be presented and a discussion of how awareness resources could support emergency response will be stated too.

3   Drones to the Rescue: A Technological Solution

Drones to the rescue is a collaborative and technological solution designed and imple-mented to support decision makers into their practical action through drones [10]. This artifact was developed having in mind three aspects: (i) the professionals cannot go to the location of the accident to explore what happened, (ii) time saving, and (iii) the necessity for more special details of the scene, when an in-person exploration can cause damage or hurt for the professionals.

Time is a precious variable in emergency management. However, decision makers need reliable information about the current event to direct efforts. Eventually, in order to support the emergency response, it is necessary to call in specialists from specific areas, such as those who have knowledge of fire or liquid or gas leaks, radioactive leaks, among others. In this context, when there is the possibility of aerial visualization of the scenario, as in some cases of fires, landslides or floods, it is possible to be much more assertive in decision making.

Generally, it is recommended that data captured at the emergency scene go through an analysis process. In the event of aerial image capture, these should be forwarded to specialists; which may, in the course of the analysis, make relevant observations and notes of the situation, and then be directed to the decision makers. Currently, several computational technologies have been used to support the decision-making process, such as: (i) capture tools, (ii) image processing tools (2D / 3D mapping for example) and (iii) collaborative tools that can handle photos, text and files, instant messengers, email applications and cloud file storage services (remote server).

Drones to the Rescue solution, when fed with aerial images of the emergency scene, allows in its first version: (i) to make the content available on the web; (ii) share the content; (iii) display the images in an organized manner; (iv) Insert graphic markings on images; (v) View and edit comments; (vi) Display map content and (vii) Responsive operation (desktop and mobile). This solution seeks to support agents involved in emergency response as well as decision makers through the availability of images, analyzed by experts.

This proposed solution involves two modules responsible for drone capture images, where the images are available in the cloud and a third developed module. This latter is a web system, the central theme of this work, which allows responses and collaborative editing of captured images. Considering an emergency scenario, this solution proposes that agents involved can act according to the following steps. Figure 1 illustrates it.

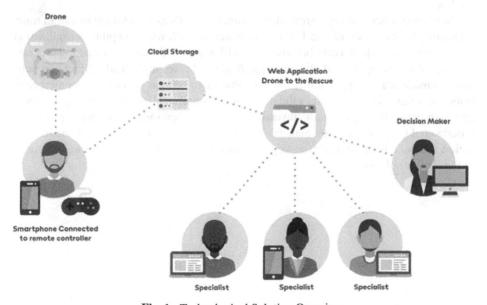

Fig. 1. Technological Solution Overview

(1) A qualified agent takes off a drone from the emergency location.
(2) The agent commands the drone flight over emergency location.
(3) After finding scenes of interest, the agent remotely triggers photo capture by the drone camera.
(4) The agent downloads the captured images to your mobile phone through the application.
(5) The downloaded images are recognized by a second application present on the pilot's phone. This app starts the process of uploading images to a cloud folder.
(6) The images are available on a cloud storage service.
(7) Experts and other contributors access the page of a third application, available on the Web.
(8) Users view the images obtained and their locations; use the app's features to edit images (inserting and / or changing comments) to aggregate information to support decision making.
(9) Users view changes made by other collaborating agents and can make new considerations and edits to images.
(10) Decision makers access the platform and refer to the original and edited content to support decision making regarding subsequent actions.

In this solution, the camera attached to the drone is the source of the images, which serve as the central element in the solution. Figure 2 represents the flow made by an image. The solution allows visualization and collaborative interaction, and also provides full support for images taken by other means such as smartphone cameras, satellite images, drawings, among others. However, in this paper we emphasize only drone images. This solution, applied in an emergency scenario, requires: a drone, a smartphone with web connection and drone compatibility, and a web-connected device for use by the third module.

In an emergency's situation reliable information needs to be obtained in a short time. Therefore, the existence of a technology resource that allows the capture, visualization and processing of data in a collaborative way, will subsidize the decision-making process.

After the development of *Drones to the Rescue*, this technological artifact was validated considering the applicability of this software to support specialists in emergency response actions. Details of this validation can be found in [10]. The next step of emergency response through drones' investigation is the identification of how awareness criteria could support decision makers. In the next section, we present how the investigation was conducted through a survey and discuss how the results will improve *Drones to the Rescue* solution.

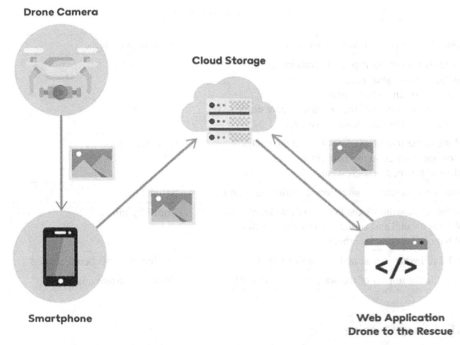

Fig. 2. Image's capture and treatment flow.

4 Emergency Response Through Awareness: A Survey to Investigate Awareness Criteria in Drone's Solution

As presented in the background section, some research [21]; [20]; [23]; [24] defend the contextualization of actions in a situation to improve awareness development. Based on it, some questions were proposed, and, in this research, we raised six awareness criteria that follow (Table 1).

The main goal of this research is to investigate how awareness criteria are considered in real emergency response and how these criteria can support a drone's technological solution, especially *Drones to the Rescue* [10]. To do it, we planned, executed and analyzed the answers of a survey conducted with real experts from the Firefight Department, Civil Defense, Military Police, and Armed Forces of Rio de Janeiro and Minas Gerais - Brazil. In the next sections we provide the details of this survey and discuss the results achieved.

Table 1. Awareness Criteria.

Questions to contextualize situations	Awareness Criteria
What is the common goal of those involved? What is being analyzed? How important is the action? What is the source of the problems being discussed? Which locations are being considered?	Common Goal
What is the role of each involved in the context? How far can I go in my participation? How to proceed in each scenario?	Role definition
How to represent the situation scenario and analysis?	Artifact use
What relationships exist between those involved? Who is around and acting in the actions performed? What can be done by others?	Authority impact
Who did what in past actions (authorship)?	Preview analysis being applied
What is the impact of the actions implemented?	Correlate current analyses

4.1 Survey Planning

This survey was designed by three researchers and experts in the field of emergency response. It was designed considering the contextual question to support the awareness investigation and the six criteria presented in Table 1. To collect data with experts, the researchers designed a questionnaire with six main questions, in addition to identity questions, and scenarios to illustrate an emergency supported by drones. In summary, for each question, a contextual aspect (scenario) was presented to support the respondents' understanding.

Each main question was considered taking into account the six sensitization criteria. All questions aim to understand awareness considering a real case of emergency. Table 2 presents the questions answered by the experts and their relationship with the awareness criteria.

The questionnaire presents closed questions, and for each of them the respondents could choose between the following options: prime, very important, important, not very important, indifferent and irrelevant. The data collection was planned to be open during seven days: from 01/17/2022 to 01/24/2022. The researchers sent the survey's invite for known specialists and groups by Email, WhatsApp and social media.

Table 2. Correlation between scenario/questionnaire and awareness criteria.

Scenario (S) and Question (Q)	Awareness Criteria
S1: It is known that it is possible, for an emergency, to define the main objective of the team before attending to it (ex: it was defined that the main objective is to identify survivors, or that the main objective is to identify possible points that can lead to new disasters within a disaster, etc.) Q1: What level of importance do you give to the definition of the team's goal in an emergency response?	Common Goal
S2: Consider that there is someone (a professional involved) with the role of acting in charge of the main actions to be taken during the emergency and that there is a clear definition of the role of each of the professionals involved in the occurrence Q2: How important is the clear definition of roles in an emergency response situation?	Role definition
S3: Imagine that, if any of the professionals involved in the emergency, who are viewing the drone images, identify a possible victim. Aware that the web system (where the generated images are viewed) that accompanies the drone also allows the point in the generated image to be marked with an observation and that the others involved in the occurrence can later signal at that marked point that they agree or disagree with what was flagged (thus giving a view of consensus or dissent) Q3: How important would you rate the use of a web system to identify a victim in the scene?	Artifact use
S4: It is considered that, in an image generated by a drone, about a disaster, it is possible to signal an area (a stretch of ground or a set of points in coordinate) as having already been analyzed by all professionals involved in the emergency, giving the awareness to everyone that the area has already been the target of everyone's analysis effort Q4: What level of importance would you attribute to the use of a system that allows a signalization of an area analyzed by others specialists?	Preview analysis being applied
S5: Consider that there is a definition of the role of each of the professionals involved in the analysis of the images of the disaster, and that each one of those involved is marked with a symbol (icon) that explicitly characterizes him (eg, risk analyst, etc.) Q5: Do you think that viewing the representation of each of those involved can change your awareness of the facts reported by them?	Authority impact

(continued)

Table 2. (*continued*)

Scenario (S) and Question (Q)	Awareness Criteria
S6: Consider that, when analyzing the facts presented in an emergency, it is possible to identify and mark some relevant point in the images generated by the drone and that these points can be related (if there is a relationship) by each of those involved, still allowing you to have access to information that shows what was related by whom and why of the relationship Q6: What level of importance would you attribute to the use of a system that would allow you to relate analyzed points?	Correlate current analyzes

4.2 Survey Execution and Results

The questionnaire was open for data collection over the seven days initially planned. In total, we had 30 answers from specialists with experience in emergency response with drone's solution. Among them, 40% firefighters; 20% police; 26,67% civil defense; 3,34% navy, and 10% expert civil servants in Brazil. The graphics below (Figs. 3, 4, 5, 6, 7, 8) present the data collected for each question of Table 2 and show the position of this sample.

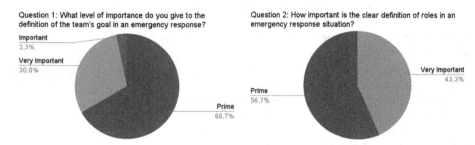

Fig. 3. Data of Common Goal.   **Fig. 4.** Data of Role definition.

As can be observed in the graphics above (Figs. 3, 4, 5, 6, 7, 8), all the respondents believe that criteria like common goal, role definition, artifact use, preview analysis being applied, authority impact, and correlate current analyzes, will influence, in a significant way, the emergency response actions. This result, from real specialists, indicate that a solution that offers real and instant aerial images of a region via drone to support physical rescues and decision-making, must provide awareness resources.

Analyzing the suggestions above, and the results of this survey, we can confirm that awareness criteria are present in emergence response actions. These criteria are demanded by specialists in technological solutions that operate or are operated by drones. Functions that provide, for instance: (a) a tracking of images, (b) communication between co-workers, or (c) a different perspective for a known scene; are a way to improve the understanding of actions in an emergency scenario.

Question 3: How important would you rate the use of a web system to identify a victim in the scene?

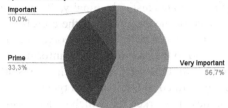

Question 4: What level of importance would you attribute to the use of a system that allows a sinalization of an area analyzed

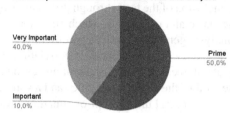

Fig. 5. Data of artifact use.

Fig. 6. Data of preview analysis being applied.

Question 5: Do you think that viewing the representation of each of those involved can change your perception of the facts

Question 6: What level of importance would you attribute to the use of a system that would allow you to relate analyzed points?

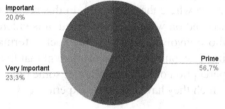

Fig. 7. Data of Authority impact.

Fig. 8. Data of Correlate current analyze

Scenarios and the questions defined are correlated in this work to web application functionalities (an integral part of the Drone ao Resgate solution) can implement, aiming to promote aspects of awareness to its users. With the result of the answers given through scenarios and questions 1 and 2, it is possible to define that it is important that there are mechanisms for coordinating teams in an emergency, and that, with them, the objectives of the rescue mission can be clearly defined, as well as which stakeholders are responsible for the strategy part of the operation (strategic level), coordination (management level) and for the operationalization part (operational level). Having, in the web solution, clear indications of this information, can speed up the process of identifying each one of those involved and the nature of the contribution that each one can make in the execution of the rescue operation. The scenario and question 3, in turn, showed that the implementation of features that, in a possible rescue coordination, are useful to inform those involved that a signal made by one of those involved in the rescue, is corroborated or not by others involved, signaling that more than one involved, in this case, had the same awareness about a fact. The scenario and question 4 brought results that show the need to implement functionalities aimed at the awareness, individually and collectively, that all others involved in the operation have already directed their efforts to a certain analyzed area, thus suggesting that multiple perspectives were used in the analysis of an area impacted by a disaster. The results generated with the scenario and question 5 show that it is relevant to implement features whose association with iconographic elements allows those involved in the rescue to quickly perceive that the feedbacks given in the application are specific to some type of professional, which can impact their analysis and conclusion of the facts through different insights generated instantly. Finally, there is the scenario and question 6, which show the relevance of the awareness of the correlation analysis generated between information placed in the system by those involved in the emergency. This awareness of correlations can lead to the creation of new information that will feed the system, generating new awareness for those involved, which can restart several of the analysis activities and awareness generated so far, in an emergency.

In [26, 27] the concept of situational awareness is worked on, which concerns the awareness of elements and possible events in a disaster, for example, correlating temporal order and space where they occurred, thus managing to make predictions of possible actions in future actions. The model presented [26] shows the representation of the impacted environment whose observation leads to situational awareness with the selection of a mental model that works with objectives and plans, enabling a set of steps that will originate actions to be taken in the analyzed situation, considering time and space where they occurred. In this research, it is possible that situational awareness is worked on while new information is entered into the web system from the analysis of those involved in the rescue. Such information may be specific to individual analysis, image capture by drone equipment that flies over the affected area or resulting from the perception of the perception of some other individual, when faced with a situation with which they have extensive experience.

5   Conclusion and Future Work

This research presents a study of an emergency response through awareness making use of Drones. The focus is the investigation of six awareness criteria and how they can improve a technological drone solution to support decision makers and physical rescue. To achieve this result, a survey was conducted with specialists in emergency response from the Army, Civil Defense and Fire Department.

The results show that awareness criteria are important to emergency response based on drone's technological solution. They can bring a better understanding of an emergency scenario and support innovative solutions.

In Correia [10], some suggestions were made by specialists to improve the Drones to the Rescue solution, in a work effort that can be considered the basis of the research presented in this article. Analyzing these suggestions, combined with the results obtained and with the observations of possible implementations for Drones to the Rescue, made at the end of Subsect. 4.2, it becomes possible to present the points listed below, as items that must be considered in the implementation of a web solution that supports awareness:

- Access control is captured and edited, preventing leaks of content restricted to those involved in the operation. Therefore, it will be necessary to develop a specific module for this purpose. In this sense, coordination and awareness of coordination can be better worked with different levels of access and functionalities.
- Optimize the organization of captured images by grouping them according to their origin and image versioning, allowing their tracking. This will help the web solution to display captured images with good performance, allowing quick awareness based

on available images, including the historical evolution of events by the history of available images.

- Treatment not only of images, but also of videos captured by the drone. The clear and objective awareness of the items identified in an image must not contain dubiousness, which can impact the awareness of those involved.
- Live streaming, where it will be important to have low latency and no streaming delay, so a good internet connection is essential. In this sense, the awareness may change as new information is seen and analyzed by those involved.
- Display the geographic coordinates of the drone on the map. It reinforces the idea of the awareness that those involved in the rescue are having access to the same points analyzed by all those involved.
- Report new captured data via email or SMS using an active message triggering system to stakeholders. This will allow the awareness that information has been sent, that it has been viewed or not, or that it has not been considered in an analysis.
- Support autonomous flight for 3D mapping, together with an app connected to the drone, so that the drone operation takes place autonomously, so that it is possible to form a 3D map after processing the images. At this point, sizing information is added that can help in different analyses, based on the awareness of specific stakeholders. As an example, you can change the awareness of a place in the disaster based on relief information, steep or difficult to access areas.

Awareness can be achieved even in distributed teams [28], if there is a data network that has databases accessible by different mechanisms that work in a distributed way, constantly updated by different nodes of the same network. In this sense, the participating group, each contributing with their perception of the facts, will create a sharing community, generating, as the work suggests, a sense of belonging. In Drones to Rescue, group work is essential and indispensable in an emergency. All the research carried out showed that the implementations that were suggested in this and other sections, corroborate so that those involved have a clear perception of the impacts and contributions of their actions during the emergency, reinforcing the feeling of community.

As a limitation of this study, it is important to highlight that it was carried out in a situation simulated emergency response. In this sense, the daily and real challenges faced in environments of uncertainty and scarce time, such as a real emergency, were not taken into account. This can impact the responses obtained by the participants, although those involved are professionals linked to this type of emergency, several of them with practical experience with the use of drones (this information was not collected). In future research, the different times of experience in rescues should be considered in the research.

In the next steps, all six investigated criteria (common purpose, role definition, artifact usage, applied visualization analysis, authority impact, and correlated current analyses) will be introduced as new functional requirements in the Drones to the Rescue solution, starting with the functional requirements highlighted in the previous section. Also as a next step in this research, we are planning to evaluate the Drones to the Rescue solution enhanced by other experts, in real emergency scenarios, in addition to increasing the interview samples to validate the identification of new criteria to be considered. Our interest at this stage is to assess the quality of rescues and decision making based on an awareness solution.

Acknowledgments. We thank all the specialist's team for their commitment and availability during this research development. This research was supported by Faperj - E-26/211.367/2019 (248406) and E-26/202.876/2018.

References

1. Correia, A., Severino, I., Nunes, I.L., Simões-Marques, M.: Knowledge management in the development of an intelligent system to support emergency response. In: Nunes, I. (eds.) Advances in Human Factors and Systems Interaction. AHFE 2017. Advances in Intelligent Systems and Computing, vol, 592. Springer, Cham (2018). https://doi.org/10.1007/978-3-319-60366-7_11
2. Klein, G.A., Orasanu, J., Calderwood, R., Zsambok, E. (eds.): Decision Making in Action: Models and Methods, pp. 138–147. Ablex Publishing Corporation Norwood, New Jersey (1993)
3. Qudrat-Ullah, H.: Modelling and simulation in service of energy policy. In: The 7th International Conference on Applied Energy – ICAE2015 (2015). https://doi.org/10.1016/j.egypro.2015.07.558
4. França, J.B.S., Dias, A.F.S., Neiva, F.W., Borges, M.R.S.: Towards projected impacts on emergency domains through a conceptual framework. In: Proceedings of the 14th International Conference on Information Systems for Crisis Response And Management, Albi, France (2017)
5. Vivacqua, A.S., Borges, M.R.S.: Taking advantage of collective knowledge in emergency response systems. J. Netw. Comput. Appl. **35**(1), 189–1982 (2012)
6. Sermet, Y., Demir, I.: Flood action VR: a virtual reality framework for disaster awareness and emergency response training. ACM SIGGRAPH 2019 Posters pp. 1–2 (2019)
7. Gasaway, R.B.: Situational Awareness for Emergency Response. Fire Engineering Books (2013)
8. Gilman, D.: Unmanned Aerial Vehicles in Humanitarian Response. Matthew Easton (2014)
9. Kerasidou, X., Büscher, M., Liegl, M.: Don't Drone? Negotiating ethics of RPAS in emergency response. Short Paper - Ethical Legal and Social Issues Proceedings of the ISCRAM 2015 Conference, Kristiansand (2015)
10. Correia, H.R., et al.: Drones to the rescue: a support solution for emergency response. In: 17th International Conference on Information Systems for Crisis Response and Management. Springer, Cham (2020)
11. Correia, H.R., da Costa Rubim, I., da Silva Dias, A.F., dos Santos França, J.B., da Silva Borges, M.R.. Emergency response supported by drones and experts perceptions. In: Murayama, Y., Velev, D., Zlateva, P. (eds.) Information Technology in Disaster Risk Reduction. ITDRR 2020. IFIP Advances in Information and Communication Technology, vol. 622. Springer, Cham (2021). https://doi.org/10.1007/978-3-030-81469-4_23
12. Maturana, H.R., Varela, F.J.: The Tree of Knowledge - The Biological Roots of Human Understanding. Shambhala Publications Inc, United State of America (1987)
13. Lindell, M.K., Prater, C., Perry, R.W.: Introduction to Emergency Management. 1st edn. Wiley (2007)
14. Haddow, G.D., Bullock, J.A., Coppola, D.P.: Introduction to Emergency Management. Butterworth-Heinemann (2017)
15. Chen, R., Sharman, R., Rao, H.R., Upadhyaya, S.J.: Coordination in emergency response management. Commun. ACM **51**(5), 66–73 (2008)

16. Chowdhury, S., Emelogu, A., Marufuzzaman, M., Nurre, S.G., Bian, L.: Drones for disaster response and relief operations: a continuous approximation model. Int. J. Prod. Econ. **188**, 167–184 (2017)
17. Amukele, T.K., Sokoll, L.J., Pepper, D., Howard, D.P., Street, J.: Can unmanned aerial systems (drones) be used for the routine transport of chemistry, hematology, and coagulation laboratory specimens?, PLOS ONE (2015)
18. Lally, H.T., O'Connor, I., Jensen, O.P., Graham, C.T.: Can drones be used to conduct water sampling in aquatic environments? a review. Sci. Total Environ. **670**, 569–575 (2019)
19. Bjørn, P., et al.: Immersive Cooperative Work Environments (CWE): designing human-building interaction in virtual reality. Comput. Supp. Coop. Work (CSCW), 1–41 (2021)
20. Cravo, M.F.S.S., Sousa, R.A., Racca, B.S., França, J.B.S.: Conceituando a Percepção em Sistemas Colaborativos: a Busca por Sistemas Sensíveis a Percepção. In: Desenho De Pesquisa - Simpósio Brasileiro De Sistemas Colaborativos (SBSC), 17 2021. Online Event. **Proc.** [...]. Sociedade Brasileira de Computação, Porto Alegre, pp. 7–12 (2021). <in Portuguese>
21. Gerosa, M.A.: Analysis and design of awareness elements in collaborative digital environments: a case study in the AulaNet learning environment. J. Interact. Learn. Res. **14**(3), 315–332 (2003)
22. Gerosa, M., Fuks, H., Lucena, C.: Elementos de percepção como forma de facilitar a colaboração em cursos via Internet. In: XII Simpósio Brasileiro De Informática na Educação - SBIE 2001, Vitória, ES. Anais do XII Simpósio Brasileiro de Informática na Educação (2001). <in portuguese>
23. de Lima, Dhanielly Paulina R., Gerosa, M.A., de Magalhães Netto, J.F.: Using awareness information to enhance online discussion forums: a systematic mapping study. In: 2018 IEEE Frontiers in Education Conference (FIE). IEEE (2018)
24. França, J.B.S., de Souza, R.S., Dias, A.F.S., Borges, M.R.S.: ImpactMap: a collaborative environment to support impact projection of complex decision. In: Information Technology in Disaster Risk Reduction: 4th IFIP TC 5 DCITDRR International Conference, ITDRR 2019, Kyiv, Ukraine, 9–10 October 2019, Revised Selected Papers, vol. 575. Springer Nature (2020)
25. Lee, S., Har, D., Kum, D.: Drone-assisted disaster management: finding victims via infrared camera and lidar sensor fusion. In: 3rd Asia-Pacific World Congress on Computer Science and Engineering (APWC on CSE), pp. 84–89 (2016)
26. Endsley, M.R.: Toward a theory of situation awareness in dynamic systems. Hum. Fact. J. **37**(1), 32–64 (1995)
27. Harrald, J., Jefferson, T.: Shared situational awareness in emergency management mitigation and response. In: 2007 40th Annual Hawaii International Conference on System Sciences (HICSS 2007), Waikoloa, HI, p. 23 (2007)
28. Dourish, P., Bly, S.: Portholes: supporting awareness in a distributed work group. In: Proceedings of the CHI 1992 Conference on Human Factors in Computing Systems, Monterey, CA USA, pp. 541–547. ACM Press, New York (1992)

Telecommunications, Sensors and Drones

Application of the Fuel Cell Vehicle to Support ICT in Emergency Response

Yasuhiro Soshino[1,2](✉) (iD)

[1] Disaster Management Research Institute, Japanese Red Cross College of Nursing, 4-1-3, Hiroo, Shibuya-Ku, Tokyo 150-0012, Japan
y-soshino@jrcdmri.redcross.ac.jp
[2] Japanese Red Cross
Kumamoto Hospital, 2-1-1, Nagamine-Minami, Higashi-Ku, Kumamoto City, Kumamoto 861-8520, Japan

Abstract. Ensuring the telecommunication services is one of the key pillars for the disaster response. However, the past studies pointed out that the lack of electricity causes significant negative effect in the service continuity of telecommunication in emergencies. Using the vehicle to establish a mobile and off-grid telecommunication site is one of the solutions in emergencies. Recently, the vehicle with the external power supply functions becomes popular as the progress of the electric vehicles in our society. Therefore, this study aims to assess the practical effectiveness of the application of the fuel cell vehicle to support the telecommunication services in emergencies. The medical fuel cell vehicle with telecommunication functions and the external power supply functions was developed. In the field test, various functions in the M-FCV such as the external power supply, the real-time image sharing, the vehicle management application were tested to support the telecommunication in emergencies. In addition, in a disaster response drill, the M-FCV was utilized to establish the field telecommunication unit by using its functions. To ensure the electricity to support the telecommunication services in emergencies, the application of fuel cell vehicles is considered as an effective solution.

Keywords: Fuel Cell Vehicle · Power Supply in Emergencies · ICT and Energy in Emergencies

1 Introduction

In the 21st century, Japan needs to respond two different types of disaster. The first type of disaster can be called as "silent disasters" such as the super aging, rapid population decrease, aging of social infrastructure, and the vulnerability in energy supply. While these silent disasters gradually increase the vulnerability against natural disasters, there is a growing concern about the occurrence of catastrophic natural disasters in Japan. Nankai Trough Earthquake and Tsunami is one of the National Crisis Disasters such as the Tokyo Inland Earthquake and the catastrophic floods in Tokyo. In addition, in 2022,

T. Gjøsæter et al. (Eds.): ITDRR 2022, IFIP AICT 672, pp. 89–100, 2023.
https://doi.org/10.1007/978-3-031-34207-3_6

the Japan Cabinet Office announced the expected damage in the future earthquake and tsunami in the northern part of Japan. According to the report, approximately two hundred thousand of people may be killed by the earthquake, tsunami, and the low temperature in the disaster affected areas where the blackout is expected due to the earthquake [1]. In fact, recent natural disasters revealed the concern about the blackouts in Japan. The 2018 Hokkaido Eastern Iburi Earthquake caused the historical blackout. Due to this blackout, approximately, 140 thousand landlines were disturbed and 6,500 cellular base station stopped the services [2]. The 2019 Typhoon Faxai caused the blackout in Boso Peninsula in Chiba, Japan caused the serious blackout which disturbed 67 landline base stations and 1936 cellular base stations were affected by a major power outage [3]. Previous studies pointed out the importance of the telecommunication in emergencies. To exchange the information to coordinate relief operations, emergency networks must be sustained to operate in difficult situations [4]. Communication network outage is caused by power outage in natural disasters such as Hurricane Sandy [5]. According to the damage assessment on the communication network caused by Hurricane Katrina, one of the common vulnerable points of failure is the link between power supply and telecommunication networks. The main reason of telecommunication outages was the lack of electricity in communication site. This caused by the low availability of the backup generators [6]. For the information and telecommunication, a power blackout causes significant impact. The backup capacities such as UPS and emergency generators for key communication facilities become unusable after such reserve capacities are exhausted after a few hours or days [7]. To provide a resilient solution for the major failure caused by natural disasters, microgrids with distributed generation are effective approaches [8].

For the rapid restoration of the communication services, several studies proposed the mobile unit consist of power supply unit and communication equipment. The application of vehicles as the mobile telecommunication base stations is possible solutions since vehicles can supply the electricity [9, 10].

While vehicles are used as the communication base stations in various pro-jects, recently, electric vehicles with power supply function such as Electric Vehicles (EVs), Hybrid Vehicles (HVs), Plug-in Hybrid Vehicles (PHVs), and Fuel Cell Vehicles (FCVs) are commercialized. Among these electric vehicles, Hybrid, Plug-in Hybrid, and Fuel Cell Vehicles, which can generate electricity, can be used as Mobile Power Plant even in emergencies. In particular, Fuel Cell Vehicles are free from the challenges of producing poisoning gases and large noise while fuel cell vehicles can produce large amount of electricity.

Therefore, this study aims to assess the practical effectiveness of the application of the fuel cell vehicle as the telecommunication base in emergencies. Following the introduction, section two explains the background of the medical fuel cell vehicle project by the Japanese Red Cross Kumamoto Hospital and Toyota. Section three presents the overviews of the medical fuel cell vehicle project. The results of the field tests are presented in the section four. The discussion will be described in the section five and the section six concludes this study.

2   Introduction

In November 2000, the Japanese Red Cross Kumamoto Hospital was firstly nominated as a hub hospital for the global medical relief activities in the Japanese Red Cross Society. After the 2001 Gujarat Earthquake, the hospital started the research and development of the field hospital equipment. Field hospital consists of various equipment to rapidly establish the basic hospital infrastructure by using tents, generators, water supply equipment, sanitation equipment and telecommunication equipment. In this sense, the field hospital is the assembly of movable infrastructure functions. While the usual hospital's infrastructure is established on the land, the field hospital's infrastructure is mobile to flexibly respond to the needs in the disaster affected areas. In addition, field hospital equipment can be used for other humanitarian purposes. For example, in the 2004 Niigata Chuetsu Earthquake, the hospital deployed the field hospital equipment to accommodate the refugees. However, in the 2011 Great East Japan Earthquake and Tsunami, the hospital faced the limitation in using the field hospital equipment to improve the living conditions of the refugees. Only one field hospital equipment was not sufficient to respond to such catastrophic disaster in the wide geographic areas.

Therefore, in 2013, the hospital proposed the "Smart Design Shelter Concept" (see Fig. 1) to prepare for the future catastrophic disasters in Japan. This concept proposes the daily uses of the mobile infrastructure such as solar batteries (see Fig. 2), water-recycling shower system, and the water-recycling toilet (see Fig. 3) system in schools, parks, stadiums, hospitals and other public facilities to be used as refugee centers in emergencies. Once disaster occurs, these mobile infrastructures can be transported to the disaster affected areas. Based on this concept, the hospital started the research and development of the mobile infrastructures and these mobile infrastructures were deployed in the 2015 Kumamoto Earthquake, 2018 Western Japan Floods, and 2020 Kumamoto Floods relief operations.

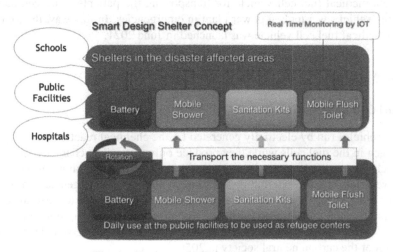

Fig. 1. The Smart Design Shelter Concept

Fig. 2. Solar Battery in the Field Hospital   **Fig. 3.** The Mobile Flush Toilet

On the other hand, in 1992, Toyota started the development of fuel cell vehicles and the first commercial models were launched in 1996. Toyota has an idea that Eco-friendly vehicles contribute to society and environment only when the vehicles come into widespread use. Based on this idea, Toyota is trying to promote fuel cell vehicles as the solutions for the social challenges by effectively utilizing the external power supply function, which is the unique strength of the fuel cell vehicles. For example, Toyota proposed a model to utilize a Fuel Cell Bus as a community transportation in peacetime while deploy the community bus to the refugee center to supply electricity in emergencies.

In this way, both organizations shared the same approach to prepare for disasters by the daily uses of mobile infrastructures. Based on this idea, since July 2020, both organizations started the discussion on the effective utilization of fuel cell vehicles in medical services and disaster response. As a result, both organizations proposed a model to utilize a medical fuel cell vehicle for transporting the patients in peacetime while deploy the vehicle as a mobile power plant in emergencies. In this way, the joint field test on a medical fuel cell vehicle was launched in June 2021.

3   The Medical Fuel Cell Vehicle "Doctor Car NEO"

3.1   Fuel Cell Vehicles

Fuel cell vehicles run by electricity generated by the chemical reaction with Hydrogen and Oxygen in the fuel cells while they produce only water. The characteristics of fuel cell vehicles are zero emission, silent (low noises), short fuel charging time compare to electric vehicles, and the external power supply function in emergencies. In the 2018 Hokkaido Iburi Eastern Earthquake, fuel cell vehicles were deployed to the refugee center in Muroran to supply electricity for lighting equipment, television, mobile phones. In Japan, fuel cell vehicles are expected to replace the present engine vehicles toward the realization of the carbon neutral society in 2050.

3.2   Medical Fuel Cell Vehicle "Doctor Car NEO"

The medical fuel cell vehicle (hereafter M-FCV) "Doctor Car NEO" (see Figs. 4 and 5) is developed based on Toyota Coaster Minibus by using the Toyota Fuel Cell System for the fuel cell vehicle "Mirai" as its power source. Compared to the hospital's medical vehicle based on Toyota Coaster Minibus with the diesel engine, the medical fuel cell vehicle enjoys a low-noise and low-vibration driving experience.

The M-FCV has the external power supply function (9kW maximum output, approximately 90kWh supply capacity). To supply the better quality of electricity for the medical equipment, a medical UPS is installed in the power supply system. For the infection control in the vehicle, M-FCV introduced an air conditioning system with an exhaust system with HEPA filter.

Fig. 4. The Medical Fuel Cell Vehicle "Doctor Car NEO"

3.3   Technical Features

Power Supply. Figure 6 shows the external power supply functions in the M-FCV. The fuel cell system provides electricity to the outlets installed inside and outside of the vehicle. on the outside of the vehicle at each side, there are external outlets for the power supply to medical equipment and other instrument in emergencies. One receptacle is also equipped to receive the shore power. To provide better quality of the electricity to medical equipment, the vehicle has a medical UPS connected to the inside and outside outlets. One DC outlet for rapid charging is also installed. two levels of headings should be numbered.

Fig. 5. The Treatment Room in the M-FCV

Fig. 6. The External Power Supply Functions

Image Sharing System. Figure 7 shows the image sharing system which links between the M-FCV and the hospital in transporting the patient. In emergencies, the M-FCV functions the mobile on-site headquarters by using this system. The M-FCV has two cameras which is installed behind the windscreen to capture the images around the vehicle and in the treatment space to share the condition of the patient. In emergencies, the camera in the treatment room could be used for tele-meeting with other stakeholders in relief operation. The vehicle has three large monitors to show the present location of the vehicle and other information such as the patient' physical information by the medical monitor. The Wi-Fi router is equipped in the vehicle for internet communication. In emergencies, the mobile satellite phones can be installed to ensure the internet communication in the disaster affected areas by supplying electricity from the M-FCV.

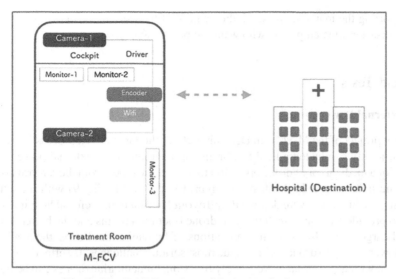

Fig. 7. The Brief Overview of the image sharing system

Vehicle Management Application. Figure 8 shows the image of the vehicle management application. This application shares the information on the present location, destination, amount of fuel, possible milage or external power supply, and the location of the Hydrogen Stations. In addition, this application links with the other application

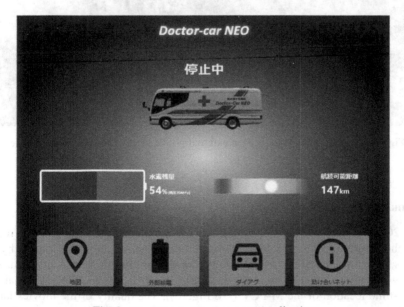

Fig. 8. The Vehicle Management Application

for supporting the matching between the owners of the external power supply vehicles and the disaster affected people who want the power supply supports.

4 Field Tests

4.1 External Power Supply

As a pilot project of the M-FCV, in December 2020, the Japanese Red Cross Kumamoto Hospital jointly conducted a field test on the application of the external power supply vehicle for a medical cargo drone operation to deliver the blood from the referral hospital to a clinic in an island. In this test, two hybrid vehicles (see Fig. 9) with the external power supply functions were deployed by Toyota Kyushu to the referral hospital and an island to provide electricity with the field drone operation rooms and the batteries of the medical cargo drone. In emergency operations of humanitarian drones, the availability of the power supply to drones is one of the most serious challenges. By effectively utilize the vehicle with the external power supply function, humanitarian drones can be flexibly dispatched even from the point where the electricity is not available.

Fig. 9. Battery Charing by using the external power supply function of the vehicle

4.2 Image Sharing System

In July 2021, the field test of the image sharing system was conducted in Mt. Aso region, where the severe floods struck in 2012. In this field test, the movies captured by two cameras, which are installed behind the windscreen and in the treatment room, were shared with the operation room at the Japanese Red Cross Kumamoto Hospital with the real-time location of the M-FCV (see Fig. 10). The quality of the movies largely depends on the connectivity of the mobile phone transmission, however, as long as the connection is ensured, the movie and photos are clearly shown in the laptops at the operation room of the hospital. In the 2011 Great East Japan and Tsunami disaster response, the hospital deployed the medical relief convoys to the disaster affected areas. On the way, the deployed medical team had to stop to report the present locations and the road conditions to the headquarters in the hospital. By using the image sharing system, the information sharing between the deployed relief team and the headquarters could become easy as long as the telecommunication is available.

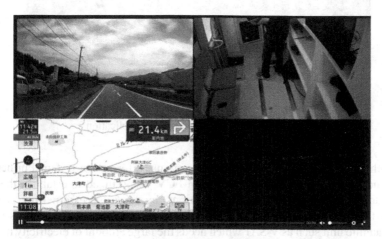

Fig. 10. The field test of the real-time image sharing system in the M-FCV

4.3   Vehicle Management Application

In November 2021, the field test of the vehicle management application (see Fig. 11) was conducted by deploying the M-FCV and a hybrid vehicle with the external power supply function. By using the application, the power supply support by the M-FCV and the hybrid vehicle was requested from two places in Nanjo City of Okinawa. The M-FCV was deployed to the Nanjo City Hall and the hybrid vehicle was deployed to an island of Kudaka. In the past disaster response by using the vehicle with the external power supply function, there were several problems such as the needs matching between the disaster affected people and the power supply vehicles, monitoring of the location and the fuel consumption of the power supply vehicles, and the decision making of the appropriate schedule to deploy the replacing vehicles for refueling. The vehicle management would be a new solution for these challenges on vehicle management in emergencies.

4.4   The Mobile Telecommunication Unit

To examine the possibility to utilize the telecommunication system in the M-FCV, the vehicle was deployed to the disaster response drill in Nanjo City of Okinawa in November 2021. In this drill, the M-FCV was used as an on-site emergency headquarters by using the space and the telecommunication system. A main monitor in the M-FCV showed the movie taken by an assessment drone (see Fig. 12), the location of the other external power

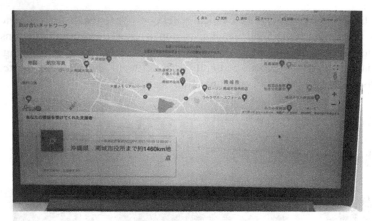

Fig. 11. The vehicle management application

supply vehicles (see Fig. 13), and the disaster response information system. Furthermore, the external power supply function of the M-FCV was utilized to establish the triage post. In addition to support these ICT functions, by using the external power supply function, the M-FCV can supply the electricity to the mobile satellite phones and the mobile satellite unit such as V-SAT which needs the large amount of electricity to ensure the large data transmission in the disaster affected areas.

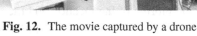

Fig. 12. The movie captured by a drone   **Fig. 13.** The vehicle management system

5   Discussions

This study aimed to assess the practical effectiveness of the application of fuel cell vehicles to support the ICT services in emergencies. The field tests of the M-FCV identified the practical value of fuel cell vehicles to support the ICT services in emergencies with its unique external power supply function. While the recent study proposed the utilization of the electric vehicle to establish the information network in emergencies [11], this study presented the new approach by using the fuel cell vehicles. Different from electric vehicles, fuel cell vehicles can generate the large amount of electricity which is useful to support ICT equipment which requires large power supply in emergencies. In addition, compared to the conventional emergency telecommunication vehicles with engines and generators, the application of fuel cell vehicles can alleviate the stress of the disaster affected people and relief workers by reducing the annoying noises and exhaust gas. Furthermore, the application of fuel cell vehicles contributes to reduce the incidents in disaster affected areas caused by generators and vehicles. In the 2011 Great East Japan Earthquake and Tsunami, uses of electric generators caused a number of carbon monoxide cases [12]. Therefore, by the application of fuel cell vehicles, which can supply electricity without producing the toxic gas, the number of the carbon monoxide poisoning cases can be decreased in disaster affected areas especially in winter.

In terms of the environmentally friendly disaster response, fuel cell vehicles are possible solution to achieve the carbon neutral in emergency response. In 2021, International Committee of Red Cross (ICRC) and International Federation of Red Cross and Red Crescent Societies (IFRC) adopted the Climate and Environment Charter for Humanitarian Organizations. This charter encourages all the humanitarian charter to adapt the changes of disasters caused by the climate change, and to mitigate the impact on environment caused by the activities of humanitarian organizations themselves [13].

The limitation of this study is the lack of the deployments in the real disaster response operations. Therefore, the serious challenges in the supply chain management of hydrogen in emergencies is not tested in this study. In fact, even in peacetime, quite limited number of fuel cell stations are available in Japan. The supply of hydrogen should be maintained even in emergencies if relief organizations seriously want to deploy fuel cell vehicles in the disaster affected areas. Furthermore, this study did not try the power supply from the M-FCV to the actual ICT service facilities such as mobile phone hubs. Further field tests are required to confirm the effectiveness of fuel cell vehicles to support the existing telecommunication facilities. For example, in Japan, pre-install of the V2H (Vehicle to Home) system in public facilities is proposed to ensure the power supply by fuel cell vehicles, electric vehicles and other vehicles with the external power supply functions. By pre-install of the power receiving facility from fuel cell vehicles, the resilience of telecommunication facilities can be enhanced.

6 Conclusion

This study aimed to assess the practical effectiveness of the application of fuel cell vehicles as the telecommunication base to support ICT in emergencies. The field tests of the M-FCV with the ICT functions and the external power supply functions revealed the effectiveness of the M-FCV as a movable telecommunication hub in the disaster affected areas. As fuel cell vehicles are widely used in communities, they become the practical solutions to support ICT services in emergencies. In this sense, the application of fuel cell vehicles is one of the future solutions to ensure the ICT service continuity in emergences that contributes the realization of the resilient and sustainable society.

References

1. Cabinet Office, Government of Japan, Explanatory material, Report on the mega-earthquake preparedness working group (2022). https://www.bousai.go.jp/jishin/nihonkaiko_chishima/WG/pdf/220322/shiryo02.pdf. Accessed 11 July 2022
2. Ministry of Internal Affairs and Communications, Hokkaido Eastern Iburi Earthquake, Damage and recovery of telecommunication and broadcast tin Blackout (2018). https://www.soumu.go.jp/main_content/000585075.pdf. Accessed 11 July 2022
3. Onga, H.: Disaster preparedness on ensuring telecommunication in emergencies, Resilient ICT symposium (2021). https://www.nict.go.jp/resil/symposium2021/lde9n2000001pim5-att/a1617331988490.pdf. Accessed 11 July 2022
4. Gomes, T., et al.: A survey of strategies for communication networks to protect against large-scale natural disasters. In: 2016 8th International Workshop on Resilient Networks Design and Modeling (RNDM), Halmstad, Sweden, pp. 11–12 (2016)
5. Kwasinski, A.: Lessons from Field Damage Assessments about Communication Networks Power Supply and Infrastructure Performance during Natural Disasters with a focus on Hurricane Sandy (2013). http://users.ece.utexas.edu/~kwasinski/1569715143%20Kwasinski%20paper%20FCC-NR2013%20submitted.pdf. Accessed 11 July 2022
6. Kwasinski, A., Weaver, W.W., Chapman, L.P., Krein, T.P.: Telecommunications power plant damage assessment for Hurricane Katrina–Site survey and follow-up results. IEEE Syst. J. **3**(3), 277–287 (2009)
7. Petermann, T., Bradke, H., Lüllmann, A., Poetzsch, M., Riehm, U.: What happens during a blackout , Consequences of a prolonged and wide-ranging power outage, Final Report, Report for the Committee on Education, Research and Technology Assessment, Office of Technology Assessment at the German Bundestag (2011). https://publikationen.bibliothek.kit.edu/1000103292. Accessed 11 July 2022
8. Chen, C., Wang, J., Qiu, F., Zhao, D.: Resilient distribution system by microgrids formation after natural disasters. IEEE Trans. Smart Grid **7**(2), 958–966 (2016)
9. Sakano, T., et al.: Bringing movable and deployable networks to disaster areas: development and field test of MDRU. IEEE Netw. **30**(1), 86–91 (2016)
10. Randall, G.W., Conrad, J.M., Vaughn, G., Randall, M. E., Shadwell, Jr., P.F.: Technical capabilities of the IEEE MOVE emergency relief vehicle. In: 2016 IEEE Global Humanitarian Technology Conference (GHTC) Proceedings, Seattle, WA, USA, pp. 261–266 (2016)
11. Mase, K., Gao, J.: Electric vehicle-based ad-hoc networking for large scale disasters design principles and prototype development. In: 2013 IEEE Eleventh International Symposium on Autonomous Decentralized Systems, Mexico City, Mexico, pp.1–6 (2013)
12. Iseki, K., Hayashida, A., Shikama, Y., Goto, K., Tase, C.: An outbreak of carbon monoxide poisoning in Yamagata prefecture following the great east Japan earthquake. Asia Pac. Jo. Med. Toxicol. **2**(2), 37–41 (2013)
13. ICRC/IFRC, The Climate and Environment Charter for Humanitarian Organizations. https://www.climate-charter.org/wp-content/uploads/2022/05/ClimateEnvironmentCharter-EN.pdf. Accessed 11 July 2022

COVID-19 Sāvdhān: Harnessing the Telecom Infrastructure for COVID-19 Management

Saurabh Basu⏺, Suvam Suvabrata Behera(✉) ⏺, Sandeep Sharma⏺,
Anugandula Naveen Kumar, Sumit Kumar Jha, Sabyasachi Majumdar,
Niraj Kant Kushwaha, Arun Yadav, and Pankaj Kumar Dalela

Centre for Development of Telematics, Mehrauli, New Delhi, India
saurabh.basu.cs@gmail.com, suvambehera27@gmail.com,
sandeepsharmax97@gmail.com, naveen987naveen123@gmail.com, {skjha,
niraj.kushwaha,arun.yadav}@cdot.in, sabyasachi3.cse@gmail.com,
pdalela@gmail.com

Abstract. The tremendous challenges brought on by the COVID-19 pandemic has brought to light the significance of inclusive and effective risk communication as a top priority for preparedness and response in health emergencies. A comprehensive emergency management strategy must include effective communication systems assisted with state-of-the-art Information and Communication Technologies (ICTs). For enabling communication, SMS messages utilizing the vast telecommunication sector have proven to be a very efficient tool. Messages should be precise, scientifically accurate, context-sensitive, entrusted, understandable, as well as relevant for the segment of society they are intended for. Geotargeting helps in reducing over-alerting by minimizing the annoyance and the subsequent opt-out behavior caused by unnecessary alerts. This study provides an in-depth description of the established platform known as 'COVID-19 Sāvdhān', which allows for the SMS dissemination of pandemic-related messages to the geo-targeted population, including but not limited to information about vaccination, quarantine facilities, testing centers, hotspots, lockdown, essential supplies, and law and order situations. The platform been widely used to disseminate more than 3.4 billion targeted SMS in 10 different languages across the length and breadth of India during COVID situation.

Keywords: Risk communication · Information dissemination · Pandemic management · COVID-19 · Common Alerting Protocol

1 Introduction

The new coronavirus (COVID-19) outbreak and dissemination have had disastrous effects on both the human population and the global economy. Over 228 countries and territories in the world have been affected by the Coronavirus pandemic. This included most urban clusters and even rural regions. According to the WHO COVID-19 Dashboard, there have been 572,239,451 confirmed cases of COVID-19 worldwide, with 6,390,401 deaths as of July 29, 2022 [1]. The fact is that while it took it took ninety-three days to reach the first million infections, it only took thirteen days to reach the second million [2].

© IFIP International Federation for Information Processing 2023
Published by Springer Nature Switzerland AG 2023
T. Gjøsæter et al. (Eds.): ITDRR 2022, IFIP AICT 672, pp. 101–117, 2023.
https://doi.org/10.1007/978-3-031-34207-3_7

India has not been spared from the severe death toll and economic damage that COVID-19 has caused over the world. There have been 44,019,811 verified COVID-19 instances as of July 31, 2022, of which 143,676 are active cases, 43,349,778 have been treated or released from the hospital, and 526,357 are recorded fatalities [3]. The case fatality rate (CFR) is the ratio between confirmed deaths and confirmed cases. Compared to the stated global CFR of 5.64%, the fatality rate in India is relatively low at 3.30% on June 18, 2020, yet India still had the highest number of confirmed cases in Asia [4]. The world's worst-affected nations and regions' COVID-19 figures for CFR have been published in Fig. 1.

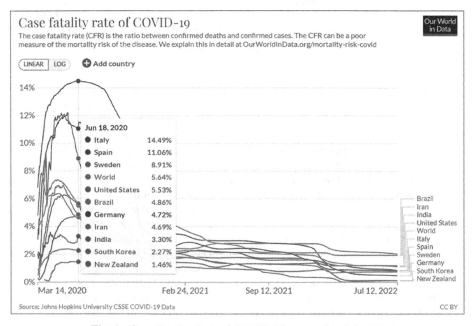

Fig. 1. Case Fatality Rate of COVID-19 across the globe [5].

Information and communications technology (ICT) has become increasingly important in these challenging circumstances for both addressing the pandemic's issues and adapting to daily life's new realities. The management of pandemics is intrinsically linked to mass communication. The decade's success depends on communication in all its forms. Almost every component of any hazard-mitigation approach is based on it. The capabilities of communications, data-gathering, and data-management technology have evolved in lockstep with our growing understanding of the causes, behavior, and mitigation of natural calamities. Indeed, one of the key factors in the realization that technology might significantly reduce the consequences of pandemic is advancements in the fields of telecommunications and computer sciences.

The COVID-19 epidemic has brought to light the vital role that the technology and telecommunications sectors play in ensuring that organizations, governments, and communities are linked and operating effectively. People all throughout the world are relying on technology for information, social communication, and work from home because of the pandemic's socioeconomic devastation. Particularly during this unprecedented time, the telecom industry has demonstrated its importance for both enterprises and individuals, contributing to the flourishing of society. Telecom infrastructure can be used to help the needy, the administration, and coordinators to better handle the pandemic situation as created during COVID-19 in practically all crisis situations like that caused by coronavirus.

COVID-19 has led to a growth in the number of policy tools being employed at various levels of governments around the world to combat the pandemic. The Right to Information during a heath emergency must be a fundamental human right [6]. Despite widespread agreement on the crucial importance of timely disclosures of COVID-19 information, the transmission of epidemic information as a policy tool has gotten little attention in comparison to travel bans, lockdowns, social isolation, and economic stimulus package [7]. Looking into this, the importance of sending geo-targeted emergency messages which has been proven to be a promising communication tool to rapidly disseminate information and promote preventive behavior among the public during epidemic outbreaks is highlighted in this paper.

There is a widespread use of and access to smartphone and mobile devices in India, with mobile phone technology penetration at nearly 100% worldwide. Mobile telecom network today spans most of the country today. The overall tele-density of India stood at 85.91 as on December 31, 2021 [8]. Short Message service (SMS) is one of the most effective communication media as it is device independent and supports major Indian vernacular languages. Mobile technology especially Short Message Service (SMS) has huge impact in the communication system of modern civilization. The paper also mentions a usability analysis of SMS for pandemic management alert system.

For effective communication related to COVID-19, utilizing the potential of ICT infrastructure, Centre for Development of Telematics (C-DOT) has developed a system called **COVID-19 Sāvdhān** through which COVID messages are disseminated in the form of SMS to the population of the target area. SMS is also able to reach people who do not have smartphone or internet access. According to the International Telecommunication Union (ITU), almost half of the world's population (46.4%) is still not connected to the Internet, yet 97% of the world's population lives within reach of a mobile cellular signal and has 108 mobile-cellular subscriptions per 100 people worldwide [9]. SMS messaging can therefore be used to widely reach a section of the population of each country, in order to combat a disease from which no part of the population is protected. Location based messaging ensures end-to-end reach, thereby reducing the burden on such infrastructure in times of pandemic and also reducing network congestion. Through this COVID-19 Sāvdhān Platform, all the stakeholder agencies of the Central, State, and Local Governments are able to integrate at one place and automatically disseminate any important information related to their work to the population of the target area identified through postal zip codes or drawing customized polygon over map using geo-intelligent tools.

The paper is organized as follows: Sect. 2 provides background information along with similar works done in this field. Section 3 gives detailed description along with implementation details of the established platform for enabling geo-targeted dissemi-nation of SMS by authorities to the general population in local languages. Section 4 presents statistics on the platform's use in actual situations. Concluding remarks are provided in Sect. 5.

2 Background and Related Work

Effective pandemic management necessitates the timely and efficient exchange of pandemic-related information among various stakeholders before, during, and after any pandemic situation, for which telecommunications/ICTs play an important role. Techno-logical advancements have opened new opportunities for supporting any kind of disaster resilience, the same applies to COVID-19.

The area of work includes leveraging technology for enabling effective commu-nication and dissemination of targeted warnings to the vulnerable section of society supported by efficient ICT systems and building an ecosystem for pandemic manage-ment solutions to assist in better regulation of COVID-19. Sakurai and Murayama [10] have highlighted about the use of information technology in a wide range of disasters including natural, radiological, chemical, infectious disease outbreak, and human-caused crises [11] at different disaster management stages such as disaster response, recovery, preparedness and risk reduction. From local government's perspective, essential roles of information systems, i.e., information record, exchange and process, are critical in effective disaster management. Information record and exchange are initial functions of information systems prior to a disaster, while information process and exchange become core to disaster relief operations. Rattien [12] has mentioned the role of com-munication in hazard mitigation and disaster management. Mass communication plays a definitive role in the transition in thinking and action away from post-disaster relief and towards preparedness and hazard mitigation. Manalu, E. P. S., et al. [13] empha-sized the crucial function of telecommunications in a crisis management scenario, that includes connecting, informing, and ultimately saving the lives of those affected by the disaster; and restoring connectivity to affected region so that government can connect with the citizens. The significance of emergency risk communication in public health emergency planning and response has been discussed by Seeger, Matthew W., et al. [14]. The effective management of emergencies during the COVID-19 pandemic crisis depends critically on communication. Any emergency preparation programme should aim to increase the country's capacity to recognize and respond to a variety of public health emergencies, such as emerging infectious diseases and natural disasters [15].

Despite of the availability of pandemic management systems, there is a gap between health authorities and administrators and the common public victims to be specific for which a lot of people get affected in the COVID-19 pandemic and that led to a greater loss to the development of the country. In the existing ecosystem, there is lack of co-ordination between different authorities, and limited utilization of communication media, resulting in less audience reach. The existing system does not cater to wide area coverage, because it lacks geo-fencing intelligence due to which the effectiveness of the alert messages decreases. Certain populations are more at-risk than others during a pandemic and health systems are required to have targeted risk messaging to ensure that those populations have access to necessary protective materials and information [16]. Elazab, A., B. Shababa, and H. Hefny mentioned about the importance of Location Based Messaging Services in Risk Reduction Management [17], whether in natural disasters, or human made risks, and in many other areas that require informing numbers of people caught up in the scope of a particular area, to identify them in emergencies to help save their health and their life processes. Regardless the recipient's phone numbers or their segments (age, gender, the address in the contract with service provider, state, and if they use a post-paid or pre-paid line). The effectiveness of geo-targeted alerts is also mentioned in [18]. According to the study presented in [19], health authorities should take into account sending emergency alert text messages to the public in order to give them with correct and reliable information, which could lessen the impact of infodemics.

3   COVID-19 Sāvdhān: Enabling Targeted Messaging

3.1   Need and Importance of Targeted Messaging

The role of communication technology has been recognized as integral to disaster management for a long time. With rapid advances in Information and Communication Technology (ICT) in the last decades, the interoperability and integration of various communication systems including internet, mobile, landline, fax, e-mail, radio and television is increasingly becoming functional and has begun to transform the lives of people and communities.

The massive telecom infrastructure in India i.e., 1.15 billion wireless mobile subscribers, [20] is not being used to its potential. At the same time, the existing alerting system lacks geo-fencing intelligence, due to this, warning message is delivered to lots of people and is not relevant to most of them thus reducing the effectiveness of the alert messages. The existing system that was in place for alerting or notifying public through SMS, was mostly based on bulk messaging and also there was prior requirement of the subscriber's phone number. The COVID-19 pandemic outbreak in 2020, did not provide time to prepare and prevent it through awareness generation. Geo-fencing is defined as the mechanism that allows an administrator or operator to set up triggers or alerts so when a device enters (or exits) the boundaries defined by the administrator, an alert is issued. Geofencing is used by Retail stores to notify shoppers about deals only when they're at the boundary of their shop or mall.

The COVID-19 Sāvdhān system, having capability of targeted messaging provided a framework to authorities of Indian states and union territories to disseminate advisories, instructions directly to public without any pre-subscription through phone numbers in a location-based manner.

With the advancement of Mobile technologies, dissemination of geo-targeted SMS has become a reality. Figure 2 describes how geo-targeted messaging works. The persons connected to the mobile tower present in the geo-targeted area will only receive the SMS. With this mechanism, the seasonal population of tourists currently present in the affected area can also be warned.

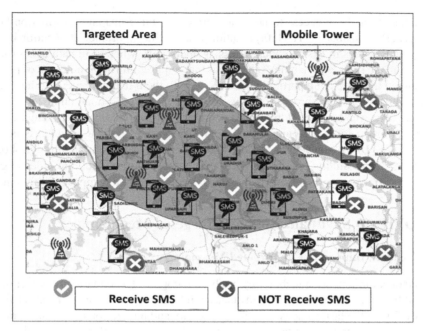

Fig. 2. Location Based Mobile Users Notification Mechanism using geo-fencing intelligence.

3.2 System Architecture and Information Flow

The COVID-19 Sāvdhān application enables officials to reach out to all mobile customers in any Containment Zone up to the level of individual mobile towers and deliver targeted messages regarding health, wellness, water supply etc. through SMS in local language.

COVID-19 Sāvdhān is an integrated platform facilitated by the Department of Telecommunications (DoT), Government of India through which Central and State Government Authorities are able to seamlessly integrate under one umbrella and disseminate any important information and advisories related to COVID-19 pandemic to a target area population (catering both local population and roamers) identified through zip codes and customized polygons. In coordination with DoT Field Offices in the States, the COVID-19 Sāvdhān platform enables dissemination of important information from government sources to the people of specific areas through SMS alerts in English and Indian vernacular languages, as easily understood by the local people, with the help of active Telecom Service Providers (TSPs) in the area. The targeted communication could include any COVID-19 mitigation measures including alerts on quarantine centers, supply of essential commodities, law and order issues, new COVID-19 hot zones etc. Various Government Authorities can directly reach to the people by harnessing the significant penetration of mobile phones in India through this platform. Internationally recognized Common Alerting Protocol (an ITU-T 1303.x recommendation) has been adopted in this platform for emergency Communication.

The information to be disseminated by various stakeholder agencies involved may be about but not limited to:

- Vaccination centers, vaccine doses eligibility information.
- Opening of a COVID test centre in a specific residential area.
- About any existing/new Quarantine or Isolation facility in that area.
- Supply of Essential commodities by the Civil supplies Department in that area.
- Alert on new hot zone of COVID Positive cases in that area, Containment Zones/hotspots to warn the people to stay at home and be more watchful.
- Alert on law-and-order issues/lockdown information for people in specific areas.

The major stakeholders include the Central and State Authorities, Department of Telecommunications (DoT) Licensed Service Area (LSA) field units, and Telecom Service Providers. There are a total of 36 States/Union Territories with corresponding 22 DoT LSA units, and 4 major Telecom service providers (BSNL, Reliance Jio, Airtel, and Vodafone-Idea). The working model of the platform is shown in Fig. 3.

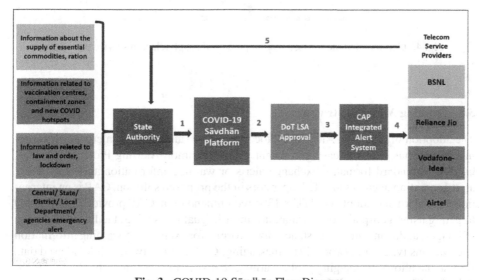

Fig. 3. COVID-19 Sāvdhān Flow Diagram.

- The COVID-19 Sāvdhān platform enables users of authorized agencies to access the service through a secure login via multi-factor authentication.
- The information to be disseminated by the different departments is fed into the platform by authorized State Authority officers.
- This information is due approved from the corresponding DoT LSA units' officers.
- The approved information passes through the developed CAP Integrated Alert System to give out a readable format of SMS. This SMS is disseminated to the target area residents (identified by their zip codes or customized polygons) through the active Telecom Service Providers like Airtel, Vodafone-Idea, Reliance Jio and BSNL.

– The targeted audience get the COVID-19 related required information through SMS on their mobile phones without the need to subscribe notifications or installation of the App on the phone.
– After successful completion of the dissemination of SMSs, dissemination statistics for the sent messages is available for records.
– The geo-targeted alert dissemination from platform consists of following steps as displayed in Fig. 4.

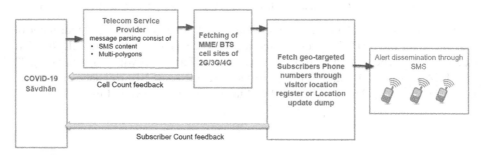

Fig. 4. Geo-targeted alert dissemination process through telecom service providers

3.3 Defining Message Structure

The adoption of Common Alerting Protocol (CAP), a standardized emergency messaging format, has been increasing in recent years. Common Alerting Protocol (CAP) is used as a standard format to exchange alerts or warning information among different alert generating agencies and TSP operators in the proposed solution. CAP is an international standard and adopted as ITU x.1303 recommendation. CAP provides geo-graphic targeting using geospatial representations, multilingual messaging, facility of inclusion of images, audio and video and standardized format for exchanging warning information over various types of networks [21], messaging. CAP is a lightweight XML-based data format that allows exchanging public warnings between the alerting technologies. Technologies. The use of CAP for alerting services has been used as part of many alerting systems, such as the Integrated Public Alert and Warning System (IPAWS) by the Federal Emergency Management Agency (FEMA) in the USA for warning dissemination through diverse media [22]. Other countries including Canada, Germany, Australia and Italy have also adopted CAP. The basic structure of the CAP message used is depicted in Fig. 5.

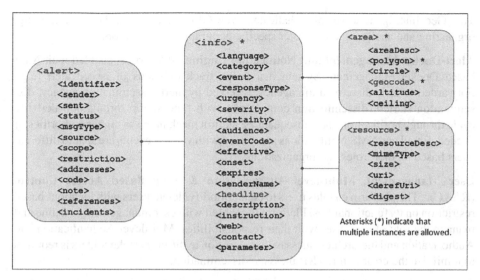

Fig. 5. Structure of CAP message.

The <alert> block provides the basic information regarding the COVID-19 related message which includes the purpose of the alert, its source, and an identifier that allows the alert to be uniquely identified among all other messages. The <info> block inside <alert> provides the details of the event, its severity defining the intensity, certainty that defines the confidence or probability, and urgency defining the available time to prepare for the concerned event. The effective and expiry date, description, and other additional information for the event may also be provided. The emergency message to be disseminated as SMS to mobile users is defined under <headline> tag in <info> block. The <area> block describes the targeted geographical area where the COVID-19 information is to be disseminated.

3.4 Features and Functionalities

CAP Message Generator, Validator, Aggregator, and Dispatcher. COVID related alerts and advisories are fed by multiple Central and State Government Authorities, which are generated and mapped to internationally adopted standardized CAP format. CAP Validator receives generated CAP alerts and validates it as per ITU CAP standard. Only the validated CAP file is processed and transferred to different interfaces. The CAP aggregator facilitates the aggregation of multiple generated similar alerts by different agencies for easing the dissemination process. The alert is finally dispatched to different interfaces of telecom service providers through CAP dispatcher for public dissemination.

Geo Intelligent Engine. Open Geospatial Consortium (OGC) compliant Geo-Location Management Module with Interactive User Interface allows users to demarcate one or more areas on a digital map. GUI allows operator to define CAP message and CAP polygons visually, and extraction and identification of cell sites in geo-fenced area.

This Geo-Intelligent server plus dedicated Web GIS infrastructure helps in creating, organizing and analyzing the disaster specific geographic information.

Alert-Docket Management and Notification Engine. Platform is enabled with Alert based Docket Management System that keeps track of status of issued alert (e.g., Forwarded to alert dissemination agency, received by alert dissemination agency, dissemination started, dissemination completed.) with time stamp throughout alert life cycle through notification and subsequent escalation mechanism to higher authorities, if needed. Email and SMS Notifications associated with various events are sent to different users based on their roles and organizations.

User Management, Multi-level Authorization & Role Based Access Control (RBAC). The platform enables users to create/modify/delete users with location- based restriction on its functionalities. Platform is enabled with user management to define and manage the role of each user with their responsibilities. Multilevel Authentication and Authorization and hierarchical message acceleration to different stakeholders is required to minimize the error before alert message dissemination.

Configuration and Log Management. Configuration management functionality of the platform enables the controlling authority (i.e., administrator) to establish the operating procedures (e.g., alert issuing procedure, alert specific authorization) and functionality (e.g., alert status notification, SMS dissemination report) based on defined Standard Operating Procedures. Also, record of all log messages is maintained through log management module, which helps to administer and facilitate the generation, transmission, analysis, storage, archiving and disposal of the log data created within the system. It is useful in identifying malicious activities (if any) to protect the platform from external vulnerabilities.

Report Management. Report Generator module is used to generate report for authorities providing status of all alerts in the specified timeframe in pdf or excel format along with information of statistics of alerts in the form of graphical representations for analysis and record purposes.

Regional Language Support. Platform also supports dissemination of alert message in English and different Indian vernacular languages including Assamese, Bengali, Gujarati, Kannada, Kashmiri, Malayalam, Marathi, Nepali, Odia, Punjabi, Sanskrit, Sindhi, Tamil, Telugu and Urdu. Platform facilitates users to type/input text content in supported languages.

Targeted Population and Subscriber Predictor. In case of SMS dissemination, number of mobile towers within the selected area and approximate mobile users in the targeted area in proportion with state wise mobile subscriber data periodically published by Telecom Regulatory Authority of India (TRAI) is displayed to authorities for aiding decision-making process. However, this figure can be used for rough estimation, actual number of mobile subscribers to whom SMS has been disseminated is notified by telecom service provider after completion of dissemination.

Area and Message Template Management. User can either use these area templates or create a new area based on its requirement. Pre-defined vulnerable areas (like-COVID hotpots, containment zones, etc.) can be configured for dissemination in the system. It saves time for area selection during critical time. Users can also create different covid related specific messages templates and save as draft for future.

Task Scheduler. Task scheduler helps in scheduling the tasks like alert dissemination, without any manual intervention in an automated manner. It helps in generating periodic alerts or sending an alert in odd hours (Fig. 6).

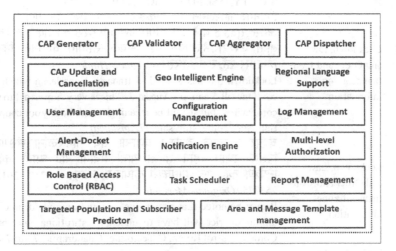

Fig. 6. Major Functionalities of COVID-19 Sāvdhān Platform.

4 Platform Usage and Statistics

4.1 Usage Scenarios and Message Content Analysis

The risk communication during health emergencies such as COVID-19 should address the information requirements for local, state, and central authorities, community, and the public at large in all phases i.e., before, during, and after emergency. The messages should be reliable, clear, simple, useful, scientifically accurate, context-sensitive, action oriented, and understandable for the common public. The developed platform is used for disseminating precautionary messages related to COVID-19 pandemic to the targeted population in their vernacular languages in different situations. The summary of different types of messages disseminated is provided in Table 1.

Table 1. Sample messages disseminated using COVID-19 Sāvdhān platform.

S. No.	Usage Scenario	SMS Disseminated
1	Lockdown, Law and Order and Containment zones information	IN VIEW OF THE COVID 19 PANDEMIC SITUATION, PAKYONG AND RONGLI SUB-DIVISION HAS BEEN PLACED UNDER COMPLETE LOCKDOWN. YOU ARE REQUESTED TO STAY AT HOME FOR YOUR OWN SAFETY. ISSUED BY GOVT. OF SIKKIM.
3	Lockdown, Law and Order and Containment zones information	ईटानगर-नहारलगुन में लॉकडाउन 3.0 शुरू हो गया है जो 3 अगस्त,सुबह 5 बजे तक रहेगा।कोरोना वायरस को रोकने के लिए ये बहुत ज़रूरी है,लेकिन यह आपके सहयोग के बिना निरर्थक होगा।घर रहें, सुरक्षित रहें। *(Original- Hindi)* Lockdown 3.0 has started in Itanagar Naharlagun which will continue till 5 a.m. on August 3. This is very important to stop coronavirus, but it will be meaningless without your cooperation. Stay home, stay safe. *(Translated)*
5	Lockdown, Law and Order and Containment zones information	चंद्रपुर जिल्ह्यात बाहेरुन येणाऱ्या सर्व नागरिकांना संस्थात्मक विलगीकरणात रहावे लागेल याची सर्वांनी नोंद घ्यावी. कोरोना नियंत्रण कक्ष, जिल्हाधिकारी कार्यालय, चंद्रपूर - 07172-261226, 253275 *(Original- Marathi)* It may be noted that all persons coming from outside in Chandrapur district will have to undergo institutional quarantine. Corona Control Room, Collectorate, Chandrapur *(Translated)*
6	Lockdown, Law and Order and Containment zones information	All religious and social gatherings are banned upto 14.4.20 by Govt. Legal action shall be taken under DM Act and 188 IPC against violators-Yamunanagar Police
7	Supply of essential commodities	Under PMGKAY, All AAY, PHH Ration Card holders will be provided 5KG FREE Rice per person for April to June 2020 in addition to their monthly quota. FCSD, SIKKIM
9	Supply of essential commodities	రేషన్ సమస్యకు 08612326776 కాల్ చేయండి. జిల్లా కలెక్టర్, నెల్లూరు. *(Original – Telugu)* Call 08612326776 for ration problem. District Collector, Nellore *(Translated)*
10	COVID-19 Testing	This is to inform all entering the state from Banderdewa Checkgate that antigen test is being carried out from 6AM-6PM everyday at the gate. As no one is allowed to enter the state without test, hence all are requested to strictly adhere and arrive within the period of 6AM-6PM.Issued by DIPR Locations for Rapid Antigen Tests in ICR: Banderdewa check

(continued)

Table 1. (*continued*)

12	COVID-19 Testing	gate, Lekhi CCC, TRIHMS, Ashoka hotel kiosk, Zoo road CCC, RKMH Itanagar, Heema Hospital, Niba Hospital Naharlagun. The rate for the RAT at the Govt facilities are Rs 250/- for APST/State/Central Govt employees and Rs 500/- for Non APST. Issued by DIPR
13	Scientifically Accurate Information	Did you know? COVID-19 infection occurs in two phases. Phase 1-Viral Phase ranges from start of 1st day of symptoms to 5th day. Phase2-Hyper inflammatory/Hypersensitivity phase ranges from Day 5-8. Early testing at the onset of symptoms on Day 1 is crucial to save lives. Call 14410 for information.
14	Scientifically Accurate Information	State Data reveals that from all age groups, the maximum number of fatalities due to COVID-19 belong to unvaccinated population group, indicating that severity of infection is higher, leading to lower chances of recovery and survival in non vaccinated people. Please get vaccinated on your turn.
15	Vaccination Information	As per GOI guidelines, COVID-19 vaccination has been deemed safe even for lactating women. Register now at cowin.gov.in and get vaccinated when your turn arrives.
16	Vaccination Information	Mild headaches, pain/swelling at injection site, fever, irritability are common side effects after COVID-19 vaccine and will subside in few days. Do not hesitate to vaccinate.
17	Advisories	A Corona affected person travelled in Haryana Roadways Bus HR58A-9541 which started at 8.30AM from Delhi to Yamunanagar on 11 March. Persons who travelled by this bus should inform on number 100. Yamunanagar Police.
18	Advisories	ହାତ ଧୋଇବା, ମାସ୍କ ପିନ୍ଧିବା, ସାମାଜିକ ଦୂରତା ନିୟମ ପାଳିବା, ଜନ ଗହଳିରୁ ଦୂରରେ ରହିବା, ତେବେ କରୋନାକୁ ଜିତିବା- ସୂଚନା ଓ ଲୋକ ସମ୍ପର୍କ ବିଭାଗ, ଓଡ଼ିଶା ସରକାର *(Original- Odia)* Washing hands, wearing masks, social distancing, staying away from public gatherings should be the only way to win over corona: Odisha govt *(Translated)*

4.2 Message Dissemination Statistics

During COVID-19 pandemic situation, the service of this system (known as 'COVID-19 Sāvdhān') has been rigorously used by 26 State & Union Territory authorities for sending nearly 3.4 billion of SMS in 10 different languages (Bengali, Gujarati, Hindi, Kannada, Malayalam, Marathi, Odia, Tamil, Telugu, and English) to the citizens of India related to COVID-19 mitigation measures including alerts on quarantine centers, supply of essential commodities, law and order issues, new COVID-19 hot zones etc. Figure 7 shows the usage of the platform by different authorities of States/UTs and total area targeted for dissemination of COVID related advisories and alerts is shown in Fig. 8. Figure 9 presents the screenshots of some messages received by the public.

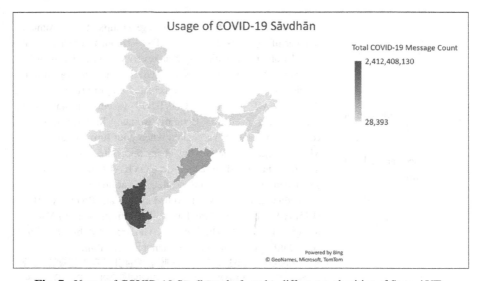

Fig. 7. Usage of COVID-19 Sāvdhān platform by different authorities of States/ UTs.

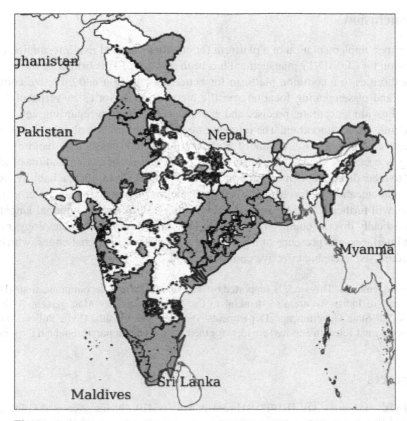

Fig. 8. Targeted Area for dissemination of COVID-related advisories and alerts

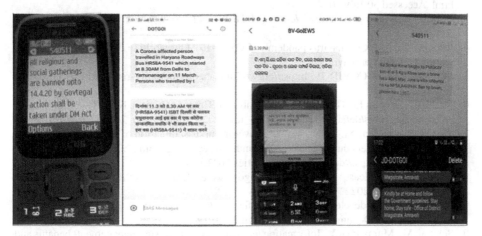

Fig. 9. Screenshots of actual received messages

5 Conclusion

In this paper, implementation of a platform for enabling targeted risk information communication for COVID-19 management has been discussed. This brings all the responsible authorities to a common platform for better coordination and effective communication and disseminating location specific alerts and advisories in vernacular languages. Providing accurate, precise, and actionable information regarding any hazard or pandemic is very important. The immense penetration of mobile phones makes SMS an effective communication channel for alerting. Targeted messaging, avoiding over-alerting is necessary. The same platform can be extended for dissemination of alerts related to other disasters or emergency situations. To enable last mile reachability, use of other communication media channels including satellite, broadcasting, and internet technologies will further extend the outreach. Providing information in regional languages in linguistically diverse country like India is very important. Multi-technology, multi-variant interfaces, and presence of legacy infrastructures pose big challenges, which are being addressed to enable effective communication.

Acknowledgements. This work is supported by the Department of Telecommunications (DoT), Government of India. We are also thankful to the National Disaster Management Authority (NDMA), all State Governments' Departments/Agencies, viz. Health, Civil, Police, SDMA, logistics, etc., and Telecom Service Providers for their continuous support throughout the journey.

References

1. WHO Coronavirus (COVID-19) Dashboard. https://covid19.who.int/. Accessed 31 July 2022
2. Covid-19 outbreak. https://www.hindustantimes.com/india-news/covid-19-outbreak-it-took-the-world-13-days-to-get-its-second-million-cases/story-EUpP3YyAvbrnEF5Zq3qO0H.html. Accessed 30 July 2022
3. Ministry of Health and Family Welfare (MoHFW). https://www.mohfw.gov.in. Accessed 31 July 2022
4. Ritchie, H., et al.: Coronavirus pandemic (COVID-19). Our world in data (2020). https://ourworldindata.org/coronavirus
5. Mortality Risk of COVID-19. https://ourworldindata.org/mortality-risk-covid. Accessed 12 July 2022
6. Mendel, T., Notess L.: The Right to Information in Times of Crisis. UNESCO (2020). https://en.unesco.org/sites/default/files/unesco_ati_iduai2020_english_sep_24.pdf
7. Wu, X., Shi, L., Lu, X., Li, X., Ma, L.: Government dissemination of epidemic information as a policy instrument during COVID-19 pandemic: evidence from Chinese cities. Cities **125**, 103658 (2022). https://doi.org/10.1016/j.cities.2022.103658
8. TRAI Press Release. https://www.trai.gov.in/sites/default/files/PR_No.12of2022_0.pdf. Accessed 29 July 2022
9. Measuring digital development Facts and figures 2019, ITU (2019). https://www.itu.int/en/ITU-D/Statistics/Documents/facts/FactsFigures2019.pdf
10. Sakurai, M., Murayama, Y.: Information technologies and disaster management–benefits and issues. Prog. Disaster Sci. **2**, 100012 (2019). https://doi.org/10.1016/j.pdisas.2019.100012
11. Ayyub, B.M., McGill, W.L., Kaminskiy, M.: Critical asset and portfolio risk analysis: an all-hazards framework. Risk Anal. **27**, 789–801 (2007). https://doi.org/10.1111/j.1539-6924.2007.00911.x

12. Rattien, S.: The role of the media in hazard mitigation and disaster management. Disasters **14**, 36–45 (1990). https://doi.org/10.1111/j.1467-7717.1990.tb00970.x
13. Manalu, E.P.S., Muditomo A., Adriana, D., Trisnowati, Y., Kesuma P., Z., Dwiyani H., R.: Role of information technology for successful responses to Covid-19 pandemic. In: 2020 International Conference on Information Management and Technology (ICIMTech), pp. 415–420. IEEE (2020). https://doi.org/10.1109/ICIMTech50083.2020.9211290
14. Seeger, M.W., et al.: A conceptual model for evaluating emergency risk communication in public health. Health Secur. **16**(3), 193–203 (2018). https://doi.org/10.1089/hs.2018.0020
15. Hodge, J.G., Gostin, L.O., Vernick, J.S.: The pandemic and all-hazards preparedness act: improving public health emergency response. JAMA **297**(15), 1708–1711 (2007). https://doi.org/10.1001/jama.297.15.1708
16. Driedger, S.M., Maier, R., Sanguins, J., Carter, S., Bartlett, J.: Pandemic H1N1 targeted messaging for Manitoba Metis: an evaluation of a risk communication intervention. Aboriginal Policy Stud. **3**(1–2) (2014)
17. Elazab, A., Shabana, B., Hefny, H.: Location based services classifications. Int. Res. J. Adv. Eng. Sci. **3**(2), 40–48 (2018)
18. Parker, A.M., Jackson, B.A.: Exploring the effect of the diffusion of geo-targeted emergency alerts: the application of agent-based modeling to understanding the spread of messages from the wireless emergency alerts systems. United States. Department of Homeland Security; United States. Department of Homeland Security. Science and Technology Directorate (2015)
19. Lee, M., You, M.: Effects of COVID-19 emergency alert text messages on practicing preventive behaviors: cross-sectional web-based survey in South Korea. J. Med. Internet Res. **23**(2), e24165 (2021). https://doi.org/10.2196/24165
20. Wireless subscribers across India 2010–2021, Statista. https://www.statista.com/statistics/328 003/wireless-subscribers-in-india/. Accessed 25 July 2022
21. Common alerting protocol (CAP 1.2). https://www.itu.int/en/ITU-D/Emergency-Telecommu nications/Documents/2020/T-REC-X.1303bis-201403-.pdf
22. Purvis, L.K., Jortner, J.N., Arpin, B.K., Ramos, B.J., Glaser, R.F.: Integrated Public Alert and Warning System (IPAWS). Sandia National Lab. (SNL-CA), Livermore, CA (United States); Sandia National Lab. (SNL-NM), Albuquerque, NM (United States), Technical report (2007)

Collapsed Building Detection Using Multiple Object Tracking from Aerial Videos and Analysis of Effective Filming Techniques of Drones

Shono Fujita[1]([⊠]) [iD] and Michinori Hatayama[2] [iD]

[1] Graduate School of Informatics, Kyoto University, 36-1 Yoshidahommachi, Sakyo-Ku, Kyoto-City, Kyoto 606-8501, Japan
`fujita.shono.32x@st.kyoto-u.ac.jp`
[2] Disaster Prevention Research Institute, Kyoto University, Gokasho, Uji-City, Kyoto 611-0011, Japan
`hatayama@dimsis.dpri.kyoto-u.ac.jp`

Abstract. Earthquake destroyed many buildings, especially wooden ones, in Japan. Collecting information regarding collapsed buildings during the emergency phase (i.e., 72 h after a disaster) is difficult but essential for rescue activities. This study developed an automatic model to detect collapsed buildings using multiple object tracking (MOT) from aerial videos. Roof damage and pancake collapse are destructions unique to traditional Japanese buildings. Previous studies that detected collapsed buildings using the features of debris or damage failed to discriminate between collapsed and held-up buildings when the buildings have the above Japanese feature. Therefore, this study used the deep learning MOT model to classify collapsed and held-up buildings regardless of debris appearance. The recall and precision of each track of collapsed buildings were 29.1% and 36.7%, respectively, based on cross-validation with the drone video of the 2016 Kumamoto Earthquake. Analysis between the recall and other factors indicated that the aspect ratio, speed, and appearance time of the buildings were significant features for the detection. In the relationship between recall and these factors, we deduce that the recall of track increases to 63.9% if the drone operator films aerial videos effectively. Moreover, this study analyzed effective drone filming and flying way to satisfy some conditions for detection. This result provides recommended filming guides to drone operators for future earthquakes.

Keywords: Multiple Object Detection Keyword · Collapsed Building · Aerial Video

1 Introduction

Previous earthquakes in Japan damaged many buildings, especially wooden buildings. The Great Hanshin-Awaji earthquake damaged about 640,00 buildings [1] and killed over 4,200 people from suffocation or crushing deaths at the hands of collapsed buildings

T. Gjøsæter et al. (Eds.): ITDRR 2022, IFIP AICT 672, pp. 118–135, 2023.
https://doi.org/10.1007/978-3-031-34207-3_8

[2]. The Great East Japan Earthquake damaged about 280,000 buildings by seismic motion and tsunami [3]. The 2016 Kumamoto earthquake damaged or collapsed about 200,000 buildings [4]. Because building damage causes human injury, disaster response headquarters and fire brigades need the information on these damaged buildings as quickly as possible. However, the information on damaged or collapsed buildings was challenging to obtain during these earthquakes. In the Great East Japan Earthquake, 25% of fire departments in three affected prefectures could not receive the 119 calls due to communication network interruptions [5]. In the 2016 Kumamoto earthquake, fire brigades could not organize and analyze information of damage reported by each fire station because of a lack of staff [6]. In the 2016 Kumamoto and 2018 Northern Osaka earthquakes, there was an overflow of 119 calls that did not merit the dispatch of firefighters [7–9], which led to inefficient rescue operations. In the 2016 Kumamoto earthquake, because fire brigades could not obtain accurate information on damaged buildings and victims, they investigated all buildings in the area. However, this operation required abundant manpower, support staff from other local governments, and equipment [6]. We expect that disaster response headquarters and fire brigades cannot gather damage information for future large earthquake disasters that require a large number of human resources and equipment.

Therefore, disaster response headquarters and fire brigades have to actively collect information on damaged buildings. This study develops an automatic model to detect collapsed buildings during earthquakes from aerial videos, mainly drone videos. Drone videos can collect extensive information from a bird's eye view at a low cost in places that cannot be reached by people.

Currently, 52.9% (383/724) of fire departments in Japan have drones that can capture damage situations due to earthquakes, landslides, fire, or toxic gas accidents [10]. Moreover, disaster response organizations, such as local governments or fire brigades, have helicopters to capture disasters in aerial videos [11]. From this, the Japanese disaster response organization recommends using aerial movies, drones, and helicopters to capture damage situations. However, it is difficult for disaster response organization teams to find each damaged or collapsed building in real time from the many buildings shown in aerial videos. Therefore, this study uses a deep learning model to automatically detect collapsed buildings from aerial videos. It also analyzes effective filming and flying techniques for drones to detect collapsed buildings through deep learning.

2 Related Study

2.1 Detection of Damaged Buildings

Previous studies presented various models to detect damaged or collapsed buildings. Vetrivel et al. developed a damage building detection model through deep learning, 3D point cloud features, and multiple-kernel learning [12]. Cusicanqui et al. [13] and Yamazaki et al. [14] constructed 3D point clouds of buildings from aerial images and videos for effective structure assessments. Although this 3D point cloud analysis effectively assesses individual buildings, it is still difficult to detect many buildings in the affected areas because of the large calculation volume and small area covered in the videos.

Our previous study detected roof damage from aerial images through deep learning to ensure more rapid and efficient damage investigation of buildings in Japan [15–17]. Miura et al. [18] also estimated damaged buildings from the detection of roof damage and roof covered with blue sheets from aerial images through deep learning. Calantropio et al. [19] extracted building regions through deep learning segmentation and detected damaged buildings. Ortho aerial images obtained above can detect roof damage, which can help assess building body damage, in large areas. However, these images cannot detect collapsed buildings without roof damage, where rescuers or injured people are likely located because these images cannot discriminate between vertical displacements of collapsed buildings.

Yamazaki et al. made fragility curves of Japanese buildings based on damage survey data from the 2016 Kumamoto earthquake [20]. These curves represent building damage probability corresponding to the peak ground velocity of earthquakes. The National Research Institute for Earth Science and Disaster Resilience in Japan supplies the estimated number of damaged buildings on the website based on fragility curves during the disaster [21]. The fragility curves estimate the number of individual damaged buildings in 250 m mesh areas. Japanese local governments can use this system to capture a rough damage overview.

Xie et al. [22], Khajwal et al. [23], and Shishido et al. [24] proposed a crowdsourcing system to collect information on damaged buildings from aerial images. Volunteer cooperation such as crowdsourcing is effective during restoration and reconstruction. However, it takes more time to complete these tasks in the emergency phase, which lasts 72 h during disasters.

This study uses aerial videos, especially drone videos, to automatically detect collapsed buildings through deep learning. Aerial videos can detect individual collapsed buildings with vertical displacement and without roof damage from an oblique angle. Moreover, aerial videos are effective during the emergency phase because of minimal calculation volume and filming labor.

2.2 Detection from Aerial Videos

Qi et al. detected collapsed buildings through image processing from aerial videos in areas affected by the earthquake [25]. They detected debris of collapsed buildings from the disorder of texture in images using the HOG feature, a histogram of gradient direction of luminance. Pi et al. detected flood areas, undamaged roofs, damaged roofs, cars, debris, and vegetation by object detection from aerial videos in areas affected by hurricanes [26]. Object detection is an image recognition task that classifies and localizes object place by bbox, which is a circumscribed quadrangle of an object. Zhu et al. detected damaged buildings using the original model (MSNet) with object detection from aerial videos in areas affected by hurricanes [27]. This MSNet used building bbox and segmentation mask of damage regions, such as debris and roof.

Japanese traditional buildings often suffer damaged roofs, especially tile roofs during earthquakes or typhoons. Prior to the ammendment in the building standard in 1981, tile roofs of buildings did not have to be fixed to the roof base. Currently, the number of tile roofs that sustain damage in disasters is decreasing because of revised strict building standards, the use of light raw materials, and a decrease in the number of people using tile roofs. Hence, many old buildings, or buildings without sufficient countermeasures, may still be affected in the future. These studies [25–27] detected collapsed buildings mainly using debris and damaged parts in videos. Even if buildings did not collapse, these detection systems that focus on debris overly react to roof damage in Japan (Fig. 1). Because fire brigades aim to locate collapsed buildings, where rescuers or injured people are likely located, information on a large number of buildings with light damage limits their rescue activity. Additionally, Japanese buildings, especially wooden ones, may cause pancake collapse, indicating that the collapsed story is crushed flat during earthquakes [28–30]. In this collapse pattern, the appearance of the building body, such as the wall and roof, may be intact, except for the crushed story. Because many of the crushed story cannot be seen well, these buildings cannot be detected based only on debris or damage regions. Considering the above feature of Japanese buildings, this study classifies collapsed buildings using object detection of deep learning regardless of debris appearance. In other words, the unique point of this study is to focus on not debris or damaged buildings but collapsed buildings.

Moreover, this study uses multiple object tracking (MOT), which is a type of technique applied to object detection. MOT detects an object by drawing a bbox in each frame and associating the same object among different frames in the video to follow the object tracking. Thus, disaster response organizations can grasp the number of collapsed buildings and confirm individual detected buildings after this tracking.

Fig. 1. Image visualizing MSNet [27] applied to damaged Japanese buildings in Mashiki city

3   System Use Flow

Figure 2 shows the usage flow of the proposed system. First, MOT detects collapsed buildings from an aerial video filmed by drones or helicopters. Then, the detected collapsed buildings are visualized in the video. Finally, the headquarter staff, such as fire brigades and local governments, watch this video to grasp individual collapsed buildings and rough damage overview in real time. Therefore, object detection is expected to be an effective interface for users to visualize collapsed buildings.

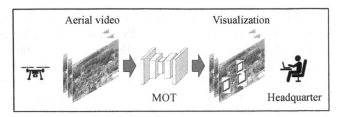

Fig. 2. Usage flow of the proposed system

4 Dataset

4.1 Video Dataset

To develop the detection model, this study uses aerial videos and images filmed by drones in Mashiki city of Kumamoto prefecture after the 2016 Kumamoto earthquake. The 2016 Kumamoto earthquake occurred on April 14 and 16, 2016; the maximum seismic intensity was 7, and the moment magnitude scale was 7.0. The number of deaths reported was 273, and 198,258 buildings were damaged [4]. Mashiki city had large damage to buildings, mainly wooden buildings. The dataset is 6 aerial videos and 659 aerial images of one drone flight (hereinafter referred to as ODF). The durations of the six aerial videos are 2 s (51 frames), 2 s (56 frames), 6 min and 56 s (12,472 frames), 7 min and 37 s (13,683 frames), 7 min and 40 s (13,776 frames), and 7 min and 52 s (14,138 frames). The image sizes of these videos is $3,840 \times 2,160$, and the image size of ODF is $4,608 \times 3456$. The frame rate of these videos is 30 fps, and the average altitude of the drone was about 60–75 m.

4.2 Annotation Dataset

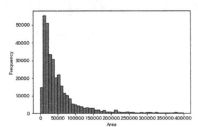 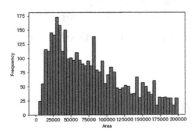

Fig. 3. Histogram of the annotation data by bbox areas (left: video data, right: ODF image data)

Bbox of collapsed buildings for MOT was annotated using the annotation tool "Computer Vision Annotation Tools." We annotated one image out of every ten frames and compensated remain nine frames by linear interpolation. The following are the annotation rules:

- Target objects are buildings that collapses, especially pancake collapse, and those with dropped roofs, where rescuers or injured people are likely located.

- We exclude buildings whose collapse and dropped roofs cannot be recognized, such as those distant and unclear buildings.
- We judge collapse and dropped roofs from only the target frame. We do not use the information of the same building in other frames. Annotation can change in different frames for the same building.
- Bbox is drawn for one continuous building.
- Targets include warehouses.
- The classification class is only collapse.

Figure 3 shows the histogram of these annotation data by bbox areas (the number of pixel). This study calls the annotated data an "answer" in contrast to estimation data. Figure 4 shows a captured image of the annotation tool with the video of Mashiki city.

Fig. 4. Captured image of the annotation tool with the Mashiki city video

5 Training MOT Model

5.1 Dataset for Cross-Validation

Each frame image of these 6 videos is divided into eight classes based on four regions (Fig. 5) to make training, validation, and test data for cross-validation. The eight classes are "only A," "only B," "only C," and "only D" (i.e., frames showing only buildings in A, B, C, and D regions) and "A and B," "B and C," "C and D," and "D and A" (i.e., frames showing buildings in both regions A and B, B and C, C and D, and D and A). The images of ODF are also divided into these eight classes. Table 1 shows the cross-validation dataset. We use these data classifications to avoid using the same buildings among training, validation, and test data. Training data update parameters of the model and validation data decide training epoch to prevent overfitting, and test data evaluate the model accuracy after training. Using the data in Table 1, the validation and test data can be accurately evaluated. Test data use only video data to consider the practical usage of this model. "Annotation" in Table 1 means each bbox of an object.

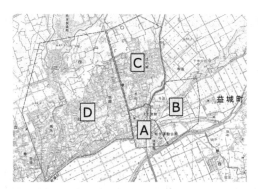

Fig. 5. Region classification for cross-validation

Table 1. Breakdown of data in cross-validation

	Training data	Validation data	Test data
1st	Video and ODF of "only C," "C and D," "only D"	Video and ODF of "only B"	Video of "only A"
	16,004 images, 102,618 annotations, 435 tracks	9,746 images, 12,983 annotations, 104 tracks	3,893 images, 14,287 annotations, 71 tracks
2nd	Video and ODF of "only D," "D and A," "only A"	Video and ODF of "only C"	Video of "only B"
	10,428 images, 100,704 annotations, 467 tracks	6,499 images, 36,459 annotations, 203 tracks	9,619 images, 12,771 annotations, 52 tracks
3rd	Video and ODF of "only A," "A and B," "only B"	Video and ODF of "only D"	Video of "only C"
	19,185 images, 41,379 annotations, 366 tracks	1,921 images, 24,696 annotations, 137 tracks	6,436 images, 35,674 annotations, 88 tracks
4th	Video and ODF of "only B", "B and C", "only C"	Video and ODF of "only A"	Video of "only D"
	17,689 images, 51,650 annotations, 342 tracks	4,014 images, 14,838 annotations, 166 tracks	1,921 images, 24,696 annotations, 137 tracks

5.2 MOT Model

This study uses ByteTrack [31] as the MOT model, which has high tracking accuracy and speed. ByteTrack uses a detected object with low confidence level, which other MOT models normally discard, when the detected object overlaps a large region with the object predicted by using the Kalman filter from a former track. The model can detect objects with occlusion, which implies hidden in front of other objects, or decrease ID switch, which indicates switching object identity to other objects.

5.3 Training Experiment

This study trained Bytetrack by the above dataset in Table 1 for cross-validation four times. The backbone for object detection is YOLOX-m [32], and fine-tuning is executed using a pre-trained backbone model by the COCO dataset. The input image size was 800×1440, batch size was 1, basic learning rate per image was 0.0001/64, max training epoch was 100, and other hyper parameters were the same as the default value in the GitHub code [33]. This experiment used GeForce RTX 2080 SUPER. The training times of the first to fourth train were approximately 36 h, 26 h and a half, 38 h, and 38 h. The upper part of Fig. 6 shows the transition of training data loss. The lower-left- and lower-right-hand sides of the figure show the validated data transition of average precision (AP50–95) and average recall (AR50–95) of the COCO dataset version, which implies an average from 50% to 95% of the IoU threshold. In the test MOT model, we used the trained model with high AP and AR, as shown in Fig. 6. Selected models in the first to fourth train were trained models of 5, 4, 3, and 2 epochs.

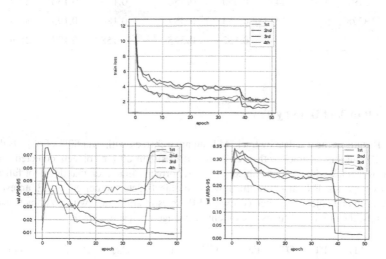

Fig. 6. Upper: training loss transition, lower left: validation AP50–95 transition, lower right: validation AR50–95 transition

6 Evaluation of the MOT Model

6.1 Result of the Test Data by an Annotation

Table 2 shows the cross-validation result by an object, which implies each bbox in track. These experiments set 0.4 to the threshold of detection confidence, which was lower than the default because preventing overlook of collapsed buildings (FN data) is important for rescue activity. In Table 2, TP is the correct detection to answer data, FP is an incorrect estimation, FN is overlooked answer data, AP50 is the average precision of the COCO dataset version, IDF1 indicates MOT accuracy, and inference time is measured by one image. This experiment set 0.5 as the threshold IoU of correct detection. The IoU has an overlapped ratio between true bbox and estimated bbox. From this result, because recall was lower than precision, the number of detections of the model tended to be small. Moreover, because the average inference time was 25.0 ms (i.e., an inference speed of 40.0 fps), the MOT model can run with aerial videos of 30 fps in real time.

Table 2. Results of the test data by annotation. TP: correct detections of answer data, FP: incorrect estimations, FN: overlooked answer data, AP50: average precision on the COCO dataset, IDF1: an indication of MOT accuracy

	TP↑	FP↓	FN↓	Recall↑	Precision↑	AP50↑	IDF1↑	Inference time (ms)↓
1st	2080	2277	12207	0.146	0.477	0.119	0.202	23.0
2nd	3047	7921	9724	0.239	0.278	0.149	0.255	22.4
3rd	3197	5787	32477	0.090	0.356	0.178	0.136	23.7
4th	3278	5192	21418	0.133	0.387	0.186	0.193	30.8
Average				**0.152**	**0.375**	0.158	0.197	**25.0**

6.2 Result of Test Data by Track

Table 3. Results of the test data by track. MT: an answer track with over 80% of objects detected correctly, PT: an answer track with over 20% and less than 80% of objects detected correctly, OT: an answer track with even one object detected correctly in a track that does not fall into the MT or PT categories, FN: an answer track with no objects detected correctly. CE: an estimation track with even one object estimated correctly, FP: an estimation track with no objects estimated correctly. IDs: the number of times track identity changed in a single track.

	MT	PT	OT	FN↓	CE↑	FP↓	IDs↓	Recall↑	Precision↑
1st	4	7	4	56	18	39	3	0.211	0.316
2nd	2	9	8	33	22	40	9	0.365	0.355
3rd	4	9	13	62	30	53	8	0.295	0.361
4th	6	18	16	97	43	53	5	0.292	0.448
Average								**0.291**	**0.367**

Table 3 shows the result of cross-validation by track. In the table, MT, PT, OT, and FN are the numbers for the answer data. Specifically, MT is an answer track that has over 80% of objects detected correctly in the track, PT is an answer track that has over

20% below 80% of objects detected correctly in the track, OT is an answer track that has even one object detected correctly in the track but MT and PT, and FN is an answer track that has no objects detected correctly in the track. Alternatively, CE and FP are the numbers for estimation data. Specifically, CE is an estimation track that has even one object estimated correctly in the track, and FP is an estimation track with no objects estimated correctly in the track. Meanwhile, IDs are the number of times changing track identity in one track. Recall is the ratio of the sum of MT, PT, and OT to the total answer track, and precision is the ratio of CE to the total estimation track. If users consider the track with even one detected object by the model as a collapsed building, they can detect 29.1% of collapsed buildings with 63.3% of no collapsed building detected incorrectly.

6.3 Analysis of Accuracy and Other Factors

This section analyzes the relationship between recall of answer track in Table 3 and other factors. Because recall is calculated from denominator of the answer data, other factors such as bbox size and the appearance time of real collapsed data annotated in the experiment can also be used. However, precision is calculated from the denominator of the data of estimated collapsed buildings. Because other factors obtained from the estimation data are not real values, they cannot be used in the analysis. Hence, we focus on recall in this section. Moreover, recall may also be considered as a more important measure of performance in disaster scenarios because it enables us to focus on reducing overlooked collapsed buildings, which is critical for locating survivors in a timely manner. These other factors are the average bbox area (the number of the pixel) converted to 800×1440, bbox aspect ratio (width/height), displacement pixel of bbox center from the former frame (bbox speed), and appearance time (number of frames) of an object in each answer track. Figure 7 shows the histogram of the answer track in each rank and recall of the answer track by each rank. If the "correct value" of the detected answer track was set to 1, the "correct value" of the not detected answer track was set to 0. Each correlation coefficient between "correct value" and area, aspect ratio, speed, and appearance time was -0.007, -0.358, -0.204, and 0.251, respectively. From this result and in Fig. 7, the smaller the aspect ratio, the slower speed and longer appearance time, and the higher the model recall. The speed and appearance time results also apply to humans and can be predicted easily. The result of the aspect ratio indicates that an object whose aspect ratio is large (i.e., the object watched from an angle close to the horizon) is difficult for the MOT model to detect. This result may indicate that being able to see collapsed story, mainly the first story, located in the lower part of the building, is important for collapse detection.

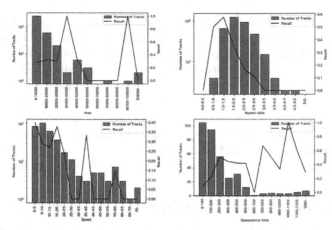

Fig. 7. Histogram and recall of answer track by other factors (upper left: area, upper right: aspect ratio, lower left: speed, lower right: appearance time)

6.4 Qualitative Analysis

Figure 8 shows an image visualizing the bbox of answers and estimation. These estimation images indicate that the MOT model can detect collapsed buildings without large debris or damage, which is a specific feature of Japanese buildings. The image shows the number of estimated collapsed buildings in the upper-left part. This number enables the user to capture a rough damage overview. The color of the bbox corresponds to the detection confidence level to tell collapsed buildings with a high degree of probability of being correctly estimated to users.

Figure 9 shows an example of the building with the following feature of FN and FP track data. In all 248 FN tracks in Table 3, which is an overlooked track, there were two features in common with some data. First, 60 (24.1%) buildings did not suffer roof damage. This implies that the MOT model use information about roof damage in addition to the building body as food for thought to detect collapsed buildings. Second, 30 (12.1%) buildings' collapsed story (wall) was not seen because of the angle, other buildings, or obstacles. In the annotation task, these buildings were judged from the roof position to the ground or inclination of the buildings as collapsed. This result matches the fact that the small building aspect ratio is suitable for the detection of the MOT model discussed in Sect. 6.3.

Fig. 8. Image visualizing bbox of answer (left) and estimation (right)

In all 185 FP tracks in Table 3, which were incorrect estimations, there were three features in common with some data. First, 78 (42.2%) buildings had roof damage. This feature has the same tendency as the above first feature of FN. Second, 20 (10.8%) buildings had the incorrect bbox shape and size against the answer bbox, although they could point to collapsed buildings. However, users can understand collapsed buildings from these incorrect detections because they have only mistaken their shapes or sizes. Third, 19 (10.3%) buildings did not collapse judging from an angle at that time, but collapsed judging from another angle. This difference in annotation labels resulted from the third annotation rule discussed in Sect. 4.2. This result suggests that the MOT model can possibly extract features of collapsed buildings that humans cannot understand because these buildings actually collapsed.

Fig. 9. Example of FN and FP features (upper left: building without roof damage, upper right: building whose collapsed story cannot be seen, lower left: building with damage, lower center: building who's detected bbox is bad, lower right: building collapsed in fact)

7 Effective Videography and Flight Techniques for Aerial Drones

7.1 Necessary Conditions for Video Capture and Flight Simulation

In Subsect. 6.3, we determined that the aspect ratio, speed, and appearance time of buildings in videos are important features to identify damaged buildings. When we set tracks with an average aspect ratio of less than 2, a speed of less than 30 pixels per frame, and an appearance time of more than 200 frames (6.66 s) in this experiment, we found that recall increased to 63.9% (53/83). This implies that 63.9% of collapsed buildings can be detected if drone operators adopt more optimal videography and flight techniques. From this result, we executed a simulation of video capture during a drone flight satisfying the following necessary conditions to determine a set of effective flight and videography techniques for drones.

(1) The aspect ratio of each bbox in the track should be less than 2 so that the average aspect ratio can be less than 2.
(2) The average speed of the buildings in the track should be less than 30 pixels per frame.
(3) The appearance time should be more than 200 frames.
(4) The area of the building bboxes ($h_b \times w_b$ of Fig. 10) in a 3,840 × 2,160 video should be more than 10,000 pixels.
(5) The length of building walls (h_w in Fig. 11) in 3,840 × 2,160 video should be more than 20 pixels.

The necessary condition (4) and (5) were added to avoid the buildings shown in the video from being too small to detect building body and collapsed stories (walls), which is important to detect collapses as described under FN in the second feature of Sect. 6.4.

7.2   Altitude and Camera Angle

Figure 10 shows videographic and flight techniques used in this simulation. The z-, y- and x-axes respectively indicate the vertical direction, the direction of flight, and the direction perpendicular to the y-z plane. The drone proceeded in a straight line, and the height of the drone H and the camera angle θ_D to the z-axis in the y-z plane remained constant. This simulation assumed buildings to be rectangular solids, and that their front sides were orthogonal to the direction of flight of the drone. The side shape of the buildings in the x-y plane was a W_b square with a height of H_b. The buildings were two stories and the first story was collapsed. Considering the average gross floor area 126.63 m^2 of Japanese detached houses [34], W_b was set as $\sqrt{126.63/2}$ (m). From the minimum ceiling height of the Japanese Building Standard Law, H_b was set as 2.1 (m). At a certain H and θ_D, the simulation calculated the trapezoid area in Fig. 10, where the building satisfied the necessary conditions (1), (4) and (5), and the rectangle area (ASA) where the building always fell within the area within which the conditions were satisfied even if the drone continued to fly in the same direction. This simulation determined the most effective H and θ_D to maximize ASA.

In reference to the diagonal viewing angle of 84° and image size of 3840 × 2160 of DJI Mavic 3 drones [35], this simulation utilized a horizontal view angle $\theta_h = 47.6°$ and a vertical view angle $\theta_v = 76.2°$. In calculating ASA, this simulation utilized a building located in the left-right center of the video plane. Figure 11 left and right show the location relation from the perspective of the x- and z-axes, where h_b, h_w and w_b are the bbox height, the building wall height and the bbox width, respectively. In this simulation, we examined whether the necessary conditions (1), (4) and (5) were satisfied in all combinations among θ_D (integer from 0 to 90), H (integer from H_b to 150) and l (an integer in range when the building appeared in the video plane). Then, we calculated ASA in all of θ_D and H from the maximum l, minimum l, and minimum l_2 satisfying the above conditions at a given θ_D and H. Figure 12 shows the result, and the maximum ASA (red cross in Fig. 12) was 19,739 m^2 at $\theta_D = 33°$, $H = 106$ m.

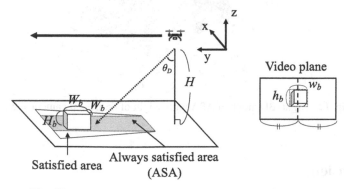

Fig. 10. Videography methods for drones in the simulation

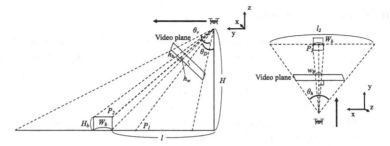

Fig. 11. Location relation viewed from the x-axis (left) and z-axis (right)

7.3 Drone Speed and Area Covered

At the maximum ASA value, the depth of ASA region appearing in video plane was 570 pixels. When the building appeared in the ASA in video plane for 200 frames (necessary condition (3)), the building speed in the video was 2.85 pixels per frame, which satisfies the necessary condition (2). In this case, the drone can have maximum speed 57.78 km/h calculated from an ASA length 107 m. With a battery life of 46 min [35], a vehicle could film an area of 8.10 km^2 in a single flight based on an ASA width of 182 m. These effective flight and videography techniques with optimal θ_D, H and maximum speed can be used to survey an area of 8.10 km^2 area with 63.9% recall in a single flight.

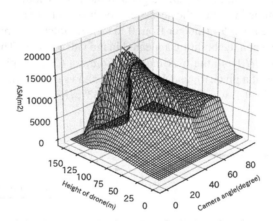

Fig. 12. (right) 3D graph of ASA with height of drone and camera angle

8   Conclusion

This study developed an automatic MOT model to detect collapsed buildings in earthquakes from aerial videos and analyzed effective filming of drone aerial videos. To focus on collapse and address building damage features, such as roof damage and pancake collapse of Japan, this study used object detection, especially the MOT model, of deep learning, instead of debris feature detection. From the cross-validation result using aerial videos of the 2016 Kumamoto earthquake, recall and precision of the MOT model by track were 29.1% and 36.7%, respectively. The results of the analysis between recall and other factors indicated that the aspect ratio, speed, and appearance time of buildings were important features for the detection. However, the number of detected collapsed buildings was often lower than the actual number. Qualitative analysis indicated that the MOT model could detect buildings with pancake collapse without large debris and damage, specific to Japanese buildings. However, the detection of the MOT model relied on information about roof damage. Finally, this study indicated that track recall increases to 63.9% if drone operators effectively film aerial videos. Then, we analyzed effective drone videography and flight techniques to maintain this recall using the filming simulation. We determined the optimal altitude and camera angle to be 106 m and 36°, respectively, and that a single flight can film an area of some 8.10 km².

In the future, another MOT model should be analyzed for improved accuracy, along with possible hyperparameter configurations and training processes. In addition to improving accuracy, the allowed recall and precision should be analyzed through a questionnaire or investigation. Calculation or simulation of more practical flight and videography techniques for aerial drones is also crucial. In addition to disaster response personnel, this system may also be effective to help drone operators determine where to fly. An analysis of types of residential areas that are difficult for this model to recognize would enable operators to select areas on which to focus. Moreover, the practical implementation of this system must be considered, including methods of sending videos and associated server architectures and communication frameworks. Finally, the proposed model can also be combined with geospatial information to produce maps to facilitate rescue activities.

Acknowledgements. This work is supported by JSPS KAKENHI Grant Number JP 22J15895.

References

1. Fire and Disaster Management Agency in Japan: Final report about the Great Hanshin-Awaji Earthquake. https://www.fdma.go.jp/disaster/info/assets/post1.pdf. Accessed 5 July 2022. (in Japanese)
2. Hyogo Prefecture Medical Association: Actual state of affairs of human damage by the Great Hanshin-Awaji Earthquake. https://www.hyogo.med.or.jp/jmat-hyogo/day-after/siryo/. Accessed 5 July 2022. (in Japanese)
3. Disaster response headquarters of Fukushima prefecture: No. 1778 damage report of the 2011 off the Pacific coast of Tohoku Earthquake. https://www.pref.fukushima.lg.jp/uploaded/life/620025_1725169_misc.pdf. Accessed 5 July 2022. (in Japanese)
4. Disaster response headquarters of Kumamoto prefecture: No. 325 damage report of the 2016 Kumamoto Earthquake. https://www.pref.kumamoto.jp/uploaded/attachment/182677.pdf. Accessed 5 July 2022. (in Japanese)
5. Fire and Disaster Management Agency in Japan: Report of review meeting about ideal way of effective initial activity of firefighter headquarter in large-scale disasters. https://www.fdma.go.jp/singi_kento/kento/items/kento004_01_houkoku.pdf. Accessed 5 July 2022. (in Japanese)

6. Kumamoto city fire department. Activity record journal of Kumamoto city fire department in the 2016 Kumamoto Earthquake. https://www.city.kumamoto.jp/common/UploadFileDsp.aspx?c_id=5&id=19060&sub_id=1&flid=134936. Accessed 5 July 2022. (in Japanese)
7. Tv Asahi news site. https://news.tv-asahi.co.jp/news_society/articles/000074837.html. Accessed July 2022. (in Japanese)
8. Murakami, H.: Study on rescue and emergency activities by Kumamoto City fire department after the 2016 Kumamoto earthquake - comparison with the 2004 Niigata Chuuetsu and the 2005 West off Fukuoka Prefecture earthquakes. Report of Tono Research Institute of Earthquake Science, vol. 41, pp. 93–98 (2017). (in Japanese)
9. The Sankei News. https://www.sankei.com/article/20200115-7M7FDUJP2RLLDJDFXYP23H4J3E/. Accessed 5 July 2022. (in Japanese)
10. Fire and Disaster Management Agency in Japan: Notice about promotion of drone usage of the fire brigade in disaster response. https://www.fdma.go.jp/laws/tutatsu/items/040331_drone.pdf. Accessed 5 July 2022 (in Japanese)
11. Nazarov, E.: Emergency response management in Japan, final research report. ASIAN disaster reduction center, FY2011A program (2011)
12. Anand, V., Markus, G., Norman, K., Francesco, N., George, V.: Disaster damage detection through synergistic use of deep learning and 3D point cloud features derived from very high-resolution oblique aerial images, and multiple-kernel-learning. ISPRS J. Photogramm. Remote Sens. 140, 45–59 (2018)
13. Johnny, C., Norman, K., Francesco, N.: Usability of aerial video footage for 3-D scene reconstruction and structural damage assessment. Nat. Hazards Earth Syst. Sci. 18(6), 1583–1598 (2018)
14. Yamazaki, F., Kubo, K., Tanabe, R., Liu, W.: Damage assessment and 3D modeling by UAV flights after the 2016 Kumamoto, Japan earthquake. In: The IEEE International Geoscience and Remote Sensing Symposium (IGARSS), Fort Worth, TX, USA, pp. 3182–3185 (2017)
15. Fujita, S., Hatayama, M.: Estimation method for roof-damaged buildings from aero-photo images during earthquakes using deep learning. Inf. Syst. Front. 25(1), 351–363 (2021)
16. Fujita, S., Hatayama, M.: Automatic calculation of damage rate of roofs based on image segmentation. In: 6th IFIP WG 5.15 International Conference, ITDRR 2021, pp. 3–22, Morioka, Japan, (2022)
17. Fujita, S., Hatayama, M.: Rapid and accurate detection of building damage investigation using an automatic method to calculate roof damage rate. IDRiM J. 12(1), 89–111 (2022)
18. Miura, H., Aridome, T., Matsuoka, M.: Deep learning-based identification of collapsed, non-collapsed and blue tarp-covered buildings from post-disaster aerial images. Remote Sens. 12(12) (2020)
19. Calantropio, A., Chiabrando, F., Codastefano, M., Bourke, E.: Deep learning for automatic building damage assessment: application in post-disaster scenarios using UAV data. ISPRS Ann. Photogramm. Remote Sens. Spat. Inf. Sci. V-1-2021, 113–120 (2021)
20. Yamazaki, F., et al.: Development of fragility curves of Japanese buildings based on the 2016 Kumamoto earthquake. In: The 2019 Pacific Conference on Earthquake Engineering, Auckland, New Zealand (2019)
21. Kusaka, A., Nakamura, H., Fujiwara, H., Okano, H.: Bayesian updating of damaged building distribution in post-earthquake assessment. In: The 16th World Conference on Earthquake, 16WCEE 2017, Santiago Chile (2017)
22. Xie, S., et al.: Crowdsourcing rapid assessment of collapsed buildings early after the earthquake based on aerial remote sensing image: a case study of Yushu earthquake. Remote Sens. 8(9) (2016)
23. Khajwal, A.B., Noshadravan, A.: An uncertainty-aware framework for reliable disaster damage assessment via crowdsourcing. Int. J. Disaster Risk Reduct. 55 (2021)

24. Shishido, H., Kobayashi, K., Kameda, Y., Kitahara, I.: Method to generate building damage maps by combining aerial image processing and crowdsourcing. J. Disaster Res. **16**(5), 827–839 (2021)
25. Qi, J., et al.: Search and rescue rotary-wing UAV and its application to the Lushan Ms 7.0 earthquake. J. Field Robot. **33**(3), 290–321 (2016)
26. Pi, Y., Nath, N.D., Behzadan, A.H.: Convolutional neural networks for object detection in aerial imagery for disaster response and recovery. Adv. Eng. Inform. **43** (2020)
27. Zhu, X., Liang, J., Hauptmann, A.: MSNet: a multilevel instance segmentation network for natural disaster damage assessment in aerial videos. In: The IEEE/CVF Winter Conference on Applications of Computer Vision (WACV), pp. 2023–2032 (2021)
28. Scawthorn, C., Yanev, P.I.: Preliminary report 17 January 1995, Hyogo-ken Nambu, Japanese earthquake. Eng. Struct. **17**(3), 146–157 (1995)
29. Okada, S., Takai, N.: Classifications of structural types and damage patterns of buildings for earthquake field investigation. In: 12th World Conference on Earthquake Engineering, Auckland, New Zealand (2000)
30. Scawthorn, C.: Building aspects of the 2004 Niigata Ken Chuetsu, Japan, Earthquake. Earthq. Spectra **22**(1), 75–88 (2006)
31. Zhang, Y., et al.: Bytetrack: multi-object tracking by associating every detection box. arXiv preprint arXiv:2110.06864 (2021)
32. Ge, Z., Liu, S., Wang, F., Li, Z., Sun, J.: Yolox: exceeding yolo series in 2021. arXiv preprint arXiv:2107.08430 (2021)
33. GitHub - ifzhang/ByteTrack: [ECCV 2022] ByteTrack: Multi-Object Tracking by Associating Every Detection Box. https://github.com/ifzhang/ByteTrack. Accessed 7 July 2022
34. Ministry of Internal Affairs and Communications: Result summary of basic tabulation about housing and households in housiPng and land survey. https://www.stat.go.jp/data/jyutaku/2018/pdf/kihon_gaiyou.pdf. Accessed 29 July 2022. (in Japanese)
35. DJI: Mavic 3 specification. https://www.dji.com/jp/mavic-3/specs. Accessed 29 July 2022. (in Japanese)

Challenges and Implementation of CBRN Sensor Networks in Urban Areas

Walter Seböck$^{(\boxtimes)}$ ⓘ, Bettina Biron ⓘ, and Bettina Pospisil ⓘ

University of Continuing Education Krems, Dr.-Karl-Dorrek-Straße 30, 3500 Krems an Der Donau, Austria

`{walter.seboeck,bettina.biron,bettina.pospisil}@donau-uni.ac.at`

Abstract. The threat posed by chemical, biological, radiological, and nuclear (CBRN) agents is considered greater than ever before. Technological advances offer new opportunities for prevention and decontamination in the fight against terrorism, but also pose new challenges for affected areas, companies, and forces. This article is based on the project "CBRN - City Sensor Network". The aim was to use stationary sensor networks to achieve early, automatic detection, identification, and protection against attacks with CBRN substances in public enclosed spaces with a focus on transport companies. In this paper, special attention is given to the challenges and factors that need to be considered when implementing sensor networks for emergency plans from a social science perspective. In doing so, processes and factors were defined to enable blue light organisations to limit damages faster, increase the safety of their own employees and improve the reconstruction of accidents. With a mix of methods, social science developed a phase model that depict the process of detecting and determining CBRN and extracted the challenges of implementation and deployment into a theme map.

Keywords: CBRN · Counterterrorism · Technology Implementation · Emergency Management

1 Introduction

The prospect of non-state actors, including terrorists and their supporters, gaining access to, and using Weapons of Mass Destruction (WMD)/Chemical Biological, Radiological and Nuclear (CBRN) materials is a serious threat to international peace and security. Over the years, terrorist groups have tested new ways and means to acquire and use more dangerous weapons to maximize damage and incite terror, including weapons incorporating CBRN materials. With advancements being made in technology and the expansion of legal and illegal commercial channels, including on the dark web, some of these weapons have become continuously more accessible. In addition, the United Nation Office of Counter-Terrorism (UNOCT) has observed an increasing frequency of terrorist attacks on so-called "soft targets" such as urban centres [1, 2]. As much as the topic is increasingly coming into the focus of security organisations, practical experiences of the emergency forces and data situation, especially as far as accidents

© IFIP International Federation for Information Processing 2023
Published by Springer Nature Switzerland AG 2023
T. Gjøsæter et al. (Eds.): ITDRR 2022, IFIP AICT 672, pp. 136–149, 2023.
https://doi.org/10.1007/978-3-031-34207-3_9

and terrorist attacks are concerned, are still relatively manageable at present: the sarin attack on the Tokyo underground in 1995 and a similar incident in Matsumoto a year earlier were fortunately so far the only use of nerve agents in a large-scale terrorist attack, some experiments with anthrax letters (Antrax) in the USA also remained basically one of the few incidents of bioterrorism that remains in the public perception [3]. The same applies to deliberate criminal use of polonium-210 in the Litvinenko case [4].

Since it must be assumed, that attacks of this kind are likely to occur more frequently, governments and international organisations have launched comprehensive programmes in recent years to accelerate the development of effective counterstrategies. For example, fifty heads of state and government from around the world took part in a crisis simulation of a radiological terrorist attack as part of a nuclear security summit in 2016 [5]. In 2018, the UN Secretary-General launched the UN Global Counter-Terrorism Coordination Compact, a coordination framework that synchronize 38 UN agencies as well as INTERPOL and the World Customs Organisation. [6, 7]. National programmes, for example the civil security research programme *KIRAS* and the defence research programme FORTE in Austria, are also dedicated to this important topic with funding programmes for security research. The aim of the project "CBRN - City Sensor Network"[1], on which this paper is based, was to minimize hazards from CBRN substances in public spaces, especially in traffic stations, by developing technical measures for prevention, detection, and assessment, of the hazard potential and for intervention, evacuation and recovery in CBRN situations. The primary focus was to find efficient approaches to significantly increase the safety of both the emergency services and the population in the event of threats from weapons of mass destruction and to develop and refine the necessary processes and information technology resources (sensor networks, visualisations) together with those responsible.

To address this challenge, scientific studies recommend not only increased awareness in society, but also new approaches to faster hazard detection, training of responders, and further development of existing equipment [8]. Technological tools can support employees at various stages of emergency management from gathering information to communication, decision-making and infrastructure survivability [9–12], there are several challenges emergency organizations face during the implementation of new technologies [13]. While literature suggests the implementation of technical systems, there is a lack of knowledge how to realize the recent processes for employees interacting with a new system.

Pennathur et.al. [14] emphasize: "Often, decisions regarding the implementation of such technologies are made with limited foreknowledge of the degree to which such systems will alter existing work practices and impact work performance (negatively as well as positively)". Therefore, it is necessary to understand existing processes, activities, but also attitudes of potential users in order to include them in the technology development. Only in this way those functions, that are necessary for the users, can be optimally covered by the new technologies [14]. This is what makes them meaningful

---

[1] The results of this article are based on the research project "CBRN City Sensor Network", which was funded within the framework of the security research programme KIRAS of the Federal Ministry of Agriculture, Regional Planning and Tourism in Austria.

and increases their acceptance and useability [15]. Thus, literature highlights the importance of asking those persons, handling incidents, for their experiences and needs. The present research work is novel insofar, as it does not only ask technicians for the perfect possible solution, but asks those in operational processes for their experiences of how a technological solution would and could fit in. The main research question of the present paper is therefore, which challenges employees of mobility partners and strategic partners face in incident handling and where they see opportunities for technical support. Special consideration was given to the topic of a CBRN-city sensor network and how it could affect information flow, decision-making as well as existing manual and automated processes.

2   Challenges and Approaches in Urban Areas

One of the main challenges for rapid and targeted countermeasures by the security authorities in the case of CBRN substances is the relatively lengthy process of detection and identification. More precise knowledge of the hazardous substance and its dispersion in the affected area, e.g., in underground stations, is often significantly delayed due to the lack of special detectors in an emergency. This is only possible after the arrival of emergency forces with special equipment. In the case of the attack in Tokyo, for example, it took hours to identify the chemical substance used, which led to a total of around 6,000 casualties and 13 deaths. [3]. A circumstance which, then as now, makes time one of the most important factors in countermeasures. Real-time measurement integrated into interdisciplinary response processes is therefore urgently needed to be able to support transport operators and emergency forces equipped with NBC protection measures in an efficient and targeted manner.

Reliable sensors or sensor networks for detection, identification, monitoring and preservation of evidence are considered key technologies before, during and after a CBRN incident [16]. Prior to a CBRN incident, detectors can be used for continuous monitoring to either prevent a CBRN incident (Detect-to-Protect) or to provide early warning in the event of an incident (Detect-to-Treat). During a CBRN incident, detectors are needed to determine the exact nature and extent of the CBRN agent. After a CBRN incident, detectors are essential for three main tasks: (i) to confirm the results of early identification, (ii) to collect evidence of the use of internationally prohibited substances (forensic aspects), (iii) to confirm that the area can be safely re-inhabited after decontamination [3].

These are already used in the chemical and petrochemical industry to warn of dangerous concentrations of chemical substances. For example, the data from a fixed sensor network can be used to visualise and mathematically model a spreading gas cloud, which provides emergency services with important information, e.g., for planning evacuations. In addition, current research is increasingly addressing the challenges of CBRN threats in underground tunnels, for example, in order to be able to detect the ingress of water and explosions [17].

2.1 Relevant Technical Concepts

In addition to operational sensor networks, this field is also advancing secure wireless data transmission, sensor data compression, and data interpolation and dispersion calculation. A good example is the wireless sensor network for monitoring the port of Brisbane in Australia, which can detect liquid gas, radioactive radiation, wind direction and speed, and dust concentrations, and is based on wireless communication modules [18]. A similar approach to wireless data transmission is emerging from a combination of fixed and mobile sensors, specifically designed for monitoring the transport of dangerous goods over long distances [19].

Another step against terror is the use of drones to safely detect clouds of poison gas, etc. Drone swarms - multiple unmanned systems capable of coordinating their actions to achieve common goals - have significant implications for the future of warfare, including enabling more effective CBRN countermeasures through prevention and detection. At the same time, many CBRN-related applications of drone swarm technology pose significant technical challenges even for sophisticated states, and even more so for non-state actors whose capabilities are far more limited, so there is considerable uncertainty about whether, to what extent and when drone swarm technology will complement, challenge or replace CBRN weapons. The main advantages are that both heavy and light gas scenarios can be covered, environmental models provide direct indications of potentially vulnerable regions, gas samples can be taken almost free of downwind and levitation effects, and contamination is actively countered [20].

Even though these approaches show very practical and implementable technological developments, challenges remain in monitoring transport infrastructure for potentially catastrophic, including terrorist, events involving chemical or nuclear agents. Due to the location of monitoring sites, as well as not least the maintenance intensity, costs and space requirements, concrete information for emergency forces in CBRN situations can often only be provided in a cumbersome manner in traffic stations. An essential factor of measures also concerns the implementation and communication of the emergency forces and their different emergency management [21].

Therefore, the core idea in the project "CBRN - City Sensor Network" was to link early warning systems with the deployment procedures of the emergency services and infrastructure providers to inform the emergency services as quickly as possible about the threat situation to increase their safety by selecting the appropriate equipment and to evacuate the affected civilian population effectively and quickly out of a possible danger zone.

3 Methodology

3.1 Technical Approaches

Since the paper concentrates on the socio-scientific aspects, the technical implementation and test runs of the sensor technology will be briefly discussed at this point. Three identical sensor boxes were constructed, two of which were mounted in underground stations and the third used for laboratory tests. Each sensor box consists of several actively ventilated chemical sensors and one sensor for radioactive radiation.

The selection of gases to be detected was based on international lists of hazardous substances and threat analysis. Due to the required tests for commissioning and also tests in the underground area, only substances for which test gases were available were selected. Outside the laboratories in the public area, the choice for testing purposes fell on a non-toxic, odourless, non-explosive gas. For communication with the control system, LTE mobile modems were used which communicate in an encrypted and secured VPN (Virtual Private Network) due to the sensitivity of the sensor data. It was important to the person in charge to use real data for this simulation to establish the greatest possible reference to reality.

The chemical gas dispersion tests involved the vaporisation of a simulated warfare agent that had been deployed. The scientific closer examination of the dispersion of a gas and its effects on people and material in a closed system, such as an underground set and the underground system, was possible by means of air samples and their analysis and was recorded quantitatively.

Another requirement was the possibility of quantitative proof of the simulation agent using analytical methods to be able to describe the effects on people and material and to determine air flows in the system of the underground and on train stations. The movement of the trains also contributes to the dynamics in the system. The strength and direction of the air flow depend on a variety of parameters, which is why there is still a need for further research in modelling the formation of different hazardous substances. One finding was that a sensor system on the platforms is sufficient to trigger a gas alarm. This information is sufficient for the emergency services to initiate appropriate evacuation measures and to enter the area only with appropriate safety equipment. The spatial and physical conditions are far too complex to automatically certify an area-wide decontamination. For the final clearance or all-clear, it is imperative that a specialist from the emergency services be present.

When positioning the sensor systems, it is also important to ensure that the largest possible air volume is monitored. Shielding by pillars, wall projections etc. should be avoided to increase the catchment area of the sensor system. During installation, it is also important to ensure that the air can flow freely in the vicinity of the sensor system or the intake points.

3.2   Social Science Methodology

It is important to survey the respective processes in the event of an incident and to obtain and evaluate assessments from the respective responsible organisations. For this reason, the social sciences partners in the project "CBRN City Sensor Network" conducted a qualitative data collection using guided expert interviews (Lamnek 2005). Ten experts of all relevant institutions in the Austrian field of mobility and all necessary operational organisations which are responsible from the CBRN emergency to the evacuation were interviewed between April 2019 and March 2020. The insights of procedures of the mobility partners "Österreichischen Bundesbahnen (ÖBB)" - the Austrian national train service - and "Wiener Linien (WL)" – the public transport service of the capital city of Vienna-, of the strategic partner Federal Ministry of the Interior for procedures of police and army in this context and experts for hazardous goods of the Vienna Fire Brigade were covered in this process. These persons were chosen due to their responsibility, knowledge and experiences in the coordination of the respective procedure and operational plan in the event of an incident in the transport companies (railway and underground). This made it possible to gain important insights into the respective steps and sequences, challenges and needs.

The results obtained were supported and deepened in the context of ongoing workshops with the experts and the project consortium, as well as with an open, non-participatory observation of the incident practice game testing the function and usability of the sensor boxes and procedures of the operation in railway stations and subways according to Lueger (2000).

In the context of the workshops the findings of the interviews were discussed and developed further. The aim of those workshops was, to incorporate different disciplines and ask how the consortium could face the needs of those employees responsible for incident handling. Finally, all emergency organizations – police, fire brigade and rescue service – and mobility partners took part in an incident practice game, where the processes of a CBRN-incident as well as the interaction with a sensor-interface got trained. As a result, it was possible to see, where the organizations faced difficulties in working with a sensor-interface and where there was a need for further adaptations. The interviews as well as the workshops and the incident practice game where recorded, transcribed and finally interpreted by drawing on the context analysis of Mayring (2000).

Operational procedures are defined differently depending on the organisation (military, blue-light organisations, etc.). The most differentiated aspect exists in the military sector, in that every soldier is provided with personal NBC protective equipment and, depending on the degree of specialisation, corresponding tasks are assigned in the event of CBRN. Crisis teams are set up to deal with major incidents or catastrophes (support for the head of operations; coordination of emergency forces such as the fire brigade, rescue services, police, armed forces and third parties). Typical security control systems in military and civilian operations therefore focus on creating a common level of information. These are usually fed by their own reporting lines, automated status recording (resources, task forces, etc.) and externally supplied data. The exchange of information between security control systems is necessary as soon as several forces are involved in a crisis. (Federal Ministry of the Interior Austria 2022).

4   Results

4.1   Process of an Operation in the Context of a CBRN Incident

In the following, the tasks regarding deployment and evacuation procedures as well as the development of an emergency plan will be discussed in more detail, as this is one of the most essential points in the introduction of new technologies. In the interviews and discussions with the stakeholders, the existing deployment and evacuation procedures and, among other things, the importance of emergency management in the participating companies were identified. The emergency management must grow with the experiences of the employees and the institution and should always be oriented towards the doctrine of uniformity. Because only an emergency management that is as comprehensible and uncomplicated to implement as possible is a good emergency management. Based on the knowledge acquired, it did not seem to make much sense to develop a completely new concept, as this would be a plan handed down to those concerned and not one that had emerged from practice. For this reason, and based on the existing plans, the focus was placed on possible adaptations of the emergency plans regarding CBRN situations.

Since the processing of a CBRN scenario involves working through an emergency in successive steps, a phase model was created to make the procedure clearer (see Fig. 1). However, the linear procedure illustrated here is a simplified representation of the processes that take place. Due to the involvement of many different actors, they often work on different tasks at the same time, or the boundaries between the individual phases become increasingly blurred in practice. Furthermore, the diagram - like other incident diagrams - can be understood as a cycle. Thus, after each successful follow-up, there is again the possibility of an incident, which must always be expected. Nevertheless, the graphic representation helps both with an initial orientation for approaching the topic and with the theoretical representation of the individual phases.

The process diagram shows the need for decisions before the arrival of the emergency forces and thus for technical support at the beginning of the CBRN incident. The phase model clearly explains that currently, after detection, alerting and initial response, detection and determination is often not defined until the arrival of the emergency forces and from that point on the specific measures can be defined. This also proves the relevance of automated procedures in the detection of CBRN substances. An effective sensor network quickly detects the release of hazardous substances and transmits all information in real time to all forces involved. In this way

– first measures can be initiated immediately (e.g. evacuations),
– the emergency organisations are fully informed from the time of the alert, and
– the required equipment is already known at the time of deployment, which significantly increases safety.

In addition, it was possible to specify more precisely what role the demonstrator of a future technical system to be developed can take on in cooperation with specialised human personnel. Insights into current emergency management, for example regarding the delineation of areas of responsibility in terms of space, type of emergency and time, as well as existing communication and workflow processes, therefore, prove to be particularly relevant in similar research approaches. The direct connection to the information and control systems of infrastructure operators and security authorities to enable rapid alerting and display of all relevant information is another essential point for integrating a complex technical system and its usable data efficiently and practically into the already existing deployment and emergency management process. This sensor-based data fusion triggers predefined processes, this sensor-based early detection enables adapted initial measures (before the arrival of the emergency services) [24]. These measures help the emergency services to move out quickly with the right equipment, protect people and improve the reconstruction of accidents.

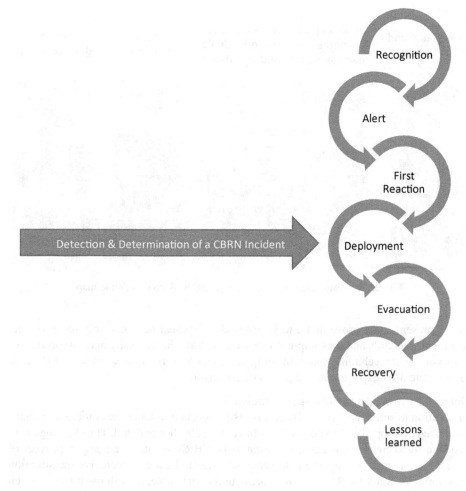

Fig. 1. Process of a CBRN scenario

4.2 Recognition, Adaptation, Connectivity and Acceptance

In this way, topics can be formulated that the emergency services are confronted with to integrate a complex technical system or its action-guiding information into the existing operation and emergency management process in a meaningful way. Drawing on the interviews as well as discussions and observation, five areas are formulated here in which different challenges arise in dealing with a CBRN sensor.

Evaluated challenges and factors in implementing sensor networks for emergency plans (Fig. 2):

The five areas are: (1) the detection and appropriate response to CBRN incidents, (2) the adaptation of the sensor to the existing emergency management framework, (3) the connectivity of the sensor to people and situations, (4) the acceptance of the sensor by users, and (5) the further development of emergency management. The results

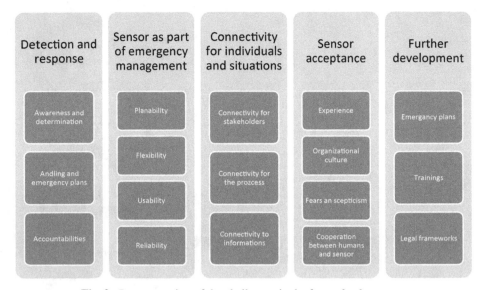

Fig. 2. Representation of the challenges in the form of a theme map

of the present study prove that a technology development does not only have to meet technical standards and thus impressively demonstrate the necessity and importance of involving future technology users in complementary and critical areas of work to be able to integrate their experiences and points of criticism.

Detect CBRN incidents and respond efficiently
In addition to sensitivity to the issue, it is also important to know that emergency plans have been developed and responsibilities have been clarified in detail. The challenge here is primarily to create the necessary awareness of CBRN situations among employees of the affected companies and the emergency services to be able to perceive the situation appropriately. Since CBRN substances are usually not visible, hazardous situations often only become recognisable through their effects. If a suspicion arises, the appropriate equipment is needed to detect and prove the presence of the hazardous substance. This challenge could be solved by a technical sensor that triggers an alarm when CBRN substances are detected. However, when this occurs, adequate and predefined measures are also needed for the correct handling of this additional information.

Requirements for the technical sensor
A sensor as part of an emergency management system requires plannability, flexibility regarding different events, intuitive operability, and of course reliable results. To be a player in emergency management, a technical sensor must fulfil certain framework conditions. For example, the tool should be oriented towards usability by users and the principles of consistency and flexibility. The sensor should not be considered as a single component, but as part of a system or a network and should adapt to the given framework conditions. This means, on the one hand, that the integration of a sensor into the application process should be regulated in advance in terms of plannability and, on the other hand, that the information provided by the sensor should be used flexibly.

Connectivity

Regarding the overall operational workflow in CBRN events, one of the most important challenges is the necessary connectivity of a sensor to existing processes and information channels. This connectivity means, on the one hand, that the actors in a CBRN situation have different responsibilities that require different types of information. Accordingly, the target groups need to be differentiated and the sensor needs to be adapted to the needs of different responders, such as rescue or firefighters. In this way, each organisation would be able to access the information that helps it to fulfil its tasks and the complexity for the staff is not unnecessarily increased. On the other hand, connectivity means that the information provided by the sensor can be supplemented by additional observations. The sensor provides very meaningful information, but at the same time it is not all-encompassing. The sensor is limited to measuring quantitative key figures that can be interpreted in terms of substance, concentration, and dispersion. In an incident, however, much more information is collected in the phases of perception, reporting, assessment, and review of the situation. This qualitative information, which humans gather through observation, experience, or even gut feeling, is of great importance for situation assessment. For example, the sensor can detect a CBRN situation, but not whether it was brought about intentionally (e.g., terror) or unintentionally (e.g., accident).

Acceptance of the technology

Even if there is awareness that CBRN incidents are a real danger, this does not automatically mean that the actors of the different organisations approve or accept a technical sensor for detection. This acceptance of the technical device is an essential prerequisite to ensure cooperation between humans and sensors. The different structures of the emergency services look back on different experiences, which, in combination with the organisational culture, influence their attitude and relationship to technologies. Scepticism about the benefits of a technology as well as fear of dependency or rationalisation through technologies are reasons for the rejection of new devices. For acceptance of new tools, especially in dangerous operations, it is necessary to find out employees' concerns, take them seriously and address them through training and education. Organisations can support staff in this by emphasising the high importance of these devices for information gathering and thus encourage them in their tasks. Technical devices such as the CBRN sensor are thus a much-needed support for staff, not a substitute for them.

Further development of emergency management

As a CBRN sensor leads to changes in the emergency process, its development should simultaneously address the further development of existing emergency plans, the training of staff and the clarification of framework conditions. Emergency management is largely oriented to the requirements of third parties (laws, standards) and can therefore only be designed to a certain extent. It consists of predefined essential elements but must be flexible enough to respond to the specific circumstances of an emergency. The basic tenor of the expert interviews was that emergency management must always be regulated in advance, as this is the only way to relieve the burden on individual employees in the field. For some actors, the early increase in information goes hand in hand with an increase in responsibility and necessity. Mobility partners are particularly affected by this. They need information on the most appropriate measures in such situations and further development of existing emergency plans for CBRN situations. When developing a sensor, the employees who will use the tool should always be considered. They are confronted with a new problem and new tasks that require sensitisation and training to respond appropriately. Furthermore, the handling of the CBRN sensor needs to be learned and practised. Finally, the integration of a new technical device requires the definition of legal framework conditions. Thus, already during the development, it should be considered who is responsible for the output of the sensor, the monitoring of the data, the financing and maintenance of the devices and possible false alarms.

It is crucial that the additional information is of low complexity and can be easily integrated into existing processes. For response organisations with CBRN competence (e.g., fire brigades' pollutant bases), on the other hand, a different depth of information is necessary to better understand the course, nature and spread of the incident and to be able to initiate measures. The third important perspective concerns the detailed technical evaluation of incidents, e.g., for forensic evaluations, for which detailed measurement data overviews are needed. Thus, by linking the individual sensor data, it is possible to find out from which source a measured value exceedance originated, how it spread and whether there is a danger for other locations, e.g., if a radioactive source is transported.

5   Conclusion

The present paper illustrates, that sensor-technology could ease and secure the job of emergency employees and those involved in incident handling. However, the developed model shows, that there are several aspects, that must be kept in mind, when thinking about implementing a technology in such complex and safety-relevant processes. From a social science perspective, technology development must fulfil far more requirements than the purely technical ones. One can conclude that the development of sensor-technology must consider the framework conditions of the current CBRN deployment processes and emergency management itself, as well as the connectivity for people and situations. Technological tools are no standalone actors, but solely offer a greater extend on information. It is the task of the emergency employee making sense of this information, incorporating it into the situation and linking it to their situational-awareness and knowledge arising from their yearlong experience. Thus, their acceptance of the new technological tool is crucial and a major component of the further development of emergency management.

A hazardous situation is always "exceptional" if the lack of knowledge, material or human resources requires central coordination to maintain the ability to cope. A particular challenge here is the separation of responsibilities and the multitude of preparedness plans to achieve congruence and optimal coping capacities with shared planning responsibilities. The diverse alliance between private companies, research institutions and (public) users provides a good basis for innovative and needs-based solutions. These remarks paint a clear picture of the need for permanent staff training to be able to use these assistive technologies competently and sensibly. At the interface between the technical system and the users or representatives of relevant stakeholders (human-machine interface), different socio-demographic as well as business needs can have a significant impact on the control, visualisation, and communication of information. In addition to the obvious disadvantage, one-sided usability also entails operational risks, as the system may not be operated optimally in difficult situations.

As a conclusion, and based on the presented findings, the following factors can be defined for successful counter-terror strategies around CBRN sensor networks - especially for transport companies:

- Cost-effective sensor technology for use in a dense, large-area C(B)R(N) sensor network.
- Robust integration and networking of sensors and IT systems.
- Connectable implementation Methods for computer-based situational awareness, decision support and information distribution.
- Sensor data fusion, preparation, and provision of initial information for the start of the crisis team's work, situation assessments and operational planning.
- Threat analysis and development of instructions for immediate action
- Adaptation of operational procedures and crisis management in case of emergency as well as for the rapid recovery of the affected area (decontamination) with safety in mind.

Overtaking the perspective of social sciences, the results of this study show once again that technology development must fulfil far more requirements than the purely technical ones. Using the example of a CBRN sensor, the interviews, and discussions with experts in incident handling showed, that there is potential for technological solutions, solely if these technologies follow certain aspects. One can conclude that the development of sensor-technology must consider the framework conditions of the current CBRN deployment processes and emergency management itself, as well as the connectivity for people and situations, the acceptance by users and the further development of emergency management. A hazardous situation is always "exceptional" if the lack of knowledge, material or human resources requires central coordination to maintain the ability to cope.

A particular challenge here is the separation of responsibilities and the multitude of preparedness plans to achieve congruence and optimal coping capacities with shared planning responsibilities.

The diverse alliance between private companies, research institutions and (public) users provides a good basis for innovative and needs-based solutions. These remarks paint a clear picture of the need for permanent staff training to be able to use these assistive technologies competently and sensibly.

At the interface between the technical system and the users or representatives of relevant stakeholders (human-machine interface), different socio-demographic as well as business needs can have a significant impact on the control, visualisation, and communication of information. In addition to the obvious disadvantage, one-sided usability also entails operational risks, as the system may not be operated optimally in difficult situations. Finally, insights gained from the study provide an ideal basis for e.g., the development of a prototype tool that would meet the requirements of the various stakeholders, be practical to implement or integrate into existing processes, and offer the hoped-for added value.

The highly integrative approach together with stakeholders created an enormous knowledge gain in the use of technology to improve stakeholder interaction in CBRN incidents. Through a broad and very in-depth involvement of relevant stakeholder groups, an optimal dispersion of knowledge in CBRN incidents in stakeholder organizations was created. Thus, the knowledge gained in CBRN processes and dispersion behavior of CBRN substances (especially CBRN specialists) can be incorporated into follow-up projects or other CBRN settings, as well as being considered in trainings. Especially in the field of CBRN sensing there is still a considerable need for research to be able to achieve the sensitivity, specificity, flexibility, and form factor for the intended application. In this regard, the developed sensor box as well as the findings of the interdisciplinary test series can serve as a common research platform to explore further sensor solutions and conduct algorithmic research. In particular, the sensor network solution benefits from the creation of CBRN-specific forms of representation that may be relevant to stakeholders outside of the CBRN-CSN sensor network. Furthermore, it is possible to bring a similar perspective to the military domain, where Austria is a pioneer in the CBRN context regarding reconnaissance and surveillance.

References

1. Germann, J.-P.: Politisch motivierte Kriminalität mit CBRN-Tatmitteln. In: Freudenberg, D., Goertz, S., Maninger, S. (eds.) Terrorismus als hybride Bedrohung des 21. Jahrhunderts. SP, pp. 147–182. Springer, Wiesbaden (2019). https://doi.org/10.1007/978-3-658-20919-3_6
2. UNOCT: Chemical biological, radiological and nuclear terrorism | Office of Counter-Terrorism. https://www.un.org/counterterrorism/cct/chemical-biological-radiological-and-nuclear-terrorism. Accessed 30 November 2022
3. Richardt, A., Hülseweh, B., Niemeyer, B., Sabath, F. (eds.): CBRN Protection: Managing the Threat of Chemical, Biological, Radioactive and Nuclear Weapons. Wiley-VCH, Weinheim (2013)
4. Schmiermund, T.: Das Chemiewissen für die Feuerwehr. Springer, Heidelberg (2019). https://doi.org/10.1007/978-3-662-56606-0
5. Koblentz, G.D.: Emerging technologies and the future of CBRN terrorism. Wash. Q. **43**, 177–196 (2020). https://doi.org/10.1080/0163660X.2020.1770969
6. Behr, H.: Die Antiterrorismuspolitik der UN seit dem Jahr 2001. Vereinte Nationen: German Review on the United Nations, vol. 65, pp. 147–152 (2017)
7. United Nations: Global Programme on the Protection of Vulnerable Targets. https://www.un.org/counterterrorism/global-programme-protection-vulnerable-targets
8. Chroust, G., Rainer, K., Sturm, N., Roth, M., Ziehesberger, P.: Improving Resilience of Critical Human Systems in CBRN-Emergencies: Challenges for First Responders, Waterloo (2010)
9. Sakurai, M., Murayama, Y.: Information technologies and disaster management – benefits and issues. Prog. Disaster Sci. **2**, 100012 (2019). https://doi.org/10.1016/j.pdisas.2019.100012
10. Reddick, C.: Information technology and emergency management: preparedness and planning in US states. Disasters **35**, 45–61 (2011). https://doi.org/10.1111/j.1467-7717.2010.01192.x
11. Rao, G., Madan, A.: A study exploring the link between attachment styles and social networking habits of adolescents in urban Bangladore. Int. J. Sci. Res. Publ. **3** (2013)
12. Perry, R.W., Lindell, M.K.: Preparedness for emergency response: guidelines for the emergency planning process. Disasters **27**, 336–350 (2003). https://doi.org/10.1111/j.0361-3666.2003.00237.x
13. Rogers, C., Scally, E.J.: Police use of technology: insights from the literature. IJES **7**, 100–110 (2018). https://doi.org/10.1108/IJES-03-2017-0012
14. Pennathur, P.R., Bisantz, A.M., Fairbanks, R.J., Perry, S.J., Zwemer, F., Wears, R.L.: Assessing the impact of computerization on work practice: information technology in emergency departments. Proc. Hum. Factors Ergon. Soc. Annu. Meet. **51**, 377–381 (2007). https://doi.org/10.1177/154193120705100448

15. Grabowski, M., Rowen, A., Rancy, J.-P.: Evaluation of wearable immersive augmented reality technology in safety-critical systems. Saf. Sci. **103**, 23–32 (2018). https://doi.org/10.1016/j. ssci.2017.11.013
16. Hülseweh, B., Marschall, H., Rambousky, R., Richardt, A.: Why are reliable CBRN detector technologies needed? In: Richardt, A., Hülseweh, B., Niemeyer, B., Sabath, F. (eds.) CBRN Protection, pp. 167–178. Wiley (2013). https://doi.org/10.1002/9783527650163.ch6
17. Vincke, J., Kempf, S., Schnelle, N., Horch, C., Schäfer, F.: A concept for an ultra-low power sensor network - detecting and monitoring disaster events in underground metro systems: In: Proceedings of the 6th International Conference on Sensor Networks, pp. 150–155. SCITEPRESS - Science and Technology Publications, Porto, Portugal (2017). https://doi. org/10.5220/0006186901500155
18. Ahmadi, A., Bigdeli, A., Baktashmotlagh, M., Lovell, B.C.: A wireless mesh sensor network for hazard and safety monitoring at the Port of Brisbane. In: 37th Annual IEEE Conference on Local Computer Networks, Clearwater Beach, FL, USA, pp. 180–183. IEEE (2012). https:// doi.org/10.1109/LCN.2012.6423601
19. Tan, Q., et al.: A hazardous chemical-oriented monitoring and tracking system based on sensor network. Int. J. Distrib. Sens. Netw. **10**, 410476 (2014). https://doi.org/10.1155/2014/410476
20. Kallenborn, Z., Bleek, P.C.: Swarming destruction: drone swarms and chemical, biological, radiological, and nuclear weapons. Nonprolif. Rev. **25**, 523–543 (2018). https://doi.org/10. 1080/10736700.2018.1546902
21. Benolli, F., Guidotti, M., Bisogni, F.: The CBRN threat. Perspective of an interagency response. In: Jacobs, G., Suojanen, I., Horton, K.E., Bayerl, P.S. (eds.) International Security Management. ASTSA, pp. 429–448. Springer, Cham (2021). https://doi.org/10.1007/978-3- 030-42523-4_29
22. Lueger, M.: Grundlagen qualitativer Feldforschung: Methodologie-Organisierung- Materialanalyse. UTB (2000)
23. Bundesministerium für Inneres Österreich: Krisen- und Katastrophenmanagement. Zivilschutz in Österreich. Staatliches Krisen- und Katastrophenschutzmanagement (SKKM), Österreich (2022)
24. Castanedo, F.: A review of data fusion techniques. Sci. World J. **2013**, 1–19 (2013). https:// doi.org/10.1155/2013/704504

Collaborative Emergency Management

Developing Information Systems
for Collaborative Emergency Management:
Requirements Analysis and Prototyping

Sofie Pilemalm[1,2] ⓘ, Bjørn Erik Munkvold[1](✉) ⓘ, and Jaziar Radianti[1] ⓘ

[1] Centre for Integrated Emergency Management, University of Agder, Kristiansand, Norway
bjorn.e.munkvold@uia.no
[2] Centre for Advanced Research in Emergency Response, Linköping University, Linköping,
Sweden

Abstract. The paper presents needs and requirements for information systems support for collaborative emergency management, developed in collaboration with emergency management stakeholders in Norway. The requirements focus on three basic elements for shared situation awareness (SA) in inter-agency emergency response: terminology harmonization, map-based common operational picture (COP), and support for evaluation and learning from incidents. Building on core design principles for emergency management information systems, prototypes have been developed for these three areas and validated with potential users. The paper contributes with a user-centric approach in identifying and designing information systems support for collaborative emergency management together with stakeholders, moving from needs to requirements to design proposals and covering core elements of COPs needed for shared SA. The collected requirements and prototypes developed may serve as a basis for further development of standardized solutions for inter-agency emergency operations.

Keywords: Emergency management · Common Operational Picture · Situation Awareness · User participation · Design principles · Terminology harmonization · Map support

1 Introduction

The recent decades have witnessed an increase in frequency and severity of natural and man-made disasters, requiring large-scale and complex response operations involving extensive inter-agency collaboration. During any disaster, there is a need to make quick, correct, and strategic decisions at different organizational levels and among the agencies involved. Adequate decisions in turn depend on high-quality situation awareness (SA), i.e., the perception of environmental elements and events concerning time or space, meaning, and their future status [1]. Establishing SA is often challenging at the individual or team level and even more so when joint SA across agencies must be achieved.

© IFIP International Federation for Information Processing 2023
Published by Springer Nature Switzerland AG 2023
T. Gjøsæter et al. (Eds.): ITDRR 2022, IFIP AICT 672, pp. 153–169, 2023.
https://doi.org/10.1007/978-3-031-34207-3_10

The use of information systems (IS) for developing and presenting common operational pictures (COP) supporting joint emergency response is one approach to improved SA [2, 3]. Even if COPs lack a univocal definition, they can be seen as a structure for available information to be collectively transformed by the actors into knowledge and a representation of this knowledge that provides a process and basis for further decisions and actions [4]. COP solutions often incorporate the use of geographical information systems (GIS), to be able to visualize the locations, available resources, and dynamics of a crisis event on a map. However, COPs also come with multifaceted challenges: lack of a systematic overview of information elements that are critical to share in different crisis scenarios; lack of a common map interface in place using standard symbols; and different terminologies used across disciplines, resulting in possible communication and coordination problems [5]. Further, even with access to a shared COP, this may still result in multiple interpretations and a lack of a common situational understanding among the actors involved [4, 5].

Almost two decades ago, Turoff et al. [6] presented fundamental design principles for developing a general "dynamic emergency response management information system", one of these principles being that such a system needs to support "an open and flat communication process". Yet, emergency management (EM) practice is still characterized by uncoordinated efforts where different agencies develop and implement IT solutions according to their sector-specific needs, without consideration for interoperability and information exchange with solutions used by collaborating agencies [7, 8]. The result is a fragmented landscape of different solutions that lack functionality for seamless sharing of information. To address these challenges, this study reports from a research project that focuses on enhanced IS support for collaborative emergency management, to establish COPs and shared SA among multiple stakeholders and agencies involved in joint operations.

Based on extensive interaction with Norwegian emergency management practitioners, the paper presents identified needs and requirements for information systems support for collaborative emergency management. The requirements focus on three basic elements for shared situation awareness (SA) in inter-agency emergency response: terminology harmonization, map-based COPs, and support for evaluation and learning from incidents through replay functionality in a map interface. Building on core design principles for emergency management information systems [6], we have developed prototypes supporting these three areas and validated these with potential users. The requirements and prototypes presented may serve as a basis for further development of standardized IS support for inter-agency emergency operations.

2   Background

In this section, we first briefly present challenges related to fragmented technology support and the lack of interoperable IS for emergency management. We then present related work on COPs for inter-agency collaboration and briefly review the design principles suggested by Turoff et al. [6].

2.1 Needs for Interoperable IS in Emergency Management

Emergency management is an area in continuous expansion and change, involving increasing threats from terror attacks, natural disasters, pandemics, and warfare. Global warming has resulted in dry summers and an increase of wildfires – globally but also in geographical areas not previously affected, e.g., the Swedish forest fires in 2014 and 2018. The Covid-19 pandemic struck in early 2020 and we have a current global security threat. All of these events make the dilemmas of fragmentation of information technology and IS increasingly visible and urgent. Many countries have decentralized crisis management systems. Such arrangement has consequences in terms of various software systems in use and lack of inter-organizational data access which limits the efficient sharing of information during crises [7, 8]. For instance, an earlier study in Germany identified 170 different ICT systems in use for supporting crisis management [9]. Similarly, studies of Scandinavian emergency management practice have identified how a range of various digital map systems is currently used by first responder agencies (police, fire, health services), municipalities, government organizations, and volunteer organizations) [10]. This severely inhibits the possibilities for inter-agency collaboration in emergency response. Our study aims to contribute insight into how the needs, requirements, and design of IS support can be used to improve such collaboration in crisis management.

2.2 Common Operational Pictures and Situation Awareness

A COP is a display or a series of displays of relevant operational information from a situation, showing, e.g., position of units, infrastructure, weather information, events, and decisions. While the COP concept lacks a univocal definition, some recurring elements are significant: structure, representation, processes, and management [11]. A COP is often manifested as a geographical representation combined with a checklist that describes the characteristics of the response operation [4]. During the past decades, there has been a focus on the potential of map-based COPs to increase common SA since it can capture and visualize the dynamics of crises. It can thus both be used in the crisis response phase when actors and agencies share information and make joint decisions, as well as for evaluation and learning purposes. SA, in its turn, can be described as the perception of environmental elements and events with respect to time or space, the comprehension of their meaning, and the projection of their future status [1]. It plays an important role in situations where the environment is complex, and the actors need to ascertain critical cues to determine which decisions to make.

While research points at opportunities, corresponding practice tends to progress slowly. For instance, the Swedish Civil Contingencies Agency (MSB) published a report in 2016 pointing out the need for shared information and COPs among the Swedish response organizations [12]. Similarly, the Norwegian Ministry of Justice and Public Defense [13] in a government white paper pointed to how different terminology in use by the different responders for depicting the same concepts represents a challenge for information sharing and shared situational understanding in emergency management.

As pointed to by McNeese et al. [11], COPs are typically developed from non-user-centric perspectives and are being defined in technological terms that are not necessarily in the best interests of users. They defined this as a critical research gap since "success results from representations and visualizations that are highly user-centric, rather than just computationally-convenient or designed strictly from a programmer's mindset" [11, p. 468]. The specific focus of our study is thus on eliciting needs and requirements for COPs and shared SA that originate from emergency management practitioners.

2.3   Design Principles for Emergency Management IS

The work by Murray Turoff and colleagues on design principles for what they term a Dynamic Emergency Response Management Information System (DERMIS) represents a seminal contribution in conceptualizing design requirements for IS support for EM [6]. Based on an analysis of the role and tasks of first responders and emergency management personnel, they present an extensive framework of design premises, design concepts, and design principles. From this framework, Table 1 presents six (out of eight) design principles that have been influential on the prototype services developed in this study and that we consider to be important for the development of any such service. The principles were selected based on their relevance to the first prototype versions and their focus on core functionality. The two remaining principles, referred to as "content as address" (i.e., forming ad hoc groups based on common content interests) and "psychological and sociological factors", will be focused in further development of the prototypes.

Table 1.   Selected design principles for Emergency Management Information Systems (based on [6])

Design Principle	Description
System Directory	The system directory should provide a hierarchical structure for the data and information currently in the system
Information Source and Timeliness	All data brought into the system dealing with the ongoing emergency should be identified by its human or database source, by its time of occurrence, by its status, and by its location (where appropriate)
Open Multi-Directional Communication	The system should be viewed as an open and flat communication process among all those involved in reacting to the disaster
Up-to-Date Information and Data	Data that reaches a user and/or his/her interface device must be updated whenever it is viewed on the screen
Link Relevant Information and Data	An item of data and its semantic links to other data are treated as one unit of information that is simultaneously created or updated
Authority, Responsibility and Accountability	Authority in an emergency flows down to where the actions are taking place

These design principles are then referred to in Sect. 5 where we present the design prototypes developed in our project.

3   Methods

3.1   Data Collection and Analysis

The study is a part of the INSITU project (insitu.uia.no) funded by the Research Council of Norway, running from 2019 to 2022. The project was conducted in close cooperation with stakeholders from Norwegian authorities and emergency management organizations for requirements analysis, participatory design, and validation of project deliverables related to enhanced information systems support for collaborative emergency management.

The results reported in this study are based on a combination of several research methods. First, we collected and analyzed several types of documents, including national regulations, emergency plans and guidelines, government white papers, and reports from exercises and evaluations. The document analysis served both as a basis for developing the interview guides and as sources for complementary information, see further detail reported in [10, 14].

A total of 23 semi-structured interviews have been conducted with Norwegian emergency management stakeholders and system vendors, including the following roles: incident commanders from first responders (police and fire), emergency dispatchers from command-and-control centres, municipal emergency coordinators, and providers and developers of map services. The interviews focused on the following topics: current practice for collecting and sharing information; terminology resources in use and experienced challenges related to lack of terminology harmonization; existing use of map systems and current practice for sharing geospatial information with collaborating partners; and current practice for the technology-supported evaluation and learning from incidents. Most of the interviews were recorded and transcribed in full.

Further, we conducted a two-day workshop in autumn 2019 with 24 participants from 20 organizations. This included national directorates, authorities, and first responders, thus enabling a broad representation of stakeholders from the emergency management domain covering strategic, operational, and tactical levels. The focus of the workshop was, based on current practices and needs for improvement, to elicit requirements for information systems support for collaborative emergency management.

The workshop was organized in three main sessions. First, a group roundtable discussions and experience exchange on current practice for establishing COPs and common situational understanding and, second, brainstorming on the stakeholders' needs for improvement. The participants were divided into four smaller groups where the aim was to have representation from various stakeholders, emergency organizations, and different organizational levels in each group. The groups worked with four different themes relating to various aspects of the COP(s). The groups rotated to attend the presentation of each theme so that each group had a chance to provide feedback on the brainstorming results of the other groups. On the second day, we employed "World Café" - a design method drawing on various design principles requiring active participation of stakeholders and group dynamics [15]. A café-like atmosphere is manifested through the establishment of four small groups working at round tables about a topic guided by a moderator. The same four groups rotated into different tables to discuss the various themes. The data collected in the brainstorming phase served as input. The results were then shared in the larger group at the end of the workshop. The workshop outputs were requirements identified in relation to the thematic focus areas of the project. Extensive notes were taken from the different sessions by project members specifically assigned this role. Material developed by the groups (flip-over sheets, post-it notes) was also collected.

The interview transcripts and material from the workshop were analyzed together using thematic analysis [16], identifying current practice and needs as a basis for developing requirements specifications for the different focus areas of the project: terminology harmonization, map-based COPs, and support for evaluation and learning from incidents.

3.2 Design Approach

The need to actively involve end-users in systems development and to anchor design solutions and requirements in user needs has been known for decades, sometimes referred to as participatory design and related to a socio-technical view on information systems [17]. In later stages of the IS development process, this can be related to practical views on design theory [18] where it is used to explain the means-ends relationship as a practical and prescriptive causal mechanism to justify design components. The particular DERMIS design principles also reflect the socio-technical system view at a more theoretical level and is thus motivated by this more general view on information systems. According to the socio-technical system view an information system consists of organizations, personnel, methods, equipment, and technological artifacts intertwined in implementing the assignments [19]. The DERMIS design principles clearly include all these factors.

In this study, we actively involved the users in the two-day workshop, letting them interact with each other and identify common practices and needs relating to both system functionality (technology) and organizational support. We then sorted the needs, prioritized them, and linked them to systems requirements complemented with requirements descriptions as is common in requirements engineering [20]. Where relevant, our requirements were also linked to basic design principles for emergency management information systems [6].

4   User Needs and Requirements

In this section, we present the empirical results in terms of the identified user needs and resulting core requirements for collaborative EM support related to terminology harmonization, map-based COP, and support for evaluation and learning from incidents.

4.1 Terminology Harmonization

Currently, terminologies for crisis management are fragmented and not maintained in a single repository, according to the respondents in the workshop. The Handbook for the Norwegian Rescue Services published in 2018 contains definitions of terms and acronyms to be used across sectors, but this is not exhaustive in terms of emergency scenarios covered and actors involved. The respondents expressed their needs for harmonization of terms used in large-scale emergencies involving collaboration between different sectors and levels in the respective organizations. Requests here, among other things concerned joint locations, repositories, overviews, consolidated lists. Common needs and related requirements are listed in Table 2.

Table 2. Needs and Requirements for Terminology Harmonization

Needs	Requirement Description
Easy access to joint use of terminology	Support for seamless and simple ways to access terms and symbols for joint use in training and practice
National online location of terminology support	The system should include a national authoritative online joint location for the terminology and search service
Joint terminology repository	The system shall provide a terminology repository for emergency map services including terminologies, glossaries, and dictionaries
Feedback channel	The system should include a simple feedback channel for comments from the users
Overview of properties of terms	The system shall include an overview of the properties of terms for harmonization, e.g., orthography or sound for audio communications
Consolidated list	The system shall include a consolidated list of sources of terminologies and symbols
Automated support	The system should provide automated support for collection and verification of sources to assure that the source owners can continue to maintain their sources

4.2 Map-Based COP

The analysis of current practices documented a need for common map support for a COP in larger emergency scenarios involving inter-sectoral collaboration. At the organizational level, the stakeholders requested a national-level standard for sharing information and the importance of having a joint repository for all Norwegian emergency map services and a standardized template with map overlays. Related to this, they also expressed a need for a common symbolization and a standardized usage of map symbols.

Regarding technology support, several of the respondents pointed to the need for sharing the same map-based COP interface across different agencies and to be able to transfer data or images, resources, and events in real-time. The map solution should be intuitive and made available as a unified system both internally and externally. Further, the respondents stated a need for visualization in terms of a map or a graphic representing both static information (e.g., critical infrastructure) and thematic layers supporting dynamic and situation-specific information such as weather forecasts, resources, and movement of personnel. Having a complete resource overview across agencies and organizations was here considered to be useful. At the same time, it should be possible to adapt the map displays to each stakeholder's needs, to avoid maps being 'cluttered'. One must also consider possible security issues resulting from the aggregation of different information elements that become sensitive when combined, such as the location of communications infrastructure. The main needs and corresponding requirements for map support are condensed in Table 3.

Table 3. Needs and Requirements for Map-Based COP

Need	Requirement description
National standards for sharing of map-based information	The map support shall be based on a national level standard for providing and sharing information, for multi-agency data access. It should provide dynamic integration of real-time geographic content across various emergency responders
Joint map repository	The map support shall provide a joint repository of thematic maps available in Norwegian emergency management, available as web map services
Common operation symbology	The map support shall include a repository of common operation cartographic symbols along with the standards of their usage
Overview and adaption	The map support shall provide overviews and layers with reduced content to be used in simplified operational map interfaces for various stakeholders
Rules to prevent information overload	The map support shall include rules for reducing information to be shown in a single map-based interface to prevent visual clutter and information overload

4.3 Learning from Incidents and Evaluation

As for evaluation and learning from incidents, the respondents in the workshop suggested that the COP should provide *"fact-based"* and *"objective"* information. It was also deemed important that the information provided is dynamic, with time scales, time logs and stamps, and continuously updated COPs that monitor the crisis development, to be able to reconstruct events and do systematic follow-ups. Some respondents also requested a decision repository and a COP with the capability to aggregate reports, generate action plans from reports, and extract statistical data. Further, the need for joint, inter-organizational after-action-reviews, vertical and horizontal evaluations at the management and/or operational level, and evaluations across sectors was recurrently pointed out. At the structural level, the respondents requested simplified national guidelines including support to develop concepts and training courses for evaluation, to develop common and regular routines for evaluations, to focus more on best practices, and to develop standards for evaluation, and regulations of how information should be stored, owned, and distributed. Some respondents also requested similar evaluation methodologies across organizations for synergy effects. Table 4 summarizes the identified needs and corresponding requirements for supporting evaluations and learning from incidents.

Table 4. Needs and Requirements for Evaluation and Learning from Incidents

Need	Requirement description
Fact-based, objective evaluation	The system should support objective and fact-based evaluation based on time stamps, maps, logs, and symbols, including descriptions of what facts users can access in the COP solution
Repository of evaluations and stakeholders	The system should include a repository that collects actors and agencies relevant to emergency management and systemizes them horizontally and vertically, to be accessible for cross-agency evaluations
Replay of incident timeline	The system should collect and present digital, dynamic, and aggregated information, replay events according to the timeline, and have updating functions for time stamps, maps, logs, and symbols
Repository for decisions	The system should store decisions taken during an exercise or operation for re-construction of the decision-making process
Repository for lessons identified	The system should store best practices, lessons identified and outcomes of previous evaluations

5   Development of Prototype Services

Based on the collected user needs and requirements, our research project has designed and developed prototype services for terminology harmonization, map-based COP for inter-agency collaboration, and support for evaluation and learning. This section briefly presents these prototypes.

5.1 Prototype for Terminology Harmonization

Considering terminology harmonization, a central requirement was that the COP should include a joint repository including glossaries and harmonized terms providing translations when first responders from several sectors may have a different understanding of terms and concepts. In the design phase, this was addressed by proposing a way to apply the Norwegian Public Management Standard for concept harmonization or concept differentiation to existing glossaries in crisis management. Also, supporting actions for harmonization and introducing aspects of oral and written communication related to similarities of sounds and meaning, were suggested. In total, concepts from around thirty terminology sources (Norway, EU, UN) covering Norwegian or English concepts were collected. Some of these sources cover many language combinations, including the General Multilingual Environmental Thesaurus (GEMET), with over five hundred combinations each. This is integrated into an online resource, TERMER, where stakeholders can search across the word lists from the national rescue handbook, and all the known sector-specific sources to facilitate further harmonization. The online resource also includes a feedback functionality so that users can comment on both existing and missing concepts. This reflects Turoff et al.'s [6] design principle of *Authority, Responsibility and Accountability* (See Table 1), as the glossary is intended to be coordinated at national level while being interactively accessible to the emergency organizations.

The TERMER online terminology resource can be installed on the emergency organizations' web page, then supporting terminology search on all contents of the pages including pdf documents. This is in line with the design principle to *Link Relevant Information and Data* [6] (see Table 1). According to this principle, a data item and its semantic links to other data are treated as one unit of information that is simultaneously created or updated. Figure 1 shows an example of the installation of TERMER on the web page of the Norwegian Joint Rescue Coordination Centre (JRCC) (www.hovedredn ingssentralen.no).

5.2 Design of Map-Based COPs for Collaborative Emergency Management

The stakeholders expressed a basic need for a national standard and service for emergency-related maps. While the Norwegian Directorate for Civil Protection (DSB) offers a map service with thematic layers related to different emergency scenarios and resources (e.g., forest fire), this is not in widespread use among emergency stakeholders and is also not well known. This is partly because the system is not intuitive in use with a complex user interface, and also because the technology on which the system is based now appears somewhat outdated. There is currently a national initiative on establishing a digital map repository that can also support emergency management, led by the Norwegian Mapping Authority. However, this process seems rather slow and is still at the planning stage. The project, therefore, designed a 'lightweight' and easy-to-use application for map-based information sharing supporting collaborative emergency management, which can be used on different devices (laptop, iPad, mobile phone).

Figure 2 shows a screenshot of the application. The system includes functionality where the organization in charge of the emergency response can create an event in the system and then invite collaborating stakeholders/agencies at different organizational

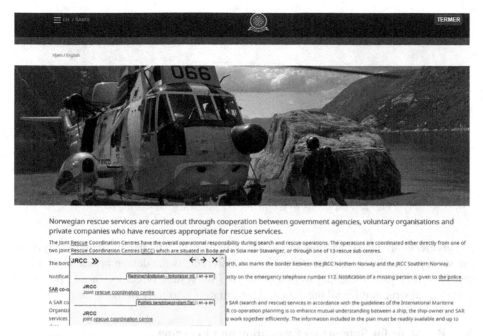

Fig. 1. Screenshot from use of the TERMER application at the JRCC web page

levels (tactical, operational, strategic) to share information in the same map interface. This reflects the design principle of *Authority, Responsibility and Accountability* [6] (ref. Table 1) according to which there needs to be clear accountability of who is taking what actions. Each user can create, for instance, an event or point of interest (POI) and place symbols, the position of units, on the map. The example in Fig. 2 depicts a safe zone for a traffic accident with hazardous material. A simplified situation report can also be generated, based on the actions performed by the users. As to requirements for information sharing, a chat function is also included to enable the stakeholders to quickly communicate their actions and share information with each other. It is possible to filter information depending on whom you want to share information with (all or selected actors) and whether or not information can be shared with the media.

The functionality of this application reflects the design principle of *Up-to-date Information and Data*, according to which data from the emergency system that reaches a user and/or their interface device must be up-to-date, whenever it is viewed on the screen [6]. Further, it also reflects the design principle of *Open Multi-Directional Communication*, according to which any emergency management system should be viewed as an open and flat communication process among all those involved in reacting to the disaster (ibid.).

As to the need for common map symbols, GIS experts in our project team collected and analyzed official emergency map symbol repositories in use by different emergency responders and system vendors in Norway. They then extended the symbol set, symbol modification, and grouping of symbols. Symbols could relate to info-types such as electricity, water, waste, weather, crimes, operations, activities, and statistics. Concepts of symbol standardization and harmonization were also proposed, all reflecting

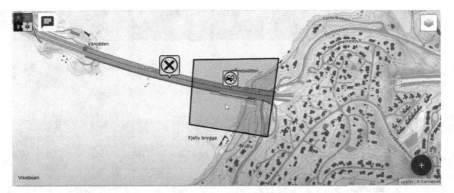

Fig. 2. Screenshot of the map-based information sharing tool

requirements of standardization and joint symbols [21]. The use of thematic layers at the strategic, tactical, and operational levels also reflects the design principle of a *System Directory* [6]. According to this principle, the system directory should provide a hierarchical structure for all the data and information currently in the system.

5.3   Prototype for Supporting Evaluation and Learning

As to evaluation, we chose to focus on the requirements for replaying incidents to enable objective, fact-based evaluations as this was jointly stated among the stakeholders participating in the requirement workshop. In the prototype for map-based information sharing, we thus also included a replay function for information sharing, chat communication, and decisions taken during the incident, displayed at various speeds based on a timeline indicator. It is also possible to freeze the timeline and take screenshots if you want to explore something in more detail. When a user replays the event, it is possible to register evaluation notes (e.g., something went wrong here, why?) that can be used in later evaluations, thus reflecting the requirement of a repository of lessons learned. The replay function is displayed in Fig. 3, reflecting the design principle of *Up-to-date Information and Data* [6].

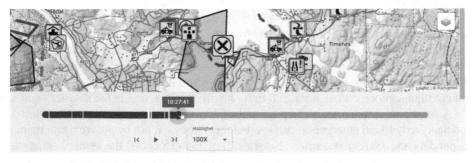

Fig. 3. Replay function in the map-based evaluation tool

6 Discussion

In this section, we reflect on the results of our project this far, considering extant related research. We also briefly discuss associated implementation challenges and transferability of the study results.

6.1 Improving Inter-agency Collaboration with Map-Based COPs

As stated in the study introduction, the need for joint crisis management operations and inter-agency collaboration is substantial and will likely increase in the future. COPs for improved common SA are certainly no new phenomenon but technological advancements have provided new opportunities, e.g., in terms of map-based COPs with real-time information updates. In this context, former research has provided important contributions in the form of concepts, architectures, and tools for supporting situation awareness and COP [2–4]. Yet, as described previously, the landscape is still fragmented with individual response organizations and agencies developing their own solutions without focusing on interoperability and supporting collaborative operations.

Also internationally, there is a lack of universal solutions supporting a COP. The International Forum to Advance First Responder Innovation [22] points out that there is a major gap in first responders' ability to collect data from traditional (e.g., weather maps, sensor readings) and nontraditional (e.g., social media) information sources, and to integrate this data into a user-configurable COP. It has also been pointed out, that even with access to a shared COP space, this may still result in multiple interpretations and a lack of a common SA among the actors involved [5].

The requirements elicited in our study and the resulting prototypes are intended to contribute to progress further in establishing systems support for COPs adapted to the need of the different emergency stakeholders. The identified needs and requirements are both technical and organizational and thus in line with the socio-technical system view [19]. However, as discussed in the next section, for these requirements and prototypes to be taken further requires addressing implementation challenges concerning organizational resources, training, and even legislation related to data privacy and secrecy.

6.2 Stakeholder Involvement in Design and Evaluation of Emergency Management Systems

The need to involve stakeholders is crucial in any IS development process [20] and perhaps even more so in emergency management. This is because solutions that are not solidly based on user needs may have fatal consequences. Our study is based on principles of active user participation in combination with the socio-technical system view, [19] and design principles applied to emergency systems [6]. This should be seen as a major contribution of the study, i.e., that it presents extensive requirements for collaborative emergency management support as stated by the involved stakeholders and based on these developing prototypes in an application domain where technology development often is fragmented and non-user-centric [11].

The stakeholders have also been involved in further validation of the design proposals and prototypes, including focus group interviews and exercises. In a digital table-top exercise in spring 2021 using a forest fire scenario, we studied how access to a common map system could possibly support shared situation awareness among emergency stakeholders at the local, regional, and national levels. The exercise involved eighty participants from the fire services in three municipalities, the police, the county's emergency management, municipal emergency managers, GIS experts at national and local levels, the public road authority, and critical infrastructure operators. While illustrating the potential for improved inter-agency SA through a map-based COP, the exercise also documented the need for developing more specific information sharing procedures for use of this service to be effective across the tactical, operational, and strategic levels of the emergency response. Another table-top exercise took place in spring 2022, involving 8 stakeholders from various agencies and response organizations and focusing on the information sharing and replay function. The results from this exercise served to validate how the replay functionality as implemented in our prototype could contribute to the more systematic evaluation and learning from incidents.

As clearly illustrated in the results of this study, besides addressing the technological and functional requirements there are also several requirements at the organizational, inter-agency, and structural levels that could be more challenging to solve. As the stakeholders pointed to, supporting the need for common systems for map-based COP requires coordination at the national level, also providing the required funding and personnel resources for development and maintenance. As mentioned in Sect. 4.2, this overall support is further related to concrete needs for sharing the same map-based COP interface across different agencies and transfer information in real-time. How this is done, i.e., establishing a control mechanism, must likely be worked out together with the command-and-control center, which is typically established for an emergency and where all agencies have representatives. Also, considering the security issues relating to aggregation of information elements, additional design principles such as "securing classified information or having a system to control user access to classified information" must likely be integrated in mature protypes and real implementations.

In relation to the above, different areas in our suggested solution concept may have different prospects of being implemented. For instance, as to terminology harmonization, the TERMER online resource is developed by a private company that is a project partner specializing in terminology services and thus may have a good possibility for turning the prototype into a commercial product. While the replay function for evaluation is much dependent on organizational and national structural support, the function must be accompanied by training, after-action-review processes, and processes for (inter-) organizational knowledge transfer, if it is to enable best practice and double-loop learning [14].

Finally, a basic design premise formulated by Turoff et al. is also relevant to bring into focus here: "An emergency system that is not used on a regular basis before an emergency will never be of use in an actual emergency" [6, p. 6]. In line with this, the prototype services developed in our project can also be used to support work practices of emergency management professionals outside emergency situations, related to joint terminology (e.g., in preparedness planning) and map-based information sharing in training and exercises.

7 Conclusion

In the study reported in this article, we have collected and analyzed needs and requirements from emergency stakeholders in various sectors and organizational levels and facilitated interaction among these in a requirements elicitation workshop. Based on this we have developed prototype applications supporting terminology harmonization, common map symbols, map-based support for information sharing and COP, and support for objective and fact-based evaluation and learning from incidents through the replay of actions in the map-based COP. The requirements and prototypes have been further validated by stakeholders and prospective users in focus group interviews, workshops, and exercises.

Recent technological developments have enhanced the possibilities to produce and enhance map-based development, representations, and visualization of COP functionality. As illustrated in our study, this enables the development of systems support that addresses essential design principles for emergency management information systems as defined by Turoff et al. [6]. The study thus also documents the continued importance of these design principles presented nearly two decades ago.

Our study contributes with a user-centric approach in identifying comprehensive requirements for IS support for collaborative emergency managers together with stakeholders, moving from needs to requirements to design proposals and covering core elements of COPs needed for improved joint SA. The collected requirements and prototypes developed may serve as a basis for further development of standardized solutions. As presented earlier in the paper, the TERMER resource is already implemented by the Norwegian Joint Rescue Coordination Centre, and the Norwegian Directorate for Civil Protection (DSB) has expressed interest in using the map service developed in our project as a demonstrator in the process of further design and development of a national system for emergency map support.

While the context of this study is limited to emergency management practice in Norway, the requirements for the COPs for cross-sectoral collaboration are considered to have broader relevance to researchers and practitioners in the emergency management domain. Thus, since the need for inter-agency collaboration will likely increase in the future and basic needs for information retrieval, sharing, improved SA, and evaluation are similar across national contexts. However, the prototyped functions have been developed for a decentralized emergency management system and may thus be most relevant to similar organizational structures. Future work should also focus more on challenges to organizational implementation of the support systems that need to be addressed for diffusing these solutions in the community of emergency management stakeholders. This work could build further on design principles from Turoff et al. [6] related to psychological and sociological factors, as well as extending these with new design principles relating to system security.

Acknowledgements. The authors acknowledge their project partners in INSITU for developing the prototypes referred to in this paper. The INSITU project is funded by the Research Council of Norway, SAMRISK grant #295848.

References

1. Endsley, M.R.: Toward a theory of situation awareness in dynamic systems. Hum. Factors **37**(1), 32–64 (1995)
2. Luokkala, P., Nikander, J., Korpi, J., Virrantaus, K., Torkki, P.: Developing a concept of a context-aware common operational picture. Saf. Sci. **93**, 277–295 (2017)
3. Van Dijk, H.: Situation awareness in crisis situations: development of a user-defined operational picture. In: Proceedings of the 12th International ISCRAM Conference, Kristiansand, Norway (2015)
4. Wolbers, J., Boersma, K.: The common operational picture as collective sensemaking. J. Contingencies Crisis Manag. **21**(4), 186–199 (2013)
5. Steen-Tveit, K., Munkvold, B.E.: From common operational picture to common situational understanding: an analysis based on practitioner perspectives. Saf. Sci. **142**, 105381 (2021)
6. Turoff, M., Chumer, M., Van de Walle, B., Yao, X.: The design of a dynamic emergency response management information system (DERMIS). J. Inf. Technol. Theory Appl. (JITTA) **5**(4), 1–35 (2004)
7. Grottenberg, L., Njå, O.: Applying a systems safety approach to the development of GIS in the Norwegian emergency management domain. In: Cepin, M., Bris, R. (eds.) Safety and Reliability. Theory and Applications, pp. 484–491. CRC Press (2017)
8. Meum, T., Munkvold, B.E.: Information infrastructure for crisis response coordination: a study of local emergency management in Norwegian municipalities. In: Proceedings of the 10th International ISCRAM Conference, Baden-Baden, Germany, pp. 84–88 (2013)
9. Neuhaus, C., Giebel, D., Hannappel, M., Färfers, S.: Crisis management systems in Germany - a status report about the current functions and developments of private and public crisis management systems in Germany. In: Proceedings of the 9th International ISCRAM Conference, Vancouver, Canada (2012)
10. Opach, T., Rød, J.K., Munkvold, B.E., Radianti, J., Steen-Tveit, K., Grottenberg, L.O.: Map-based interfaces for common operational picture. In: Proceedings of the 17th International ISCRAM Conference, Blacksburg, VA, USA, pp. 506–516 (2020)
11. McNeese, M.D., Pfaff, M.S., Connors, E.S., Obieta, J.F., Terrell, I.S., Friedenberg, M.A.: Multiple vantage points of the common operational picture: supporting international teamwork. In: Proceedings of the Human Factors and Ergonomics Society Annual Meeting. SAGE Publications, Los Angeles, CA (2016)
12. Landgren, J., Borglund, E.: Att skapa och analysera lägesbilder vid samhällsstörningar. Swedish Civil Contingencies Agency (MSB) (2016)
13. Meld.St.10: Risk in a Safe and Secure Society. Norwegian Ministry of Justice and Public Security (2016–2017)
14. Pilemalm, S., Radianti, J., Munkvold, B.E., Majchrzak, T.A., Steen-Tveit, K.: Turning common operational picture data into double-loop learning from crises - can vision meet reality? In: Proceedings of the 18th International ISCRAM Conference, Blacksburg, VA, USA (2021)
15. Nunez, H.C., Rybels, S., Coppens, T., Valderrama Pineda, A.F.: World café as a participatory approach to facilitate the implementation process of problem-based learning. J. Probl. Based Learn. High. Educ. **8**(1), 19–40 (2020)
16. Bowen, G.A.: Document analysis as a qualitative research method. Qual. Res. J. **9**(2), 27–40 (2009)

17. Schuler, D., Namioka, A.: Participatory Design: Principles and Practices. CRC Press (1993)
18. Markus, M.L., Majchrzak, A., Gasser, L.: A design theory for systems that support emergent knowledge processes. MIS Q. **26**(3), 179–212 (2002)
19. Orlikowski, W.J., Iacono, C.S.: Research commentary: desperately seeking the "IT" in IT research - a call to theorizing the IT artifact. Inf. Syst. Res. **12**(2), 121–134 (2001)
20. Aveson, D., Fitzgerald, G.: Methodologies for developing information systems: a historical perspective. In: Avison, D., Elliot, S., Krogstie, J., Pries-Heje, J. (eds.) IFIP WCC TC8 2006. IFIP International Federation for Information Processing, vol. 214, pp. 27–38. Springer, Boston (2006). https://doi.org/10.1007/978-0-387-34732-5_3
21. Opach, T., Rød, J.K.: A user-centric optimization of emergency map symbols to facilitate common operational picture. Cartogr. Geogr. Inf. Sci. **49**(2), 134–153 (2021)
22. IFAFRI: Capability Gap 4 "Deep Dive" Analysis Synopsis. The International Forum to Advance First Responder Innovation (2018)

Shortcomings of Netcentric Operations During the COVID-19 Pandemic

Abir Agray and Kenny Meesters[✉] [iD]

Tilburg University, 5037AB Tilburg, The Netherlands
`k.j.m.g.meesters@tilburguniversity.edu`

Abstract. As the COVID-19 pandemic is a multi-agency, long-lasting crisis with a complex information structure, the netcentric approach in the crisis operations would be expected to show its advantages. However, the implementation of netcentric operations seems to be met with challenges during the COVID-19 pandemic. This research investigates the capability of organizations to adapt the netcentric approach, specifically in relation to information sharing in changing contexts. Thereby, the factors that influence inter-organizational information sharing within netcentric operations are examined. It can be concluded that in practice, re-applying the principles of netcentric operations to a different context can be challenging. More specifically, over time, the netcentric operations become ingrained in process, systems, and tools. While this codified and institutionalized netcentric approach supports the daily information exchange in emergencies, it also reduces the ability of organizations to adapt their approaches to new requirements dictated by changing circumstances.

Keywords: Netcentric Operations · Information Sharing · Crisis Response · COVID-19 · Information Systems

1 Introduction

At the end of February 2020, the first COVID-19 case in the Netherlands was detected. Since not much was known about the virus or its effects, it has been hard to coordinate the crisis by the government. The virus also had and still has a great impact on not only the healthcare sector but also on the societal aspects across the nation. This crisis therefore brings uncertainty across several sectors. To reduce this uncertainty and support the development of the response to the emergency, having access to information is vital. As The Prime Minister Mark Rutte of the Netherlands therefore stated: "We are making 100% of the decisions based on 50% of information". The importance of information management to obtain, process and share this information within crisis response also came to light during the response to COVID-19 pandemic. Since the COVID-19 pandemic affects the whole country, several emergency organizations from all levels need to work together. It is important for all these organizations to have accurate information to anticipate effectively. However, information sharing among all these organizations during a crisis with such large scope is not always done effectively which in turns affects the coordination of the crisis.

© IFIP International Federation for Information Processing 2023
Published by Springer Nature Switzerland AG 2023
T. Gjøsæter et al. (Eds.): ITDRR 2022, IFIP AICT 672, pp. 170–184, 2023.
https://doi.org/10.1007/978-3-031-34207-3_11

Past disasters have shown that there are a number of challenges associated with coordinating crisis response [1]. Researchers argue that coordination is often suboptimal among governments, humanitarian organizations, and volunteers [2]. According to previous studies these problems that occur in crisis coordination can often be attributed to the fast-changing network, time pressure, uncertainty and unpredictability of information needs and flows [3, 4]. To overcome these problems netcentric operations have evolved as a coordination mechanism [5]. The aim of this coordination mechanism is to improve situational awareness among organizations by sharing real-time data about each other's actions and the crisis [5]. Thus, netcentric operations should cause organizations to have the right information at the right time [6].

As the COVID-19 pandemic is a multi-agency, long-lasting crisis with a complex information structure, netcentric operations would be expected to show its advantages. Theoretically it should provide agility and self-synchronization of crisis response teams [7]. Netcentric operations should increase efficiency, security, agility and shared situational awareness [6]. However, the implementation of netcentric operations seems to be met with challenges during the COVID-19 pandemic. Since the scope of this crisis involves the whole country, a large collaboration network needed to be set up with organizations that never worked together before. In order to coordinate such a crisis, other processes and structures are needed to gain capabilities to be more agile and therefore adapt faster to any given situation [8].

This research is set up to understand the capability of organizations to adapt the netcentric approach to information sharing in changing circumstances and operational contexts. Thereby, the factors that influence inter-organizational information sharing within netcentric operations will be examined. The general factors that influence inter-organizational information sharing have been researched by several scholars and can be attributed to organizational, technological, and political determinants [9]. However, how these factors influence inter-organizational information sharing during a crisis within a network centric context is not researched yet [10]. This research aims to bridge the gap between information management within crisis response by examining how organizational, technological, and political factors influence inter-organizational information sharing within a network centric context.

2 Research Method

This research consists of three main phases (Fig. 1). The first one is the preliminary research phase. This phase consists of the literature review and explorative interviews. The literature was analyzed by following the steps of Wolfswinkel, Furtmueller & Wilderom [11]. The second stage includes in-depth interviews and analysis of existing interview scripts as a case study. According to Charmaz [12], a sample size is not relevant during a case study. Therefore, interviews were held until no other new theoretical insights were found [12]. That is when a total of 10 interviews was reached during the interviews and when a total of 4 interview scripts were analyzed. All the interviews were recorded, and an interview script was written afterwards. Also, the second stage of the research method includes the analysis of the data.

The first set of interviews will be analyzed by using template coding techniques [13]. When all the interview scripts are coded, an occurrence table will be set up. This table shows how many times a code was discussed during all the interviews. Lastly, the conclusion and discussion will be drawn.

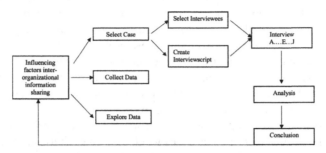

Fig. 1. Research Method

3   Related Work

3.1   Netcentric Operations

The term network centric operations find its origin in the military. In its essence, network centric operations imply the autonomy and empowering of individuals in their ability to adapt to the changing environment/circumstances. This high level of adaptability is achieved by leveraging technical and human capabilities [10]. Alberts et al. [14], define four tenets that describe the benefits of network centric operations. These four tenets include the improvement of information sharing, collaboration, and shared situational awareness. Network centric operations also compresses the strategic, tactical, and operational echelons and emphasizes the need to operate across organizational boundaries [14].

This indicates that the process of sharing data and information is not done on a "command and control" basis anymore but from a network point of view. This does not imply however, that the command-and-control method is not used at all anymore. The method had just been adjusted because there was a need for decentralized information sharing so groups in the field could anticipate faster to the current situation [5]. A pure hierarchical coordination mechanism lacks this ability [14].

Researchers have shown that network centric operations improve (shared) situational awareness by overcoming two main drawbacks: time and information. It helps to improve information sharing in dynamic situations where multiple actors are involved. This coordination mechanism however includes more than just information sharing [15].

There are capabilities necessary to achieve the benefits of network centric operations. These capabilities can be attributed to four domains [7]:

1. Social domain: includes the nature of interaction.
2. Cognitive domain: includes the creation of rules, responsibilities, roles and constraints.

3. Information domain: includes the allocation of resources (information assets and access) and establishing rules for information sharing.
4. Physical domain: includes the allocation of resources (materiel).

In order to control a certain situation in which different organizations are involved, synchronization of plans among these organizations is needed. Synchronization requires shared awareness across domains. In order to achieve shared awareness, organizations need to share a common understanding of the situation by sharing information [16].

Network centric operations have evolved in crisis management to tackle the disadvantages which a hierarchical coordination mechanism brings. When a hierarchical coordination mechanism is used, tactical groups tend to ignore information unless it is provided by a higher level of command. All decisions are made at the top of the hierarchy. The theoretical advantages of using network centric operations in crisis management are therefore the right information is provided at the right time to the right people. Network centric operations also should increase efficiency, security, agility and shared situational awareness. However, the concept of network centric operations requires a change within and among organizations, policies and their technological infrastructure [17]. To be able to work with a network centric coordination mechanism, it is important that each organization within the network has accurate information, that the information is shared among all organizations, that there are shared goals and values and that organizations are willing to achieve those goals together [18]. However, research shows that network centric conditions among organizations are still not met. Evaluation shows that there is no real inter-organizational coordination, the goals are diverse and not shared, organizations do not have access to information and information systems are not used optimally [18]. Finally, within a context where a high level of agility is needed, like the COVID-19 pandemic, the capability to adapt to these circumstances is still questioned by researchers [8].

3.2 Information Sharing Within Netcentric Operations

Information sharing can be described as the extent to which critical information is communicated to others [19]. Information sharing can occur on several levels. Depending on the complexity of a certain situation and the organizations that are involved, information sharing can evolve from intra-organizational to interorganizational to intergovernmental. The more complex a situation is and the larger the scale, the higher the evolvement of information sharing. Since the scope of this research is on a certain crisis situation within the Netherlands and organizations in crisis response operate independently during a crisis in this context [10]. The focus will be on inter-organizational information sharing.

Inter-organizational information sharing can be defined as "the cross-boundary information sharing that takes place among multiple organizations as opposed to among multiple units within the same organization" [9]. This definition will be used in this research to describe the term. During a crisis, multiple organizations need to share information on all levels (operational, tactical and strategic). Several problems occur during a crisis within the process of information sharing and coordination since 1) the network changes rapidly, 2) time pressure, 3) uncertainty, 4) unpredictability of information needs and flows. Information sharing within network centric operations should lead to coordination, the improvement of information quality and collaboration [3, 4]. However, it also could involve the threats of information overload and responsibility dilution [10, 20].

Thus, the sharing of information could be useful however, there are several drawbacks when information is shared. Besides the threat of information overload and responsibility dilution [10, 21], there is also a possibility of coordination neglect. Coordination neglect is described as a cognitive problem that finds it roots in the theories people use to coordinate and organize with others [22]. Within network centric operations, coordination neglect could be a pitfall because much information and data are being shared without knowing for whom the information is important and for which cause the information will be used. Many information is being shared within the network but little to no attention is given to the integration of this information. Emergency responders can therefore not anticipate shared information [5].

Many studies have discussed the determinants of inter-organizational information sharing among public organizations [23, 24]. These determinants could be mainly addressed to three categories: organizational, technological and political. Research states that organizational and technological determinants play a more important role in interorganizational information sharing [9]. However, since the factors are not yet tested within the scope of a research like this one, all the three determinants will be considered.

3.3 Organizational Determinants

Effective inter-organizational information sharing is affected by several determinants. The benefits for the organization that comes with inter-organizational information sharing, are problem solving and the expansion of the professional network. However, there are also some disadvantages that organizational determinants have on the sharing of information. These disadvantages can be attributed to several factors.

Organizational culture influences coordination and the sharing of information, common values, interests, and norms - which are all part of the organizational culture - make it easier to coordinate all sorts of activities among different organizations. Thereby, incompatible cultures may cause less interaction and less mutual trust across organizations [25]. Organizational culture also shapes the assumptions within an organization about information. Specifically, about what information is and how it should be managed. It also shapes the process of how information and knowledge is created and distributed within organizations [26].

Thus, culture influences inter-organizational information sharing because it shapes the creation, distribution, and assumptions of information. To measure culture within organizations in this research, the following definition will be used: "a property of the collective reflecting deeper phenomena based on symbolic meanings and shared meaning about core values, beliefs, and underlying ideologies and assumptions" [27]. This definition of culture is chosen because it can be applied on the inter-organizational level of analysis which is the level of analysis of this research [27].

Another factor that influences information sharing is trust. Several researchers examined the influence of trust on coordination [28]. This factor has been proved critical for organizational settings where risk is involved [29]. It also influences knowledge sharing directly and indirectly among organizations as it serves as a replacement for monitoring and verifying information [30]. Researchers also suggest that communities that have strong relationships function better during a crisis because of the high level of trust. Hence, trust building among public emergency organizations is essential to overcome a crisis [31]. It also influences information sharing. Therefore, the influence of trust on inter-organizational information sharing will be measured in this research. Since this research focuses on interorganizational information sharing, the level of trust that will be measured is also on the inter-organizational level. Thereby, the levels that are developed by Sako [32] will be used to measure trust. These include: 1) knowing the other party will do what they said they would; 2) willingness to participate 3) two-way understanding; 4) being predictable [33].

The effective sharing of information across multiple organizations is essential for effectiveness during an uncertain event. If emergency responders are not in contact with each other, it is difficult to remain successful in managing a crisis [31]. Effective communication processes allow organizations to make well informed decisions about how to proceed in synergy with others in the network to achieve the overall goal of solving a certain crisis [34]. Research has highlighted the importance of inter-organizational communication when carrying out responses in a successful way [35]. During a crisis, communication does not only occur at the top levels of the involved organizations, but it occurs among almost all levels of the organizations in the network [31], due to the dynamic nature of a crisis. These organizations need to work together and communicate with each other. Many times, this results in informal inter-organizational communication among different levels of different organizations [35].

To measure effective communication during a crisis, three elements could be taken into account. The first one is measuring the output and effectiveness of the process. The second one includes measuring the impact and the last one is measuring the outcomes. One could use all the three measurement types or simply choose one that is in line with the needs of the research [36]. In this research, effective communication will be measured by measuring the output and effectiveness of the process because this research is not only about communication which makes measuring the impact and the outcomes of the communication process out of the reach of this scope. Thus, the key messages which are communicated and how (formal vs. informal communication process) will be considered. This will provide insight into how information is communicated during a crisis among organizations and will show the usability and effectiveness of the formal communication channels which are set up.

3.4 Technological Determinants

Technology is crucial during a crisis because it provides organizations to overcome communication barriers like geographic distances and enables communication with emergency responders in the field [37]. Therefore, technological determinants that could influence inter-organizational information sharing are also taken into account. Technology has the potential to transform how organizations work and facilitates inter-organizational information sharing in a networked environment. Researchers examined that in order to realize the benefits that come with the use of technology, organizations should integrate their information across organizational boundaries. Studies define the sharing of information and data integration with the emphasis on technological elements [38].

Technical infrastructure includes the structure needed to search and exchange information [31] and has the capacity to facilitate communication among organizations. This capacity is embedded in the social context in which the technical structure occurs. Some researchers argue that, in the current high-tech environment, it is important to develop robust processes that facilitate information exchange [39]. Technological determinants could influence inter-organizational information sharing positively and negatively. The benefits of technology that are associated with interorganizational information sharing are, the streamline of data management and the contribution to information infrastructure. The barriers that may occur with technology are incompatibility and inconsistent data structures [9, 40].

In order to support inter-organizational information sharing, organizations need compatible technology to communicate [40]. Technological compatibility substantially affects the performance of interorganizational information sharing initiatives. Thus, incompatibility between the technical resources of participating organizations could represent a major barrier. Compatible technology can be defined according to Rogers, as the degree to which an innovation is perceived as consistent with the existing values and beliefs, past and present experiences, and needs of the users [41]. Tornatzky & Klein [42] further elaborated on this definition and made a distinction between two types of compatibility namely, 1) cognitive compatibility. This indicates that there exists compatibility with what people feel or think about an innovation. Furthermore, there also exists 2) practical compatibility which indicates compatibility with what people do [41, 42]. Both types of compatibility will be considered to examine if the used technology is compatible during a crisis.

The second technological barrier, data structures, includes conflicting data definitions among organizations. This may result in organizations not understanding the data and information that is shared [40]. These two barriers mainly arise because of the lack of IT [9]. IT standards imply common and accepted data formats, transmission protocols and hardware that supports the sharing of information among organizations [43]. Thus, technological factors play an essential role in crisis management. The three technological factors that will be examined during this research are compatible technology, IT standards and data structures since these factors are essential within crisis response [37]. It will be examined if the used technology is compatible if there are IT standards and data structures and how these three factors either improve or worsen inter-organizational information sharing.

3.5 Political Determinants

The influence of politics has become greater over the time during crises [18]. A crisis can be seen as a window of opportunity for politics as well as the initiation of policy in the political system in which they occur. Politics seem to be infiltrating crisis management and crises therefore should be more viewed through the lenses of politics [44]. The term 'political' is thus intended as political or strategic interference that are not necessarily related to the crisis response activities [45]. The factors which are described in this paragraph all may lead to this interference.

Political determinants influence the sharing of information among public organizations in several ways [9]. Firstly, public organizations are influenced by the political environment in the country wherein they operate. This influence from the central government has an impact on the decision-making processes and the collaborative network of the local agencies. Therefore, it also influences information sharing among local government organizations [46]. Since this research aims to examine interorganizational information sharing among emergency organizations within the public sector, the political environment will also be taken into consideration. There will be looked at if the central government promotes information sharing and provides the resources to share information among organizations [46].

Second, legislation and principles need to be considered. Legislation can affect interorganizational information sharing by creating a governance framework for information sharing among different agencies [9]. Researchers argue that public agencies can only gather and store information regarding the task they have. In many cases, agencies are unaware under what law or policy they can share the information. This includes concerns over privacy. Sensitive information, like citizen identities, need to be protected [9, 47]. Some ambiguous legal frameworks can lead to sanctioning/prevention of information sharing, resulting in 1) organizations making decisions based on what they feel and understand from regulations and 2) non-collaborative organizations because of the fear of making mistakes [46].

Another barrier that influences the sharing of information is the resistance to share because information is a source of power and a symbol of authority [40, 48, 49] argue that the relationship between two or more organizations is often characterized by power asymmetry. This implies that when a more powerful organization perceives the potential benefits of information sharing with other organizations, it would exercise its power and request them to share their information. The higher the power of an organization is, the more important it is for the other organizations to maintain a good relationship even if that could bring negative consequences (e.g. opportunistic behavior of the other party) [49]. This political/power distance between organizations could also result in barriers for organizations to establish and sustain their engagement in a network for information and knowledge sharing [9]. Since organizations within crisis response also deal with organizations that have more power and authority (like within governmental hierarchy structures), this factor could also play a role in inter-organizational information sharing.

4 Results

Table 1 shows how many times a certain variable occurred during the in-depth interviews. The results in the occurrence table were drawn after coding the interview scripts. A significant result was that all the interviewees know the term network centric operations. However, the meaning of this term was interpreted in a different way by interviewees. Most significantly, netcentric operations was most frequently associated with the information sharing system that is used during a crisis named LCMS. Also, the effectiveness of network centric operations during COVID-19 was questioned by interviewees. Thereby, the lack of effective information management when using this coordination mechanism was addressed as a main concern. One of the interviewees described this concern as follows:

"Network centric operations within Safety Regions is still in its infancy. We have -in a manner of speaking- not yet outgrown the toddler phase of network centric operations ... In which manner you should manage your information and the way in which we train people to do so, should be improved significantly in the Netherlands. Also, the focus of network centric operations lays on sudden disasters. But there is no understanding of network centric operations during a long-term disaster."

-Employee Ministry of Justice and Security

Table 1. Code occurrences.

Code	Sub-Code	Definition	Total
Organizational	Culture	*a property of the collective reflecting deeper phenomena based on symbolic meanings and shared meaning about core values, beliefs, and underlying ideologies and assumptions*	33
	Trust	*1) knowing the other party will do what they said they would. 2) willingness to participate 3) two-way understanding; 4) being predictable*	14
	Communication Process	*The key messages which are communicated and how (formal vs. informal communication process) they are communicated*	51
Technological	Compatible Technology	*The degree to which an innovation is perceived as consistent with the existing values and beliefs, past and present experiences, user needs*	63
	Data Structures	*Conflicting data definitions among organizations*	9
	IT Standards	*Common and accepted data formats, transmission protocols and hardware that supports the sharing of information among organizations*	22
Political	Political Environment	*The influence from the central government on the decision-making processes*	41
	Legislation & Principles	*Legal frameworks in a certain country*	24
	Power & Authority	*Political/power distance between organization*	5

4.1 Organizational Determinants

Firstly, interviewees state that employees of emergency organizations are trained in how to share information during a crisis. These trainings emphasize the use of the information sharing system LCMS. However, they are not taught the underlying concepts of why they should share information with each other. As stated in the literature, culture influences inter-organizational information sharing because it shapes the creation, distribution and assumptions of information. With not training people in the underlying concepts of why and how information should be shared, organizations do not see the purpose of information sharing but rather see information sharing as a burden in the long run. During the COVID-19 pandemic this is exactly what happens. Interviewees stated that at the start of the pandemic, organizations shared their information with each other. However, in the long run, organizations stopped with the sharing of information because they did not see the purpose anymore. Besides the given training, organizational culture also influences the sharing of information in another manner. As reviewed in the literature, subcultures of organizations have different requirements for the use and outputs of information. Interviewees also state that different subcultures influence the sharing of information. For example, during the COVID-19 pandemic hospitals needed to share information with the operational divisions of the Safety Regions. However, since hospitals are known for their 'consensus culture' and everything needs to be discussed and agreed upon, the receiving of information from these organizations goes much slower.

Furthermore, the communication process also influences inter-organizational information sharing. Most formal communication during COVID-19 goes through the information sharing system LCMS. The shortcomings of this system are described in the previous part of the discussion. During the interviews it appeared that informal communication was much more important than the formal ones. If a crisis responder needs something from other organizations quickly, informal communication processes are being used. This results in information not being shared with the whole network. Other organizations who also need this information therefore do not receive the required information.

4.2 Technological Determinants

As stated in the literature review, compatible technology affects the performance of inter-organizational information sharing. The incompatibility of technology and the lack of IT standards result in a barrier of information sharing. All interviewees stated that the used system to share information with (LCMS) is not compatible/fulfilling enough. It is characterized as outdated and too static. Thus, the current system is perceived as a barrier to inter-organizational information sharing. However, it is also stated by interviewees that individuals who work on a daily basis with LCMS, are able to filter and find the information that they need in an effective way. Hence, the question is, if the compatibility of the system itself is the real barrier here.

Even though all the interviewees stated that the information sharing system is not compatible, the real barrier appears to be rather organizational. It is hard for organizations who do not work with the system on a daily basis, to receive the information that they want out of the system. A real drawback is that people who are using the system on a daily basis, do not want to use another information sharing system that could be more compatible.

Organizations seem to be not willing to let go the "this is how we work" idea and therefore more compatible information sharing systems cannot be implemented easily. During a long-term crisis like the COVID-19 pandemic, the inability/willingness to let go of old processes and tools results in a major drawback when it comes to interorganizational information sharing. This phenomenon may be attributed to the organizational culture. Even though organizations know that the crisis won't be over soon, and that information sharing could be done a lot more effectively if tools and processes were changed, the rigid culture within those organizations acts as a barrier.

4.3 Political Determinants

The political environment has an influence on inter-organizational information sharing and coordination of the COVID-19 crisis. The crisis structure in the Netherlands is organized hierarchically. Thus, it is set up beforehand who has authority about a crisis situation. In this case, the COVID-19 pandemic is a nationwide crisis. Therefore, the national Government takes the measures and Safety Regions can take additional measures for their region if necessary. The political environment influences inter-organizational information sharing by facilitating tools that can be used to share information among organizations. Also, when organizations are not willing to share information anymore, organizations which are higher in the hierarchy, can use their authority to pull information from other organizations. Besides the political environment, legislation and principles also appeared to be significant in this particular case study. The GDPR and the privacy of citizens were especially discussed by interviewees. Since the COVID-19 pandemic involves privacy-sensitive information about individuals, organizations are reluctant to share information with other organizations. As stated in the literature, ambiguous legal frameworks can result in 1) organizations making decisions based on what they feel and understand from the policies and 2) non-collaborative organizations because of the fear of making mistakes. Some organizations do not share information with others and use the GDPR as an argument. However, when organizations/individuals with authority or a higher rank ask for the same information, organizations are suddenly more willing to share.

5 Discussion

As stated in the literature review, network centric operations have evolved to create shared situational awareness and to adapt faster to uncertain situations like a crisis. However, network centric operations bring its own pitfalls like the threat of information overload, responsibility dilution and coordination neglect.

This case study shows that all the disadvantages of network centric operations occur during this crisis. Firstly, the problem of information overload during the COVID-19 pandemic, is associated by experts with the incompatibility of the used information sharing system (LCMS). The information sharing system is not able to create visualizations and to filter information. Although the information sharing system is perceived as incompatible, the underlying problem of information overload is not the technology that is used to manage and share information. The problem rather lies in organizations not knowing who needs what information for what purpose and when, which can be attributed to the problem of coordination neglect. Because the information is centrally available within the network and everyone has access to the shared information without further formal communication, the gap between the information offered and information need cannot be fulfilled. One interviewee stated the following:

"However, there is one caveat when all the information is shared. When you share too much information, you get lost and cannot see the bigger picture anymore. The point is, the one who manages the information sharing systems must realize the following: who needs this information and what is relevant now, what is relevant later or just irrelevant?"

-Manager Safety Region.

Secondly, the threat of responsibility dilution also occurs during the COVID-19 pandemic among organizations. Responsibility dilution is that the sharing of information may result in false impressions among strategic levels. Interviewees state that the strategic level indeed sometimes interferes because of the information that is available. This causes strategic levels to interfere in matters while it is not their responsibility. The responsibility of these decisions lies with the operational levels, but because all information is available, organizations are sometimes inclined to interfere with the course of events. Another interviewee stated the following:

"Noticeable -even during a sudden disaster- is the fact that the strategic and operational levels become intertwined and this does not always contribute in a positive manner to the crisis. Directors sometimes lose themselves in the operational aspects while this is not their task."

-Employee Safety Region

It can be discussed that organizations within a network centric context lack the ability to manage information effectively during a crisis due to this coordination mechanism. Due to the high number of organizations involved in the network, it is hard to know who needs what information and when. Also, during a crisis, the network of organizations may change on the basis of the needs to overcome the crisis. This makes sharing and managing information even harder. What is needed is the use of a "facilitating" organization whose only purpose is to bridge the gap between the information offered and the information needed by organizations.

However, with this structure, the coordination mechanism cannot be called network centric because a central managing organization becomes included. A so-called hybrid approach like the one that is introduced by [10], could be a possible solution. Hybrid approaches retain the strengths of network centric and hierarchical coordination mechanisms while overcoming the limitations of both. This approach uses an information coordination node which links new, environment-related information to prior information and knowledge to gain situational awareness [10].

6 Conclusion

It can be concluded that in theory, netcentric operations should bring many advantages within crisis response. Especially considering the complex actor environments that crisis response today is. As the number of actors increases, the effectiveness of exchange of information becomes key. Netcentric approaches can support the effective exchange of information between actors in such a network. However, in practice, applying the principles of netcentric operations can be challenging. More specifically, over time, the netcentric operations become ingrained in process, systems and tools. While this codified netcentric approach supports the daily information exchange in emergencies, it can also reduce the ability of an organization to adapt to new circumstances. For example, when the actor environment changes.

Also, netcentric operations cause information overload, responsibility dilution and coordination neglect during a crisis with a large scope. The problems can all be attributed to organizations not being able to manage their information within the network. Thereby, the most difficult part is organizations not knowing who needs what information and when. During a long-term crisis, this part becomes even harder because the network keeps changing and the number of organizations also grows when the crisis keeps going on. The amount of available information only gets larger. Managing information in such large networks with the use of a netcentric approach becomes difficult.

Lastly, crisis responders equate netcentric operations to the technological aspects instead of the underlying concepts. This is because crisis responders are only trained on the implementation part of netcentric operations. The emphasis during the training thereby lies on processes and systems. Due to this operational inset of netcentric operations, the whole concept is institutionalized which results in the way of working becoming rigid and the adaption to new circumstances becomes difficult.

References

1. Militello, L.G., Patterson, E.S., Bowman, L., Wears, R.: Information flow during crisis management: challenges to coordination in the emergency operations center. Cognit. Technol. Work, 25–31 (2007)
2. McEntire: Coordinating multi-organizational responses to disaster: lessons from the March 28, 2000, Fort Worth tornado. Disaster Prev. Manag., 369–379 (2002)
3. Bharosa, N., Lee, J.K., Janssen, M.: Challenges and obstacles in sharing and coordinating information during multi-agency disaster response: propositions from field exercises. Inf. Syst. Front. 12(1), 49–65 (2010)
4. Reddy, M.C., Paul, S.A., Abraham, J., McNeese, M., DeFlitch, C., Yen, J.: Challenges to effective crisis management: using information and communication technologies to coordinate emergency medical services and emergency department teams. Int. J. Med. Inform., 259–269 (2009)
5. Wolbers, J., Boersma, F.K., de Heer, J.: Netcentrisch werken in ontwikkeling (2012)
6. Calderon-Meza, G.: An analysis of the effects of net-centric operations using multi-agent adaptive behavior, vol. 213. George Mason University (2011)
7. Alberts, D.S., Hayes, R.E.: DoD Command and Control Research Program. CCRP, pp. 8–98 (2007)

8. Janssen, M., & Van der Voort, H.: Agile and adaptive governance in crisis response: lessons from the COVID-19 pandemic. Int. J. Inf. Manag. **55** (2020)

9. Gil-Garcia, J.R., Sayogo, D.S.: Government inter-organizational information sharing initiatives: understanding the main determinants of success. Gov. Inf. Q., 572–582 (2016)

10. Bharosa, N., Janssen, M., Tan, Y.H.: A research agenda for information quality assurance in public safety networks: information orchestration as the middle ground between hierarchical and netcentric approaches. Cognit. Technol. Work, 203–216 (2011)

11. Wolfswinkel, J.F., Furtmueller, E., Wilderom, C.P.M.: Using grounded theory as a method for rigorously reviewing literature. Eur. J. Inf. Syst. **22**(1), 45–55 (2013)

12. Charmaz, K.: Constructing Grounded Theory: A Practical Guide Through Qualitative Analysis. Sage Publications, London (2006)

13. Blair, E.: A reflexive exploration of two qualitative data coding techniques. J. Methods Meas. Soc. Sci., 14–29 (2015)

14. Alberts, D.S., Garstka, J.J., Stein, F.P.: Network-Centric Warfare: Developing and Leveraging Information Superiority, vol. 2. CCRP Publication Series, Washington (2002)

15. Van De Ven, J., Van Rijk, R., Essens, P., Frinking, E.: Network centric operations in crisis management. In: 5th International ISCRAM Conference, Washington, DC, USA, May 2008

16. Van de Ven, A.H., Walker, G.: The dynamics of interorganizational coordination. Adm. Sci. Q., 598–621 (1984)

17. Calderón-Meza, G.: An Analysis of the Effects of Net-Centric Operations Using Multi-Agent Adaptive Behavior. George Mason University (2011)

18. Van Santen, W., Jonker, C., Wijngaards, N.: Crisis decision making through a shared integrative negotiation mental model. Int. J. Emerg. Manag. **6**(3–4), 342–355 (2009)

19. Li, S., Lin, B.: Accessing information sharing and information quality in supply chain management, 1641–1656 (2006)

20. Gonzalez, R.A.: Coordination and its ICT support in crisis response: confronting the information-processing view of coordination with a case study. In: Proceedings of the 41st Annual Hawaii International Conference on System Sciences (HICSS 2008), p. 28. IEEE (2008)

21. Bruijn, H.D.: One Fight, One Team: the 9/11 Commission Report on Intelligence, Fragmentation and Information, pp. 267–287. Blackwell Publishing (2006)

22. Heath, C., Staudenmayer, N.: Coordination Neglect: How Lay Theories of Organizing Complicate Coordination in Organizations, pp. 153–191. Elsevier Science Inc. (2000)

23. Pardo, T.A., Gil-Garcia, J.R., Burke, G.B.: Sustainable cross-boundary information sharing. Center for Technology in Government, University at Albany, State University of New York, Albany, New York, U.S.A, pp. 422–438 (2008)

24. Drake, D.B., Steckler, N.A., Koch, M.J.: Information sharing in and across government agencies. Soc. Sci. Comput. Rev., 67–84 (2004)

25. Jamil, I., Panday, P.: Inter-organizational coordination and corruption in urban policy implementation in Bangladesh: a case of Rajshahi city corporation. Int. J. Public Adm., 352–366 (2012)

26. Long, D., Fahey, L.: Diagnosing cultural barriers to knowledge management. Acad. Manag. Exec., 113–127 (2000)

27. Ostroff, C., Kinicki, A.J., Muhammad, R.S.: Organizational culture and climate. In: Handbook of Psychology, pp. 643–670 (2013)

28. Saab, D.J., Tapia, A., Maitland, C., Maldonado, E., Tchouakeu, L.M.N.: Inter-organizational coordination in the wild: trust building and collaboration among field-level ICT workers in humanitarian relief organizations. Voluntas Int. J. Volunt. Nonprofit Organ. **24**, 194–213 (2013)

29. Huang, Y.H.: Trust and relational commitment in corporate crises: the effects of crisis communicative strategy and form of crisis response. J. Public Relat. Res., 297–327 (2008)

30. McNeish, J., Mann, I.J.S.: Knowledge sharing and trust in organizations. J. Knowl. Manag. **38** (2010)
31. Kapucu, N.: Interagency communication networks during emergencies: boundary spanners in multiagency coordination. Am. Rev. Public Adm., 207–225 (2006)
32. Sako, M.: Price, Quality and Trust: Inter-firm Relations in Britain and Japan, no. 18. Cambridge University Press, Cambridge (1992)
33. Cousins, P.D.: A conceptual model for managing long-term inter-organisational relationships, 71–82 (2001)
34. Comfort, L.K., Kapucu, N.: Inter-organizational coordination in extreme events: the world trade center attacks, September 11, 2001. Nat. Hazards **39**(2), 309 (2006)
35. Hossain, L., Khalili, S., Uddin, S.: Inter-organizational coordination dynamics during crisis. J. Decis. Syst., 383–396 (2011)
36. Paine, D.: How to measure your results in a crisis, vol. 9. The Institute for Public Relations (2002)
37. Fischer, D., Posegga, O., Fischbach, K.: Communication barriers in crisis management: a literature review. In: Twenty-Fourth European Conference on Information Systems (ECIS), vol. 18 (2016)
38. Gil-Garcia, J.R., Chun, S.A., Janssen, M.: Government information sharing and integration: combining the social and the technical. Inf. Polity **14**(1, 2), 1–10 (2009)
39. Paturas, J.L, Smith, S.R., Albanese, J., Waite, G.: Inter-organisational response to disasters. J. Bus. Contin. Emerg. Plan., 347–358 (2015)
40. Dawes, S.S: Interagency information shoring: expected benefits, manageable risks. J. Policy Anal. Manag., 377–394 (1996)
41. Agarwal, R., Karahanna, E.: On the multi-dimensional nature of compatibility beliefs in technology acceptance. Digit **16** (1998)
42. Tornatzky, L.G., Klein, K.J.: Innovation characteristics and innovation adoption-implementation: a meta-analysis of findings. IEEE Trans. Eng. Manag. **1**, 28–45 (1982)
43. Tchouakeu, L.M.N., Maitland, C.F., Tapia, A.H., Bajpai, K.: Humanitarian organizational collaboration: information technologies as necessary but not sufficient. In: ISCRAM, May 2011
44. Hart, P., Heyse, L., Boin, A.: Guest editorial introduction new trends in crisis management practice and crisis management research: setting the agenda. J. Conting. Crisis Manag., 181–189 (2001)
45. Kalkman, J.P., Kerstholt, J.H., Roelofs, M.: Crisis response team decision-making as a bureau-political process. Conting. Crisis Manag., 480–490 (2018)
46. Bigdeli, Z., Kamal, M., de Cesare, S.: Information sharing through inter-organisational systems in local government. Transform. Gov. People Process Policy, 148–176 (2013)
47. Lam, W.: Barriers to e-government integration. J. Enterp. Inf. Manag., 511–530 (2005)
48. Landsbergen Jr., D., Wolken Jr., G.: Realizing the promise: government information systems and the fourth generation of information technology. Public Adm. Rev. **2001** (2001)
49. Ke, W., Wei, K.: Factors affecting trading partners' knowledge sharing: using the lens of transaction cost economics and socio-political theories . Electron. Commer. Res. Appl., 297–308 (2007)

Work as Imagined vs Work as Done: The Case of an Under Development Risk and Resilience Research Centre During the Antonov An-12 Crash Emergency in Greece

Ioannis M. Dokas[1]([✉]) [iD], Anastasia K. Paschalidou[2] [iD], Konstantinos Chouvardas[3], Ilias Petrou[2] [iD], Kyriaki Psistaki[2], Sofia Christoforou[4], Valkaniotis Sotiris[1] [iD], Panagiotis Argyrakis[1] [iD], Apostolos Zeleskidis[1] [iD], Stavroula Charalabidou[1] [iD], and Apostolos Vasileiou[1] [iD]

[1] Civil Engineering Department, Democritus University of Thrace, Komotini, Greece
idokas@civil.duth.gr
[2] Department of Forestry and Management of the Environment and Natural Resources, Democritus University of Thrace, Komotini, Greece
apascha@fmenr.duth.gr
[3] Civil Protection Agency REMTH, Marousi, Greece
[4] General Directorate of Inspectorate, Marousi, Greece
s.christoforou@prv.ypeka.gr

Abstract. The Risk and Resilience Assessment Center (RiskAC) of East Macedonia and Thrace Region (REMTH) is a research project aiming at supporting decision-making on the repression and prevention of disasters in the geographical region of REMTH in Greece. The project's objective is to establish a new, properly equipped, and organized research center up to the Technological Readiness Level 5 (TRL5) by August 2023, dedicated to risk and resilience assessment studies of possible hazardous scenarios within REMTH. This paper will present the gaps identified between work as imagined vs. work as done by the RiskAC center, which is currently under development, during a plane crash emergency in REMTH in July 2022. Although RiskAC analyses related to the plane crash emergency validated that the project achieved the goal of creating a center that reached the TRL 5 maturity level, it identified points for further improving its processes. Lastly, the paper highlights the importance of considering safety via creating Concept of Operation Documents, among other things, as early as possible as essential aspects in effective operating such systems.

Keywords: RiskAC · Plane Crash Emergency · Antonov A-12 · Risk Assessment. Air Pollution · ALOHA · ADMS5

T. Gjøsæter et al. (Eds.): ITDRR 2022, IFIP AICT 672, pp. 185–196, 2023.
https://doi.org/10.1007/978-3-031-34207-3_12

1 Introduction

The Risk and Resilience Assessment Center (RiskAC) of the Region of East Macedonian and Thrace (REMTH) in Greece is a 30-month research project aiming at establishing, by the mid of 2023, a new properly equipped, and organized research center up to the Technological Readiness Level 5 (TRL5) to support decision-making on the repression and prevention of disasters in the geographical region of REMTH in Greece.

Creating a research infrastructure on natural hazard risk assessments and their effects is not new. Well-established and successful research teams specializing in specific hazards (i.e., earthquakes, floods, forest fires, meteorological hazards, etc.) exist in Greek institutions. However, what is missing **is a system** to truly enhance risk and resilience assessment studies, where the output of a specific hazard assessment scenario created by one team could affect the analysis or could be considered as input to the assessment scenario of other hazards created by another team in the same geographical area region. The RiskAC project has the ambition to fill this gap. Because such a goal was considered ambitious from the beginning, it was decided to set TRL5 as a goal that could realistically be achieved within 30 months by the RiskAC team.

The novelty of the RiskAC project is that it adopts a holistic approach to risk and resilience studies for a specific region. This means that RiskAC adopts the view that, in many cases, natural and technological hazards within a specific geographical region have causal relationships over time. For instance, a forest fire during summertime in a region may be a causal factor for landslides during springtime in that region. Thus, experts in different types of hazards should be "encouraged" via a new type of system, in this case, the RiskAC research center, to monitor and study a specific region and together establish the necessary culture to achieve seamless collaboration and exchange of information between them, and through that to effectively support decision-makers in being proactive about the challenges that expected due to the climate crisis.

One task of the research team during the end of 2021 was to begin creating a high-level description document on the needs, assumptions, and procedures that should be defined, monitored, and be in place, so that the RiskAC center continues operating and fulfilling its aims after the end of the project, together with a description of the processes and interactions between RiskAC elements (humans and technological elements) when the center will be in "active mode". That is, when the Civil Protection Agency of REMTH, for instance, or some other organization request RiskAC's contribution for decision support. At the General Assembly of the RiskAC consortium in December 2021, an initial draft of the document was presented, discussed, and accepted as the basis for more detailed analysis, possibly in the form of a Concept of Operations Document. That document represented a rough and imaginary sketch of how RiskAC research center will operate when it is in "active mode" (i.e., work as imagined – WAI) when it reaches the appropriate maturity level.

Around April 2022 major project supplies, such as sensors, instruments, computers, consumable reagents, servers, and software began to arrive on site. By the end of June 2022, most supplies were received. In addition, the training sessions of members of the research group on specific software, such as the Air Pollution Modeling Software ADMS-5, were completed. Given that major components of the RiskAC research center were on site, the assembly and configuration of the research center began at the end of June. During the same period, the team began the process of devising the scenarios based on which the basic elements of the RiskAC center will be tested in a 'simulated' or somewhat realistic environment to validate that the center has reached the TRL 5 maturity level.

That process was interrupted when on the night of the 16th of July, a cargo Antonov An-12 aircraft carrying 11.5 tons of munitions from Serbia to Bangladesh crashed in the region of Kavala in REMTH [1]. Regardless that RiskAC center was "under construction" a request was made to assess the direction and dispersion of the air pollutant byproducts of the crash. That was not a test on a simulated environment, it was a real case for decision support. As a result, the research team engaged for the first time in the "active mode" of the RiskAC research center. This paper will present the gaps identified between the work described in the document presented in the RiskAC General Assembly in December 2021 against the work done (i.e., work as done – WAD) during the Antonov An-12 plane crash emergency.

Although the analyses of RiskAC researchers related to the plane crash emergency validated that the project achieved the goal of creating a center that outreached TRL 5 maturity level, points for further improving its processes have been identified.

2   Previous Works

A distinction between the system task description, or WAI, and the cognitive tasks, or WAD was proposed in 1983 by [2]. That played a role in the early discussions about resilience engineering. WAI stipulates how work should be done to achieve the intended results and WAD refers to how such work is actually done under varying circumstances [3]. In the emergency management literature, works like the ones of [4, 5], and [6] examine to what extent procedures and steps described in written documents, such as Standard Operating Procedures (SOP), were implemented or omitted when a sociotechnical system operates to address real emergencies or operates in a simulated environments or during periodic emergency management drills.

In the same rationale [7] utilized the Event Management SOP TimeLine (EMSTL), as a method to visualize the gaps between the SOP of the event under emergency management conditions and the activities carried out in the field during periodic exercises utilizing data gathering and experiences from real operational situations to raise awareness of the need for cultural change in the organization. The same authors found that only about one-third of the steps of emergency SOPs were carried out as prescribed and made a call for a change in the system.

On the other hand, works such as, [8] and [9] point out that organizational traits like overreliance on rules and written procedures, excessive specialization of tasks, failure to learn from near misses, and absence of shared perception of urgency hinder organizational personnel from behaving and reacting to emergencies naturally without trammeling resulting from hindering WAD from being displayed during exercises or real emergencies.

Studies on the gap between WAI and WAD indicate that the variability of a system during its operational phase is typically much greater than the variability implied in the task descriptions in its SOP documents. In short, the actual work is often more complex than the work described in written procedures. Nonetheless, identifying these gaps can help organizations introduce better guidelines and SOPs' and possibly initiate a cultural transformation of the system itself.

3 RiskAC: Research Groups and Physical Deliverables

RiskAC is comprised of 10 research groups, as shown in Table 1. Each group has one coordinator/director who holds academic staff position in a university or is a senior researcher in a research institute with track record and expertise in the scientific field that the group is focused at. Young researchers were also members of each group. By the first year of the project most of the 53 positions for young researchers which were required to support the needs of each RiskAC group were filled.

Table 1. The ten groups of RiskAC.

Logo	Group Name
	Project Coordination and Critical Infrastructure Interdependencies
	Fire Hazard
	Air Pollution and Meteorology
	Hydrological Hazard
	Engineering Infrastructure
	ICT
	Cultural Capital
	Human Health and Land Microbiology
	Geotechnical - Geological Hazard and GIS
	Seismic Hazard

RiskAC has a modular structure by design. This means that additional groups specialized in a domain (e.g., radiological hazards group), can be included, depending on the hazard, risk, and resilience analysis needs of the authorities and organizations of

REMTH in the future. The 10 groups shown in Table 1 were initially chosen based on the:

a) Frequency of occurrence of a hazard in REMTH in the past, such as floods, forest fires, landslides and rockfalls, and industrial accidents that may disperse toxic fumes.
b) Hazards that may be characterized as being of low in frequency but high in negative consequences, such as climate change, and earthquakes.
c) Things that may be affected by a hazard occurrence in REMTH, such as public and environmental health, cities and critical infrastructures, human activities, and cultural monuments.
d) Teams that provide the necessary technological resources, hardware, and information processing support to the entire RiskAC system.

Two are the main physical deliverables of the project. The first is a data fusion and analysis room, which has the look of a control room. The second, is a mobile data collection unit in the form of a trailer. The trailer unit is designed to be equipped with sensors, solar panels, batteries, hardware, and software. Its purpose is to collect sensor data from specific geographical locations, when needed, like in the cases of technological accidents, and transmit them to the data fusion and analysis room to be analyzed by the research groups. The data fusion and analysis room will be a 100 m^2 approximately room located in the Civil Engineering Department of Democritus University of Thrace, equipped with the necessary ICT networks, double monitor workstations, server to store and process large volume of sensor data, control room displays in the wall to monitor multiple data and information streams, and shared space for coordinated – collaborative work during emergencies.

4 Work as Imagined

Three operational modes for the RiakAC research center were identified in the December 2021 document that presented a high-level description of its needs, assumptions, and procedures. These modes are presented in Table 2.

The December 2021 document also described the processes and interactions between RiskAC elements when the center would be in an Active operational Mode. To enter in Active Mode, a request for decision support by a public or private organization should be received by RiskAC (See Fig. 1). In the case, however, where there is a forecast for a hazardous event by let's say the National Meteorological Service, then the forecast could act as trigger for RiskAC to change its operational mode to Active Mode. The request, when is received, or when a forecast is perceived, is communicated to the Lead Coordinator who first validates the request or the forecast and then activates the most relevant RiskAC groups based on the nature and characteristics of the hazard that occurred or forecasted. The ICT group Coordinator is also informed.

The Lead Coordinator meet physically or remotely with the Coordinators of the activated RiskAC groups to assess, based on the information and data at hand, if what has been requested has been studied in the past as possible hazard scenario and its assessment already exists in the servers of RiskAC, or new assessment must be conducted by RiskAC group/s to respond to the request. The Coordinator of the ICT group participates in the meeting.

Table 2. RiskAC operational modes.

No	Operational Mode Name	Description
1	Idle Mode	No hazard or other event occurs in REMTH, nor is there a forecast for occurrence. During this period the RiskAC personnel should: a) monitor the environment for events or signs indicating the occurrence of a hazard, b) upgrade/maintain the equipment and instruments of the center, c) gain new knowledge and skills
2	Active Mode	A hazardous event occurred or is expected to occur in REMTH. A request for decision support by private or public organizations is received. In this operational mode, the personnel of RiskAC is active in gathering and analyzing data and information to produce as soon as possible scientifically sound assessments and deliver them to those who request them
3	Validation and Performance Evaluation Mode	After Active Operational Mode ends, the personnel of RiskAC engages in activities aiming at validating the outcomes of the produced assessments. In addition, reflect on how work was done during Active Mode to identify aspects that can be further improved. Evaluate the overall performance of the RiskAC center

If the requested assessment has been analyzed in the past as a possible scenario and exists in the server, then it is extracted from the server and reviewed. The Coordinator of the group responsible for the assessment recommends to the Lead Coordinator whether the results from the retrieved assessment are sound and valid for the requested case or not. If the recommendation of the Coordinator is that the outputs of the assessment are valid for the case at hand then the Lead Coordinator grants the "publication" of the assessment or its submission to the organization that requested the support of RiskAC. The "publication" of the assessment is executed by the ICT group which depending on the file types of the assessment could be uploaded to the WebGIS server of RiskAC, if the files are GIS compatible or submitted to a specific server, medium, or channel.

If what is requested hasn't been analyzed by RiskAC groups in the past, then the Coordinator/s of the groups involved recommend if a new assessment can be fulfilled or not for the case at hand during the meeting with the Lead Coordinator and the Technical Support Coordinator. If a new assessment cannot be fulfilled, then the Lead Coordination contacts the organization who requested the support of RiskAC explaining why their request cannot be supported. If a new assessment can be done, then the Lead Coordinator

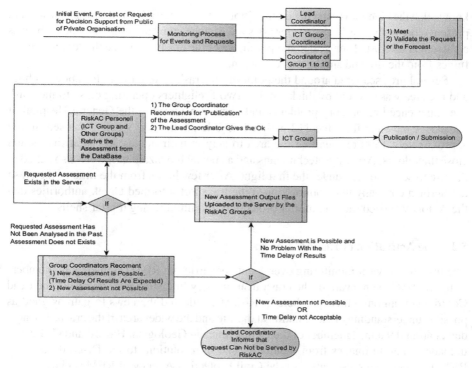

Fig. 1. Description of RiskAC's Active Operational Mode.

informs the organization who requested the support of RiskAC that the request can be supported but with a time delay. If the specified time delay is not an issue, then all actions necessary to produce the assessment are executed by the RiskAC groups. When the assessment has been completed its results are reviewed and the Coordinator/s of the group/s involved in the assessment recommends to the Lead Coordinator whether the results are sound and valid or not. If the recommendation of the Coordinator/s is that the outputs of the assessment are valid for the case at hand, then the Lead Coordinator grants the "publication" of the assessment or its submission to the organization who requested the support of RiskAC.

5   Work as Done: The Case of Antnonov An-12 Crash

5.1   The Crash

On Saturday, 16th July 2022, a cargo Antonov An-12 aircraft transporting 11.5 tons of ammunition and flying from Serbia to Bangladesh crashed due to engine problems killing all eight crew members in the region of Kavala in REMTH very close to Palaiochori and Antifilippoi villages. The aircraft was flying from Serbia to its final destination Bangladesh. The aircraft crashed at around 23:54 EEST.

The fire department and the police deployed to the area immediately. Initially, it was known that the plane cargo is classified as "dangerous". After a while it become known that the plane was carrying ammunition. At first, they removed civilians who were present close to the crash site to offer assistance, since many assumed that the plane was a passenger aircraft. Then sealed the perimeter of the crash site since the toxicity of the fumes from the fire and smoke was unknown.

Several fires scattered around the point of the crash were burning for about an hour and the area was covered by thick smoke. Two firefighters operating close to the crash site experienced respiratory problems and were transferred to the General Hospital of Kavala. A message from the 112 national mobile phone alert service was sent to the approximately 1500 residents of the area to stay in their homes and wear masks and close their doors. Army Pyrotechnicians and a special biohazard unit were also called to the site to scan the area under the first light. After few hours from the time of the crash the Serbian company that commissioned the transport informed Greek authorities that the Antonov carried training mortar projectiles and illuminating mortar shells.

5.2   The Activation of RiskAC Center

The process of tweet monitoring over events occurring in REMTH made key members of the RiskAC team aware of the crash from its very first moments. As result, the Lead Coordinator, among other members of RiskAC, followed the news to gain as good as possible understanding of the situation at the site and the wider area of the crash. The next day at around 9 a.m. a member of the Geotechnical – Geological Hazard and GIS group uploaded satellite images from Sentinel-2 (10 m resolution) to the Discord server of RiskAC, where a representative of the Civil Protection Agency of REMTH has access, showing the exact location of the crash and how many meters the plane crawl to the ground during its crash.

At noon, the Lead Coordinator received a call from the Civil Protection Agency of REMTH. The talk focused on assessing, given its under construction status, if RiskAC can contribute to the situation with useful scientific support. Based on the nature and characteristics of the event, the interactions between the Lead Coordinator with the Coordinators of the Groups that can contribute to the situation at hand, and the state of the infrastructure of the center at that point in time, a decision was made to provide scientific support in relation to the dispersion of air pollution to the area during the first hours from the time of the crash.

The decision which was made resulted ad changing the operational mode of the Air Pollution and Meteorology Group from Idle to Active Mode and of specific members of the Geotechnical – Geological Hazard and GIS team to Standby Mode so as to be ready to act when needed via the provision of data and resources, such as raster GIS files of Digital Elevation Models (DIM) of the area, satellite images, uploading files to the RiskAC's WebGIS server.

After working with her team for a couple of hours the Coordinator of the Air Pollution and Meteorology Group informed the Lead Coordinator about their decision to proceed with the creation of a potential chemical release model for the first hour from the crash, utilizing Meteorological data which were immediately available for the area by the National Observatory of Athens together with the US EPA software ALOHA [10].

After the review of ALOHA software results, the group was planning to utilize the ADMS5 software [11] to model the dispersion of particles with diameters that are generally 2.5 μm and smaller (PM$_{2.5}$) at the ground level for the first 4 h from the crash. A major factor to utilize ALOHA first was the estimated time needed to create and review the model, which was significantly shorter compared to the alternative of utilizing ADMS5.

On Sunday afternoon the 17th, the results from ALOHA software were ready to be reviewed. At 21:40 EEST a virtual meeting was held between the members of the Air Pollution and Meteorology Group the Lead Coordinator and a representative from the Civil Protection Agency of REMTH for this purpose. After about 30 min of discussion on the model, its assumptions, and its results, the output of the assessment (see Fig. 2) was accepted, and the results were submitted to the Civil Protection Agency of REMTH to be used for decision support.

Fig. 2. Indicative representation of the ALOHA analysis results.

The Group then focused its attention on the creation of PM$_{2.5}$ dispersion model, utilizing the recently acquired ADMS5 software. In this case, DIM raster file depicting the elevation and topography around the crash site was integrated into the ADMS5. At 18:00 on the 18th of July the results of the ADMS5 analysis were scheduled to be reviewed. A virtual meeting was held at 18:00 with the same participants as with the virtual meeting a day before. The Coordinator of the Group expressed the need to further refine the model, and everybody agreed with her. On Thursday the 21st another meeting was held where it was decided that the results of the ADMS5 model (see Fig. 3) are acceptable, and the results were sent to the Civil Protection Agency of REMTH for decision support. In addition, it was decided to upload the results of the analysis to the WebGIS server of RiskAC.

In overall the results of the analyses indicated that the depression of the air pollution was covering an area with a hart like shape of 4.6 km^2 northeast to the point of the crash away from the two villages nearby.

Fig. 3. Indicative representation of the ADMS5 analysis results.

6   Conclusions

6.1   Identified Gaps

The Antonov An-12 crash was the first time where RiskAC behaved as a center for decision support. Regardless of being in under-construction phase, the interaction of RiskAC members between them and between software and hardware was flawless. In addition, the communication and collaboration between RiskAC and the Civil Protection Agency of REMTH were carried out without any problems.

There were, however lessons learned to further improve the document describing the Active Mode of operations. One aspect that was missing and revealed through the RiskAC reaction to the crash was the need to introduce the notion of Standby Mode into the document. Indeed, certain members of the Geotechnical-Geological Hazard and GIS Group were standing by their phones to react and provide support in specific time periods during the timeline of the process. But their actions and support at those specific points in time were of importance. For example, the immediate provision of the DIM GIS raster file to the Air Pollution and Meteorology Group was of importance to properly create an acceptable PM2.2 desperation model.

Thus, while one Group can be in Active Mode, members of other groups can be in Standby Mode and other groups in Idle Mode. In addition, the Geotechnical-Geological Hazard and GIS Group, in this case, were acting in a supporting role similar to what was imagined and expected by the ICT group. The ICT group would have been very active in this case if the trailer mobile data collection unit was assembled and ready to be deployed at the scene of the crash. But unfortunately, the trailer was not entirely constructed and wasn't ready to be deployed.

A point of improvement for RiskAC based on the crash case is the time duration required to produce reliable results when utilizing specific modeling tools and approaches. For instance, while the ALOHA model produced acceptable results within a few hours after the accident, the ADMS5 model results took several days to be produced. This delay can be explained, however, due to the fact that the Meteorological Group members finished their training on the ADMS5 software a few weeks before the crash and didn't have the time to gain the ideal level of experience on its use. Thus, the crash highlighted the need to constantly gain experience and training in using RiskAC software models and resources.

Lastly, a significant lesson learned through this case was the need to establish collaboration with organizations that own calibrated sensor data in REMTH, which can be accessed and utilized without major time delays. In the case of the crash, the meteorological data to be used in the models were acquired after a few hours of the crash by the open sensor network data of the National Observatory of Athens. If that data were unavailable or received after several days, then it would not be possible for RiskAC to offer valuable service in this case.

6.2 Validation and Impact

RiskAC was officially invited to present the results of its assessments in a meeting with the stakeholders involved in managing the incident on Friday the 22nd of July in the city of Kavala. In that meeting, the RiskAC assessment results were validated in a way, by the decision of authorities to seal an area around the crash site like the area shown in Fig. 3 during the first days of the crash. Furthermore, the RiskAC air pollution dispersion maps are utilized by environmental inspectors to set up the soil and leaf sample plans for detailed chemical analysis.

Overall, the reaction and behavior of the RiskAC project team in the Antonov An-12 crash have shown that the project, within approximately 19 months, developed a system whose basic components were capable of providing decision support in real emergencies within REMTH. The performance of RiskAC in the Antonov An-12 crash indicates that the research center has reached and overshot the target of the TRL 5 maturity level. Much work needs to be done by the team, however, so the RiskAC center, as a system, to reach a higher level of maturity. The lessons learned and the experience gained from this event contribute to its continuous improvement and development.

Having also a brief description of how the RiskAC system will behave to provide decision support in case of such events has also helped to produce the outputs it produced in this case. It was as if everybody within RiskAC knew how to interact and when to act. That highlights the importance of having in place as early as possible a Concept of Operations document for such systems.

Acknowledgements. We acknowledge support of this work by the project "Risk and Resilience Assessment Center – Prefecture of East Macedonia and Thrace – Greece." (MIS 5047293) which is implemented under the Action "Reinforcement of the Research and Innovation Infrastructure", funded by the Operational Programme "Competitiveness, Entrepreneurship and Innovation" (NSRF 2014–2020) and co-financed by Greece and the European Union (European Regional Development Fund).

Co-financed by Greece and the European Union

References

1. BBC, Greece plane crash: Cargo aircraft was carrying weapons to Bangladesh. bbc.com/news/world-europe-62195005. Accessed 31 Jul 2022
2. Hollnagel, E., Woods, D.D.: Cognitive systems engineering: new wine in new bottles. Int. J. Man Mach. Stud. **18**(6), 583–600 (1983)
3. Wreathall, J.: Properties of resilient organizations: an initial view. In: Resilience Engineering: Concepts and Precepts, pp. 275–286. Ashgate Publishing, Aldershot (2006)
4. de Carvalho, P.V.R., Arce, D., Passos, C., Huber, G.J., Borges, M., Gomes, J.O.: A participatory approach to improve resilience in command and control (C2) systems: a case study in the Rio de Janeiro C2 system. In: At the 6th Resilience Engineering Symposium, Lisbon Portugal (2015)
5. Huber, G., Righi, A.W., Lemos, C., Emygdio, K., Gomes, J.O., Carvalho, P.V.: Firefighting emergency response exercise? An analysis of standardization and resilience. In: Proceedings of the 13th International Conference on Information Systems for Crisis Response and Management. Rio de Janeiro (2016)
6. Righi, A., Saurin, T.: Complex socio-technical systems: characterization and management guidelines. Appl. Ergon. **50**(1), 19–30 (2015)
7. de Carvalho, P.V.R., Righi, A.W., Huber, G.J., Lemos, C.d.F., Jatoba, A., Gomes, J.O.: Reflections on work as done (WAD) and work as imagined (WAI) in an emergency response organization: a study on firefighters training exercises. Appl. Ergon. **68**, 28–41 (2018)
8. Webb, G.R., Chevreau, F.-R.: Planning to improvise: the importance of creativity and flexibility in crisis response. Int. J. Emerg. Manag. **3**(1), 66–72 (2006)
9. Roux-Dufort, C., Vidaillet, B.: The difficulties of improvising in a crisis situation: a case study. Int. Stud. Manag. Organ. **33**(1), 86–115 (2003)
10. US EPA, ALOHA Software. https://www.epa.gov/cameo/aloha-software. Accessed 31 Jul 2022
11. Cambridge Environmental Research Consultants (CERC) Software, ADMS 5 – Industrial Air Pollution Modelling Software. https://www.environmental-expert.com/software/adms-5-industrial-air-pollution-modelling-software-18344. Accessed 31 Jul 2022

A Business Continuity Robustness Assessment Approach Through Disruption's Sociological Indicators

Oussema Ben Amara[1](✉) iD, Daouda Kamissoko[1](✉) iD, Ygal Fijalkow[2](✉) iD, and Frederick Benaben[1](✉) iD

[1] Centre Génie Industriel, IMT Mines Albi, University of Toulouse, Campus Jarlard, Route De Teillet, Albi, France
{oussema.ben_amara,daouda.kamissoko,
frederick.benaben}@mines-albi.fr
[2] CERTOP Laboratory, INU Champollion, University of Toulouse, Place de Verdun, Albi, France
ygal.fijalkow@univ-jfc.fr

Abstract. During the last years, International Organizations for Standardization have been developing many quality management tools which are being implemented by several types of organizations. These tools are especially being implemented to manage disasters and reduce activity disruptions' consequences. However, monitoring the performance of the organizational norm requires developing metrics and assessment tools that can be used easily and on a daily basis to make organizations more resilient to crisis situations. The management tool that this research work considers is the "Business Continuity Plan" known as BCP. One way to assess this type of plan is to define, design then test quantifying and qualifying keys to measure its robustness.

Keywords: Business Continuity Management · Sociological factors · Robustness · Assessment tools · Risk Management

1 Introduction

The pandemic of COVID 19 along with the decisions that followed its arrival according to the World Economic Situation Report (WESR) 2021 [1, 2] is a such an important crisis during the last century. The aim of protecting employment and productivity emphasizes the role of the Sustainable Development Goals (SDGs) as a guarantee and impetus for the resilience of countries, businesses and communities. To develop their capacity for future crises, public authorities in many countries have sought to act in the face of the danger posed by the COVID crisis, taking measures to prevent them, to detect the threats, and then try to deal with them. In this research work, the robustness of the Business Continuity Management (BCM) is our main interest. In fact, a BCM is the "holistic management process that identifies potential threats to an organization and the impact those threats,

T. Gjøsæter et al. (Eds.): ITDRR 2022, IFIP AICT 672, pp. 197–212, 2023.
https://doi.org/10.1007/978-3-031-34207-3_13

if realized, can cause on business operations, and provides a framework for building organizational resilience with the capability of an effective response that safeguards the interests of key interested parties, reputation, brand and value-creating activities". While a BCP is the "document containing the critical information that an organization requires to continue value-creating operations during an unplanned event" [2, 3].

Whereas, **robustness**, explicitly links system dynamics with performance measurements. Therefore, **resilience** concepts about the nature of persistence and transformation in complex systems can be linked to performance measurements and used to make a decision-making framework for **sustainability** operational. Robustness is probably the clearest of these three concepts (robustness, resilience and sustainability), judging by the consistency or accuracy of its use in the literature [4].

Hence, this research work aims at the following:

a. Define and explain: (i) **the pillars of a BCP** and (ii) **the dependencies of a BCP's robustness** (Sect. 3).
b. Propose a **BCP robustness assessment grid** based on (a), (Sect. 4).
c. Introduce a **case study** then define, design and test **sociological indicators to assess the robustness of the BCP** (Sects. 4 and 5).

2   State of the Art: Setting the Scene and Literature Review

Business continuity (BC) is the organization's ability to continue to deliver products or provide services with a predefined level of acceptable capability following a disruption. Business continuity management is the process of implementing and maintaining BC to prevent loss and prepare for, mitigate, and manage disruptions [5].

In general, business continuity is unique to an organization. However, its implementation can have implications that may extend to the wider community and other third parties. An organization may have external organizations that it depends on and conversely other organizations that depend on it. Therefore, effective business continuity contributes to a more resilient society [6]. A BCP must function in practice as well as in theory. The goal for an organization should be to be able to address all issues in a controlled and methodical manner without having to open the business continuity guidelines, which should be understood and memorized [7].

Organizations might become overly dependent on the checklists given in existing standards. A BCP is likely to be more helpful if it is utilized as a general support tool to solve any type of crisis rather than only as a guide for a set of predetermined eventualities (although some specific situations could have checklists prepared). These checklists for predetermined circumstances must be developed during the business continuity planning phase and kept up to date during the subsequent maintenance procedure. Managers should learn how to think strategically in risky contexts, which is arguably as essential as learning how to minimize risks or uncertainties [8].

To maintain these checklists for the BCP in particular, the pillars of such a plan should be identified so that the aspects to measure could be determined and thus through designed indicators their assessment could be possible. An example for this demonstration could be that in [9], instead of making use of safety audit type of techniques, which are typically rather time-consuming, more attention was rather be paid on safety indicators, and in particular those that measure the remote organizational factors. The utilization of indicators will facilitate the demand for a 'speedy' evaluation and will also provide quantitative statements of the states of the organizational factors. The indicator values are based on registrations of observable variables carried out during a predefined time period. These values must then be transformed to a "state" for each of the organizational factors. Thus, we only rely on observations/registrations and not on interviews, questionnaires, etc., which are much more time-consuming. However, this puts high demands on the validity of the chosen indicators, both individually and in terms of the total coverage.

Using the same logic in the case of this research work, the term **"rating" or "qualifying" the business continuity factors refers to determining the quality or "goodness" of the factors**. It is a measure of a particular factor's "state." The weighting of organizational elements **indicates an evaluation of the robustness that these factors have on the BCP**, either directly or indirectly.

As stated in [6], a resilient society is tied up with robust business continuity. The following section will thus cite and explain the "factors" or "pillars" that this work considers for the BCP and its robustness. However, in the next sections the indicators and the use of the evaluation tool are demonstrated based on the proposed evaluation grid and the factors considered in its design, definition and calculation of the robustness qualifying indicators.

3   Robustness Assessment Grid for BCPs

Through this section, the proposal of our robustness assessment grid is explained. In fact, to design this grid two major factors were considered: (a) the pillars of a BCP; its most important parts and configurations, and (b) the dependencies of a BCP's robustness; what does the robustness of these plans actually rely on.

3.1   The Pillars of BCP

Figure 1, below shows the main four pillars of a BCP that we are considering in this research work and that are inspired from the ISO 22301:2019 [6]. These four pillars are explained in details in the following paragraphs.

1. Commitment

    The commitment, defined as the involvement of the resources, within one organization regardless of its nature and role can be demonstrated by:

    - Staff training: Guiding and supporting individuals to contribute to the effectiveness of the BCMS (Business Continuity Management System), promoting continuous improvement and assisting other relevant managers to demonstrate leadership and commitment as it applies to their areas of responsibility.
    - Informative meetings: ensuring that BCMS requirements are integrated into the organization's business processes, ensuring that the necessary resources for the BCMS are available and communicating the importance of effective business continuity and compliance with the BCMS requirements.

Fig. 1. BCP main pillars

- Staff awareness: guide the staff and raise their awareness of the subject of business continuity.

2. Policy

A policy is an organization's method of conduct or a principle of action and could be basically established by:

- Certifications: including and certifying a commitment and know-how to meet applicable requirements.
- Control of standards: Maintaining the certifications level and frequency and providing a framework for setting business continuity objectives.
- Hierarchy and assigned responsibilities (department/team and manager): Defining the responsibilities and authorities, and designing who has the responsibility and authority to: (i) ensure that the BCMS complies with the requirements of this document and (ii) report to the executive desk on the BCMS performance.
- Control of recurring or non-recurring disruptions: including a commitment to continuous improvement of the SMCA and thus better managing the upcoming disruptions. This also implies an estimation of the frequency of the danger (e.g. absenteeism from work) and its potential damage.

3. Support

The business continuity support is the proactive business process that allows identifying potential threats, vulnerabilities, and weaknesses within one organization, and it can be verified and enhanced by the following measures:

- Documentation of a BCP: the organization's BCMS shall include: (i) documented information required by the BCP and (ii) documented information that the organization determines is necessary for the effectiveness of the BCMS.
- Integration of a BCP into the organization's IS (Information System): the documented information required by the BCMS must be controlled to ensure that: (i) it is integrated in the IS and available and fit for use, where and when needed, (ii) it is adequately protected against loss of confidentiality, inappropriate use or loss of integrity, and (iii) it is well-stored and preserved; including readability preservation, version change control, and information retention and disposal.

4. Operation

The operation within an organization is the business's day-to-day value-creating organizational activities and it can be enhanced by:

- Fallback site: a default site can which is defined for the scenario of a major risk that could cause an important disruption of the organization's main activities.
- Use of telecommuting, subcontracting or mutual aid agreements: to have other alternatives to work in the case of difficulties in the workplace under the existing conditions.
- Acquisition of specific equipment on the day of the disaster: equipment needed for fires, attacks, floods and other major risks.

3.2   Factors of the Robustness of BCPs

To start with defining the robustness dependencies and afterward indicators for a BCP, a definition for the robustness itself should be adapted in this concept. Resilience should be as well distinguished from the robustness to avoid any possible misconceptions. Overall, the definitions of robustness and resilience are different in all domains, but we note that they have strong similarities. For robustness, most research works speak of an 'initial state' and of the fact that robustness is qualified in relation to the disturbance that should not modify it or its main functionalities. For resilience, the research works establish a consensus on the capacity of the system to adapt to a disturbance until it returns to the initial state of the system. This adaptation is often described in two phases: the reaction to the disturbance and the response to a return to the initial state [10].

Vulnerability should be as well defined since it belongs to same context and can impact the robustness and resilience of an organization. Vulnerability is typically described as an underlying condition that is distinct from the risky events that may cause the outcome [11]. Sometimes the literature is vague about what constitutes loss or damage, and whether it matters to whom the losses or damages accrue. The literature on disaster management divides vulnerability into two categories: (a) disaster prevention, and (b) disaster response [12].

Thus, the definition that would be adapted in our case is the following: "Robustness corresponds to the ability of the organization to survive and stay under control by the emergence of new organizational patterns, keeping its most important or "vital" activities in continuity when a disruption of any given type occurs." [13].

Therefore, three types of robustness are distinguished:

a. "Absolute" robustness: total invariance to disturbances.
b. "Tolerated" robustness: variance within a robustness zone.
c. "Mastered" or "controlled" robustness: "Mastered" secondary functions are derived from the main invariant function [14].

The second type of robustness is where this research work is situated as the indicators designed within this paper measure the organization's capacity to deal with a "tolerated" disturbance and maintain its most important activities accordingly.

Through the interpretation of the ISO 22313:2020 [5], and as shown by Fig. 2. Below, the robustness of a BCP could be impacted by:

a. Physical layout of the organization: the organization's premises; its various offices, production units, administrative offices, storage facilities, etc.
b. Customers and staff satisfaction: the impact of the organization's services on satisfying the customers' and/or staff's needs and meeting their expectations.
c. Internal management of the staff and skilled workers: the management strategy deployed, the communication to the staff, their evaluation, dispatching, conflict resolution, etc.

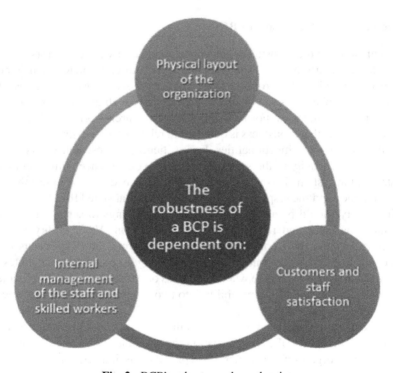

Fig. 2. BCP's robustness dependencies

3.3 The Proposed Evaluation Grid

Based on 2.1 and 2.2, a robustness assessment grid for business continuity plans has been developed. This grid allows a freedom of twelve degrees in order to place sociological indicators of robustness. It includes: (a) 3 repartition layers which represent the dependencies of the robustness of a BCP and (b) 4 improvement axes which consist of BCP main pillars: operation, policy, support and commitment. The Fig. 3. Below represents namely the evaluation grid and its composition.

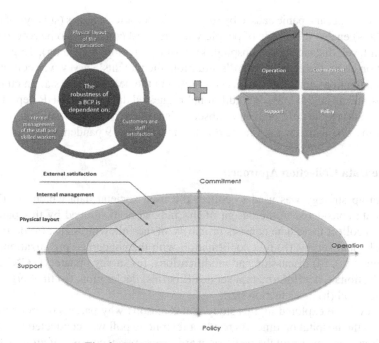

Fig. 3. The BCP robustness evaluation grid

4 Robustness Indicators Proposed from the Sociological Study of the Case Study

To test this research work's empirical proposal, a case study was considered. In the following paragraphs, we will start by introducing the case study and how the used data was collected. Afterwards, the calculation of the sociological robustness indicators will be explained which we will lead us to their definition and representation. In the following section, the classification of these indicators is detailed in order to justify the evaluation's grid usability and its interpretation in a real-life situation and a practical field.

4.1 Introduction to the Case Study

In fact, this implementation took place in a pediatric ward of a public middle-sized healthcare organization in a city with a population of around 50,000 people in the southwest of France. During the first wave of the COVID-19 pandemic, non-Covid-19 patients had limited access to health care [15]. This was the situation in France, particularly in our case study. As a result, a sociological survey was constructed and addressed to the patients. In the event of a pandemic (such as the COVID-19 pandemic), the hospital is compelled to manage a "crisis inside a crisis." It must understand the reasons for hospital worker and patient absences (renunciation of treatment). Individual and group human elements must be included in the business continuity plan, including the reasons for absence as well as collective mental representations of threat and risk (fear of being exposed to a viral threat, panic, and panic caused by rumors). Sociological studies (surveys of patients and workers) enable the profile of people who are most concerned to be recorded (age, education level, distance to the hospital, kind of occupation, and so on). To get further information about the pediatric ward's situation, the patients' survey was completed by some investigations and observations conducted in the health services as an ethnologist in the hospital as in [16] and some additional requested data from the HR department of the staff to survey the development of absenteeism in the pediatric ward before, during, and after the first lockdown in France due to the COVID-19 pandemic.

4.2   The Data Collection Approach

A bottom-up strategy was used to collect the used societal data which are the only type of data considered in the design of the indicators mentioned by this paper. The strategy to collect these data consists primarily of the following steps: (a) definition of the sociological survey, (b) first confirmation with the concerned organization, survey development (c), (d) discussion and modifications, (e) survey update, (f) CNIL (Commission Nationale de l'Informatique et des Libertés) declaration, (g) final organization acceptance, and (h) investigation start.

The key issue explored by this study is the reasons why parents do not bring their children to the hospital on time. As result, a telephone poll was conducted to interview the children's parents about the pediatric ward. This survey consists of around 44 items and was completed by 673 parents of children being treated by this department.

As a result, the parents' responses were recorded using LimeSurvey (a statistical survey and polling program) and then analyzed. In fact, the current study intends to extract certain essential data from the responses of the parents to the survey such as information reflecting their professional stability, life balance, age, distance to hospital, impression regarding the pediatric ward and so on. These essential figures are utilized in the calculation of the sociological indicators of the robustness of the BCP.

4.3   The Crisis Type

In our case, the study of the pediatric ward during the COVID-19 pandemic, the crisis the hospital is facing is actually an event-driven crisis and of a hyper-crisis form (see Fig. 4 for definition). In fact, the hyper-crises can be mostly external as a pandemic or a significant natural disaster such as the Icelandic volcano "Eyjafjallajökull" eruption in 2010 that lead to a cancellation of 95,000 flights and a US$1.7 billion loss for the airline industry [17]. Major crises can be mostly external as well but with less "worldwide" damage. As per the internal crises, they do basically happen within the firm and affect only its activity and stakeholders. From another perspective based on the occurrence of a crisis, crises can be either frequently occurrent on a daily-basis or related to a certain event such as a storm or a flood [18]. Given this explanation, the crisis that we are dealing with "the COVID-19" and that our case study "the pediatric ward" is facing is basically of an (event-driven; hyper-crisis) nature.

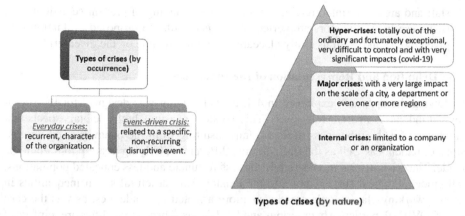

Fig. 4. Types of crises [18]

4.4 Explanation of the Basis for Calculating the Indicators

To obtain a final designed and tested version of the sociological robustness indicators regarding of the case study, several steps were followed:

a. ***Data clustering:*** It mainly consist of dividing the data into several categories, such as during the first lockdown and the same period in 2019, absence due to pandemic reasons and causes, socio-professional situation (level of education and nature of work: manager, employee, etc.), economic situation (monthly income, work situation: suspended, unemployed, etc.), professional situation during the first lockdown, and the parental residence.

b. ***Relevant plots representation:*** After the sociological data was separated, the necessary digitized responses were utilized to create certain essential graphs, such as displaying the dispatching of appointments during the first lockdown and the parents' refusal based on their employability status.

c. ***Key figures extractions:*** Some essential statistics were taken from multiple graphs and processing and put in a "Societal Performance Indicators (SPI) dashboard" so that these key figures may serve as the foundation of the β-version indicators calculation.

d. ***β-version indicators calculation:*** Some indicators were determined based on the retrieved important figures as mentioned above. The planned ratios essentially measure the cancellation of appointments during the first lockout, the parents' dropout rates for their children's appointments, the parents' satisfaction with the pediatric ward, and the rate of not attending appointments owing to COVID-19 dread. The ratios are all between 0 and 1, These metrics measure basically: (i) patient satisfaction, (ii) the frequency of interruptions (dropout rates, health effects, not attending appointments, etc.), and (iii) their influence.

e. ***Final γ-version indicators calculation:*** Based on the previous steps and the β-version indicators, the γ-version of the indicators was then designed and calculated. The difference consists basically of: (i) the final version indicators qualify and quantify accurately the pillars and factors explained in 3.1 and 3.2, (ii) the indicators assess the robustness of the BCP regarding the societal facet including both patients and the staff and are easily interpretable for the decision-making of preventive actions, and (iii) these final indicators are perfectly matched with the proposed evaluation grid given by 3.3 and are thus easily placeable and interpretable on the given grid.

4.5   Definition and Representation of the Indicators

Following the approach explained in 4.4, a final version was designed for the sociological indicators of BCP robustness. This version measures both societal aspects that are crucial for the robustness of these plans resulting from the behaviors and impressions of patients as well as the staff. To this, different underlying assumptions could be made. The crisis affects more strongly the less fortunate and less educated populations. All epidemiological surveys point to the existence of structural social inequalities in health: working-class people are always more affected by epidemics, as was the case with COVID19, particularly in serious and fatal forms. These inequalities are reinforced by the decrease in hospital credits. The fewer staff there are, the more important the social capital of the patients is. As a matter of fact, the more the patient belongs to a working-class environment, the less resources he or she has to get out of it on his or her own if the hospital is failing. The hospital therefore plays an essential role in protecting the most working-class environments [19]. Besides, in normal times the hospital staff is insufficient and is often absent because the working conditions are difficult. During the COVID-19 Crisis, the staff gets sick like everybody else, is exhausted because of the high demand on them and is afraid for themselves and their families because they are very exposed to illness and disease. While they are essential, they are potentially missing from the organization.

Therefore, the designed indicators ultimately measure: (a) the relative attendance of the staff (the attendance during the first lockdown period in France: 17/03/2020 to 11/05/2020, compared with the absence during the same period in 2019): the collective absence of the pediatric ward personnel was amplified by 6.25 between the first lockdown period in France and the same time the previous year, (b) the capacity of the pediatric ward, (c) the overall satisfaction rate of the patients' parents, (d) the patient's fear regarding the sanitary situation, (e) the service occupancy and (f) the attendance of the staff during the first lockdown period in France.

The Fig. 5, below illustrates these γ-version indicators, their definitions and formulas. It should be noted that TsppC, TipC, TrpcpC and TrppC are sociological robustness indicators resulting from the beta-version of this dashboard and which measure accordingly the **pediatric service parents' satisfaction rate** during the first lockdown, the **health impact rate of children in the pediatric ward** during the same period, the **rate of not attending appointments by fear of becoming infected with COVID-19** and **parent dropout rates for their children's appointments** during the first lockdown.

Once these indicators were calculated, we proceeded to calculate their values and to visualize them in a dashboard. The representation of these ratios is given by the Fig. 6. Below. To interpret these values and evaluate their influence on the robustness of the BCP, we conducted a placement of these indicators in the robustness evaluation grid explained in Sect. 1. In the following section, the classification of the indicators and their signification is treated.

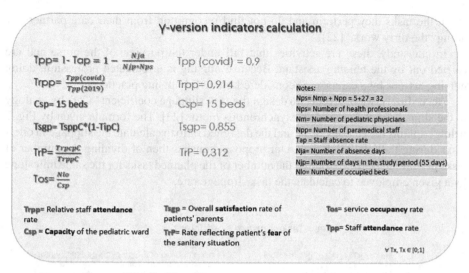

Fig. 5. The γ-version indicators calculation

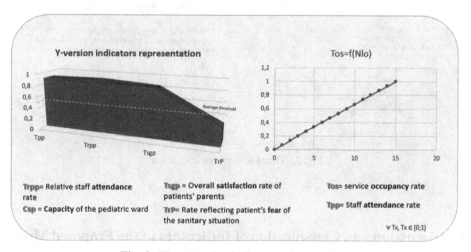

Fig. 6. The γ-version indicators representation

The Task Slippage Coefficient One more exceptional ratio was designed according to a key phenomenon in the sociology of organizations known as "Task Slippage".

In fact, task "slippage" or "shifting" is the performance of acts that are not related to the duties or rank of the performer [20, 21]. Task shifting therefore raises the issue of accountability, which does not seem to be addressed in the day-to-day work. There are several reasons for this: (a) cyclical reasons such as lack of personnel or an overload of work that results mostly into "occasional" task slippage, (b) structural reasons since the nursing profession is characteristically in the face of a staff shortage [20, 22] or (c) reasons linked to the strategies of the actors; the caregivers do not have a positive feeling about the tasks they perform and do not find recognition from their care partners by doing "the dirty work" [22].

In our study, these are activities that fall under the purview of the nurse and are carried out by the nursing assistant. Because nursing is a regulated profession, doing nursing actions by a caretaker is considered unlawful nursing practice.

Accordingly, we proceeded to design the task slippage coefficient "Cgt" by analogy to the slippage in the case of an asynchronous motor [23]. The formula given by Fig. 7 below explains the analogy made and the designed ratio to calculate the slippage in one's tasks during their daily job time. Our proposal consists then of dividing the number of tasks performed per milestone by the number of the planned tasks for the same milestone by a given employee to calculate the task slippage rate.

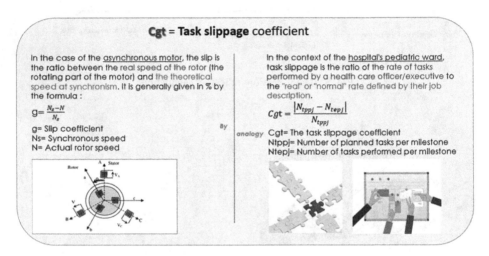

Fig. 7. The task slippage coefficient

5   Discussion and Classification of Indicators in the Proposed Model

5.1   The Classification of the Indicators in the Model

Once the sociological indicators were designed and formulated for measuring the robustness of a BCP, the process of their classification within the BCP robustness assessment grid explained in Sect. 2 was started.

The grid counts 3 layers namely physical layout, internal management and external satisfaction, and 4 axes namely operation, commitment, support and policy. As a result of this topology the evaluation grid counts 12 intersection points known as "classification patches".

These classification patches are the spots on which the sociological indicators are placed as shown by Fig. 8. Below. For example, the axis "Operation" holds the indicator representing the capacity of the pediatric ward "Csp" in between the physical layout and the internal management layers. Whereas the relative staff attendance rate "Trpp" is held by the commitment axis and located in between the internal management and the external satisfaction layers. To this, the following representation is written:

- Csp = OPL-IM = (Physical layout, Internal management) Operation
- Trpp = OIM-ES = (Internal management, External satisfaction) Commitment

Following the same approach, all of the indicators and the classification patches could be assigned and represented.

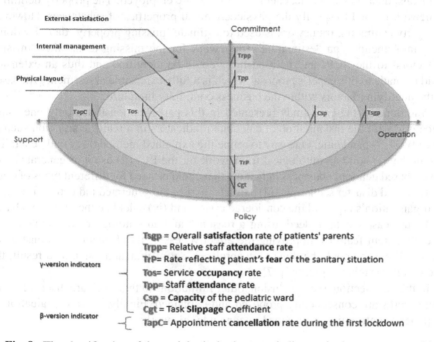

Fig. 8. The classification of the sociological robustness indicators in the assessment grid

5.2 Discussion of the Previous Findings

These indicators once calculated make the qualification of the robustness of the BCP feasible on the four different axes. Since these indicators are basically ratios between 0 and 1, an estimation of "how robust the pillar is" on a certain axis in a given zone can be easily made and thus this helps to adapt the business continuity strategy. So that it would be possible to "evaluate" or "qualify" the main factors of the BCP, the indicators assess these elements' quality. It is a measure of the "state" of a certain element, basically the four axes in the evaluation grid. The grading of organizational aspects represents an assessment of the impact that these factors have, either directly or indirectly, on the BCP, which are given by the three layers on the grid. This would also lead to think of an assessment tool for this evaluation grid itself in order to maintain its efficiency and guarantee a continuous self-improvement modality such as in [24].

Not to forget that the assessment tool suggested by this paper is completely extensible. For instance, it consists simply of 4 axes, 3 layers and thus 12 classification patches as explained previously but if other sub-factors to its design basis could be considered, these axes and layers would be increased and thus multiply the number of the classification patches and accordingly the indicators to design and to place. For example, the risk assessment and mapping framework suggested in [25], offers an extensible substance database that includes information on the structural and physicochemical properties of chemicals in order to define hazardous substances found in plant units. To identify chemicals, data such as name, chemical number are employed. The property definition framework is used to specify the physicochemical properties of substances. However, a property estimating framework is used to estimate 'missing property' data. By doing such; implementing an "estimating" framework for the missing data, other 'missing subfactors' to the BCPs and its robustness could be identified and thus an extension could be made to this paper's proposal which is a fully extensible assessment grid based on the qualifying factors within the business continuity literature.

Additionally, the case study presented in this paper demonstrates only one usage of the grid with the instantiation of calculated indicators in a real-life situation such as the COVID-19 pandemic. One way to refine the explained methodology and generalize it could be: (i) build an ontological framework for the BC, (ii) use it to generate some survey-based generic robustness indicators that could be used for different types of organizations and disaster scenarios, (iii) extract a part of the generated indicators following the organization's type and the considered crisis, and (iv) calculate the indicators based on the use case's data. Indeed, using a reasoner and an ontology could semantically generalize item features, improving the effectiveness of the decision tree constructed in [26]. The same could be done to generalize a set of indicators and, as a result, the potential threats they represent [27].

In the next section, the conclusion, other limitations to this work are discussed. The future works are consequently proposed and explained. Finally, an auto-evaluation of the paper's contribution is provided to conclude this work.

6   Conclusion

This research work proposes an assessment grid for the robustness of BCP and tests this proposal using sociological indicators designed following a societal data collection and interpretation approach. Whereas the proposal was tested considering one case study and its societal data, several other types of data can be used as well which will lead to other robustness indicators. In fact, not only societal data can be used and sociological indicators to assess the robustness of a BCP but rather other types of data (financial, technical, etc.) that we don't discuss in this paper.

Another limitation of this work and thus an improvement future work possibility is that the evaluation consists simply of 4 axes (operation, policy, commitment and support), 3 layers (physical layout, internal management and external satisfaction) and thus 12 classification patches but by considering the sub-factors of the robustness factors themselves and/or the sub-pillars of the BCP pillars theses axes and layers could massively increase and thus the classification patches would be multiplied. This would make it possible to assess the BCP robustness more precisely using more designed robustness indicators of different types (technical, financial, social networks, etc.) and following many subfactors.

At this point, this research work allows to evaluate the robustness of the BCPs based only on sociological indicators but proposes on the other hand, from the literature, an evaluation model valid for all types of indicators and which is particularly extensible by following the same tracks of its design. This gives the possibility to three future works: (a) the extension of the robustness evaluation grid of BCPs, (b) its verification using different types of data and therefore indicators such as technical, social networks, financial and so forth and (c) its application on a second use-case of a different nature.

References

1. Zhenmin, M.L.: World Economic Situation and Prospects (2021)
2. Corrales-Estrada, A.M., Gómez-Santos, L.L., Bernal-Torres, C.A., Rodriguez-López, J.E.: sustainability and resilience organizational capabilities to enhance business continuity management: a literature review. Sustainability **13**, 8196 (2021). https://doi.org/10.3390/su1315 8196
3. ISO 22300:2021(en), security and resilience — vocabulary. https://www.iso.org/obp/ui/#iso: std:iso:22300:ed-3:v1:en
4. Anderies, J.M., Folke, C., Walker, B., Ostrom, E.: Aligning key concepts for global change policy: robustness, resilience, and sustainability. Ecol. Soc. **18**(2) (2013)
5. ISO 22313:2020(en), security and resilience—business continuity management systems—guidance on the use of ISO 22301. https://www.iso.org/obp/ui/#iso:std:iso:22313:ed-2:v1:en
6. ISO 22301:2019(en), security and resilience—business continuity management systems—requirements. https://www.iso.org/obp/ui/#iso:std:iso:22301:ed-2:v1:en
7. Lindström, J., Samuelsson, S., Hägerfors, A.: Business continuity planning methodology. Disaster Prev. Manage. Int. J. **19**(2), 243–255 (2010). https://doi.org/10.1108/096535610110 38039
8. Bazerman, M.H., Moore, D.A.: Judgment in Managerial Decision Making, 7th edn. John Wiley & Sons, Hoboken (2009)
9. Øien, K.: A framework for the establishment of organizational risk indicators. Reliab. Eng. Syst. Saf. **74**(2), 147–167 (2001). https://doi.org/10.1016/s0951-8320(01)00068-0
10. Clément, A., et al.: Robustesse, résilience : une brève synthèse des définitions au travers d'une analyse structurée de la littérature. Presented at the mosim'18 - 12ème conférence internationale de modélisation, optimisation et simulation, p. 8, June 2018
11. Webb, P.: Coping with drought and food insecurity in Ethiopia. Disasters **17**(1), 33–47 (1993). https://doi.org/10.1111/j.1467-7717.1993.tb00486.x
12. Siegel, B., Jorgensen, L.: Vulnerability: a view from different disciplines. In: Social Protection Discussion Paper Series, vol. 115 (2001)
13. Wybo, J.-l.: The role of simulation exercises in the assessment of robustness and resilience of private or public organizations. In: Pasman, H.J., Kirillov, I.A., (eds.) Resilience of Cities to Terrorist and Other Threats, pp. 491–507. Springer, Dordrecht (2008). https://doi.org/10. 1007/978-1-4020-8489-8_23
14. Clément, A.: Proposition d'indicateurs de robustesse basés sur la prise en compte des risques afin d'évaluer les tournées de transport routier de marchandises. These de doctorat, ecole nationale des mines d'albi-carmaux (2019)

15. Negrini, S., et al.: Up to 2.2 million people experiencing disability suffer collateral damage each day of Covid-19 lockdown in Europe. Eur. J. Phys. Rehabil. Med. **56**(3), 361–365 (2020). https://doi.org/10.23736/s1973-9087.20.06361-3

16. Breton, D.: Anne vega, une ethnologue à l'hôpital. L'ambiguïté du quotidien infirmier. Paris, éditions des archives contemporaines, 2000, 213 p., réf., **25**(2), 179–180, (2001). https://doi.org/10.7202/000246ar

17. Lund, K.A., Benediktsson, K.: Inhabiting a risky earth: the eyjafjallajökull eruption in 2010 and its impacts (respond to this article at http://www.therai.org.uk/at/debate). Anthropol. Today **27**(1), 6–9 (2011). https://doi.org/10.1111/j.1467-8322.2011.00781.x

18. Pearson, C.M., Mitroff, I.I.: From crisis prone to crisis prepared: a framework for crisis management. **7**(1), 48–59 (1993). https://doi.org/10.5465/ame.1993.9409142058

19. Buchet-Molfessis, C.: glissements de tâches de l'infirmier vers l'aide-soignant: le lien entre la formation initiale et le positionnement des nouveaux diplômes. recherche en soins infirmiers **92**(1), 68–94 (2008). https://doi.org/10.3917/rsi.092.0068

20. Michaud, S.: les glissements de tâches des infirmiers vers les aides-soignants: quelle stratégie le directeur des soins peut-il adopter? (2004)

21. Sainsaulieu, I.: le malaise des soignants: le travail sous pression à l'hôpital. le malaise des soignants, pp. 1–238 (2004)

22. De Barros, F.: Anne-marie arborio, un personnel invisible. Les aides-soignantes à l'hôpital, paris, anthropos-economica, coll. Sociologiques, 2001, rééd. 2012, 334 p. Corps **14**(1), 177–180 (2016). https://doi.org/10.3917/corp1.014.0177

23. Fayyad, S., Al-Rawashdeh, M.O.: Factors affect slipping of automobiles. WSEAS Trans. Syst. Control **15**, June 2020. https://doi.org/10.37394/23203.2020.15.26

24. Caffyn, S.: Development of a continuous improvement self-assessment tool. Int. J. Oper. Prod. Manage. **19**(11), 1138–1153 (1999). https://doi.org/10.1108/01443579910291050

25. Girgin, S., Krausmann, E.: RAPID-N: Rapid natech risk assessment and mapping framework. J. Loss Prev. Process Ind. **26**(6), 949–960 (2013). https://doi.org/10.1016/j.jlp.2013.10.004

26. Bouza, A., Reif, G., Bernstein, A., Gall, H.: SemTree: ontology-based decision tree algorithm for recommender systems (2008). https://doi.org/10.5167/uzh-5392

27. Daniel L. Costa, M.L.C., Samuel J. Perl, M.J.A., George J. Silowash, D.L.S.: An ontology for insider threat indicators--development and applications. Carnegie-Mellon Univ Pittsburgh Pa Software Engineering Inst (2014)

Cybersecurity and Privacy

Cyber Security Policies in Crisis Response: Exploring the Predicament of Creating Safe But Workable Systems

Joshua Stassen(✉) ⓘ, Ali Pirannejad ⓘ, and Kenny Meesters ⓘ

Tilburg University, Tilburg 5037 AB, The Netherlands
Joshuastassen@gmail.com

Abstract. As societies become more connected, the nature and response to crises are becoming increasingly complex as well. Crises can affect our societies in unpredictable ways and thus require different actors to bring information together to take appropriate actions. However, as the number and diversity of actors increases, so does the quality and variety of information systems. Especially considering the increased availability and accessibility of technologies available together, process and exchange information.

While these developments provide a high potential to improved information sharing, these options also present certain risks. Individual organizations may have measures, training, and policies in place for daily routines to mitigate these risks. During a crisis however, these measures can become a constraint, especially when sharing information in an inter-organizational and cross-boundary context. People in the crisis response team may not appreciate the risks, need to improvise, or even circumvent measures.

In this paper, we examine the increased cybersecurity risks associated with the increased use of information technologies used in and facilitating information management during a crisis response. Using a serious gaming research method we examine how, in the context of crisis response, these factors are exacerbated under the pressure of time, uncertainty and coordination challenges. From this we identify the need for increased awareness about the risks of information technologies and sharing in heterogenous stakeholder environments. Specifically, a cultural change and need for additional capacities to understand, assess, and mitigate risks involved as the number of actors, systems, and technological options keep increasing.

Keywords: Cybersecurity behavior · compliance · disaster information security management

1   Introduction

With the world as connected as today, the increasing number of crises is becoming more complex. COVID-19 caused logistical disruptions and the war in Ukraine causes price surges around the world. What a crisis is, is not so clear anymore. Due to the larger

© IFIP International Federation for Information Processing 2023
Published by Springer Nature Switzerland AG 2023
T. Gjøsæter et al. (Eds.): ITDRR 2022, IFIP AICT 672, pp. 215–229, 2023.
https://doi.org/10.1007/978-3-031-34207-3_14

group of actors involved, information is shared more frequently. Luckily, there are more tools available and there is better access towards these tools. The combination of these two trends will translate to a cooperation landscape consisting of many different actors bringing their equally different systems with them. This creates the perfect storm for cybersecurity issues. The time pressure, heterogeneity of systems and the lack of IT skills (mainly in IT risk management) that exists in crises creates an unsafe environment. At the same time, large parts of our society have become dependent on technological possibilities, companies, communities, and individual citizens. This also applies to emergency response agencies which are increasingly embracing technology to support their operations, decision-making and analysis activities. However, especially in such vital sectors, this dependency not only carries the same risks but also an increased possibility of errors because working under pressure. During the COVID-19 pandemic, attacks have been launched on governmental agencies or directly at users to disrupt essential services, steal information or seek to spread fear during the pandemic [1]. The biggest vulnerability of these systems primarily lies with the humans interacting with those systems. Most of the time, human error is the root cause of the hack [3]. Humans pose a high risk, whether this is through malicious intent or human error. There is a lack of cybersecurity understanding amongst responders. While responders are thought to prioritize their own safety and have a great understanding of how their tools function, this is not the case for IT. Especially amongst emergency responders coming from different backgrounds. If emergency responders don't know how to use their 'virtual firehose', how should these responders safely provide support during a crisis? And more important, what is stopping us from translating the same physical response reasoning to the digital response environment?

To understand this problem, it is critical to understand how people act during a crisis. In short, disasters, systems and humans are dependent on each other. Humans interact with systems, which increases not only the risks from a technical and human perspective, but also from the increased pressure that the systems and humans operate under, and their vitality in critical operations. Disasters create pressure with a high cognitive load, which incentives problematic cybersecurity behavior by humans. These factors combined can potentially even create a disaster within a disaster. In the heat of a response saving lives could be deemed more important than compliance, jeopardizing valuable information or systems. Disasters create pressure, which incentives problematic cybersecurity behavior by humans. To solve this, systems can be made very strict, but this comes at a cost of flexibility during a disaster. This inflexibility can be problematic for the ability to deal with large multidisciplinary crises like COVID-19. Flexibility is needed for future uncertain and unknown situations.

This dilemma between compliance and pressure is the focus of this paper. The following research questions are answered by this study: 'What are key characteristics of disasters and how do these characteristics influence behavior?', 'When do people start to show non-compliant behavior with their organizations cyber policy?' and 'What variables contribute to this non-compliance behavior?'. By examining the influences on compliance rates, cybersecurity in natural disasters can improve. The paper will focus on human behavior, which will show what the actual cyber risks are and provide important mitigation starting points.

2 Theoretical Background

2.1 Data Security

To measure data security, information security practitioners turn to the CIA triad. The triad consists of the terms confidentiality, integrity and availability [2, 4]. The definitions of the CIA triad are the following:

1. Unauthorized information release. An unauthorized person can read and take advantage of stored information. Unauthorized access also extends to the unauthorized usage of programs. This access to information has become the notion of confidentiality. Confidentiality refers to the preservation of authorized information access and disclosure restrictions, including means for protecting personal privacy and proprietary information.
2. Unauthorized information modification. An unauthorized person can make changes to the information that is stored. This improper information modification or destruction has become the notion of Integrity.
3. Unauthorized denial of use. An intruder can prevent a user from referring to or modifying information, becoming the notion of availability. Availability entails ensuring timely and reliable access to and the use of information.

The CIA triad provides a basic framework to establish insecure behavior. This means that in the context of the rest of the study, insecure behavior refers to a breach in confidentiality, integrity, or availability.

2.2 Compliance

But what have factors like timeliness, accessibility, load, and coordination have to do with compliance rates? In a cybersecurity context, employees tend to be influenced by the perceived costs of being compliant. These are 'costs', for example, in terms of investing extra time and effort. According to the Rational Choice Theory (RCT) employees who view compliant behavior as too costly tend to be non-compliance [5]. This is strengthened by an individual's reaction to threats. If threat appraisal by individual results in a low sense of severity and vulnerability, the individual will be inclined not to follow the policy. Weighing the perceived severity of non-compliant behavior against the 'ease of use', the Protection Motivation Theory (PMT) and Theory of Planned Behavior (TPB) state that if an employee perceives the ability to complete the security task, enjoys a positive attitude towards the security task and observes other people also actively performing the task, the employee will be likely to comply and thus can result in actual compliance [6, 7]. What does this mean in a disaster context? There is little thought of cybersecurity measures, because of the costs in time or inflexibility. Think of databases in Excel that are sent to responders but can be uncontrollably forwarded to other people. Sharing information may be beneficial to the relief effort, but a possible breach of confidentiality or integrity may pose problems. Situations were cybersecurity protocols dramatically decrease the usability through for example time costs, will trigger non-compliant behavior by the individuals interacting with the systems. The same protocols meant for security, could make an application through displayed behavior by individuals more insecure.

So, if these costs are too high, it will lead to shadow security. Shadow security can be seen as employees not complying with prescribed policies but create a more suitable alternative to the policies suggested by the organization's official security functions [8]. There are two ineffective scenarios of cyber security: 'It is impossible to comply with the set policy and get the work done' and 'current policies are irrelevant and burdensome' [9]. Both scenarios have these elements of burdensome security implementations. Perceptions of disproportionate impact upon the ability to proceed led employees to procure their own less demanding and disruptive solutions to support (in what the employees perceived as more proportionate) security behavior. There are four forms of security burdens [9]:

- Time. Time-related problems occurred in situations where employees followed the prescribed security behavior (which resulted in slower completion).
- Lack of adaptability. A lack of adaptability in IT systems to account for the changing organizational conditions. This lack of adaptability creates disruptive problems, for example, employees that did not have timely access to information necessary for their role.
- Increased cognitive load. Employees devised their own security mechanisms when the organization's password policy caused excessive cognitive load for the employees. Many felt the need to physically write down the passwords, especially for the system's accounts that rarely were used. There are five password management behaviors: (1) choosing a password for the first time, (2) changing a password, (3) letting someone else use your password, (4) taping passwords next to the computer and (5) sharing passwords with family, friends, or co-workers [10]. While the first two behaviors are neutral, the subsequent three are negative actions. One reason is that memorizing randomized and temporary passwords are problematic and inconvenient for employees [11]. The perceived inconvenience prompts workarounds like simpler passwords and writing passwords down.
- Disruption. Security restrictions could lead to situations wherein security mechanisms were blocking the tasks that needed to be done.

However, coordination can also cause disruption. As already seen in the previous section, natural disasters will involve multiple parties providing aid. Data sharing can be vital, but any organization that shares and manages the shared data must comply to one set of rules. To have every organization on the same page can be very difficult. When comparing EU, NATO, and national cybersecurity strategies, countries have different amounts of principles and there was not one single match between national policy and the EU or NATO cyber strategies [12]. This again can lead to shadow security. If cooperation between multiple parties is needed, clashes in policy can cause an impossibility for employees to comply. Employees will then make their 'own policy', caused by a lack of adaptability or disruption [9]. Translating this to natural disasters, organizations may not be allowed to share crucial information with each other or are going to be non-compliant, sharing the information in an insecure manner anyway to provide aid. Furthermore, poor intergroup coordination and communication can be problematic as well. This happens when high-level managers and low-level employees do not understand how one's behavior may influence the other [13]. Think of systems that require online connections, but the location where responders work doesn't have any internet access. This understanding of influencing behavior may lead to high-level managers not understanding the practical implications of specific policies, which can lead to shadow security practices.

2.3 Crisis Management

As already stated, information is crucial to combat disasters effectively. Without accurate and timely information, aid might be targeting the wrong areas, providing the wrong items, and being delayed [14]. Therefore, systems have functional requirements that describe their functions needed during natural disasters. These requirements consist of the following [15]:

- Relevance: the degree to which information matches the actors' intended use
- Timeliness: the degree to which received information is up to date
- Accessibility: the degree to which information is provided so that it easily can be used by the actor (this includes interoperability)
- Reliability: the degree to which the actor justifies information
- Verifiability: the degree to which there are the means to verify the information by the actor
- Load: the degree of cognitive load associated with the information

These requirements overlap with the earlier mentioned security burdens. Time and cognitive load are linked directly. Lack of adaptability and accessibility result in disruption, therefore these can be considered as disruption.

The coordination of humanitarian organizations is characterized by fragmentation. The inter-organizational differences in systems or standards strengthen this disconnect, which can hamper coordination and planning [16]. These differences could give way to the spontaneous and unstructured setup of coordination structures driven by individual leadership rather than organizational mandates and norms [17]. Own setups in a cyber context could lead to policy violations. This phenomenon has overlap with poor inter-group coordination and communication [13]. The deviation from organization mandates and norms can point to high-level managers and low-level employees do not understand how one's behavior may influence the other. There may not be an understanding of the practical implications of specific policies, which can lead to shadow security practices.

Furthermore, many different teams and parties are working together during disasters [15, 16]. It is highly likely that there are differences in policies and standards in cybersecurity policy that can lead to shadow security.

3   Research Method

This paper uses a qualitative methodology to explore what variables are relevant and what relationships do exist. The data should provide more information on the dilemma that is created due to the pressure. How do participants behave? What variables influence the decision-making of the participants? To apply this pressure a serious game was used. The serious game helps to mimic the environment of a natural disaster and aims to see when participants stop complying with the policy [18]. Decision-making in disaster risk management is not always a smooth or rational process but can be very dynamic and complex. Stakeholders have different interests, responsibilities, and opinions on managing the crisis. High-stress levels, uncertainty, time pressure, coordination and communication problems influence the decision-making process to make it even more complex [18]. The gamification in the serious game will enable the pressure, in the form of the earlier mentioned variables in the literature, on participants and help better understand the 'performance' of individuals' behavior. Comparing this to surveys, interviews or focus groups, the unique characteristic of serious games is addressing the complexity between a technical and physical environment (f.e. interactions between systems and the results) and the social-political complexity (the interactions between the various stakeholders) [19]. The participants are able the interact with these different complexities. Within the game setting, participants can explore behavior without real-life consequences. These games or simulations offer rule-biding, which limits the options participants have and makes the game playable. An option can be created by the allocated time or specific allocated paths, making it easy for serious games and simulations to mirror critical characteristics of a specific disaster [20]. The serious game can mirror concepts like time, cognitive load, disruption, and coordination. The serious game is a viable method for cases where socially desirable answers are likely [21] and looking at people's behavior.

3.1 Target Audience

For the target audience, there are some specifics. One group will consist of people who experience high-stress levels in their jobs, to mimic actual responders. Think of firefighters, police, and ambulance personnel. The same study was conducted with 'non-responders' to see if professionals trained in these crises make different choices than regular non-trained people. People with an IT background were ruled out of the study because of their possible expertise with the subject. For people who work on IT subjects, their prior knowledge will likely influence daily. The game scenario is designed so that both groups find it recognizable. The responders were targeted by using both a judgement and snowball sampling method. The first group was chosen based on their experience. Afterwards, the responders were asked to share this with colleagues. Furthermore, the non-responders were targeted via convenience sampling.

3.2 Design

There are two versions of the same game: one with the variables time stress, high cognitive load, disruption, and coordination and one without these variables. The first version will mimic the manipulation of the variables. For this study, a between-subjects design was used. Participants were randomly assigned to either the control group or the treatment group. After the participants were done with the game, a questionnaire was prompted to ask the participants' reasons. The questions in the questionnaire will link back to the answer that participants provided.

Although the situations are fictional, all are based on real-life examples, the literature review or situations discussed in the expert interviews. Third parties are not mentioned by country or name to prevent biases towards the country or name from influencing the game's outcomes. The following will be a brief rundown of the game with the reasoning behind the situations. Before starting the game, participants will be asked if they frequently work with stressful situations, like emergencies. Every 'yes' response will be directed to the treatment group. Every 'no' response will then be randomly directed to either the treatment or control group. The software ensures an even distribution of 'non-stress' participants between the treatment and control groups. The game starts with a prompt that a giant tsunami has hit a fictional island and that it is the participant's task to alleviate the suffering and save lives. The experts during the interviews stated that awareness and preparation could be used to mitigate the effects of time pressure, cognitive load, and disruption. The control group will receive additional information to mimic an awareness training or to reduce the complexity of the dilemma due to the mimicked better preparation. Every scenario has two options resembling compliance and non-compliance. A potential breach of confidentiality, integrity or availability will be seen as non-compliant behavior. The order of these answers is also randomized.

Dilemmas Presented in the Serious Game
Dilemma one deals with the potential flooding of dikes, based on the Europe floods of July 2021 [22]. This situation deals with time and disruption (as well as coordination). A foreign officer offers to fortify the dykes and asks for access to the control systems. However, the control group is alerted to the fact that it is unknown if the officer can be trusted and if given access, there is a risk that the officer, in a later stage, floods the country by opening the dikes.

Dilemma two deals with a junior responder who wants to access information through the participants' accounts. The notion of sharing accounts is based on an expert story of sharing printer access through one account. The responder needs the data now, or she cannot operate. This scenario resembles the time pressure and disruptive effects. The control group will be told that account sharing could lead to hacks, data modification or theft under their name.

Dilemma three applies a cognitive load on the participant. The treatment group will be given a complex randomized password, while the control group will receive a passphrase, which is easier to remember. This scenario is based that people have cognitive difficulty remembering complex passwords. Furthermore, an expert stated that passphrases should be used to make passwords easier to remember.

Dilemma four resembles a disruptive effect through coordination. The experts were asked the same question. The lack of cyber policy in the humanitarian sector and security culture differences were discussed during the interviews. This information formed the basis for this scenario where participants had to decide if data would be shared with an NGO with a low cyber policy.

One of the experts mentioned sleeping, dining, bathroom problems, and fatigue in the interviews. The expert also talked about situations where data is quickly shared by email without thinking of repercussions in confidentiality. The fifth dilemma is created based on this cognitive load. The participant will be told that there are a lot of different data sources and that the participant is fatigued. A responder needs data and offers to help by just emailing it. The control group is notified that this will cause a confidentiality breach.

The last dilemma is based on operating in conflict territories, like Ukraine and working with ISIS. The local authorities want to have all information on a displaced minority. The control group will be told that the data contains incriminating information on the minority and that the local authority is against this minority.

3.3 Pre-test

The pre-test was conducted with six people. Each tester played the game multiple times. In total, the game was played 16 times. The test showed that the logical flow of the game was broken with some questions. For example, the participant received both behavioral questions of question 5, while they should only receive the one that belongs to the chosen answer. This logic error is fixed in the final build of the serious game. Furthermore, the behavioral questions in the pre-test only asked why a participant chose a specific answer. However, this resulted in answers unrelated to the variables used, like time pressure. The updated behavioral questions had two questions per answer: Why did a participant select a particular answer and did the treatment variables affect the decision? The testers also found some grammatical errors, which were corrected in the final version. The answers originally contained progression points, which resemble a specific number of saved lives by performing that specific action. The testers felt that there were real dilemmas in each scenario. The testers also reported a noticeable difference between the treatment and control scenarios, reporting that the control scenarios were easier to answer due to the training and preparation ques. The progression points made the decision-making harder for the participants. However, there was a fear that participants would select answers based on the higher amount of progression points. Therefore, the decision was made to remove the progression points within the answers.

3.4 Expert Interview Process

To validate the findings from the literature review and serious game, a panel of experts was interviewed. These interviews helped to understand if the literature findings were plausible in the context of natural disasters while also providing more context concerning the variables. The experts were selected based on their knowledge of cybersecurity, disaster management or both. Cybersecurity experts needed to be at least five years active in cybersecurity, with links to societal projects. These include governmental, humanitarian, or military projects. The experts with a disaster management background should have been involved in two disaster responses (from 2010 onwards). IT professionals in the humanitarian field should have a clear link to cybersecurity (for example, writing papers on the topic). One recent or one current disaster response will be a minimum to qualify for the expert interviews of this study. Table 1 shows an overview of all the interviewed experts for this study.

The interview process was conducted five times. Because the qualitative methodology is used to explore variables and relationships, a semi-structured approach was used to ask the questions in a structured manner to validate the literature findings. In addition, the semi-structured approach enabled flexibility so that if statements were made, the expert could elaborate more on this statement. After each interview, the process was stopped, and the transcript was reviewed. If needed, the question sheet was altered to

Table 1. Overview interviewed experts

Expert	Job function	Experience
E1	Researcher and lecturer at a Dutch university	Cybersecurity lecturer with a background in IT audit (> 5 years in current role at this Dutch university) and conducted several studies on governmental IT-projects
E2	Digital Services, Information Management Branch at UN OCHA	Former Information Management Officer of UN OCHA. Former deployments to Haiti earthquake, Nepal earthquake of Philippines floods. Involved in the writing of papers dealing with cybersecurity in the humanitarian sector
E3	Disaster Management Consultant	Twenty-five years of experience in the development and humanitarian sector. Most of this time as a former UN staffer. Nowadays, predominantly working with UN agencies in evaluations, training, and capacity strengthening of national NGOs
E4	COO at cybersecurity NGO for the humanitarian sector	Cybersecurity Department of the French government (cyber crisis simulations and bilateral relations). Cyber response activities for European cybersecurity agency and World Economic Forum
E5	Head cybersecurity at NATO Support and Procurement Agency	Organization and security guidance for humanitarian or military flights. Former cybersecurity of Supreme Headquarters Allied Powers Europe (NATO)

provide additional questions concerning the expert's expertise (f.e. additional questions concerning disaster responses or military behavior) or to switch the order of questions. All questions dealing with conceptual model validation were asked in every interview. After the last interview, a saturation point was reached due to the similar answers by the experts. Furthermore, the literature suggests that five to fifteen interviews can reach saturation points [23]. Moreover, these types of cyber specialists in the humanitarian sector are hard to find. An explanation for this could be that cybersecurity is relatively novel in the humanitarian sector, as stated by one of the interviewees. The interviews were conducted either in person or via Zoom.

4   Results

There were 82 respondents in total for the game. It was decided to make three even groups of 20 respondents to compare all three groups with each other. Responses with missing or low-quality answers to the questions were deleted to get to 20 per group. However, close attention was paid to the differences between the groups to prevent influencing the results. The three groups are referred to as T1: No Stress (Treatment group 1 with no stressful jobs), T2: Stress (Treatment group 2 with stressful jobs) and C1: Control (the control group). Respondents found the game 'difficult to solve' since its participants had to make a choice that felt wrong (in terms of cybersecurity) but was necessary to save the lives. According to the respondents the game provided them with a real dilemma from time to time. All results can be found in Table 2 on page 12.

Dilemma One.   The participants received information about an officer of a foreign army who requested access to the control systems of the dykes to help fortify these dykes. The stress group (18) and no stress group (17) choose the non-compliance option and possibly breach integrity or availability notions. The most important reason for people to give the officer access to the system was that lives were hanging in the balance, so the response had to be quick, and the foreign army otherwise could not help. The participants confirmed that time and disruption greatly influenced the decision-making. As seen in Table 2, the control group mostly opted for the option of non-compliance. The participants mentioned an important reason: Trust. Because an officer asks for the controls, the participants deem this officer trustworthy—more on this in Sect. 5 discussion.

Dilemma Two.   A junior responder asked to borrow the participants' accounts to receive the data for the search and rescue grids. The no-stress group had an even split in non-compliance and compliance. The main reason for non-compliance was to save lives quickly because of the time pressure. Non-compliant behaviour resulted in a breach of confidentiality. Participants also noted that time pressure and disruption would be reasons to give the responder access. The stress group is with 14 answers more in favour of compliance. According to the participants, the responders' supervisor should resolve the authorisation problem. In the control group, 13 participants choose compliance. Although there is a compliance shift compared to the no-stress treatment group, this difference is insignificant (sig. $=0.400$).

Dilemma Three.   Respondents were asked if they would remember the password or write it down. The treatment groups received complex randomized passwords, while the control group received a passphrase. The no stress and stress treatment group had 19 and 17 participants who selected non-compliance, causing confidentiality and integrity concerns. The main reason was that people found the password too tricky to remember. The control group, however, had 17 participants choosing the compliance option. The reasoning behind this choice was that the password was easy to remember. There is a significant (sig. <0.001) difference between the groups.

Dilemma Four.   Participants received the same question as the experts did. The participants belong to an organization with high cybersecurity standards, while the approaching NGO has low cybersecurity standards. Table 2 shows that no stress and stress have similar results. Of the participants, 14 choose to comply with the policy and not give the NGO access. *'The NGO is not suited to handle the data securely and is in conflict with the culture of the own organization'* was one of the primary reasons participants complied with the policy. Within the control group, 18 participants choose the option of compliance. After comparing these numbers and running the tests, the results were that these were not significant differences (sig. =0.225).

Dilemma Five. The participants were confronted with a high cognitive load due to simulated information overload and fatigue. Within the no stress group, seven participants were non-compliant, and 13 were compliant. This result is different from the stress group, where 16 participants were compliant and four non-compliant. The provided non-compliant participants stated that the time pressure of saving lives and the information load influenced the decision. The control group had similar results in comparison to the stress treatment group. In the compliance group, participants noted that when people are tired, the possibility for mistakes is higher. Also, participants assumed that the data was confidential.

Dilemma Six. Participants were asked if the participants were inclined to share data about a minority group with the local authorities in order for the local authorities to speed up the process of returning the minority group to home. Table 2 shows that the no-stress treatment group mostly choose to share the data and be non-compliant. 16 of the 20 participants choose this option. The main reason for the participants was that otherwise, the local government was not able to help, and in this way, the process would go a lot faster. There was a little shift compared to the stress group, where 13 participants chose non-compliance. In the control group, 12 participants chose compliance and not to share any data with the local authorities. This difference between the treatment and control groups is significant (sig. =0.032) and shows how different behavior can impact the confidentiality of data.

Table 2. Results serious game.

	1. Granting access to foreign army officer		2. Junior responder asking for account details		3. Memorization of passwords		4. Coordination with NGO		5. Fatigued with an email request for data		6. Local authorities requesting information on minority	
	Non-compliance	Compliance	Non-compliance	Compliance	Non-compliance	Compliance	Non-compliance	Compliance	Non-compliance	Compliance	Non-compliance	Compliance
T1	17	3	10	10	19	1	6	14	7	13	16	4
T2	18	2	6	14	17	3	6	14	4	16	13	7
C1	16	4	7	13	3	17	2	18	4	16	8	12

5 Discussion

5.1 Dilemmas

This study aimed to find the variables that influence compliance rates of cyber policies. It is important to understand what contributes to insecure cyber behavior to resolve it successfully. Throughout the game, it became apparent that people took shortcuts to save lives. When lives are at stake, people take shortcuts or use alternative approaches to save these lives. In the first question, participants were willing to give an officer of a foreign army access to the control systems of the dykes. The main reason for this was the immediate time pressure to save lives and the fact that the foreign army could not help otherwise. In other words, disruption. The same goes for the last question, where participants were asked to share data about a minority with local authorities. Under time pressure and disruption, the treatment group shared the data with the local authorities because of this time pressure or disruptive effects. This is in line with the conducted expert interviews, which all stated that time pressure and disruptive effects could have a negative impact on compliance rates. Cognitive load influenced respondents to write down passwords and experts stated that mental fatigue can be problematic for compliance.

5.2 Culture

With technology becoming so important, it is time to take cybersecurity seriously. Fire-fighters are trained to use their equipment safely. Medical personnel will operate with an eye for hygiene and safety for their own health. It is time to teach responders the right hygiene and safety protocols for the systems that help during disaster responses. Instead of considering humans as the biggest threat, it is necessary to make them our biggest resources. Responders should be educated, which enables them to operate on 'auto-pilot' and recognize risks. Cyber awareness training is not the silver bullet in cyber defense as sometimes thought. The game showed that the intent to save life can take priority over data security. Awareness is useful for understanding but will not solve all our problems. Furthermore, we should reconsider our way of designing systems. It is often implied that more security causes less efficiency, that there is a trade-off. Cybersecurity professionals should work together with responders to design systems in a way that a system is secure and efficient. Tight systems may increase security but will hinder crisis responses or incentivize shadow security which places cyber vulnerabilities in our blind spot. Solutions also must be flexible and adaptable. Preparing for multiple scenarios for information sharing could help in the operational context of a disaster which can be different by the day. Besides a changing crisis context, the world of IT changes as well. Over time new systems and tools arise. As well as cooperation with different partners, which means different systems and different policies. Removing the responsibility from individual responders will make systems less flexible. Individual decision-making helps in complex situations but may open the door the cyber threats if training is done incorrectly. Using technology as a tool in disaster responses should be done responsibly with the right competences and skills for the users. In this way, user-centric systems can be created with all the possible scenarios in mind.

5.3 Serious Game

The serious game itself also helped the participants to understand more about the cyber-security problem at hand. Participants found the dilemmas '*difficult to answer*' and felt that they had '*to do something of which you knew it was not right (in terms of cyber-security) but had to in order to save lives*'. The participants started to think about the dilemmas and their possible solutions to the problem. A serious game can be a great starting point to create more awareness on the topic and help start a conservation about it. As confirmed by the experts, running through these scenarios also will help recognize problems in cyber policy and enable to find suitable solutions.

6   Conclusion

The serious game itself will function as a method for detecting behavioral problems concerning compliance. The serious game also helps create a discussion about the topic and scenarios at hand. We must be aware of the dependence on technology in our most vulnerable moments and be aware of our responsibilities to prevent it.

This study added cyber risks to the literature. Cyber risks are often looked at from a technical point of view, but this study adds to the human side of cyber risks. It shows what situations like natural disasters can do to compliance rates. Besides the influences of time, cognitive load and disruption, the notion of coordination was reasonably unexplored. This study managed to bridge the gap and showed how these variables influence data security through compliance. Besides the earlier-mentioned variables, the study also managed to identify another interesting variable that can influence compliance: Trust. This contribution can be a great starting point for further academic research into this topic.

We see more technology possibilities emerge. Our organizations, societies and technologies become more intertwined and mutually dependent, and we see the emergence of risks and vulnerabilities in our societies, it is an important subject to consider. Not just for (formal) emergency responders, but for any organizations, community or agency who may find themselves in a complex emergency situation (and we increasingly see this: floods, COVID-19, Ukraine).

Above all, this study functions as a call to action. It makes clear that organizations might have to rethink how their security protocols are designed. Current protocols could lead to shadow security and be a burden to many responders in the field.

6.1   Limitations and Future Research

The study contains limitations because of the decision-making in the execution of this study. The serious game contained a question concerning cognitive load. However, it appears that cognitive load was not triggered correctly. There is a good reason for this. The question deals with sleep deprivation and information overload. However, participants could play the game from the comfort of their own homes. This comfort situation most likely did not prime the treatment of cognitive load enough for the participants to feel the pressure. Trust also influences participants' cost perception in the first question, neutralizing the 'awareness training' provided. Trust also was found in the last question. The lack of trust was the primary reason for compliance. Besides, cognitive load and trust, it is likely that there are more violations of cyber policy in real-life cases. People are not consciously thinking of compliance. People are thinking about the time pressure, disruption, the saving of lives and other things. A real-life test or real-life observation could help unveil more employee behaviors. Therefore, further research in a real-life setting should provide more information on cognitive load, trust, and other possible variables.

Another limitation of this study is the point of view of the experts. Mainly the cybersecurity point of view from a humanitarian organization. As seen in the study, there are more stakeholders. It could be interesting to explore that same problem from a policymaker's or citizens point of view. Policymakers have different objectives and spending money on possible futures can be hard to justify, while regular citizens deal differently with cybersecurity during disasters. Further research needs to be conducted to gain more information on different perspectives.

Lastly, future research could be conducted into the effectiveness of mentioned mitigation methods. For example, how much influence does awareness have when people are under time pressure? Or what kind of an effect does training have? One of the experts mentioned that lack of time for training was an issue. So further research could investigate the most effective ways of training.

References

1. Hakak, S., Khan, W., Imran, M., Choo, K.: Have you been a victim of COVID-19-related cyber incidents? Survey, taxonomy and mitigation strategies. IEEE Access **8**, 124134–124144 (2020)
2. Samonas, S., Coss, D.: The CIA strikes back: redefining confidentiality, integrity and availability in security. J. Inf. Syst. Secur. 10(3) (2014)
3. IBM: Cyber Security Intelligence Index (2014). Retrieved from IBM security services: https://i.crn.com/sites/default/files/ckfinderimages/userfiles/images/crn/custom/IBM SecurityServices2014.PDF
4. Anderson, J.: Computer security technology planning study (1972)
5. Khatib, R., Barki, H.: How different rewards tend to influence employee non-compliance with information security policies. Inf. Comput. Secur. **30**, 97–116 (2021)
6. Vance, A., Siponen, M., Pahnila, S.: Motivating IS security compliance: insights from habit and protection motivation theory. Inf. Manage. **49**(3–4), 190–198 (2012)
7. Pham, H., Brennan, L., Richardson, J.: Review of behavioural theories in security compliance and research challenge. In: Informating Science and Information Technology Education Conference, pp. 65–76 (2017)
8. Ertan, A., Crossland, G., Health, C., Denny, D., Jensen, R.: Everyday Cyber Security in Organisations (2020)
9. Kirlappos, I., Parkin, S., Sasse, M.: Learning from "shadow security": why understanding non-compliance provides the basis for effective security (2014)
10. Tam, L., Glassman, M., Vandenwauver, M.: The psychology of password management: a tradeoff between security and convenience. Behav. Inf. Technol. **29**(3), 233–244 (2010)
11. Tari, F., Ozok, A., Holden, S.: A comparison of perceived and real shoulder-surfing risks between alphanumeric and graphical passwords. In: Proceedings of the Second Symposium on Usable Privacy and Security, pp. 56–66. ACM (2006)
12. Stitilis, D., Pakutinskas, P., Malinauskaite, I.: EU and NATO cybersecurity strategies and national cyber security strategies: a comparative analysis. Secur. J. **30**(4), 1151–1168 (2017)
13. Albrechtsen, E., Hovden, J.: The information security digital divide between information security managers and users. Comput. Secur. **28**(6), 476–490 (2009)
14. Van de Walle, B., Turoff, M.: Emergency reponse information systems: emerging trends and technologies. Commun. ACM **50**(3), 29–31 (2007)
15. Nespeca, V., Comes, T., Meesters, K., Brazier, T.: Towards coordinated self-organization: an actor-centered framework for the design of disaster management information systems. Int. J. Disaster Risk Reduction **51**, 101887 (2020)

16. Comes, T., Van de Walle, B., Van Wassenhove, L.: The coordination-information bubble in humanitarian response: theoretical foundations and empirical investigations. Prod. Oper. Manag. **29**(11), 2484–2507 (2020)

17. Darcy, J., Stobaugh, H., Walker, P., Maxwell, D.: The use of evidence in humanitarian decision making. ACAPS Operational Learning Paper (2013)

18. Solinska Nowak, A., et al.: An overview of serious games for disaster risk management – prospects and limitations for informing actions to arrest increasing risk. Int. J. Disaster Risk Reduction **31**, 1013–1029 (2018)

19. Mayer, I.: The gaming of policy and the politics of gaming: a review. Simul. Gaming **40**(6), 825–862 (2009)

20. Meesters, K., Olthof, I., Van de Walle, B.: Disaster in my backyard: a serious game to improve community disaster resilience. In: Proceedings of the European Conference on Games Based Learning, vol. 2, pp. 714–722 (2014)

21. Grimm, P.: Social desirability bias. Wiley International Encyclopedia of Marketing (2010)

22. United Nations: 2021 floods: UN researchers aim to better prepare for climate risks (2022). Retrieved from unric: https://unric.org/en/2021-floods-un-researchers-aim-to-better-prepare-for-climate-risks/

23. Hennink, M., Kaiser, B., Marconi, V.: Code saturation versus meaning saturation: how many interviews are enough? Qual. Health Res. **27**(4), 591–608 (2017)

InCReASE: A Dynamic Framework Towards Enhancing Situational Awareness in Cyber Incident Response

Jarl Andreassen, Martin Eileraas, Lucia Castro Herrera$^{(\boxtimes)}$ (iD),
and Nadia Saad Noori (iD)

University of Agder, Centre for Integrated Emergency Management,
Kristiansand, Norway
lucia.c.herrera@uia.no

Abstract. Protecting valuable IT assets is one of the most significant challenges that organizations face today. Cyber criminals operating beyond physical boundaries, are able to disrupt and destroy cyber infrastructure, deny organizations access to IT services, and steal sensitive data. In response, enterprises organize security operations centres at the heart of their entities with the purpose of employing socio-technical systems with capabilities to detect, analyze and respond to these threats. This exploratory study examines how such capabilities are operationalized in leading "Managed Security Service Providers" (MSSPs) providing cybersecurity operations and incident response, and looks at how situation awareness knowledge is constructed through the organizational levels of the enterprise detection and response. In this context, situational awareness span over different levels in the organization starting from team personnel, ending at top management. Our work contributes to situational awareness theory in the context of cybersecurity operations and incident response. Thus, we advance the understanding of the organizational capabilities of MSSPs to develop awareness of the cyber-threat landscape and the broader operational dynamics. By introducing InCReASE, a dynamic framework towards enhancing situation awareness in Security Operations Centers (SOC) operations and incident response; we extend existing situational awareness models, combining elements of the existing body of knowledge and our empirical findings. The presented work is a reflection on the best practices adopted by MSSPs organizations operating in Norway.

Keywords: Situational awareness · Cyber incident management · Cybersecurity situation awareness · Crisis information flow · Crisis response

1 Introduction

Cybersecurity threat actors have risen to become increasingly sophisticated, persistent and organized, posing a substantial threat to modern organizations [1]. As stated by the 2021 Verizon data breach investigations report (DBIR), external threat actors in 2020 perpetrated 80 percent of recorded data breaches, with

© IFIP International Federation for Information Processing 2023
Published by Springer Nature Switzerland AG 2023
T. Gjøsæter et al. (Eds.): ITDRR 2022, IFIP AICT 672, pp. 230–243, 2023.
https://doi.org/10.1007/978-3-031-34207-3_15

likewise 80 percent of *top threat actor varieties* in breaches committed by organized crime groups [30]. Human attackers who are well-informed, well-trained and methodical, use sophisticated tools and techniques to disrupt and destroy critical cyber-infrastructures; deny organizations access to their own IT infrastructure and services; and steal sensitive data such as intellectual property, trade secrets, and customer data. As a result, organizations may suffer from a loss of competitive advantage, productivity, reputation, and customer confidence, as well as legal penalties and direct financial loss [1].

The growing dependency on the cyberspace increasingly demands the need for situational awareness—essentially, perceiving and understanding the operational environment and accurately predicting and responding to problems that might occur [20]. Situational awareness is the process of obtaining relevant information related to the organization that is integrated into usable intelligence and re-disseminated to support informed decision making [16]. The systems and networks that operate in the cyberspace have vulnerabilities that present significant risks to both individual organizations and national security. By anticipating what might happen to these systems, organizations can develop effective countermeasures to protect their critical operations and services. Hence, situational awareness span over different levels in the organization starting from the cybersecurity team personnel, ending at the top management level. Thus, the provision of situational awareness at the different organizational levels is considered a complex process involving various sources of information, different levels of perspective, and different interpretations which trigger a complex set of decision making processes [20].

As incident response and crisis management becomes more reliant on the advances of technology, the sociotechnical system must adapt to respond to the capabilities and challenges of new technologies. Therefore, the human component is just as up-to-date as the technology [25]. With this in mind, we therefore pose the following research question addressing the practical perspective of situational awareness: "How is situational awareness knowledge constructed through the organizational levels of the Managed Security Service Providers (MSSPs)?".

The goal of this exploratory study is to develop an understanding of the concept of situational awareness and its relation to cyber-incident response; investigate its function in the context of enterprise MSSP cyber-incident response operations and examine how situational awareness knowledge is constructed through the organizational hierarchy in an MSSP enterprise. As a result, a conceptual dynamic framework is developed and validated in a Norwegian context [8]. The framework is expected to contribute to illustrating best practices in security operations teams.

The following sections of this article are organized as follows: Sect. 2 presents a background and work related to our area of study that defines our focus. Section 3 describes our research approach. Section 4 summarizes and discusses our findings, while Sect. 5 concludes.

2   Background and Related Work

Following a systematic literature review (SLR) method aligned with [18], we investigated the intersection between situational awareness, cybersecurity and organizations. Therefore, this section discusses the concepts and theoretical grounding resulted from the review of the existing body of knowledge. We present background concepts and a theoretical lens that frames and informs the formulation of a conceptual framework.

2.1   The Role of Cybersecurity in Organizations

Cybersecurity is the practice of protecting an organization's IT-related assets, including data, systems and networks, from digital attacks that may access, destroy, or change sensitive information or disturb business operations [15]. Cybersecurity involves the convergence of people, processes and technology to protect organizations, individuals or networks from digital attacks. Organizations have the responsibility to manage and preserve sensitive data while providing services to their customers and users. Therefore, organizations are called to allocate adequate resources to ensure data protection and encourage a security culture to ensure that data and internal processes are managed responsibly [2], following the principles of confidentiality, integrity and availability [29].

New threats develop on a regular basis, and each organization must ensure that it is prepared to deal with a constantly changing threat landscape. Even though organizations have significantly increased investments in cybersecurity, incident occurrences continue to rise [1]. In order to detect intrusions efficiently, a monitoring network is required with a global view. This is only possible with an architecture that can collect data from all sources. This task is usually assigned to a Security Operation Center (SOC) [4].

2.2   Security Operations Center (SOC) and Incident Response (IR)

A SOC is an organizational entity located at the heart of all security operations. The SOC is a complex structure that manages and improves an organization's total security posture. SOC's key functions are to detect, analyze, and respond to cybersecurity threats and cyber incidents by employing technology, people and processes [31].

On an abstract level, SOCs can be structured as centralized, distributed, or decentralized entities. A centralized architecture in the context of SOCs refers to the approach in which all data is transferred from various locations or subsidiaries to a single central SOC for processing. A distributed SOC resembles one single system operating across several subsidiary companies. Users have the impression that they are interacting with one single entity. All entities can retrieve, process, integrate, and deliver security information and services to other entities using the distributed system. A decentralized SOC is made up of a few

SOCs of possibly limited capability that report to one or more central SOCs [31]. Moreover, the choice of architecture should formalize the operation model of the SOC in terms of components and relationships [21].

2.3 Roles and Responsibilities

Depending on the scope and size of the SOC, different security operations teams are needed in different scales. Different tiers of analysts, as well as dedicated managers, are typical core positions within the operational hierarchy:

- **Tier 1** analysts are primarily in charge of gathering raw data and assessing alarms and alerts from system monitoring tools. They confirm, determine, or revise the criticality of alerts, as well as add important data to them [31].
- **Tier 2** analysts evaluate the more serious security incidents escalated by tier 1 analysts and conduct a more in-depth analysis using threat intelligence (Indicators of Compromise (IOC), updated rules, etc.). They must comprehend the scale of an incident and be aware of the systems that are affected on a higher level [31].
- **Tier 3** analysts are the most experienced members of a SOC's workforce. At this level, analysts must also analyze all significant security alerts, threat intelligence, and other security data provided by tier 1 and tier 2 analysts [31].
- **SOC Managers** oversee the security operations team. They provide technical assistance as needed, but most importantly, they are responsible for effectively managing the team. Evaluating team members, developing processes, assessing incident reports, and developing and implementing necessary crisis communication plans are all part of the job. They also assist with security audits, and report to the Chief Information Security Officer (CISO) or other top-level management positions [31].

It is worth noting that modern enterprise SOCs are hierarchically structured around SIEM (Security Information and Event Management) systems that allow the management and completion of key security functions with emphasis on preparation, detection and analysis processes [3].

2.4 Security Information and Event Management (SIEM)

One of the SOC's key functions is to monitor security related events from the enterprises' technology environments, including the IT network perimeter defense systems such as application servers, firewalls, databases, intrusion prevention devices, and user accounts. Each asset might be monitored using a variety of sensors and maintain log files of activity. The SOC receives event information from the sensors and log files and triggers alerts indicating possible malicious behavior, both at the perimeter of the network and in the enterprise [3]. In the wake of complex security events, SIEM has replaced Intrusion Detection and Prevention Systems (IDPS) to fulfill these goals [5]. SIEM systems are an important tool used in SOCs as they collect security events from numerous and diverse sources in enterprise networks, standardize the events to a common format, store the conformed events for forensic analysis, and correlate the events to identify malicious activities in real time [3]. They have evolved into comprehensive systems that provide a broad view of high-risk areas and proactively focus on mitigation measures aimed at lowering incident response costs and time [13].

While SIEM systems provide control over networks and systems, to be able to gain a knowledge advantage over cyber threat actors and anticipate potential threats and risks, SOC personnel needs to turn their attention into the operational environment and the current threat picture. Thus, the effectiveness of a SOC depends on its access to actionable threat intelligence among many dependencies [3].

2.5   Cyber Threat Intelligence (CTI)

The volume of cyber attacks and malware varieties has risen significantly in recent years, making it increasingly challenging for security analysts and forensic investigators to discover and protect against cybersecurity threats. To address this issue, researchers coined the term *"Threat Intelligence"* which refers to *"the set of data collected, assessed and applied in relation to security threats, threat actors, exploits, malware, vulnerabilities, and compromise indicators"* [6]. CTI provides knowledge of a malicious actor's capabilities, infrastructure, motives, goals, and resources in cyberspace [17]. In fact, CTI was established to support security practitioners in recognizing the indicators of cyber threats, extracting information about the attack techniques, and, as a result, accurately and swiftly responding to a given attack [6]. The primary goal of CTI is to gain a knowledge advantage over cyber threat actors. CTI accelerates the detection of malicious behavior at the tactical and operational levels, ideally before a malicious actor gains a foothold in the network. On a Strategic level, CTI helps decision-makers make sense of and gain insight into the relevant threat environment [26]. The use of threat intelligence enables an organization to prioritize defenses around prized assets, focusing on vulnerabilities and ways that an adversary activity can be mitigated [17]. [32] consequently states that CTI is not simply information, it is information that has been analyzed and is actionable.

2.6   Information Exchange

Reducing cybersecurity risk by enhancing cyber situational awareness in organizations increasingly depends on information sharing and collaboration among a wide range of actors, leveraging many different models, methods, and mechanisms. Information sharing is the process of sharing information about cybersecurity incidents, threats, vulnerabilities, best practices, mitigation measures and other topics [14]. Sharing of CTI is an effective way of enhancing the situation awareness of an organization and its stakeholders [32]. Moreover, to survive current and future attacks, organizations need to dedicate resources and efforts in prevention by working proactively instead of solely reactive. In the future, organizations could benefit from implementing a threat intelligence program and disclose their knowledge intra- and inter-organizationally as part of proactive cybersecurity. Stakeholders may be held responsible in the future for not sharing known threats that could affect others resulting in a breach. The core idea behind threat intelligence sharing is to create situation awareness among stakeholders through sharing information about the newest threats and vulnerabilities, and to swiftly implement the remedies [32]. In cybersecurity, receiving the right information at the right time can empower decision-makers to reduce risks, deter attackers, and enhance resilience. Sharing the right information is more than people exchanging data, it is also about the automation of machine-to-machine sharing to counter fast-moving threats [14]. Within the concepts of CTI management and especially information sharing, several authors ([1,19,24,28]) promote the concept of inter-organizational sharing networks for exchange of threat intelligence information, primarily by the use of SOCs. This gives organizations a considerable advantage when fighting against cyber threats [1].

2.7   Cybersecurity Situation Awareness

The widely applied and most common definition of situation awareness is that of [9], which from a cognitive point of view defines SA as *"the perception of the elements in the environment within a volume of time and space, the comprehension of their meaning and the projection of their status in the near future"*. [9] describes SA as part of a larger process for human cognition that is framed from an information-processing perspective. It is apparent in the literature, that authors most of the time refer to and "translate" Endsley's conceptualization into their own perspective when defining SA in cybersecurity.

For example, [10] states that *"building situation awareness requires capability to gather information from the environment, means to understand gathered information, and reflecting the gained understanding for the current environment"* [10]. Here - gather, understand and reflect are synonyms for perceive, comprehend and project. Furthermore, [1] defines SA in incident response as *"the perception of incident-related elements within the organizational environment over the course of the incident, the comprehension of their meaning within the context of the organization's cybersecurity mission and objectives, and the projection of their status in the near future"* - Here, the body of the definition is altered to fit the dynamics and attributes of organizational incident response perspective and environment. Consequently, [1] offer a more comprehensible example, framing SA as *"a problem of collecting relevant and useful information (i.e. 'collect the dots'), fusing together key elements of the information (i.e. 'connect the dots') and deriving insights from the fused information ('project from the dots')"* - much like how [27] compares SA to knitting pieces of a puzzle together. You collect the pieces ('the dots'), connect them and reflect upon the picture that emerges. Simultaneously, collecting and connecting the pieces of the puzzle are synonyms for perceiving and comprehending, while the finished puzzle represents insight of the environment of which an operator can reflect upon (projection) to inform decision-making. Moreover, [11] adds, based on the conceptualization of Endsley that *"the words "perception", "comprehension", and "projection" within cybersecurity can be taken to denote progressively increasing awareness levels ranging from (i) basic perception of important data, (ii) interpretation and combination of data into knowledge, and (iii) the ability to predict future events and their implications"*.

3   Research Approach

Through this exploratory study we develop an understanding of the concept of situation awareness (SA) and its relation to cybersecurity. In addition, we investigate the role of SA in the context of enterprise MSSP cybersecurity operations and examine how knowledge is constructed through the organizational levels of the enterprise, namely, strategic, tactical and operational. The choice of research design relates to the nature of the research problem and the type of knowledge information required to answer the research questions [7]. Thus, an interpretive qualitative approach [22] was adopted with the aim to develop an understanding of of the SA and its relation to cybersecurity and investigate its function in the context of cyber incident management.

This exploratory study examines how leading MSSP organizations are operationalized to provide security operations as a service while catering to the needs of SA. A MSSP provides outsourced monitoring and management of security devices and systems. Common services are managed firewall, intrusion detection, virtual private network, vulnerability assessment, and anti-viral services. MSSPs leverage high-availability security operation centers (either their own or from other data center providers) to provide 24/7 services aimed at reducing the number of operational security personnel an organization needs to hire, train, and retain in order to maintain an acceptable security posture [12].

In this article, we studied two large multinational and leading IT consultancy companies, MSSP1 and MSSP2 worth forty billion (4.4 billion USD) and forty-two billion NOK (4.5 billion USD) respectively. MSSP1 Operates in 7 countries and counts with more than 7,500 personnel. This company offers a full range of hardware and software from the world's top technology companies and help customers solve problems and get maximum productivity from their IT investments. MSSP2 Operates in nearly 30 countries and employs 47,000 personnel. They Help large private companies and public enterprises to take digital leadership, and is committed to creating value for customers and society with the mission of guiding their customers, partners and employees towards bold choices by leveraging digital technology to build a positive future for all. We selected these firms as they: (1) have an in-house, state of the art SOC and permanent 24/7 IR function (both internal and as-a-service) that is mature and - amongst few, approved by an unnamed (sensitive) governing function, and (2) have evolved 'best practice' IR from experiences of highly sophisticated cyber-attacks.

Table 1. Subject selection

Pseudonym	Role	Years in role
CISO	Chief Information Security Officer	5 years
Manager_SOC	(SOC) Project Manager	0.3 years
Lead_IRT	Leader of Incident Response Team	7 years
TeamLead_SOC	Leader of analytics-team within SOC	2 years
L1Analyst_SOC	Tier 1 SOC analyst	1 year
Sec_Consult	Senior Security/Technical Consultant	1 year
Product_Manager	Manager of SOC services	15 years
Lead_Onboarding	Director Onboarding	1 year
CSO	Chief Security Officer	8 years
Lead_SOC	Professional Leader of SOC	3 years

Our selection criteria for selecting informants from these organizations was focused on the qualifications in terns of role in the company and professional background that allowed them to provide us with information and knowledge specific to our object of inquiry [33]. Different roles of relevance within the organizations were interviewed to provide richness and depth to our study. We made an inquiry to our contacts in *MSSP1* and *MSSP2* and shared our interest in interviewing; both junior and senior analysts working on their SIEM platform handling daily events, the CISO or other C-suite employees of relevance, a cyber-operations leader, a SOC leader, a cybersecurity strategy leader, and an employee working with cyber threat intelligence. This resulted in a total of 11 interviews, all of which provided valuable information to our research. We were determined from the beginning to ensure anonymity of our respondents and their employer, so that they could answer honestly without fear of repercussions. Table 1 displays the main characteristics of our respondents. Our sample size counts with a wide range of experience and areas of responsibility. To avoid "elite-bias", which can occur if one bases the selection only on top management such as directors, board chairmen, etc. we included a variety of subjects in the sample at various organizational levels [23].

We based our analysis on the content of the interviews which were transcribed and subsequently analyzed and coded in NVivo, a software to aid qualitative research. By coding the transcriptions we derived answers to common questions from the different participants into categorized themes, which were beneficial to us when comparing and presenting our findings. After reading and developing an understanding of how it could be categorized, we identified specific segments related to the questions to label and categorize confirming or contradicting answers. The interviews were broken down into five sections, each of which was labeled to contain questions on the same subject. The questions vary from general questions about the candidate and their business in Part 1 to cybersecurity-related questions in Part 3 to a framework presentation in Part 5 where we wanted input on whether the framework accurately represented how incident management works in practice. Before presenting anything we had to translate the findings as the interviews were held in Norwegian, and we did it with utmost caution to prevent any translation-bias or misunderstandings. The findings section summarizes our main findings contrasted to existing theories from the literature review.

4   Summary of Findings and Discussion

We examined how MSSPs implement security operations to construct situational awareness. By looking into best practices within security operations centers (SOC) of large scale cybersecurity enterprises, we developed a generalized and holistic framework visualizing the function of an operational SOC. We examined elements t understand SA in cybersecurity incident management. In addition we identified conditional elements, functions and best practices involved to support SOCs in achieving their objectives.

Our proposed framework was then validated through interviews to eventually produce an empirically validated, final framework. In this section we present our empirical framework and discuss the findings from the validation to answer our research questions.

4.1   The Conceptual Framework

By drawing on related literature and through sense-making of the theoretical lens, we have developed a conceptual framework depicting how enterprise security operations work and are operationalized to reflect our understanding of how SA is constructed through the different organizational levels: operational, tactical and strategic. The following framework (Fig. 1 below) uses the logic of [9]'s *'Situation Awareness' process model for human cognition* and takes inspiration from [1]'s case study, combining their process model of *Situation Awareness in Cybersecurity IR* with their case unit *"FinanceCentral's"* information flow and communication pathways. The framework is modeled as a two-dimensional artifact. Cybersecurity stakeholders (L1 & L2, L3 and the SLT) are modeled across the vertical dimension representative to each of their organizational levels. The horizontal dimension models 'Situation Awareness' as of [9]'s process model for human cognition that is framed from an information-processing perspective. The "background colors" blue, green and yellow represent perception, comprehension and projection respectively through the different organizational levels. The framework features three kinds of dynamic behavior. The first is information processing behavior (data-driven vs goal-driven), the second is task behavior (escalation vs investigation) and the third is communication behavior (information flow and communication pathways) [1].

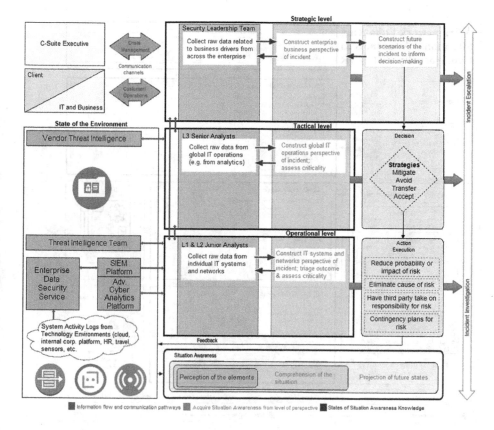

Fig. 1. A conceptual framework of SA in SOC IR

Information processing behavior is modeled using the blue arrows in Fig. 1 that allow progression through the 3 states of SA knowledge. Based on [1]'s process model, the rightward pointing blue arrows reflect that organizations can acquire increasingly higher levels of SA from data-driven processes (moving from perception to comprehension to projection). The leftward pointing blue arrows reflect that goal-driven processing such as attention-focusing existing mental models can improve lower levels of SA (moving from projection to comprehension to perception).

4.2 InCReASE: A Dynamic Framework of Situational Awareness in Cybersecurity SOC-IR

As a result of comparing the conceptual framework (Fig. 1) with our empirical inquiry, we have developed an empirically validated framework modelling how SOC-IR works and are operationalized to understand how SA is constructed through the different organizational levels of 'best practice' MSSPs. The validated framework (Fig. 2) is an outcome that uses the logic of [9]'s *'Situation*

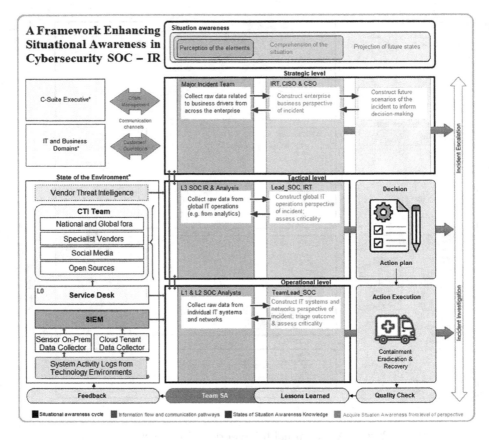

Fig. 2. InCReASE: A dynamic framework enhancing situation Awareness in cyber incident response

Awareness' process model for human cognition and, draws inspiration from [1]'s case study, the framework combines the process model of *Situation Awareness in Cybersecurity IR* with their case unit *"FinanceCentral"*'s *Information flow and communication pathways*. The framework was enhanced and validated by a process of sensemaking based on our interviews and discussions with ten cybersecurity specialists from two similar MSSPs providing cybersecurity services.

Our empirical analysis reveals that our theoretical findings were accurate before, during and after incident activities within security operations teams. Therefore, our interviews helped us to further expand some of the sections of the framework. For example, the use of SIEM platforms alongside a service desk. These two components feed raw data to L1 and L2 analysts in the SOC who collect and construct a picture of potential incidents and their criticality. Furthermore, we notice the employment of Cyber Threat Teams and Vendors that feed global IT operations data to the L3 analysts ad leaders in the SOC. Here, a decision is made whether to escalate the incident to the strategic level where an incident management team with key strategic stakeholders is formed, lines of communications are established and an enterprise business perspective of the incident is constructed. In here, various scenarios of the incident (prediction) to inform decision making. Following the decision, an action plan outlining the recovery measurements is made for execution at the operational level. Both the inquired organizations incorporate 'lessons learned' in standard operating procedures after an incident occurs. The assessment of the situation and response after an incident is critical to determine the quality and effectiveness and optimal performance of the event. This quality assurance feature is something that our studied MSSPs highlighted as missing from our framework. We have denominated this aspect as 'Quality check' which results are brought in to the lessons learned for reflection.

We argue that in future events, operators undoubtedly could be informed about some aspect of a situation of which they were not aware of before - during the 'lessons learned' of which would increase their ability to construct situational awareness. Thus, as part of the feedback onto the environment is a reflection of the acquired SA from each perspective as illustrated in Fig. 2, representing *the team's* increased knowledge of the current operational picture. The next time an incident of similar nature occur, the reflected SA knowledge sees the entire team more resilient with better awareness of the environment resulting in improved cybersecurity readiness.

The framework within the organizational levels 'operational, tactical and strategic', is modeled as a two-dimensional artifact. Cybersecurity stakeholders are modeled across the vertical dimension representative to each of their levels as inspired by [1]'s case unit and 'Situation Awareness' as of [9]'s process model for human cognition is modeled across the horizontal dimension. Also based on [9]'s model is the *Situation awareness cycle* (black arrows) which can be recognized from Fig. 2. While some of the theory-informed dimensions of the framework remain unchanged, the analysis identifies some changes and additions.

5   Conclusion

The goal of this exploratory study was first to develop an understanding of SA concepts and its role in cybersecurity; second is to investigate SA function in the context of enterprise MSSP cybersecurity operations; and third to examine how SA knowledge is constructed during incident response through the enterprise's organizational levels. To accomplish this-on a high level, we have provided an empirically validated framework, InCReASE, which models how MSSPs operationalized situational awareness in cybersecurity operations detection & response. The InCReASE framework models communication behavior and information flows between cybersecurity stakeholders, and conditional internal and external parties to coordinate the management of cybersecurity operations. Following the 'Situation awareness cycle' the MSSP projects the state of the environment through a socio-technical system which influences the SOC operations through its SIEM, CTI team and service desk. With emphasis on SA, the InCReASE framework shows how technology, people and processes either support or engage in the perception, comprehension and projection of the operational environment to construct SA knowledge across organizational levels to make informed decisions. The framework replicates how SA exists as a facilitator for decision-makers as the SA knowledge constructed in the different levels and those influencing the formulation of an action plan which initiates the execution of a decision through the incident response life cycle 'containment eradication & recovery'. Furthermore, the InCReASE framework accounts for the activities held post-incident to reflect upon the enterprise response, which we argue allows for the construction of team SA. Completing the SA cycle, the final stage 'feedback' imposes the course of action and impacts the state of the environment which is ultimately perceived by the MSSP through its *Situational Awareness* all over again.

Finally, given the nature of the organizations that were investigated in this exploratory study, a key limitation is the lack of generalization. The inquired organizations are large scale and ultimately specialized in cybersecurity services (MSSPs), thus for smaller and less capable organizations the dynamics and capability requirements of the framework could be too complicated and could differ substantially from that of e.g., an SME context. Thus, by expanding this work to include a broader range of organizational contexts, as the fewest of organizations are of the size of LSE, one could improve the overall applicability of the framework and significantly contribute to theory on the subject.

References

1. Ahmad, A., Maynard, S.B., Desouza, K.C., Kotsias, J., Whitty, M.T., Baskerville, R.L.: How can organizations develop situation awareness for incident response: a case study of management practice. Comput. Secur. **101**, 102122 (2021)
2. Arlitsch, K., Edelman, A.: Staying safe: cyber security for people and organizations. J. Libr. Adm. **54**(1), 46–56 (2014)
3. Bhatt, S., Manadhata, P.K., Zomlot, L.: The operational role of security information and event management systems. IEEE Secur. Priv. **12**(5), 35–41 (2014)
4. Bidou, R., Bourgeois, J., Spies, F.: Towards a global security architecture for intrusion detection and reaction management. In: Chae, K.-J., Yung, M. (eds.) WISA 2003. LNCS, vol. 2908, pp. 111–123. Springer, Heidelberg (2004). https://doi.org/10.1007/978-3-540-24591-9_9
5. Chopra, M., Mahapatra, C.: Significance of security information and event management (SIEM) in modern organizations. Int. J. Innovative Technol. Explor. Eng. **8**(7), 432–435 (2019)
6. Dehghantanha, A., Conti, M., Dargahi, T. (eds.): Cyber Threat Intelligence. AIS, vol. 70. Springer, Cham (2018). https://doi.org/10.1007/978-3-319-73951-9
7. Cresswell, J.W.: The Selection of a Research Design the Three Types of Designs (2008)
8. Eileraas, M., Andreassen, J.: A dynamic framework enhancing situational awareness in cybersecurity SOC-IR. Master's thesis, University of Agder (2022)
9. Endsley, M.R.: Toward a theory of situation awareness in dynamic systems. Hum. Factors **37**(1), 32–64 (1995)

10. Evesti, A., Kanstren, T., Frantti, T.: Cybersecurity situational awareness taxonomy, pp. 1–8 (2017)
11. Franke, U., Brynielsson, J.: Cyber situational awareness - a systematic review of the literature. Comput. Secur. **46**, 18–31 (2014)
12. Gartner. Managed security service provider (MSSP) (2022)
13. Gonzalez-Granadillo, G., Gonzalez-Zarzosa, S., Diaz, R.: Security information and event management (SIEM): analysis, trends, and usage in critical infrastructures. Sensors **21**(14), 4759 (2021)
14. Cristin, G., et al.: A framework for cybersecurity information sharing and risk reduction. Microsoft (2015)
15. Hasan, S., Ali, M., Kurnia, S., Thurasamy, R.: Evaluating the cyber security readiness of organizations and its influence on performance. J. Inf. Secur. Appl. **58**, 102726 (2021)
16. Horneman, A.: Situational awareness for cybersecurity: an introduction. Carnegie Mellon University's Software Engineering Institute Blog, 9 September 2019
17. Jasper, S.E.: US cyber threat intelligence sharing frameworks. Int. J. Intell. CounterIntell. **30**, 53–65 (2016)
18. Kitchenham, B., Charters, S.: Guidelines for performing systematic literature reviews in software engineering (2007)
19. Leszczyna, R., Wrobel, M.: Threat intelligence platform for the energy sector (2019)
20. Mitre.org. The MITRE corporation (2022). URL: https://www.mitre.org/
21. Muniz, J., McIntyre, G., AlFardan, N.: Security Operations Center: Building, Operating, and Maintaining Your SOC. Cisco Press, Indianapolis (2015)
22. Myers, M.D.: Qualitative research in information systems (2021)
23. Myers, M.D., Newman, M.: The qualitative interview in is research: examining the craft. Inf. Organ. **17**(1), 2–26 (2007)
24. Naseer, H., Maynard, S.B., Desouza, K.C.: Demystifying analytical information processing capability: the case of cybersecurity incident response. Decis. Support Syst. **143**, 113476 (2021)
25. Nyre-Yu, M., Gutzwiller, R.S., Caldwell, B.S.: Observing cyber security incident response: qualitative themes from field research. In: Proceedings of the Human Factors and Ergonomics Society Annual Meeting, vol. 63, pp. 437–441 (2019)
26. Oosthoek, K., Doerr, C.: Cyber threat intelligence: a product without a process? Int. J. Intell. CounterIntell. **34**(2), 300–315 (2021)
27. Rajivan, P., Cooke, N.: Impact of team collaboration on cybersecurity situational awareness. In: Liu, P., Jajodia, S., Wang, C. (eds.) Theory and Models for Cyber Situation Awareness. LNCS, vol. 10030, pp. 203–226. Springer, Cham (2017). https://doi.org/10.1007/978-3-319-61152-5_8
28. Skopik, F., Settanni, G., Fiedler, R.: A problem shared is a problem halved. Comput. Secur. **60**(C) (2016)
29. Ursillo, S., Arnold, C.: Cybersecurity is critical for all organizations - large and small (2019)
30. Verizon. 2021 data breach investigations report (2022). URL: https://www.verizon.com/business/resources/reports/2021/2021-data-breach-investigations-report.pdf
31. Vielberth, M., Böhm, F., Fichtinger, I., Pernul, G.: Security operations center: a systematic study and open challenges. IEEE Access **8**, 227756–227779 (2020)
32. Wagner, T.D., Mahbub, K., Palomar, E., Abdallah, A.E.: Cyber threat intelligence sharing: survey and research directions. Comput. Secur. **87**, 101589 (2019)
33. Yin, R.K.: Design and methods. Case Study Res. (2014)

Privacy by Design in CBRN Technologies Targeted to Vulnerable Groups: The Case of PROACTIVE

Mariano Martín Zamorano[1]([✉]) [iD], Natasha Newton[2], Virginia Bertelli[1] [iD], and Laura Petersen[3] [iD]

[1] Eticas Research and Consulting, Barcelona, Spain
martin@eticasconsutling.com
[2] Rinicom, Lancaster, UK
[3] UIC, Paris, France

Abstract. This paper provides the results of the privacy impact assessment conducted for the PROACTIVE solutions and its subsequent privacy by design integration process. PROACTIVE is a solution for fostering coordination and communication between stakeholders before and during CBRNe events focusing on providing guidance to vulnerable populations. Based on extensive fieldwork activities with practitioners and vulnerable groups, the results of the analysis reveal the main risk focus, including the need to filter data by competent authorities (data controllers) and potential solutions for each of them, which allow establishing standard procedures for systems used in similar contexts.

Keywords: Privacy by design · CBRNe technologies · Privacy impact assessment · Vulnerable groups

1 Introduction

This article examines the issue of integrating privacy by design (PbD) into technological solutions and practices related to CBRNe preparedness and response, focusing on the management of vulnerable groups' data. This issue represents a challenge at two levels. Firstly, concerning frequent tensions between those protocols aimed at prioritizing data protection in CBRNe scenarios on the one hand and the active need for personal identifiers by first responders on the other. Secondly, those aspects regarding the need for ensuring accessibility and consent to enforce privacy rights, which may find an obstacle in the differential capacities and conditions held by vulnerable populations in these contexts.

These issues are addressed in light of a technological toolkit (PROACTIVE) aimed at supporting practitioners in managing large and diverse groups of people before and during Chemical, Biological, Radiological, Nuclear and explosive (CBRNe) events. The main goal of such technology is to enhance preparedness against and response

© IFIP International Federation for Information Processing 2023
Published by Springer Nature Switzerland AG 2023
T. Gjøsæter et al. (Eds.): ITDRR 2022, IFIP AICT 672, pp. 244–258, 2023.
https://doi.org/10.1007/978-3-031-34207-3_16

to a CBRNe incident through harmonizing procedures between various categories of practitioners and better addressing the needs of vulnerable citizen groups [17].

Developed as part of the H2020 PROACTIVE project[1], the analyzed system has three main components [11]. Firstly, a collaborative web platform for communication and exchange of best practices among Law Enforcement Agencies (LEAs). This Platform for LEAs will facilitate daily operations and response to a CBRNe incident. In particular, its crisis communication system will:

- house operational documents, SOPs and communication strategies,
- collate information about incidents in the local area in terms of type, potential numbers, vulnerabilities,
- speak to the broader public at the press of a button through live notifications,
- recognize and support vulnerable citizens, in terms of wheelchair support, visual guidance, mental health needs etc.
- provide detailed pre-incident information targeted at the vulnerable citizens.

Secondly, PROACTIVE includes a Modular App for Practitioners to facilitate daily operations and response of LEAs and First Responders to a CBRNe incident. Finally, the system counts on another Mobile App adapted to various vulnerable citizen categories and sharing pre-incident public information material. This way, the App will enable all the citizens to communicate in real-time and according to their needs.

As with other CBRNe solutions, PROACTIVE technologies will manage special categories of personal information, such as health or criminal data, which require proportional safeguards in their treatment. To do so, as the literature has pointed out, both by-design and socio-technical dimensions of data protection need to be properly addressed to ensure robust data security [17, 21]. However, we do not count on empirical studies addressing privacy impact and privacy by design (PbD) mechanisms in similar CBRNe technologies. This void is even more significant concerning research involving inter-action between the police and vulnerable stakeholders using complex data governance tools. Based on the PROACTIVE case, this article seeks to fill this gap by providing an empirical-based model for privacy impact assessment [22], leading to privacy-by-design recommendations in similar contexts.

This article's qualitative methodology is based on a combination of technical analysis of the studied system and data collection techniques addressing privacy integration through actors' perceptions and technical gaps as presented by stakeholders interacting in CBRNe events from the PROACTIVE approach. This privacy impact assessment focused on the study of technical specifications through two main fieldwork phases. Firstly, two Tabletop exercises with vulnerable groups and practitioners (10 participants each), where a first response scenario, in particular a train CBRNe accident, was presented to assess potential tensions between privacy rights, technological solutions and security protocols. Secondly, a demonstration validation of the App's beta version involving both first responders and vulnerable populations (20 participants in the project's first demo) was conducted in Dortmund in May 2022 [15, 23]. Specific surveys and focus groups were held in this case. Participants were asked to provide their opinion about data

---

[1] This project has received funding from the European Union's Horizon 2020 under Grant Agreement n° 832981.

treatment, associated benefits, risks and mitigation measures based on their interaction with the App or App concept. Content analysis was applied to these activities' results to identify and classify main privacy by design risks and solutions related to tested technologies. This ongoing examination allows us to capture the socio-technical interaction leading to better integration of PbD requirements.

2 Vulnerable Populations and Privacy Policies in CBRNe Contexts

Vulnerable populations face unique challenges in CBRNe scenarios, including a lack of specific communication protocols for them (sign language, for instance) during decontamination processes [4, 9], which can impact their physical and informational privacy. Along these lines, privacy-related challenges and risks are frequently overlooked in data protection design and policy decisions. There is growing privacy literature outside privileged categories of young, white, and cisgender, seeking to understand knowledge associated with privacy practices and their implications for vulnerable communities [6, 14].

However, the normative based analysis of privacy-related inequalities in the management of vulnerable populations has not been applied to the CBRNe domain. Moreover, as pointed out by McDonald & Forte [14] this perspective often fails to notice how "structural inequalities and experiences conspire to make privacy threats and practices fundamentally different, not better or worse". Capturing this qualitative component of privacy breaches and understating power relations that lead to exploiting inequality in data management requires focusing on the experiences of those who are subject to privacy threats because of their race, religion, disability or class [13].

Following Helen Nissenbaum [16], we go beyond individual privacy to understand and analyze privacy as a function of norms in distinctive circumstances. In this framework, acceptability, particularly social expectations, must be considered in practices related to privacy violations [23]. Practices such as data sharing or access are shaped by how actors collectively define and value their rights and responsibility concerning personal data. Nissenbaum provides the example of healthcare domains where patients found it correct and legitimate to be asked for their data about sexual behaviors while they may consider the same that same inquiry inappropriate coming from other actors. Therefore, contextual integrity places social expectations and perceptions at the centre of privacy assessment.

In line with this perspective, scholars have raised concerns about the capacity of normative frameworks to capture inequalities derived from vulnerable conditions when dealing with personal identifiers, often focusing on socioeconomic factors [20]. This is particularly relevant in the context of an overwhelming exposure to accessible and, by extension, vulnerable technologies. Along these lines, empirical evidence on vulnerable populations' expectations, interests and knowledge regarding data protection needs to be translated into data protection requirements in specific CBRNe contexts. This can also provide avenues for vulnerable individuals and groups to give their views and opinions on matters that are directly relevant to their lives but on which they may not have been given the opportunity to comment before.

3   Privacy by Design in CBRNe Environments

There is scarce literature on privacy by design in CBRNe technologies. Most references concern privacy-related consequences of CBRNe prevention events, for instance, related to surveillance policies [19]. This is the case even though many CBRNe preparedness and response protocols, often led by private organizations, are subjected to strict data protection requirements and principles when implementing data-intensive solutions to related events. Such requirements need to be considered from a preventative perspective, as stated in Art. 25 GDPR "Data protection by design and by default". According to the regulation: "Taking into account the state of the art, the cost of implementation and the nature, scope, context and purposes of processing as well as the risks of varying likelihood and severity for rights and freedoms of natural persons posed by the processing", data controllers must implement before and during the processing of personal data "appropriate technical and organizational measures, such as pseudonymization, which are designed to implement data-protection principles, such as data minimization, in an effective manner and to integrate the necessary safeguards into the processing in order to meet the requirements of this Regulation and protect the rights of data subject." (Art. 25 GDPR).

The above preventative perspective within the regulation follows the core principles of the Privacy by Design (PbD) approach to technological design and development. This approach seeks to guarantee that data security mechanisms are considered and embedded in the design phase of any system, service, product or process and then throughout the data lifecycle [3]. By implementing protocols such as those mentioned in the GDPR, including data pseudonymization, developers and implementers should therefore consider privacy needs as part of the technical design while considering the potential impacts of the systems at hand on individuals' privacy [16]. The philosophy of PbD is structured around a group of seven 'foundational principles' [3]:

I. Proactive not Reactive/Preventative not Remedial or PbD anticipates and prevents privacy invasive events before they happen.
II. Privacy as the Default Setting or No action is required on the part of the individual to protect their privacy—it is built into the system, by default.
III. Privacy Embedded into Design or Privacy is integral to the system, without diminishing functionality.
IV. Full Functionality/Positive-Sum, not Zero-Sum or PbD avoids the pretense of false dichotomies, such as privacy vs. security, demonstrating that it is possible to have both.
V. End-to-End Security/Full Lifecycle Protection or PbD ensures that all data is securely retained and then securely destroyed at the end of the process, in a timely fashion.
VI. Visibility and Transparency—Keep it Open Privacy by Design aims at ensuring that all relevant information about data processing grounds and goals is available allowing independent verification.

VII. Respect for User Privacy—Keep it User-Centric.

The need to develop effective tools to implement and translate PbD principles into technical specifications and engineering practices, such as Privacy Enforcement Technologies (PET) has been stressed [18]. PET provides functionalities such as data breach alerts or firewalls, to ensure adequate and proactive action is taken to guarantee personal data integrity. Control over personal data is also achieved by integrating subsystems to assure data minimization, correct anonymization and consent of those involved [1, 8]. Other PET methods include software or protocols enabling data unlinkability (relevant data cannot be linked to any other group of relevant data outside its context), transparency (management of personal data is accessible for interested parties) and intervenability (a guaranteed intervention of subjects involved in processing their data to ensure that corrective measures or access rights can be exercised) [7].

As mentioned by Urruela Mora [21], in the exceptional circumstances of CBRNe events, "data are likely to be collected without the data subjects' consent, under highly stressful conditions, in the absence of normal infrastructure, and in the midst of political and legal uncertainty". In this framework, PbD aspects become even more relevant but have still been relegated to a secondary level of importance. Additionally, challenges in implementing common frameworks and international data protection standards in CBRNe scenarios have been underlined [10].

4   The PROACTIVE Solution: Specifications and Data Management

The PROACTIVE toolkit includes three solutions, its platform and two apps targeted to practitioners and citizens. This section will briefly describe each system's characteristics and data management in the current prototype.

4.1   The PROACTIVE Platform

The collaborative platform will include an Online Coordination Portal allowing bi-directional communication between LEAs and security-based policy makers via direct messaging and forums. Text, images, videos, audio files and PDF documents will be exchanged through the platform [11].

LEAs and Policymakers will be able to upload and download these data, and the platform will enable them to create an FAQ page with useful advice about the website itself or about particular situations in their area. Moreover, it will enable LEAs and policymakers to provide/signpost users to other relevant sites/contacts for helpful information, for example, accommodation, help lines, charities etc.

Additionally, the platform will have restricted access via a registration method and will include two types of users with their corresponding security levels, namely 'Admin and User'. Both Admin and User(s) will be able to customize the tool according to the context of a specific scenario (location - map-based), the type of incident and the policies required for particular events [11].

The system will use a GIS-based backend for the geo-located data gathered, enabling GIS-oriented data storage, management and analysis. Users will select their preferred

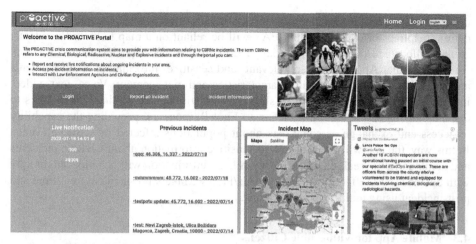

Fig. 1. PROACTIVE web prototype. Source: https://proactive-app.net/

location when they log. The LEAs will be reliant on a map to record incidents, manage/allocate resources and potentially record images of the specific incidents on a map. Personal data collected and shared by LEAs and practitioners, as well as information collected by citizens, including vulnerable populations, before and after the event, will include valid email addresses, organization, name/position and location of users.

The platform must be available via the Police Secure networks. Therefore, it will need to be certified and tested by Police IT & Digital teams to meet stability and security standards. In line with these specifications, LEAs will likely be data controllers of the system in most cases.

4.2 Mobile Application for LEA's and Policy Makers

The LEAs App will offer the same functionalities as the platform, including customization and geolocated data. The App, used by LEAs and policy makers, will allow bi-directional Communication between them via direct messaging and forums and include extended functionalities for vulnerable citizens. LEA's and policy makers will, therefore, be able to upload, download and also remove data, including personal information.

The Mobile Application will be administered by LEA's and policy makers. The App will have restricted access via a registration method and only one level of access: User. The content and credibility of the information will be up to the LEA's and Policy makers. In line with these specifications, it is likely that LEAs will be data controllers of the system in most cases. First Responders, who will be provided with access to some information will possibly act as data processors on behalf of the police.

The App must provide an option to view and validate any content uploaded to the portal and the ability to report and see an incident at a specific location using a map. Furthermore, it will give the users and vulnerable groups useful advice about the website itself or about particular situations in their area via an FAQ page, and signpost users to other relevant sites/contacts for useful information, for example, accommodation, helplines or charities. The LEA's will be reliant on a map to record incidents, manage/allocate resources and potentially record images of the specific events on a map.

The modular App administers relevant -and sensitive- information about incidents and includes references about its characteristics and management. Voice, text, video, images and PDF documents will be shared by practitioners and other stakeholders to dispatch emergency-related information to First Responders, providing the capability to access and exchange personal data about populations affected by CBRNe events. In this way, the app will allow access to sensitive information about CBRNe incidents and communities in real time. Emergency-related information will be uploaded directly with citizens (push effect), and other LEA's/Policy Makers pre-incident, real-time and post-incident using multiple media options.

4.3 Mobile App for Vulnerable Citizens

This App will allow vulnerable citizens to communicate with other citizens, LEAs and security policymakers by selecting, configuring and adapting their preferred tools according to their needs and preferences. Vulnerable citizens will be able to download and -with filter- upload data (pdf, videos, images, audio files). The App will be administered by the corresponding data controller (LEAs or authority in charge) and will have two access levels: Registered User (which enables citizens to report emergencies and view information) and Non-registered users, which enables citizens to view information but not report. Data to be processed include personal data shared by authorized users, including LEAs, public authorities and vulnerable groups using the application, such as CBRNe events' images, videos or voice.

The App provides video (for sign language support), real-time text, text-to-speech features and an intuitive user experience environment, with smart buttons and visual instructions to report emergencies and associate device data. It will be able to receive automated early warnings issued by authorities. Considering VoIP, emergency web portals, softphones and social media platforms, the system provides broad accessibility and the ability to report an incident at a specific location using a map.

It will include various settings for accessibility, including Font Size & Type, Colour of Screen to support colour blindness, no flashing images to reduce issues with epilepsy, audio options/voice control for the visually impaired/or those with dyslexia, and sign language videos for those with limited hearing [17]. It is expected that the App uses novelty (e.g., cartoon characters, pictograms or symbols) where appropriate to reduce the issue of language barriers.

The App will enable the user to select their preferred location when they log in. Moreover, it will provide the citizens with useful advice about the website itself or about particular situations in their area via an FAQ page. Included on this page will be a section prompting the information to be provided during an incident, such as the route to the event or medical symptoms. Lastly, it will signpost users to other relevant sites/contacts for useful information, for example, accommodation, helplines or charities and will reference existing apps (providing links where possible).

4.4 System Logical Topology, Security and Interoperability

The three PROACTIVE components will work interconnected by feeding and receiving data stored in the controller databases. Figure 1 shows the logical topology of an example single server deployment of the Proactive Application. The top half of the diagram shows the supported devices & web browsers (Safari, Firefox & Google Chrome), which allow the users to connect to the Server via a secure HTTPS connection. The bottom half of the diagram shows the connections & relationships between the installed components on the server (Fig. 2):

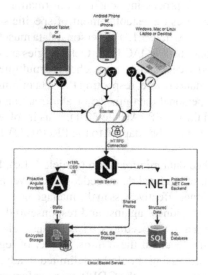

Fig. 2. PROACTIVE Linux based server. Source: [11].

The system will enforce the following security protocols by integrating SQL Data Protected by Full Drive Encryption: aes-xts 256. It will also provide Client-Server communication protected by Transport Layer Security (HTTPS). The System access is controlled by application-level authorization. Unauthorized users (not logged in) and members of the public may not view sensitive information or edit publicly accessible information directly. In addition, API Key authorization will be available for external integrations. Concerning system interoperability, the PROACTIVE platform exposes a secure REST API that allows external systems to integrate.

5 PROACTIVE High-Level Data Protection Requirements

The PROACTIVE technology has been generally framed by requirements of the General Data Protection Regulation (GDPR) [5]. Law Enforcement Agencies (LEAs) will use the PROACTIVE toolkit when processing personal data, but not always for the prevention, investigation, detection or prosecution of criminal offenses or the execution of criminal penalties. This distinction means that Directive (EU) 2016/680 of the European Parliament and the Council (known as the Police Directive) and National law enforcement regulations will apply to PROACTIVE data management only in specific circumstances. In this framework, attending to data protection principles and requirements embedded within the GDPR is even more relevant for the PROACTIVE solutions.

As already pointed out, PROACTIVE will process protected categories of data as defined in the GDPR (Art. 9.1), such as health data. The gathering and management of these data will be oriented to preparedness in case of CBRNe incidents and also include the management of further sensitive data (pictures, video, etc.) once these events occur. The toolkit must therefore ensure the rights of the most vulnerable groups in society in case of a CBRNe incident following the Respect for User Privacy principle.

In line with Art. 9 GDPR, processing sensitive information, which may also include race or disability data, requires the establishment of specific security safeguards. The integrity and confidentiality (Article 5.1,f) of personal data must be ensured both through by-design strategies and once the PROACTIVE technologies are implemented. Measures to avoid both unauthorized access and data breaches are multiple and range from correct anonymization of data-to-data erasure, respecting the data minimization principle. Security strategies to prevent personal data misuse or abuse are an essential aspect of data protection legislation and the GDPR (Article 32.1). This involves producing systematic security assessments which must be adapted to the PROACTIVE specific processes and performance.

The system must embed data minimization (Article 5,1,c). PROACTIVE must collect the minimum amount of personal data needed to achieve its purposes. These goals include increasing practitioner effectiveness in the management of a large group of people in CBRNe, enhancing preparedness against and response to these events and facilitating subsequent decontamination procedures by better articulating the different needs of stakeholders. Taking into account these aims, the set of legitimate and technically required purposes of the processing should be delimited in advance.

Other methods for securing data in the GDPR are pseudonymization and anonymization. Following Article 4(5) GDPR, pseudonymization should be applied when enabling the purposes of data collection and is in line with the protocols or technological systems at hand. Pseudonymized data is data that can no longer be attributed to a specific data subject without the use of additional information (iii). Following this principle, PROACTIVE tools pseudonymization personal data should ensure that additional information can be kept separately. It should also be subjected to technical and organizational measures to ensure that the personal data are not attributed to an identified or identifiable natural person. Other data security measures suggested in the GDPR include encryption, access control and password protection.

Data breaches should be prevented proactively both in terms of data governance and technological design. The GDPR Article 33.1 mandates to notify data subjects about data breaches without undue delay and, where possible, "*not later than 72 h after having become aware of it*". Since CBRNe attacks are often accompanied by personal data breaches and fake news dissemination, the strategy for coping with these breaches should have a holistic perspective. Notifying breaches in PROACTIVE should be integrated into a broader scope of action and address the relations to "external" stakeholders such as the media or organizations representing vulnerable persons. Although the GDPR does not specifically determine how notifications have to be produced, PROACTIVE must ensure effective communication strategies concerning data breaches. Moreover, Article 33.5 mandates properly registering personal data breaches, including all relevant information about the infringement, such as data subjects involved and remedial actions. Additional measures to be made by the data controller in case of breaches include notification to the supervisory authority as mandated in Article 34.1.

Moreover, following Article 5.1 (d), GDPR, efforts must be made to ensure that the information collected and provided by processors and controllers is accurate. Accuracy involves both classical methods for enhancing data quality, such as proper classification or erasure methodologies, but also protocols for guaranteeing the veracity of provided data. The App should also incorporate a mechanism for assessing and filtering fake news or untrustable collected information, including subsystems for avoiding algorithmic discrimination. These mechanisms also include forms of ensuring that data subjects can ask the controller to erase or rectify the data that it has regarding them (Arts. 16, 17 GDPR). Although non-trustable data that does not involve personal data is out of the scope of GDPR, it is still relevant for PROACTIVE efficiency and aims.

Finally, PROACTIVE should also consider Article 5.1 (e) on storage limitation. The systems must not keep personal data collected before and after a CBRNe incident for any longer than is reasonable for achieving the purposes for which they were collected in the first place. These original purposes, which may include providing better guidance to vulnerable groups, will determine the legal and legitimate data retention period. Still, the rationale behind data storage must be accompanied by a proportionate and rationally justifiable data storage policy in all cases.

6 Assessing and Integrating Privacy by Design into PROACTIVE

This section describes the principal risks identified during this process based on inputs provided by practitioners and vulnerable populations during fieldwork. Practitioners and interviewed vulnerable individuals, manifested or showed different issues concerning data protection, focusing on knowledge needed to ensure privacy and access control. Based on these inputs and the technical assessment of the system, the following table presents the leading solutions for integrating the above privacy-by-design principles and data protection requirements into the PROACTIVE technologies. It also systematizes critical solutions and recommendations for ensuring three pillars of PbD, data security, access controls and data protection (Table 1).

Table 1. Identified risks, applicable PbD principles and associated solutions

Main identified risks	Applicable data protection and PbD principles	Corresponding PbD solutions and enhancing technologies (both implemented and to be implemented)
Potential of the apps for collecting large amounts of nonfunctional and sensitive personal data from end users, users and also data subjects related to events (i.e., pictures taken during an event)	Data minimization, Lawfulness, fairness and transparency (Art. 5 GDPR) Proactive not Reactive, Privacy Embedded into Design	**Reducing the amount of (sensitive) data collected by the system:** • Users of the platform and mobile apps will be required to provide a valid email address only • The Mobile app will allow for both registered and anonymous users • In the case of the App for vulnerable populations, precise location information in the incident map will be replaced by "areas" to minimize privacy risks associated with the use of the app. Maps must be designed in such a way that no particular home or address can be identified (granularity of event data)
Lack of access control leading to unauthorized access to data and programs; shutdown or misuse of the systems. It could worsen one key risk identified by end users in fieldwork activities: the spreading of misinformation	Data integrity (Art. 5 GDPR) Proactive not, Reactive Privacy as the Default Setting	**Ensuring that only authorized users access personal data:** • Access control levels are provided according to 4 profiles: public user, LEA, Emergency Responder and Military. End users will be restricted and require permissions by the parent organization • Two factor authentication is used. It includes hashed IDs, usernames and passwords (user secret known). CAPTCHAs are employed to protect users from spam and password decryption • A system to check users' credentials, so this can be monitored, will be developed. It will include specific tools and protocols for mapping and registering logs to the system to be integrated into the platform. This would facilitate that they can be revoked if needed • Encrypt both communications and data before algorithmic processing to ensure that only authorized users access these data
Data security in PROACTIVE involves the above measures to protect information from unauthorized access, but also from corruption, or theft throughout its entire lifecycle	Data integrity (Art. 5 GDPR) Proactive not Reactive Privacy as the Default Setting	**Protecting PROACTIVE personal data from attacks:** • All data collected, stored, processed and retrieved by the system will be held and transferred through highly secure communication systems to prevent loss, damage or unauthorized access • NoSQL database technologies will be used for data storage and management. All personal data will be stored on encrypted volumes • Federation of the PROACTIVE App for vulnerable groups directly with other apps will be avoided to prevent privacy and security issues

(continued)

Table 1. (*continued*)

Main identified risks	Applicable data protection and PbD principles	Corresponding PbD solutions and enhancing technologies (both implemented and to be implemented)
PROACTIVE needs to ensure transparency and informed consent, which should be adapted to vulnerable groups in terms of accessibility	Accountability; Lawfulness, fairness and transparency (Art. 5 GDPR) Visibility and Transparency; Respect for User Privacy—Keep it User-Centric	**Guaranteeing informed consent from app users:** • The Apps/Web platform integrates appropriate functionalities for informed consent, already included in its *privacy policy*[a]. These tools will determine the eligibility of the person who will use the systems (+18 years old, competent authority, etc.). It ensures clear and conspicuous notice by thoroughly explaining the proposed uses of the data. All purposes for data processing, the nature of the processing and whether personal data will be shared with partners (if it will be), are among the provided details. All data used by the App from the mobile phone, including geolocation, will be included • Given the nature of the App for vulnerable groups, such as children or people with specific disabilities, accessibility will be ensured and an assent protocol will be integrated directly into the app
Sensitive personal data will be directly collected and shared through the public mobile app (i.e., pictures taken during an event). This could lead to several issues such as discrimination or false positives	Lawfulness, fairness and transparency. Data integrity, Accuracy, (Art. 5 GDPR) Proactive not Reactive Privacy as the Default Setting	**End users/data controllers should filter/monitor sensitive data** • Integrate an algorithmic subsystem to classify images and text as objectionable, detect them and avoid their exchange. Following the GDPR to automated profiling of data subjects Article 22(1) and (4), algorithms for filtering disinformation and detecting fake news or illegal data could be considered for ensuring automated identification of threats and problematic data [2, 24] • Include a system to catalog received information according to the source. In particular, tools for filtering data sources, and notifications for the removal of dispensable information should be integrated
Anticipating data breaches to minimize their impact on users	Data integrity (Art. 5 GDPR) Proactive not Reactive Privacy as the Default Setting	**Managing data breach events** • Data breaches should be prevented proactively both in technological design. In this regard, the backup functionality should also allow "freezing" a snapshot of the system over a certain period once a data breach may be integrated into the system

Source: own elaboration.

[a]See at: https://proactive-app.net/privacy

7   Discussion and Conclusions

Assessing core privacy by design and data protection principles through interaction with practitioners and potential users of the PROACTIVE technologies allowed us to identify key data protection risks concerning each step of the data life cycle. Requirements on users' data to be collected by the platform and the apps are aligned with the data minimization and purpose limitation principles since only email and names are collected. They also are proportional to the aim and features of the systems. Within the set of data to be provided by users, including email address, organization, name/position and location, all are justified under the purposes of the processing. Following the definition of "personal data" in the GDPR, which includes location data, specific minimization measures have been considered.

A second aspect addressed relates to the capacity of end users to access sensitive information. This risk required enforcing access control, particularly in relation to ongoing monitoring and registration of the activity. Moreover, the analysis of data exchanges revealed that users could upload images, videos or audio of events containing sensitive data about third parties. This entailed implementing by-design measures to ensure data privacy by making the data controller able to filter significant amounts of data and restricting the circulation of certain information, which could even increase the impact of CBRNe events. This data is not shared with the public unless it has been verified by the LEA responsible for the PROACTIVE Web Based platform and Mobile Applications.

Each action of managers and users should be registered, as well as rectified or modified data during the data breach response process. Once the system is implemented, a crisis simulation with the intervention of vulnerable groups within the implementation area should be conducted. In particular, it is recommended to perform a tabletop exercise where the incident response team addresses a data breach process, testing their performance. In this way, problems can be identified without interrupting the App workflow. The evaluation of the need for a Data Protection Impact Assessment (as mandated in Article 35.1 GDPR)must be based on the characteristics and the amount of personal data to be processed as well as on the integration of new technologies to personal data processing.

Even though the above may correspond to standard PbD solutions, some singularities particularly affecting CBRNe-inclusive technology have been spotted in the privacy impact assessment process. This includes existing issues with misinformation before and during CBRNe events [23], releasing of sensitive data, and issues with accessibility which automated or manual management of personal data by competent authorities must address. It is important to note that future iterations following the planned project workshops and field exercises may alter how data is captured and used. The ethical and legal implications will always be referenced, and an updated privacy policy will be provided if necessary.

References

1. Borking, J., Raab, C.: Laws, PETs and other technologies for privacy protection. J. Inf. Law Technol. (JILT), 1 (2001)
2. Bunker, D., Mirbabaie, M., Stieglitz, S.: Convergence behaviour of bystanders: an analysis of 2016 munich shooting twitter crisis communication. In: Proceedings of the Australasian Conference on Information Systems (2017)
3. Cavoukian, A.: Privacy by Design. The 7 Foundational Principles Implementation and Mapping of Fair Information Practices (2009). https://www.ipc.on.ca/wp-content/uploads/resources/pbd-implement-7found-principles.pdf

4. Chen, J., Wilkinson, D., Richardson, R.B., Waruszynski, B.: Issues, considerations and recommendations on emergency preparedness for vulnerable population groups. Radiat. Prot. Dosim. **134**, 3–4, 132–135 (2009)

5. Galdon Clavell, G., Valbuena Leon, M.A., Zamorano M., Marsh, I.: Legal and ethical state-of-the-art on CBRNe preparedness and response. Deliverable D8.1 of the PROACTIVE project (2021)

6. Guberek, T., McDonald, A., Simioni, S., Mhaidli, A.H., Toyama, K., Schaub, F.: Keeping a low profile? Technology, risk and privacy among undocumented immigrants. In: Proceedings of the 2018 CHI Conference on Human Factors in Computing Systems, New York, NY, pp. 114:1–114:15. CHI (2018)

7. Hansen, M.: Top 10 mistakes in system design from a privacy perspective and privacy protection goals. In: Camenisch, J., Crispo, B., Fischer-Hübner, S., Leenes, R., Russello, G. (eds.) Privacy and Identity Management for Life. Privacy and Identity 2011. IFIP AICT, vol. 375, pp. 14–31. Springer, Heidelberg (2012). https://doi.org/10.1007/978-3-642-31668-5_2

8. Heurix, J., Zimmermann, P., Neubauer, T., Fenz, S.: A taxonomy for privacy enhancing technologies. Comput. Secur. **53**, 1–17 (2015)

9. Hignett, S., Hancox, G., Edmunds Otter, M.: Chemical, biological, radiological, nuclear and explosive (CBRNe) events: systematic literature review of evacuation, triage and decontamination for vulnerable people. Int. J. Emerg. Serv. **8**(2), 175–190 (2019)

10. Jillson, I.A.: Ethical frameworks for CBRNE crises: toward shared concepts and their practical application. In: O'Mathúna, D., de Miguel Beriain, I. (eds.) Ethics and Law for Chemical, Biological, Radiological, Nuclear & Explosive Crises. The International Library of Ethics, Law and Technology, vol. 20, pp. 53–64. Springer, Cham (2019). https://doi.org/10.1007/978-3-030-11977-5_5

11. Kolev, G., Markarian, G., Polushkina, N.: Deliverable 4.1. Report on the High-level Architecture design including an interface control document. PROACTIVE (2021). https://proactive-h2020.eu/wp-content/uploads/2021/04/PROACTIVE_20210312_D4.1_V6_RINI_Report-on-the-high-level-architecture-design_revised.pdf

12. Lambert, P.: The Data Protection Officer: Profession, Rules, and Role. CRC Press, Boca Raton (2016)

13. Marwick, A., Fontaine, C., Boyd, D.: "Nobody sees it, nobody gets mad": social media, privacy, and personal responsibility among low-SES youth. Soc. Media Soc. **3**(2) (2017)

14. McDonald, N., Forte, A.: Privacy and vulnerable populations. In: Knijnenburg, B.P., Page, X., Wisniewski, P., Lipford, H.R., Proferes, N., Romano, J. (eds.) Modern Socio-Technical Perspectives on Privacy, pp. 337–363. Springer, Cham (2022). https://doi.org/10.1007/978-3-030-82786-1_15)

15. Nicholson, W., et al.: Report on the Workshop with Vulnerable Citizens. Deliverable D3.3 of the PROACTIVE project (2021). https://www.researchgate.net/publication/360106969_CBRNe_toolkit_for_policy_makers_integrating_vulnerable_groups_in_preparedness_and_response. Accessed 28 July 2022

16. Nissenbaum, H.: Privacy in Context: Technology, Policy, and the Integrity of Social Life. Stanford Law Books (2010)

17. Petersen, L., Havarneanu, G., Markarian, G., McCroneline, N.: CBRNe and vulnerable citizens: co-creating an app for that. In: 2019 International Conference on Information and Communication Technologies for Disaster Management (ICT-DM), pp. 1–4. IEEE (2019)

18. Rubinstein, I., Good, N.: Privacy by design: a counterfactual analysis of google and Facebook privacy incident. Berkeley Technol. Law J., 1333 (2012). NYU School of Law, Public Law Research Paper No. 12–43

19. Toohey, K., Taylor, T.: Surveillance and securitization: a forgotten sydney olympic legacy. Int. Rev. Sociol. Sport. **47**(3), 324–337 (2012)

20. Urban, J.M., Hoofnagle, C.J.: The privacy pragmatic as privacy vulnerable. Technical report #ID 2514381. Social Science Research Network (2014)
21. Urruela Mora, A.: The current legal framework on data protection in CBRNE crises: a general exposition. In: O'Mathúna, D.P., de Miguel Beriain, I. (eds.) Ethics and Law for Chemical, Biological, Radiological, Nuclear & Explosive Crises. TILELT, vol. 20, pp. 147–161. Springer, Cham (2019). https://doi.org/10.1007/978-3-030-11977-5_12
22. Wright, D., De Hert, P. (eds.): Privacy Impact Assessment. Springer, Dordrecht (2012). https://doi.org/10.1007/978-94-007-2543-0
23. Zamorano, M., Suarez Gonzalo, S., Clavell Galdon, G.: Legal and acceptability recommendations for PROACTIVE toolkit. Deliverable D8.2 of the PROACTIVE project (2021). https://www.researchgate.net/publication/360106969_CBRNe_toolkit_for_policy_makers_integrating_vulnerable_groups_in_preparedness_and_response
24. Zannettou, S., Sirivianos, M., Blackburn, J., Kourtellis, N.: The web of false information: rumors, fake news, hoaxes, clickbait, and various other shenanigans. Data Inf. Qual. 11(3) (2019)

Earthquake and Climate Forecasting

Transformation of an Esvecees (SVCS) Value to Spherical Coordinates as the Result of the Earthquake Forecasting Using SLHGN

Benny Benyamin Nasution$^{(\boxtimes)}$ 🆔, Abdul Rahman 🆔, M. Rikwan E. S. Manik 🆔, Rina Anugrahwaty 🆔, Liwat Tarigan 🆔, Rahmat Widia Sembiring 🆔, Indra Siregar 🆔, Ermyna Seri 🆔, Rina Walmiaty Mardi 🆔, Indri Dithisari 🆔, and Marliana Sari 🆔

Politeknik Negeri Medan, Jalan Almamater No. 1, Kampus USU, Medan 20155, Indonesia
bennynasution@polmed.ac.id

Abstract. The main issue, which has existed since the development of Single Layer Hierarchical Graph Neuron (SLHGN) started, is the representation for location data that will be fed to SLHGN structure. Similar issue, the double-value characteristics of the ordinary and current coordinate system have slowed down the enhancement of a sophisticated earthquake forecasting technology that uses SLHGN. To deal with the problem, a new way of representing locations on the earth, called Single Value Coordinate System (SVCS), has been researched and developed. Since the location of a potential earthquake—after being elaborated by the earthquake forecaster—is represented through esvecees (SVCS) values, people would have difficulties to understand and to locate it. To make the earthquake forecasting results be understandable and locatable for targeted people, those esvecees values should therefore be transformed into ordinary coordinates, which comprise longitude and latitude values. For that purpose, a technology for the transformation from esvecees values to ordinary coordinates have been successfully developed. The experiment results show that the location of a potential earthquake can now be gained as longitude and latitude values. This means that the earthquake forecasting using Single Layer Hierarchical Graph Neuron (SLHGN) is getting closer to its complete functionalities.

Keywords: Earthquake Forecasting · Single Layer Hierarchical Graph Neuron (SLHGN) · Single Value Coordinate System (SVCS) · Hierarchical Graph Neuron (HGN)

1 Introduction

It is required that an earthquake forecasting technology should be intelligent enough to generate information about not only the magnitude of the upcoming earthquake but also the time it will occur, and where the location will be. To support such an intelligent capability of the forecaster, our current earthquake forecaster utilizes the Single Layer Hierarchical Graph Neuron (SLHGN). This technology is a relatively new artificial intelligence developed since five years ago.

© IFIP International Federation for Information Processing 2023
Published by Springer Nature Switzerland AG 2023
T. Gjøsæter et al. (Eds.): ITDRR 2022, IFIP AICT 672, pp. 261–275, 2023.
https://doi.org/10.1007/978-3-031-34207-3_17

The artificial intelligence plays the main role for forecasting the magnitude, the time, and the location of a future earthquake. For this purpose, the SLHGN needs to acquire appropriate data that will be distributed to the entire elements of SLHGN. The data must therefore be sufficient and thorough. In fact, the data must contain the time-series of prior earthquakes that generally build some kind of patterns of magnitudes, time, and locations.

The patterns that are elaborated within the architecture of SLHGN are similar to multidimensional patterns. However, since the data is gathered from the whole surface of the earth, the dimensionality of the SLHGN structure is quite unique. The earthquake data should consists of spherical-shaped data that is acquired within regular time interval, and every area of the earth surface should provide with the magnitude of an earthquake.

There are some important issues related to the earthquake data, which is available for free, for instance the data provided by USGS. The location data contains two values of longitude and latitude, and the unit of both values are normally in degree. Typically, a small difference of the longitude or latitude value would not affect the cosine value of it. Moreover, the value are in floating point type, which may cost a lot of CPU-cycle while processing it. These are the beginning indications that the current coordinate system seems to be problematic for earthquake forecasting technologies.

Some other issues related to the current coordinate system lies in the natural shape of the earth, which is a sphere. A coordinate on a spherical shape does not show an area, but a point. Even though the coordinate of a point is known, it is still difficult to pinpoint it on the earth surface without a satellite support. Although it is not always straightforward [1]. Some researchers [2, 3, 4] have identified other problems in relation to spherical characteristic of the earth. Usually, the current coordinate system is converted to a 2D map. However, the conversion seems to be problematic as well [5, 6], as it may deteriorate the preciseness of the longitude and the latitude values on the map. As the effect, the distance between two points on the map cannot be so precise either, in particular on the pole areas.

On the other hand, the currently under development earthquake forecaster produces a location which pinpoints an area, rather than a point. The reason to this is that it is difficult for the technology to forecast the point of a location. Furthermore, it is very unlikely, that the same and exact point of a previous earthquake would become the epicenter of the next earthquake. Rather, an earthquake could be forecasted to occur on an area. Such an area would cover particular part of the earth crust. Up to this point of our research, the smallest area size that can be represented by the esvecees technology is within four square meters.

The location of a forecasted earthquake generated by the SLHGN has been named as single value coordinate system (SVCS), or simply esvecees. The esvecees treats the South Pole area of the earth surface as the reference area or a starting area. Different to the current one, the value of esvecees is always scalar, and everywhere on the earth surface the value of esvecees holds the same preciseness. Esvecees technology is hierarchical. It means that the length of the esvecees value represents the depth of the hierarchy. The longer the value, the smaller the area the esvecees value represents.

Esvecees technology can be extended for bigger spheres by increasing the radius size. Even though the radius size will not affect the value of esvecees itself. Just the height of the reference area needs to be moved further from or closer to the earth center. Therefore, the technology can be used for representing a location outside the earth. The esvecees technology is not just for representing the location of an area, but it can also be utilized for representing the direction from one area to another area.

As people are already used to the current coordinate system containing longitude and latitude values, it would be difficult for them to elaborate the information produced by the earthquake forecaster, when the location of the forecasted earthquake is represented through the esvecees value technology. It is therefore straightforward, that the transformation approach from an esvecees value to the current coordinate system is required. Other researchers [7, 8, 4] have also tried some kind of transformation such as using matrix, but different to esvecees conversion that uses a single value. It is also expected that the transformation approach should be consistent, wherever location the earthquake would be. By having such a transformation approach, the process of our earthquake forecasting system using SLHGN would produce effective and useful results.

2 Earthquake Forecasting Results

When an earthquake forecasting technology can work with a high accuracy, its support will possibly reduce damages and casualties in the end. By having the forecasting results very early, for instance ten hours prior to the shock hit, people may have an opportunity to be evacuated or at least to find a safe heaven where they will be protected from the furious side effects. When there is still some time available, some important belongings can also be protected or moved to a safe area as well. Such a scenario has been attempted as an approach for the earthquake risk reduction campaign for a long time, but no satisfactory results found yet.

The technology for earthquake forecasting—developed in our research—produces results that forecast not only the magnitude but also the location and the time of the earthquake. It seems to be that the magnitude is the most important parameter to be known by citizen, but the time of the occurrence and the location are as important as the magnitude. People need to know the location of the forecasting through which people can figure out whether their location is under threat or not. If the nearby location is the forecasted area, people also need to know how long they have time left for the evacuation process or for finding a safe heaven.

Our current forecasting technology produces the forecasted location using Single Value Coordinate System (SVCS) technology, simply called esvecees. This technology represent the location of an upcoming earthquake not as a point but as an area. Such a new approach would not be understandable for people for finding the location as they are not used to it. It is therefore important that the esvecees value must be transformed to the common and current coordinate system containing longitude and latitude values, prior to the submission of it publicly.

The core engine that produces the esvecees value is the SLHGN. The technology will produce an area as the result of the forecasting process. The area can be a triangle, a tetragon, a pentagon, or a hexagon. It is required that when the SLHGN produces an area as its result, it should be transformed to a number of longitude and latitude value pairs. For instance, if the result represents a pentagon area, the transformation will produce an array of five value pairs of longitude and latitude.

When the forecasted esvecees value has been transformed to longitude and latitude values, through which the effectiveness of the mobility of people and goods during the evacuation process can be increased. It is therefore important to ensure that the transformation process should have very high accuracies and preciseness. One prerequisite to achieve it is that the earthquake forecaster should produce of high accuracy and precise forecasted areas.

3 Forecasting Steps of SLHGN

The usual thing people might be interested in an earthquake forecasting technology is about when and how big an earthquake might occur in the area and its surroundings. Based on the results of the previous research on SLHGN it is shown that the SLHGN has an ability to recognize an earthquake about nine hours earlier. This should give them ample time for the evacuation process. So, people might change their thoughts to the following. In relation to an earthquake, what would happen in my place and its surroundings in nine hours' time? Such a question is actually the first part within the forecasting process using the SLHGN.

After the area and the timestamp has been determined, the next part of the forecasting process is the collection of the earthquake magnitudes from all areas across the earth surface which occurred in the last hour (the historical data). The process of the collection continues for historical data of the last two hours, three hours, up to the last eighty one hours. All the data will then be fed to the SLHGN structure. Bear in mind that the location of each earthquake (containing longitude and latitude values) must first be transformed to an esvecees value before being fed to the SLHGN. The approach of transforming a coordinate (two values) to an esvecees value will be discussed in another publication paper.

Following the nature of the earth, all the historical data is clustered within thirty two areas. Similarly, all the historical data is clustered within eighty-one-hour time-frames. This means that for instance all the earthquakes occurred between 09.00 and 10.00 o'clock will be regarded as within the same time cluster. The reason to this is based on the previous research that SLHGN has an ability to recognize only 90% of complete patterns with more than 92% accuracy.

With such an ability, the earthquake forecaster should be able to forecast an earthquake nine hours earlier. In case all the data collected, instead of eighty-one-hour time-frames, comprising only eighty-hour time-frames the SLHGN would still have a capability to forecast earthquakes. With such a condition the SLHGN can forecast an earthquake even for the next ten hours. Although such a capability of SLHGN exists and seems to be more useful, the accuracy of the forecasting capability will be less than 92%. Further, in case all the data collected only covers seventy-nine-hour time-frames, the SLHGN would still have a capability to forecast earthquakes in the next eleven hours, but with an accuracy of even lesser than 92%.

Similarly, not only in terms of the number of time-frames, the SLHGN can also be used to forecast an earthquake using a wider time frame, not hourly-based but daily-based or even weekly-based [9, 10]. But, it is logical that the accuracy would be lesser the wider the time frame would be. In case the time frame is daily-based, the historical data must be added up within a day. Similarly, when the time frame is weekly-based, the historical data must be added up within a week.

The added up earthquake magnitudes within hourly-based time frame along ninety eighty nine hours will generate a two-dimensional pattern. Since the pattern is built from every esvecees value (location), then it will generate a three-dimensional pattern. Because the architecture of SLHGN is hierarchical, the entire architecture will require four-dimensional patterns. Imagine that there are 32 polygons areas (12 pentagons and 20 hexagon) on the earth. The number of nodes within the SLHGN are 32 as well. In the layer on top of that, there are 12 nodes. The hierarchy continues to 6 and 2 nodes on the upper layers and finally on the top, there is only one single node. So, the hierarchy order is the following: 1, 2, 6, 21, and 32. In case the SLHGN requires to scrutinize patterns deeper, the hierarchy order would be: 1, 2, 6, 21, 32, 180, 360, and so on.

When the pattern has been completely built, it will be elaborated within the SLHGN architecture to be recognized. Assume that the SLHGN has properly been trained, so it means that when the current pattern has already been stored within SLHGN during the training session, the current pattern would be recognized by the SLHGN. Although the current pattern is only 90% (eighty-one-hour time-frames) of a trained pattern (ninety-hour time-frames) stored within the SLHGN architecture, the accuracy of producing correct results would be more than 92%.

The result of the forecasting process will contain earthquake magnitudes on 12 pentagons and 20 hexagons on the earth surface. The number of polygons depends on the setup architecture of the SLHGN. It can also be setup for 180 polygons, 360 polygons, and so on. From the result it can be figured out in which area the process will be focused on. Again, the result area can be a triangle, a tetragon, a pentagon, or a hexagon. However, after the seventh layer down from the top of the hierarchy the area is always a triangle. Since the result represents esvecees values, before being disseminated publicly, the esvecees values must be transformed to common coordinates that contain longitudes and latitudes.

4   Transformation of Esvecees Values to Spherical Coordinates

Before discussing the transformation process, it is important to describe the esvecees value first. As already mentioned, a coordinate depicted using the esvecees technology contains one single value only. The following are some samples of esvecees values.

```
Santiago(-70.6693, -33.4489)→    0:e>1>a9032320011231232011
London(-0.1278, 51.5074)→        0:a>13312>f10000102003013230000301
Nairobi(36.8219, -1.2921)→       0:b>12>f411013211200120212002
Tiksi(128.8645, 71.6375)→        0:c>13312>f3523122332030222103
Anchorage(-149.9003, 61.2181)→   0:d>13312>f37211113212233032111
Wellington(174.7787, -41.2924)→  0:d>>f36322030222021303113
```

From the samples above, an esvecees value always starts with a zero followed by a delimiter, a colon. The two bigger signs are also delimiters. The zero means that the esvecees value uses the lowest level of earth areas in which there are 20 hexagons and 12 pentagons on the earth surface. The following figure shows them (Fig. 1).

Fig. 1. The truncated icosahedron

If the esvecees value uses the next level (level 1) of the earth areas, there will be 120 hexagons and 12 pentagons (depicted in the figure below). However, for simplicity until the rest of the paper the discussion will always refer to level 0 of the earth area (Fig. 2).

Fig. 2. Another type of a football with 120 hexagons and 12 pentagons

The following figure shows all the 20 hexagons and 12 pentagons represented on a two dimensional format (Fig. 3).

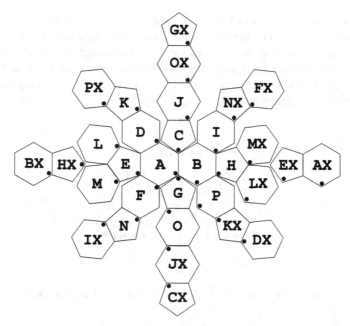

Fig. 3. The two-dimensional representation of a truncated icosahedron

In the esvecees technology, the pentagon G is chosen as the starting area of every esvecees value, and the South Pole is chosen as the starting point of every esvecees value. Why it is called as the starting point, because an esvecees value in principle represents a direction. From the South Pole, the letter after the colon shows the first direction. For instance, the esvecees value of the city of Anchorage has a letter d. The following shows all the letters on the pentagon G and the hexagon A (Fig. 4).

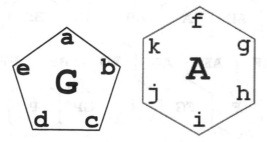

Fig. 4. The identities of corners within a pentagon and a hexagon

Note that in two dimensional format of the polygons, each of the corner a in a pentagon and the corner f in a hexagon are marked with a black dot. It can be seen from the previous data above that the esvecees value of Anchorage goes from the center of pentagon G through the corner d, about the same direction as the south-west. After going through the corner d, the next directions are: 1, 3, 3, 1, and 2. The following figure shows the meaning of those directions of 1, 2, and 3 (Fig. 5).

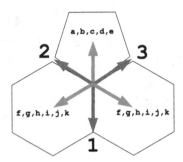

Fig. 5. The directions of 1, 2, and 3 on level 0 of earth surface

When the esvecees value represents a location/direction on level 1 of the earth surface, the following are some of the polygons including their indices (Fig. 6).

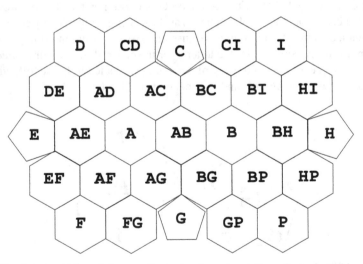

Fig. 6. The decomposition of the two-dimensional representation of a truncated icosahedron

The following are some samples of esvecees values on level 1 of the earth surface.

A →	1:a>15>f
B →	1:b>16>f
C →	1:a>15665>a
D →	1:a>156565>f
E →	1:e>16556>a
F →	1:e>15>f
G →	1:>>
H →	1:b>16556>a
I →	1:b>156565>f
P →	1:c>15>f

The following figure shows the meaning of those additional directions of 4, 5, and 6 (Fig. 7).

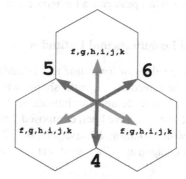

Fig. 7. Additional directions of 4, 5, and 6 on level 1 of earth surface

After the Anchorage's directions of 1, 3, 3, 1, and 2, the next direction is the letter f. It means that the direction goes into a hexagon through the corner f. After this point, the direction goes to one of the subareas of the hexagon. The direction to a subarea goes further, deeper, and deeper. The depth of the direction depends on how many digits the esvecees value would be needed. The following shows the subareas of each the pentagon and the hexagon with their corresponding indices (Fig. 8).

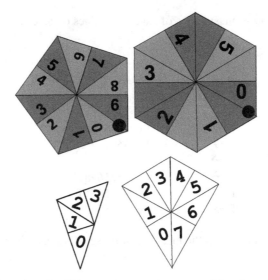

Fig. 8. The subareas within a pentagon, a hexagon, a triangle, and a tetragon

4.1 Generating Spherical Longitudes and Latitudes

The process of generating the values of longitude and latitude from those directions in an esvecees value follows the nature of the earth shape, which is a sphere. For every change of the directions, the longitude and the latitude will be calculated. In order to calculate those values, some formula have been composed through utilizing the formula of a truncated icosahedron, which contains 20 hexagons and 12 pentagons. The following are some elements within a pentagon and a hexagon that will be required in some formula (Fig. 9).

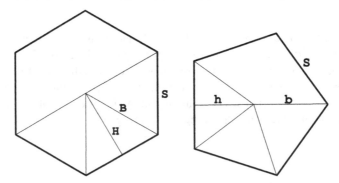

Fig. 9. The elements of a hexagon (H, B, S), and of a pentagon (h, b, S) in an icosahedron

Within a sphere, the identities of elements are appended with a letter c, stands for "curved". They are: Hc, Bc, Sc, hc, and bc. The following are those sphere elements including their positions (Fig. 10).

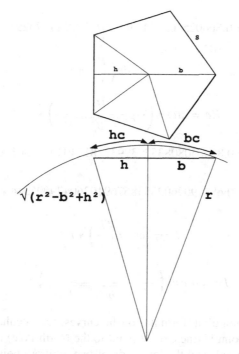

Fig. 10. Relationship between pentagon (h, b, S) of an icosahedron and of a ball (hc, bc, Sc)

When the directions go through the side of a polygon (a pentagon or a hexagon), the calculation of the side (S) length and its angle is required. Based on several resources [11–15], the following are the formulas for calculating S and Sc including their dependency to the radius (r).

$$S = \frac{4r}{\sqrt{58 + 18\sqrt{5}}} = 0.40354821233519766 * r$$

$$Sc = \frac{1}{2}d\theta, \; since\theta = 2arcsin\left(\frac{S}{2r}\right), \text{ then}$$

$$Sc = d * arcsin\left(\frac{2}{\sqrt{58 + 18\sqrt{5}}}\right) = 0.40633789992522046 * r$$

Similarly, when the directions go inside a polygon (a pentagon or a hexagon), the calculation of other elements of: B, Bc, H, Hc, b, bc, h, hc and their angles are required as well. The following are the formulas used for calculating them including their interdependency.

$$S = 2 * r * sin\left(\frac{Sc}{2 * r}\right)$$

$$B = S$$

$$H = 0.86602540378443864676372317075294 * S$$

$$Bc = arcsin\left(\frac{B}{r}\right) * r$$

$$Hc = arcsin\left(\frac{H}{\sqrt{r^2 - B^2 + H^2}}\right) * r$$

$$b = 0.85065080835203993218154049706301 * S$$

$$h = 0.68819096023558676910360479095544 * S$$

$$bc = arcsin\left(\frac{b}{r}\right) * r$$

$$hc = arcsin\left(\frac{h}{\sqrt{r^2 - b[i]^2 + h[i]^2}}\right) * r$$

After the description of all formulas of the curves, for calculating the latitude and the longitude of the point N (the closest point to the North Pole) the following are the formulas when the latitude and the longitude of two arbitrary points A and B, and the distance d between A and B are known.

$$\alpha_A = arctan\left(\frac{cos(\varphi_A) * cos(\varphi_B) * sin(\lambda_B - \lambda_A)}{sin(\varphi_B) - sin(\varphi_A) * cos(d)}\right)$$

$$\varphi_N = arccos\left(sin|\alpha_A| * cos(\varphi_A)\right)$$

$$\lambda_N = \lambda_A + sign(\alpha_A) * \left|arccos\left(\frac{tan(\varphi_A)}{tan(\varphi_N)}\right)\right|$$

On the other hand, it is important to note that every curve on the earth surface except for meridians and the equator is an orthodrome. Imagine that every orthodrome can pass two points, let say N and Y. The point N is the point from which the distance to the North Pole is the closest and the course angle on the point is the right angle (90°), and the point Y is an arbitrary point. Having all those values, it is required to calculate the latitude (φ) and the longitude (λ) of the point Y when the latitude, the longitude of the point N, and the angle (α) (to the meridian) of the curve with length (d) are known. For that purposes, the following are a number of formulas and equations required. Most of them are described and derived from [15] and [14].

$$tan(\varphi_Y) = tan(\varphi_N) * cos(\lambda_Y - \lambda_N)$$

$$\varphi_Y = arctan\left[tan(\varphi_N) * cos(\lambda_Y - \lambda_N)\right]$$

$$cos(\lambda_Y - \lambda_N) = \frac{tan(\varphi_Y)}{tan(\varphi_N)}$$

$$\varphi_Y = arcsin[cos(d) * sin(\varphi_N)]$$

$$d = arccos\left[\frac{sin(\varphi_Y)}{sin(\varphi_N)}\right]$$

$$As\ cos(\lambda_Y - \lambda_N) = \frac{tan(\varphi_Y)}{tan(\varphi_N)},\ or\ cos(\lambda_N - \lambda_Y) = \frac{tan(\varphi_Y)}{tan(\varphi_N)}$$

$$Then\ \lambda_Y = \lambda_N \pm arccos\left(\frac{tan(\varphi_Y)}{tan(\varphi_N)}\right)$$

$$\lambda_Y = \lambda_N \pm arccos\left\{\frac{tan[arcsin(cos(d) * sin(\varphi_N))]}{tan(\varphi_N)}\right\}$$

Already mentioned above, that the index of the last digit of an esvecees value represents a triangle. It is chosen that the coordinate of a triangle is its middle point. For revealing the longitude and the latitude of the middle point it is therefore required to scrutinize the characteristics of a spherical triangle. The following are the formulas for calculating an angle of a spherical triangle, which consists of three points: A, B, and C. On each point, there are angles of: α on A, β on B, and γ on C, and on the opposite of each point there are sides: a, b, and c.

$$\alpha = 2 * arctan\left(\frac{k}{sin(s-a)}\right)$$

$$\beta = 2 * arctan\left(\frac{k}{sin(s-b)}\right)$$

$$\gamma = 2 * arctan\left(\frac{k}{sin(s-c)}\right)$$

$$k = \sqrt{\left(\frac{sin(s-a) * sin(s-b) * sin(s-c)}{sin(s)}\right)}$$

$$s = \frac{a+b+c}{2}$$

5 Experiment Results

The following are the results taken during the experiment. The coordinates of six cities have been chosen as samples for the transformation of esvecees values to ordinary coordinates.

```
Santiago(-70.6693, -33.4489)→ 0:e>1>a9032320011231232011
Result: -70.66929962828182,-33.44889416566708

London(-0.1278, 51.5074)→ 0:a>13312>f10000102003013230000301
Result: -0.15257098140401332, 52.46151273060408

Nairobi(36.8219, -1.2921)→ 0:b>12>f4110132112001202120002
Result: 36.55162382776878, -7.97391061089461

Tiksi(128.8645, 71.6375)→ 0:c>13312>f3523122332030222103
Result: 128.86454164229366, 71.63750357080748

Anchorage(-149.9003, 61.2181)→ 0:d>13312>f372111132122330032111
Result: 138.71224684080312, 57.4453923345578

Wellington(174.7787, -41.2924)→ 0:d>>f3632203022202130313113
Result: 174.52800656325064, -43.99688962860224
```

After the transformation, some values are not the same as their original coordinates. The reason to this is due to two factors: 1) some coordinates are on the border of an area, 2) some coordinates are in the area of the North Pole or the South Pole. For these two problems more solutions need to be found.

6 Conclusion

The capability of the Single Layer Hierarchical Graph Neuron (SLHGN) in forecasting a future earthquake would not be useful because the results of the forecasting are represented using Single Value Coordinate System (SVCS) values, or simply called esvecees values. Not many people have understood the technology of esvecees, and only some people with of very informed technology might have read and understood it. However, it has been elaborated and tested that an esvecees value can successfully be transformed back to the ordinary coordinates, which contain longitude and latitude values. With the transformation technology from an esvecees value to longitude and latitude, not only the forecasting technology would gain benefit from it, other purposes such as GPS, distance and routing application would find the transformation useful. Having all these successful results the aim for having a better earthquake forecaster looks promising.

References

1. McCarthy, J.J., Rowton, S., Moore, D., Pavlis, D.E., Luthcke, S.B., Tsaoussi, L.S.: GEODYN Systems Description Volume 1, Greenbelt: NASA GSFC (2015)
2. Jekeli, C.: Geometric Refernce System in Geodesy. Ohio State University, Columbus (2006)
3. Panou, G., Korakitis, R.: Geodesic equations and their numerical solution in Cartesian coordinates on a triaxial elipsoid. J. Geod. Sci. 9(1), 31–42 (2017)
4. Engel, A.: Coordinate transformation algorithms for the hand-over of targets between POEMS interrogators. Eurocontrol, Brussel (2005)

5. Claessens, S.J.: Efficient transformation from Cartesian to geodetic coordinates. Comput. Geosci. **133**(1), 1–32 (2019)
6. ugli Abdufattakhov, H.M.: Coordinate systems and heights in geodesy. Eur. J. Res. Dev. Sustain. (EJRDS) **2**(11), 16–18 (2021)
7. Grewal, M.S., Weill, L.R., Andrews, A.P.: Global Positioning Systems, Inertial Navigation, and Integration. Wiley, Hoboken (2007)
8. Zeng, H.: Explicitly computing geodetic coordinates from Cartesian coordinates. Earth Planets Space **65**(4), 291–298 (2012). https://doi.org/10.5047/eps.2012.09.009
9. Nasution, B.B.: Features of single value coordinate system (SVCS) for earthquake forecasting using single layer hierarchical graph neuron (SLHGN). In: 2021 International Conference on Software Engineering & Computer Systems and 4th International Conference on Computational Science and Information Management (ICSECS-ICOCSIM), Pekan, Malaysia (2021)
10. Nasution, B.B., Sembiring, R.W., Siregar, I., Seri, E., Mardi, R.W.: Towards single value coordinate system (SVCS) for earthquake forecasting using single layer hierarchical graph neuron (SLHGN). In: Murayama, Y., Velev, D., Zlateva, P. (eds.) ITDRR 2020. IAICT, vol. 622, pp. 73–89. Springer, Cham (2021). https://doi.org/10.1007/978-3-030-81469-4_7
11. Bouman, J., Ebbing, J., Schmidt, M., Lieb, V., Fuchs, M.: Algorithm Theoretical Basis Document. GOCE+ GeoExplore, Munich (2015)
12. Badan Standardisasi Nasional: Geographic Information—Spatial Referencing by Coordinates. Badan Standardisasi Nasional, Jakarta (2011)
13. Ashby, N.: An Earth-Based Coordinate Clock Network, Boulder. National Bureau of Standards, Colorado (1975)
14. Fine, H.B., Thompson, H.D.: Coordintae Geometry. Macmillan Company, New York (1911)
15. Bronshtein, I., Semendyayev, K., Musiol, G., Muehlig, H.: Handbook of Mathematics. Springer, Berlin (2007). https://doi.org/10.1007/978-3-540-72122-2

Data Analytics of Climate Using the PCA-VARI Model Case Study in West Java, Indonesia

Devi Munandar[1] , Putri Monika[1] , Ajeng Berliana Salsabila[1] , Afrida Helen[2] ,
Atje Setiawan Abdullah[2] , and Budi Nurani Ruchjana[1](✉)

[1] Department of Mathematics, Faculty of Mathematics and Natural Sciences, Universitas
Padjadjaran, Bandung, Indonesia
budi.nurani@unpad.ac.id
[2] Department of Computer Science, Faculty of Mathematics and Natural Sciences, Universitas
Padjadjaran, Bandung, Indonesia

Abstract. Climate change occurs in the atmosphere over a long period due to the
influence of the sun, oceans, clouds, ice, land, and living organisms on each other.
This research used the Principal Component Analysis (PCA) model compounded
with Vector Autoregressive Integrated (VARI) called the PCA-VARI model to
determine climate change. PCA reduces correlated climate data to uncorrelated
data expressed as main components containing a linear combination of initial variables. In the time series model, a non-stationary multivariate comprises more than
two variables that influence each other, using differencing processes. A variety
of two models was used simultaneously to forecasting future climate data. Analysis of climate parameters uses ten measurements variable located in five areas,
namely Lembang, Bogor, Tasikmalaya, Sukabumi, and Indramayu, for twenty
years, using POWER NASA Agro-climatology datasets. The methodology follows the Knowledge Discovery in Databases (KDD) in data mining for integrated
PCA with VARI and post-processing using visualization by Impulse Response
Function (IRF). The result of forecasting in the PCA-VARI model using IRF in
the next six months showed that the effect of location climate on the response of
other regions with changes in standard deviation is similar to adjacent locations.
Meanwhile, the responses obtained varied based on the observation time for the
five areas that are not close.

Keywords: PCA-VARI Model · Climate · Forecasting · IRF · KDD

1 Introduction

Changes in the atmosphere are subject to long-term restrictions, usually from minutes
to months. Weather and climate have different meanings in climatology with time as
their dissimilarity. While the weather is a change or state of the atmosphere within a
short period, climate occurs over a long time due to temperature, humidity, rainfall,
atmospheric pressure, and others. This phenomenon can be interpreted as a stochastic
process with a sequence of place and time of climate variables and large data. Therefore,

T. Gjøsæter et al. (Eds.): ITDRR 2022, IFIP AICT 672, pp. 276–290, 2023.
https://doi.org/10.1007/978-3-031-34207-3_18

the Principal Component Analysis (PCA) process is needed to reduce variables through linear combinations or orthogonal transformations, such as marine climate applications [1]. The correlation between climate variables and time index allows univariate or multivariate modeling also need to be analyzed. This is in addition to the daily and monthly observation of various climate variables that affect weather changes. Knowledge Discovery in Database (KDD), with a theoretically three-step approach, namely preprocessing, data mining, and post-processing, is used to model climate variables. Meanwhile, those with a fairly high correlation can be modeled using Vector Autoregressive (VAR) or Vector Autoregressive integrated (VARI) as the implementation of the multivariate time series model [2]. The effect of the main climate variability, such as rainfall, humidity, and temperature, can be modeled to analyze the variance decomposition that causes an increase in malaria sufferers [3, 4].

In the scope of econometrics, the integration of PCA and VAR has significant meaning on human life caused of the influence of the climate, financial system, environmental pollution, and social media. The environmental effects influenced by vehicle exhaust emissions as a subsystem significantly affect development as an interaction with other subsystems. Integrating the two models is helpful and acts as a model that provides recommendations for these problems [5].

This study aims to combine Principal Components with integrated Vector Autoregressive through the KDD process in data mining [6]. Climate data in the West Java region of Indonesia were measured to obtain a multivariate time series model with a smaller number of variables. The acquisition of a new model from the combination of the two makes it easier to forecast and interpret the results. The Principal Component, an orthogonal transformation of the initial variable, performs the reduction process without losing much information. The percentage of cumulative variance, especially in the first Principal Component, is new data as input to the VARI model [7, 8]. Previous research outcomes explained that this examination uses this integrated model to evaluate correlation variables in this region's climate data. It contributes to the influence of the location climate for recommending community needs, such as planting season, harvest time, and analysis of disaster risk reduction, especially floods.

2 Research Methods

2.1 KDD Methods in Data Mining

Data mining is a technique for analyzing big data to obtain information through statistical and mathematical methods through artificial intelligence. This method also uses nontrivial processes to determine patterns between datasets and make predictions as a decision support system [9]. The implementation process of combining statistical and multivariate models as one of the data mining functions can be seen in Fig. 1 [10]. The two main functions of data mining are descriptive and predictive, which is an analysis of the behavior and patterns of data to be better understood and obtain information through technology [11, 12]. In the KDD stage, an in-depth data mining process is used to determine hidden patterns from climate datasets. This stage starts with preprocessing the dataset to cleaning and transforming it daily to monthly. The data mining process integrates PCA and VARI to produce a new model with the Principal Component dataset.

In the end, post-processing, as information generated in the previous stage, is visualized and interpreted as a decision support recommendation.

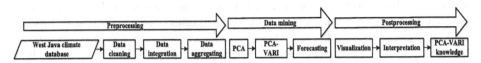

Fig. 1. Knowledge Discovery in Databases Process

2.2 PCA-VARI Model

PCA focuses on variable reduction, while VARI is a multivariate time series technique as stated in the following sub-sections.

Principal Component Analysis. Before the modeling process is conducted, the climate dataset must undergo a statistical test using the Kaiser-Meyer-Olkin (KMO) Test for Sampling Adequacy examination to determine the correlation between variables [13]. PCA specifically indicates the covariance matrix for climate variables through orthogonal transformations for its reduction [14]. It comprises $p\,k$ components, and by accomplishing PCA $p > k$. This indicates that k can clarify and change the main variables, which have the number p [15]. The vector $X' = \{X_1, X_2, X_2, ...X_n\}$ and covariance matrix Σ with p eigenvalues $\lambda_1 \geq \lambda_2 \geq \lambda_3 \geq ... \geq \lambda_p \geq 0$ indicate the occurrence of an orthogonal transformation p as follows:

$$\eta_1 = \mathbf{a}_1'X = a_{11}X_1 + a_{12}X_2 + ... + a_{1p}X_p$$
$$\vdots$$
$$\eta_p = \mathbf{a}_p'X = a_{p1}X_1 + a_{p2}X_2 + ... + a_{pp}X_p \tag{1}$$

p is made up of linear combinations, such that every variable is uncorrelated or linearly unbiased with the aid of taking only k. Therefore, the obtained $\mathrm{Var}(\eta_i) = \mathbf{a}'_i\Sigma\mathbf{a}_i$ and $\mathrm{Cov}(\eta_i, \eta_k) = \mathbf{a}_i\Sigma\mathbf{a}_k$ with $i,\ k = 1, 2, ...\ p$. To obtain the ith principal component, a delegated linear combination maximizes $\mathrm{Var}(\mathrm{a}'_i X)$ below the condition $\mathrm{a}'_i\mathrm{a}_i = 1$ and all covariates for $k < i = 0$ or $\mathrm{Cov}(\mathrm{a}'_i X, \mathrm{a}'_k X) = 0$ for $k < i$. Linear algebra [16] is described if $X' = \{X_1, X_2, X_2, ...X_n\}$ with a covariance matrix Σ comprising pairs of eigenvalues and eigenvectors $(\lambda_1, \mathbf{a}_1), (\lambda_2, \mathbf{a}_2), ...(\lambda_p, \mathbf{a}_p)$ where $\lambda_1 \geq \lambda_2 \geq \lambda_3 \geq ... \geq \lambda_p \geq 0$ in addition to $\eta_1 = \mathbf{a}'_1 X$, $\eta_2 = \mathbf{a}'_2 X$, ..., $\eta_p = \mathbf{a}'_p X$ is the first principal component, followed by $\sigma_{11} + \sigma_{22} + ... + \sigma_{pp} = \sum_{i=1}^{p} \mathrm{Var}(X_i) = \lambda_1 + \lambda_2 \geq \lambda + \geq ... + \lambda_p = \sum_{i=1}^{p} \mathrm{Var}(\eta_i)$ the quantify of the general variance for the kth principal component is $\lambda_k / \lambda_1 + \lambda_2 + ... + \lambda_p$.

Vector Autoregressive Integrated (VARI)
The method used in VARI modeling to obtain optimal results for forecasting stationary data is the Box-Jenkin procedure. It generally consists of the following steps: (i)

Identification process to ensure the data is stationary in the mean and variance. For nonstationary data, differencing processes and Box-Cox transformations are carried out until it becomes stationary. (ii) Estimation of model parameters using Ordinary Least Squared (OLS) or Maximum Likelihood Estimation (MLE). (iii) Diagnostic tests to confirm the model meets the criteria by testing the residuals of the modeling results. These conditions will return to process (i) if they are still not met until forecasting is considered possible [17].

Stationary data is a simple assumption that must be met in VARI modeling. Further analysis can be obtained assuming the statistical significance of the data is not determined at the unit root with the condition that it does not have criteria for seasonal fluctuations. The Augmented Dickey-Fuller test can meet the following autoregressive criteria: ΔZ_{t-p} in the model with $\gamma = 0$

$$\Delta Z_t = Z_t - Z_{t-1} = \alpha + \beta t + \gamma Z_{t-1} + \delta_1 \Delta Z_{t-1} + \delta_2 \Delta Z_{t-2} + \ldots + \delta_p \Delta Z_{t-p} \quad (2)$$

Z_t is series data, used to obtain ΔZ_t to t and Z_{t-1} to $\gamma \neq 0$ through linear and verification processes. If there is no unit root, $-1 < 1 + \gamma < 1$ the procedure may be stationary [18]. The presence of a unit root indicates that the data is not stationary in the mean, hence $H0: \phi = 1$. Meanwhile, if no unit root indicates stationary in the mean, $H1: \phi < 1$.

Rejection of the p-value at a significance level of less than 0.05 [19] indicates that the selection of the Box-Cox transformation is required for data that is not stationary in the variance. The determination of exponential lambda (λ) on the transformation is considered to meet the criteria if it has a value of more than 1. However, some preliminary studies stated that references are between -5 to 5 [20].

Evaluation is further needed to determine the accuracy level of modeling climate data using VARI by selecting the lag value in accordance with the Schwarz Information Criterion (SIC) [21]. Meanwhile, variable estimation using the Maximum Likelihood Estimation (MLE) [22] is a composite probability density function to obtain parameter estimates with regression values correlated using random error values in a normal distribution.

Assuming the Vector Autoregressive model is not stationary, then the differencing process is executed k times until the data is stationary, and the VARI (p, k) model is obtained. If the coefficients of p and k are 1, respectively, then the VARI $(1, 1)$ matrix is as follows:

$$\begin{bmatrix} \dot{Z}_{1,t} \\ \dot{Z}_{2,t} \\ \vdots \\ \dot{Z}_{M,t} \end{bmatrix} - \begin{bmatrix} \dot{Z}_{1,t-1} \\ \dot{Z}_{2,t-1} \\ \vdots \\ \dot{Z}_{M,t-1} \end{bmatrix} = \begin{bmatrix} \phi_{11} & \phi_{12} & \cdots & \phi_{1M} \\ \phi_{21} & \phi_{22} & \cdots & \phi_{2M} \\ \vdots & \vdots & \ddots & \vdots \\ \phi_{M1} & \phi_{M2} & \cdots & \phi_{MM} \end{bmatrix} \left(\begin{bmatrix} \dot{Z}_{1,t-1} \\ \dot{Z}_{2,t-1} \\ \vdots \\ \dot{Z}_{M,t-1} \end{bmatrix} - \begin{bmatrix} \dot{Z}_{1,t-2} \\ \dot{Z}_{2,t-2} \\ \vdots \\ \dot{Z}_{M,t-2} \end{bmatrix} \right) + \begin{bmatrix} e_{1,t} \\ e_{2,t} \\ \vdots \\ e_{M,t} \end{bmatrix}$$

or equal to

$$\dot{Z}_t - \dot{Z}_{t-1} = \mathbf{\Phi}_1(\dot{Z}_{t-1} - \dot{Z}_{t-2}) + \mathbf{e}_t \quad (3)$$

with error value is normal distribution, i.e. $e_t \overset{iid}{\sim} N(0, \sigma^2)$, and $\dot{Y}_t = \dot{Z}_{1,t} - \dot{Z}_{1,t-1}$, then satisfies with $t = 2, 3, \ldots, T$ and VARI equation

$$\dot{\mathbf{Y}}_{t((M \times (T-1)) \times 1)} = \dot{\mathbf{Y}}_{t-1((M \times (T-1)) \times (M \times M))} \mathbf{\Phi}_{((M \times M) \times 1)} + \mathbf{e}_{t((M \times (T-1)) \times 1)} \quad (4)$$

The obtained model is then tested by analyzing the residual series using white noise on the resulting parameters, assuming there is no random correlation with zero mean and constant detected variance. The null hypothesis test was also conducted on the uncorrelated residual ACF sample as a diagnostic test using the Ljung-Box.

As a statistical procedure useful for observing time series, the Granger test has a causal relationship between modeled climate variables [23]. Assuming X and Y are stationary series, to determine the ability of X Granger to produce Y can be defined as follows:

$$y_t = \alpha_0 + \sum_{i=1}^{p} \alpha_i y_{t-i} + \sum_{j=1}^{q} \beta_i x_{t-j} + a_t \text{ and } y_t = \delta_0 + \sum_{i=1}^{p} \delta_i y_{t-i} + e_t \text{ (null hypothesis}$$

model).

The impulse response function (IRF) is the feedback of the VARI model in response to some changes between the variables. IRF is used to examine the effect of a shock or a variable on itself and others from modeling in both short and long periods. According to the VARI model described in Eq. (3)

$$\Upsilon_t = \mu + \varepsilon_t + \Theta_1 \varepsilon_{t-1} + \Theta_2 \varepsilon_{t-2} + \Theta_3 \varepsilon_{t-3} + \dots$$

the Θ_s matrix is interpreted as

$$\Theta_s = \frac{\partial \Upsilon_{t+s}}{\partial \varepsilon_t'} \tag{5}$$

where i denotes row, and j represents column for recognition of Θ_s intensifying unit of jth variable at date t (ε_{jt}) to value of ith at a time $t + s$ ($\Upsilon_{i,t+s}$). The ith row, j^{th} column members of Θ_s, known as the IRF function, also continuously keeps all other variables.

3   Result and Discussion

3.1   Preprocessing of Data Mining

Before creating the PCA-VARI model, the data were first collected from climate resources of POWER NASA [27] consisting of Lembang, Bogor, Tasikmalaya, Sukabumi, and Indramayu West Java province of Indonesia from 2001 to 2020 using the daily measurement time [28].

Table 1 shows the use of the same measurement variables for each of the five locations from 2001 to 2020 [24]. The variable selection decisions were based on available data indicators in addition to the theoretical research basis and geographic location [25]. Furthermore, Table 1 also shows that eight of the overall variables indicate the climate in general [26]. The root soil wetness (rsw) and surface root wetness (srw) represent agroclimatological variables, which are included in the measurement and can affect each area. Daily data acquisition is aggregated into monthly data for simple modeling and put together in CSV file format to assist in organizing in one locality.

Table 1. Variables for Lembang, Bogor, Tasikmalaya, Sukabumi, and Indramayu regions

Lembang (LM), Bogor (BG), Tasikmalaya (TS), Sukabumi (SM), Indramayu (IN)
LM_1, BG_1, TS_1, SM_1, IN_1 = UV Index (uvi)
LM_2, BG_2, TS_2, SM_2, IN_2 = Temperature (tem)
LM_3, BG_3, TS_3, SM_3, IN_3 = Dewpoint (dew)
LM_4, BG_4, TS_4, SM_4, IN_4 = Solar radiation (sor)
LM_5, BG_5, TS_5, SM_5, IN_5 = Humidity (hum)
LM_6, BG_6, TS_6, SM_6, IN_6 = Precipitation (pre)
LM_7, BG_7, TS_7, SM_7, IN_7 = Air pressure (arp)
LM_8, BG_8, TS_8, SM_8, IN_8 = Wind speed (wsp)
LM_9, BG_9, TS_9, SM_9, IN_9 = Root soil wetness (rsw)
LM_{10}, BG_{10}, TS_{10}, SM_{10}, IN_{10} = Surface root wetness (srw)

3.2 PCA-VARI in Data Mining Process

Principal Component Recognition for PCA-VARI

The climate data verified in the preprocessing process starts by testing the data's feasibility before calculating to model the correlation value between variables simultaneously using KMO. The results obtained for the five locations were 0.6105, 0.5401, 0.7023, 0.5514, 0.6429, respectively. PCA modeling process can be continued because the test criteria obtained at the correlation of each variable is greater than 0.5.

Table 2. Estimation of eigenvalues for five climate locations

Principal component	Eigenvalue (LM)	Eigenvalue (BG)	Eigenvalue (TS)	Eigenvalue (SM)	Eigenvalue (IN)
1	4.9866	4.6862	5.5478	4.8586	5.7213
2	2.0370	2.0641	2.0896	1.9380	1.9985
3	1.3877	1.4458	0.7586	1.3608	0.8976
4	0.7657	0.7988	0.6530	0.8597	0.6560
5	0.4352	0.5566	0.4400	0.5555	0.3707
6	0.2470	0.2471	0.2422	0.2585	0.2017
7	0.0896	0.1228	0.1886	0.0896	0.1170
8	0.0493	0.0732	0.0777	0.0764	0.0315
9	0.0016	0.0050	0.0024	0.0025	0.0052
10	0.0003	0.0005	0.0001	0.0004	0.0005

Based on the results obtained in Table 2, the percentage of the cumulative variability of the main components using the correlation matrix with the minimum achievement exceeding 70% was obtained for the climatic areas of Lembang, Tasikmalaya, and

282   D. Munandar et al.

Indramayu. It is explained by two principal components, namely PC1 and PC2, with
the proportions of 70.24%, 76.37%, and 77.20%, respectively. Meanwhile, the Bogor,
Sukabumi climate region consists of three principal components, namely PC1, PC2,
and PC3, with a proportion of 81.96%, and 81.57%, respectively. The proportion of
each principal component varies based on the eigenvalues obtained from the correlation matrix. The eigenvectors corresponding to the eigenvalues for each climate location
data are linear combinations for PCA modeling. After the eigenvalues are obtained, the
eigenvectors are as in Table 3.

Table 3. Estimation of eigenvectors for five climate locations

Variable of climate	Eigenvector (PC1-LM)	Eigenvector (PC1-BG)	Eigenvector (PC1-TS)	Eigenvector (PC1-SM)	Eigenvector (PC1-IN)
uvi	−0.0768	−0.0908	−0.1070	−0.0808	−0.0509
tem	0.2259	−0.1012	−0.3800	0.2358	0.0218
dew	0.4270	0.4029	−0.4100	0.4369	0.4052
sor	0.3603	0.2320	−0.3595	0.3158	0.3702
hum	0.3886	0.4454	−0.1545	0.3960	0.3798
pre	0.3640	0.3489	−0.3422	0.3516	0.3289
arp	−0.2490	−0.2738	0.3080	−0.2539	−0.2595
wsp	−0.0324	0.1992	0.2815	−0.0856	−0.3108
rsw	0.3707	0.3930	−0.3296	0.3708	0.3648
srw	0.3834	0.4197	−0.3509	0.3969	0.3825

In Table 3 the variables with the highest positive effect on the first principal component Lembang (PC1-LM), consisted of dew point and humidity in values of 0.4270
and 0.3886. Meanwhile, on the first principal component Bogor (PC1-BG), the variance
comprises humidity and surface root wetness in values of 0.4454 and 0.4197. In contrast
to the first principal component Tasikmalaya (PC1-TS) dew point and air temperature
have a dominant variance contribution of −0.4100 and −0.3800. The minus sign is an
indication of a negative change to the variance. For first principal component, Sukabumi
(PC1-SM) dew point and surface root wetness are 0.4369 and 0.3969. Meanwhile, the
location of first principal component, Indramayu (PC1-IN), has the highest contribution
to the dew point and humidity at values of 0.4052 and 0.3798. The contribution of the
principal component for each regional climate location describes the eigenvectors of
each location to determine the most variance in dew point and humidity. This indicates
that in West Java, the two variables contributed an important role in conditions. The
role of surface root wetness is also raised as a contribution representing the principal
component, indicating the region is close to the equator. The new dataset can be seen in

Fig. 2 through linear combination processes like Eq. (1) and used to predict the inter-site climate influence based on PCA-VARI to obtain a seasonal pattern.

Identifications of PCA-VARI Locations

Stationary model using test Augmented Dickey-Fuller (ADF) and Box-Cox determined the stationary climate data in mean and variance of PC1-LM, PC1-BG, PC1-TS, PC1-SM, PC1-IN respectively as $\gamma_{1,t}$, $\gamma_{2,t}$, $\gamma_{3,t}$, $\gamma_{4,t}$, $\gamma_{5,t}$. The new variables from Principal Component were tested by applying measurements in two tests, namely i) differencing original non-stationary data for each location; and ii) differencing of new data resulting from the PCA process. The ADF and Box-Cox test values show varying values to analyze the significance of the data assumptions shown in the Table. 4. The significant value used for ADF $\alpha < 0.05$ and Box-Cox ≈ 1 to view that PCA climate data has changed. The process to stationary performs differencing is used to meet the test significant value limit.

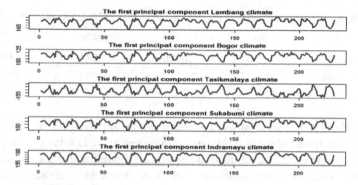

Fig. 2. New dataset after a principal component process

Table 4 shows that the first principal component data for PC1 of climate locations is not stationary in the average for $\hat{\gamma}_{1,t}$PC1-LM, $\hat{\gamma}_{1,t}$PC1-BG, $\hat{\gamma}_{1,t}$PC1-TS, and $\hat{\gamma}_{1,t}$PC1-SM. Meanwhile, for stationary data in variance where the Box-Cox value is close to 1, $\hat{\gamma}_{1,t}$PC1-IN has a sufficient value. The transformation process is conducted before differencing process at the first level to determine whether the data is stationary. The differencing process has a *p-value* of less than 5% (0.05), hence when it is more than 0.05, H_0 is rejected, indicating data is not stationary, and the Box-Cox value is close to 1.

Table 5 shows that selecting the Schwarz Information Criterion (SC) model as the PCA-VARI (1) lag sequence has a minimum value that will be used for modeling. MLE is used to calculate the model coefficients and parameter estimation. The markers in Tables 5 and 6 show the order of the lags with the first-order lag selected using the SC (n) criteria to obtain the minimum value at the significance level of $\alpha < 0.05$.

Table 4. First principal component stationary

Variable	Without different		With different	
	p-value	Box-Cox	*p-value*	Box-Cox
$\hat{\gamma}_{1,t}$PC1-LM	0.1742	0.9995	0.0001	0.9993
$\hat{\gamma}_{1,t}$PC1-BG	0.8687	0.9994	0.0001	0.9928
$\hat{\gamma}_{1,t}$PC1-TS	0.3926	0.6925	0.0001	0.9935
$\hat{\gamma}_{1,t}$PC1-SM	0.7858	0.9992	0.0001	0.9894
$\hat{\gamma}_{1,t}$PC1-IN	0.0190	0.9967	0.0001	0.9146

Table 5. Lag order criteria on the PCA-VARI model

	PCA-VARI (1)	PCA-VARI (2)	PCA-VARI (3)	PCA-VARI (4)	PCA-VARI (5)
AIC (n)	1.2771	0.9986	0.8910	0.8420	0.7677*
HQ (n)	1.7534	1.6238*	1.6650	1.7648	1.8393
SC (n)	2.4584*	2.5491	2.8107	3.1308	3.4256

Table 6 PCA-VARI modeling can be interpreted at each location, such as $\dot{Y}_{1,t}$ representing the input model of the first principal component at the Lembang location. Model interpretation occurs when the values of dew point and humidity that occurred in a month at Lembang climate decrease values by 0.1940. A change in value a month before at Indramayu climate will lead to a 0.3633 increase. When Tasikmalaya climate experiences a change in the previous month, it will increase by 0.1726. $\dot{Y}_{2,t}$ represents the first principal component of Bogor climate and interprets that a change in the values of dew point and surface root wetness, as most variances occurred a month before at Lembang and Indramayu, leads to an increase by 0.0.2954 and 0.3376. If there is a change in the last month at Tasikmalaya, it will cause an increase of 0.1441. $\dot{Y}_{3,t}$ indicate the first principal component of the Tasikmalaya. The interpretation model makes the dew point and air temperature different as most variance values occurred in the last months at Bogor climate, thereby increasing the variable value by 0.5371 times this month.

$\dot{Y}_{4,t}$ represents first principal component of the Sukabumi location, which changes most variance values of the dew point and surface root wetness. The Lembang climate that emerged in previous months caused an increase in the value by 0.2398 times. $\dot{Y}_{5,t}$ As the first principal component of Indramayu, dew point and humidity emerged in the previous month at Tasikmalaya climate, causing an increased variable value of 0.1898.

Table 6. Parameter estimation of PCA-VARI (1) model

Variable	$Y_{1,t}$	$Y_{2,t}$	$Y_{3,t}$	$Y_{4,t}$	$Y_{5,t}$
$Y_{1,t-1}$	$\hat{\phi}_{1,1}^1 = -0.1940$	$\hat{\phi}_{2,1}^1 = 0.2954$	$\hat{\phi}_{3,1}^1 = -0.1823$	$\hat{\phi}_{4,1}^1 = 0.2398$	$\hat{\phi}_{5,1}^1 = 0.3802^*$
$Y_{2,t-1}$	$\hat{\phi}_{1,1}^2 = -0.5565$	$\hat{\phi}_{2,1}^2 = -0.9009^{***}$	$\hat{\phi}_{3,1}^2 = 0.5371$	$\hat{\phi}_{4,1}^2 = -0.5573^*$	$\hat{\phi}_{5,1}^2 = -0.6341^*$
$Y_{3,t-1}$	$\hat{\phi}_{1,1}^3 = 0.1726$	$\hat{\phi}_{2,1}^3 = 0.1441$	$\hat{\phi}_{3,1}^3 = -0.6066^{***}$	$\hat{\phi}_{4,1}^3 = 0.1708$	$\hat{\phi}_{5,1}^3 = 0.1898$
$Y_{4,t-1}$	$\hat{\phi}_{1,1}^4 = 0.2018$	$\hat{\phi}_{2,1}^4 = 0.0248$	$\hat{\phi}_{3,1}^4 = -0.3161$	$\hat{\phi}_{4,1}^4 = -0.1910$	$\hat{\phi}_{5,1}^4 = 0.1170$
$Y_{5,t-1}$	$\hat{\phi}_{1,1}^5 = 0.3633^*$	$\hat{\phi}_{2,1}^5 = 0.3376^*$	$\hat{\phi}_{3,1}^5 = -0.2884$	$\hat{\phi}_{4,1}^5 = 0.2728$	$\hat{\phi}_{5,1}^5 = 0.0454$

Note: The mark of ***, **, and * show statistical significance at 0.01, 0.05 and 0.1.
Information: $Y_{1,t} = $ PC1-LM, $Y_{2,t} = $ PC1-BG, $Y_{3,t} = $ PC1-TS, $Y_{4,t} = $ PC1-SM, $Y_{5,t} = $ PC1-IN.

Table 7. PCA-VARI model estimation coefficient diagnostic test of Granger

Variable	F-Test	p-value
$Y_{1,t}$	1.1064	0.3021
$Y_{2,t}$	4.4834	0.0013
$Y_{3,t}$	1.8809	0.0328
$Y_{4,t}$	1.6996	0.0411
$Y_{5,t}$	19.626	0.0000

Table 8. PCA-VARI model estimation coefficient diagnostic test of Ljung-Box

Variable	χ^2	p-value
$Y_{1,t}$	0.1042	0.7469
$Y_{2,t}$	7.6877	0.8090
$Y_{3,t}$	0.1596	0.6895
$Y_{4,t}$	0.2052	0.6505
$Y_{5,t}$	2.5374	0.7708

Table 7 shows the Granger causality test for each first principal component of PCA-VARI model. Variables of $Y_{2,t}$, $Y_{3,t}$, $Y_{4,t}$, $Y_{5,t}$ and Granger against others with p-value $<$ 0.05 rejected H_0 and can be culminated to obtain the diagnostic model test. Meanwhile, $Y_{1,t}$ shows no Granger against others because the p-value $>$ 0.05, and the diagnostic tests gave a p-value $>$ 0.05, which is close to 1 and the significance level. The PCA-VARI model obtained a diagnostic test used to determine the multivariate time series criteria. In Table 8 it can be seen that χ^2 value is close to 1 indicating that it meets the white noise test criteria.

3.3 Interpretation and Visualization Model

The PCA-VARI model forecasting estimates between climate locations obtained in this study are represented using the Impulse Response Function (IRF). Its function is to determine the effect of one location's climate on another.

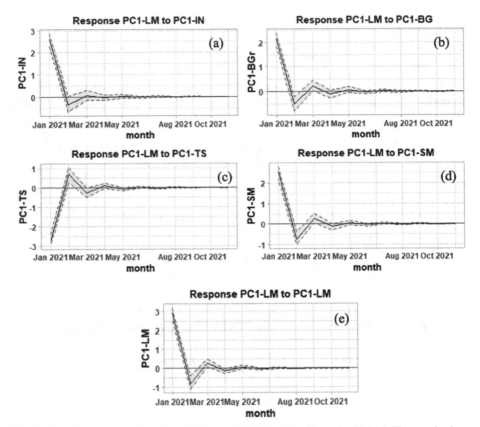

Fig. 3. Impulse response function (IRF) model PCA-VARI effect of PC1-LM. The x-axis shows the forecast for the month of the next period, and the y-axis shows the forecast standard deviation

Figure 3 shows the influence of PC1-LM on the other four regions. For instance, its effect on the value index of the Bogor location changes of standard deviation has increased in the first month of January 2021 by 2.1582, as shown in Fig. 3(b). In other words, PC1-BG comprising surface root wetness and humidity decreased to 0.5196 in February 2021 and then fluctuated until May 2021. The same pattern can be seen in Fig. 3(d), namely PC1 Sukabumi, comprising of dew point and surface root wetness, Fig. 3(e) of PC1 Indramayu with dew point and surface root wetness, and Fig. 3(a) PC1-LM Lembang.

The response by PC1-TS Tasikmalaya (humidity and air temperature) in Fig. 3(c) starts with a decrease of 2.7130 and increases in February 2021 to 0.7205. It decreases to 0.2427 in March and fluctuates until June 2021.

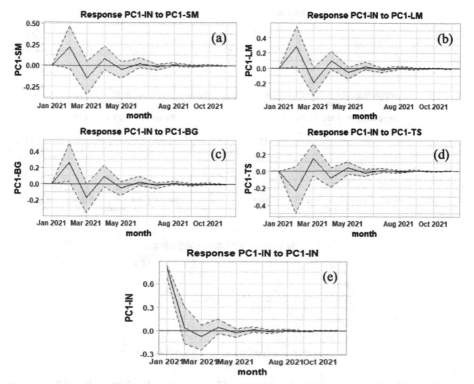

Fig. 4. Impulse response function (IRF) PCA-VARI model effect of PC1-IN (dew point and humidity).

Figure 4 IRF the effect caused by PC1-IN on PC1-LM, PC1-BG, and PC1-SM. Figure 4 (a), (b), and (c) have a similar pattern, namely there is no effect in January, with an increase above 0.2000, and a decrease to 0.2000 in February, which fluctuated to the sixth month. Meanwhile, in response to Fig. 4(e) PC1-IN experienced an increase of 0.7959 and 0.03614 in February, with a decrease in March by 0.07694, which varied until June. Significant impact is not seen until the end of the year. For the response to PC1-TS in Fig. 4(d) in January, there is no response to climate, with a decrease of 0.2295 in February and an increase of 0.15177 until July. Significant impact is not seen until the end of the year.

Figure 5 shows the IRF effect of PC1-BG on other locations with no response to PC1-LM in the first month, as shown in Fig. 5(b). However, it decreased by 0.3277 (dew point and humidity) in February 2021, increased in March by 0.2318, and fluctuated until July 2021, without a response until the end of 2021. The effect on PC1-TS in Fig. 5(c) also did not occur at the beginning of the year but increased in February by 0.2392 and decreased by 0.1633 in March, before fluctuating until June 2021. The effect to PC1-SM in Fig. 5(d) and PC1-IN in Fig. 5(a) seems to have the same pattern, starting with a positive value or increase at the beginning of the year to decreasing in February and increasing again in March. Impulse PC1-BG to PC1-TS in Fig. 5(c) has no effect from August to the end of 2021.

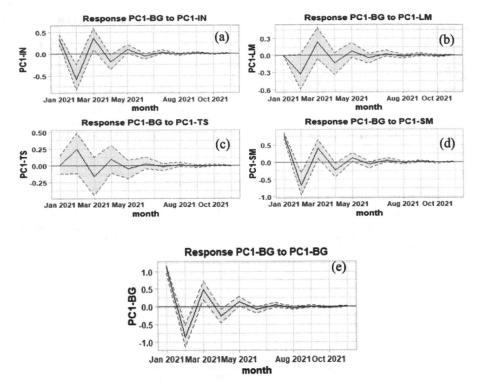

Fig. 5. Impulse response function (IRF) PCA-VARI model effect of PC1-BG

Similarly, the effect of PC1-SM and PC1-TS on the four climates of each location has the same pattern as the area adjacent to the location Bogor. However, there are differences in standard deviations for predictions each month.

4 Conclusion

The PCA-VARI model implements a multivariate time series model that reduces the number of observational variables with large data at each climate location through a linear combination of correlated and uncorrelated variables without losing much information. Quantitatively, the relationship between PCA and VARI through the computational process on a multivariate time series plays a significant role in the acquisition of forecasting results. This is common in simplifying the parameter estimation by means of the principal component, which facilitates the visualization and interpretation of the PCA-VARI model. The study analyzes time series data from daily agroclimatology with ten variables for each location. The result is the reduction of climate variables into several principal components. Following the Box-Jenkins rules, comprising of identification, parameter estimation, and model diagnostic testing, the VARI process uses the impulse response function (IRF) to determine the effect between locations of climate variables. Others respond the influence of one region with changes in increasing or decreasing the standard deviation of each climate variable. This is knowledge generated to determine future forecasts for the influence of one region on others. The forecasting results can be concluded that the climate of a location affects those whose coordinates are close together, which is proven using IRF. The influence of climate from one location to another is a recommendation such as regional development that impacts the community [29]. Furthermore, socio-economic activities contribute a positive trend to the analysis of services in improving the economy of a region [30].

Acknowledgments. The authors are grateful to the Rector of Universitas Padjadjaran, who provided financial support to disseminate research reports under the Academic Leadership Grant year 2022 and Studies Center of Modeling and Computation Faculty of Mathematics and Natural Sciences Universitas Padjadjaran. Gratefully thank the Head of the National Research and Innovation Agency (BRIN), who has supported the funding for the Doctoral Program by Research 2022. The authors are also grateful for the discussion on social media analytics through the RISE_SMA project funded by the European Union from 2019–2024.

References

1. Kishimoto, R., Shimura, T., Mori, N., Mase, H.: Statistical modeling of global mean wave height considering principal component analysis of sea level pressures and its application to future wave height projection. Hydrol. Res. Lett. **11**(1), 51–57 (2017)
2. Washington, B.J., Seymour, L.: An adapted vector autoregressive expectation maximization imputation algorithm for climate data networks. Wiley Interdiscip. Rev. Comput. Stat. **12**(6), e1494 (2020)
3. Mal, S., Singh, R.B., Huggel, C., Grover, A.: Introducing linkages between climate change, extreme events, and disaster risk reduction. In: Mal, S., Singh, R., Huggel, C. (eds.) Climate Change, Extreme Events and Disaster Risk Reduction. Sustainable Development Goals Series, pp. 1–14. Springer, Cham (2018). https://doi.org/10.1007/978-3-319-56469-2_1
4. Pretis, F.: Econometric models of climate systems: the equivalence of two-component energy balance models and cointegrated VARs (2015)
5. Mamipour, S., Yahoo, M., Jalalvandi, S.: An empirical analysis of the relationship between the environment, economy, and society: results of a PCA-VAR model for Iran. Ecol. Ind. **102**, 760–769 (2019)
6. Han, J., Kamber, M., Pei, J.: Data Mining Concepts and Techniques, 3rd edn. Elsevier Inc., Massachusetts (2012)
7. Niu, J., et al.: A comparative study on application of data mining technique in human shape clustering: principal component analysis vs. factor analysis. In: 2010 5th IEEE Conference on Industrial Electronics and Applications, pp. 2014–2018. IEEE, June 2010
8. Cerón, W.L., et al.: A principal component analysis approach to assess CHIRPS precipitation dataset for the study of climate variability of the La Plata Basin, Southern South America. Nat. Hazards **103**(1), 767–783 (2020)
9. Chandra, E., Ajitha, P.: PCA for heterogeneous data sets in a distributed data mining. In: Proceedings of the Fourth Annual ACM Bangalore Conference, pp. 1–4, March 2011
10. Munandar, D., Ruchjana, B., Abdullah, A.: Principal component analysis-vector autoregressive integrated (PCA-VARI) model using data mining approach to climate data in the West Java Region. Barekeng J. II. Mat. Ter. **16**(1), 099–112 (2022)
11. Yu, Y., Wang, D.: Similarity study of hydrological time series based on data mining. In: Atiquzzaman, M., Yen, N., Xu, Z. (eds.) BDCPS 2020. AISC, vol. 1303, pp. 1049–1055. Springer, Singapore (2021). https://doi.org/10.1007/978-981-33-4572-0_150

12. Du, X., Zhu, F.: A novel principal components analysis (PCA) method for energy absorbing structural design enhanced by data mining. Adv. Eng. Softw. **127**, 17–27 (2019)
13. Snedecor, G.W., Cochran, W.G.: Statistical Methods. Iowa State University Press (1989)
14. Singh, T., Ghosh, A., Khandelwal, N.: Dimensional reduction and feature selection: principal component analysis for data mining. Radiology **285**(3), 1055 (2017)
15. Johnson, R.A., Wichern, D.W.: Applied Multivariate Statistical Analysis, 6th edn. Pearson Prentice Hall, New Jersey (2007)
16. Anton, H., Rorrers, C.: Elementary Linear Algebra, 11th edn. Wiley, Hoboken (2014)
17. Box, G.E.P., Jenkins, G.M.: Time Series Analysis Forecasting and Control. Holden-Day. Inc. (1976)
18. Dickey, D., Fuller, W.A.: Distribution of the estimators for time series regressions with a unit root. J. Am. Stat. Assoc. **74**(366), 427–431 (1979)
19. Brockwell, P.J., Davis, R.A.: Introduction to Time Series and Forecasting, 2nd edn. Springer, New York (2002). https://doi.org/10.1007/b97391
20. Box, G.E.P., Cox, D.: An analysis of transformations. J. R. Stat. Soc. **B.26**(2), 211–252 (1964)
21. Di Asih, I.M., Rahmawati, R.: Vector autoregressive model approach for forecasting outflow cash in Central Java. J. Phys. Conf. Ser. **1025**(1), 012105 (2018)
22. Nalita, Y., Rahani, R., Tirayo, E.R., Toharudin, T., Ruchjana, B.N.: Ordinary least square and maximum likelihood estimation of VAR (1) model's parameters and it's application on Covid-19 in China 2020. J. Phys. Conf. Ser. **1722**(1), 012082 (2021)
23. Granger, C.W.J.: Investigating causal relations by econometric models and cross-spectral methods. Econometrica **37**(3), 424–438 (1969)
24. Chan, J.C., Shi, J.E.: Application of projection-pursuit principal component analysis method to climate studies. Int. J. Climatol. J. R. Meteorol. Soc. **17**(1), 103–113 (1997)
25. Shaharudin, S.M., Ahmad, N., Zainuddin, N.H., Mohamed, N.S.: Identification of rainfall patterns on hydrological simulation using robust principal component analysis. Indones. J. Electr. Eng. Comput. Sci. **11**(3), 1162–1167 (2018)
26. Shahin, M.A., Ali, M.A., Ali, A.B.M.S.: Vector autoregression (VAR) modeling and forecasting of temperature, humidity, and cloud coverage. In: Islam, T., Srivastava, P., Gupta, M., Zhu, X., Mukherjee, S. (eds.) Computational Intelligence Techniques in Earth and Environmental Sciences, pp. 29–51. Springer, Dordrecht (2014). https://doi.org/10.1007/978-94-017-8642-3_2
27. POWER NASA. https://power.larc.nasa.gov/. Accessed 21 May 2022
28. WIKIMEDIA. https://upload.wikimedia.org/wikipedia/commons/b/b9/Geocultural_regions_of_West_Java.svg. Accessed 21 May 2022
29. Gabriel, A.G., Santiago, P.N.M., Casimiro, R.R.: Mainstreaming disaster risk reduction and climate change adaptation in comprehensive development planning of the cities in Nueva Ecija in the Philippines. Int. J. Disaster Risk Sci. **12**(3), 367–80 (2021)
30. Newth, D., Gooley, G., Gunasekera, D.: Socio-economic analysis of climate services in disaster risk reduction: a perspective on pacific SIDS. Front. Environ. Sci. **9** (2021)

Social Media Analytics

Location Mention Recognition from Japanese Disaster-Related Tweets

Toshihiro Rokuse$^{(\boxtimes)}$ and Osamu Uchida$^{(\boxtimes)}$

Department of Information Media Technology, Tokai University, Hiratsuka, Kanagawa, Japan
{trokuse,o-uchida}@tokai.ac.jp

Abstract. In order to minimize the damage inflicted by large-scale disasters, it is essential to collect and disseminate information quickly and accurately. In recent years, various national agencies and local municipalities have used Twitter and other highly immediate social media to help focus their disaster relief efforts. Because the volume of information circulating on social media increases rapidly during a disaster, the ability to quickly sort out valuable posts from the massive volume of posts that appear is essential. In the case of Twitter, it is vital for early responders to identify the location of relevant tweets in order to facilitate decision making and focus their response. To help in this task, attempts have been made to use machine learning to classify genres, extract useful information, and identify locations and points of interest for groups of tweets posted during a disaster. However, since preparing training data and building a model during the early stages of a disaster are extremely challenging, using a model built on past disaster tweet data offers a promising possibility. In this study, we focus on three heavy rain disasters that occurred in Japan and examine the extraction of the location mentions in tweets using models learned from tweets posted during prior disasters.

Keywords: Disaster · Social media · Location mention · Machine learning

1 Introduction

Prompt and accurate information gathering and dissemination are critical to minimize damage in the event of a large-scale disaster. In recent years, the possibility of using highly immediate and popular social media platforms for this purpose has been the subject of increasing interest. When a disaster strikes, reports of power outages, communication failures, and other damage posted in real-time on such sites can contain information helpful in planning and executing first responses [1]. Several surveys have shown that Twitter, in particular, has been used to transmit, collect, and share information about the damage inflicted by a large-scale disaster [2]. Indeed, there is a growing movement among government agencies and local municipalities which play a key role in times of disaster to gather, disseminate, and act on information available through social media sites like Twitter [3]. However, because the volume of information circulating on social media increases rapidly during a large-scale disaster, there are still issues to be addressed if further utilization of social media is to become part of an effective disaster

© IFIP International Federation for Information Processing 2023
Published by Springer Nature Switzerland AG 2023
T. Gjøsæter et al. (Eds.): ITDRR 2022, IFIP AICT 672, pp. 293–307, 2023.
https://doi.org/10.1007/978-3-031-34207-3_19

response strategy. For example, during the earthquake that hit the northern part of Osaka Prefecture on June 18, 2018, it was revealed that at least 270,000 tweets (including re-tweets) containing the word "earthquake" were posted on Twitter during the 10 min following 8:00 a.m., immediately after the main shock was felt [4]. It has also been pointed out that more than 5,200 rescue requests posted on social media were missed during the hurricane that made landfall in Texas, USA, in August 2017 [5]. Given such experiences, there is a clear need to quickly sort out essential information from the vast number of tweets that flood the site. It is also vital for disaster responders to identify the locations noted in the tweets—that is, to extract location mentions—so that appropriate decisions can be made. Table 1 shows examples of tweets posted on Twitter that contain location mentions.

Against this background, efforts have been made to use machine learning to classify genres, extract useful information, and identify locations and points of interest for groups of tweets posted during disasters. However, preparing training data and building models in real-time when a disaster occurs are highly challenging. One of the factors that make the use of machine learning models difficult is data preparation. Since a large number of tweets with a broad range of characteristics circulate in a short period of time during a disaster, it is necessary to select the tweets to be used for learning and to annotate the collected tweets. Such tasks generally require a substantial amount of time. However, from the perspective of minimizing the damage caused by a disaster, it is important to respond quickly.

To reconcile these two conflicting requirements, building a model using tweet data from past disasters offers a promising possibility. Such models are not unprecedented. Suwaileh et al. [6], for example, attempted to extract location mentions from tweets during the 2016 flooding in Houston, Texas, USA, using a model learned from tweets posted during previous disasters. However, to the authors' knowledge, there are no cases in which location mention recognition was used for tweets written in Japanese and posted during disasters in Japan. In this study, we focus on three torrential rain disasters in Japan and examine the extraction of location mentions using a model learned from tweets posted during prior disasters. Specifically, we examine tweets posted during the heavy rain-induced disasters of July 2018, July 2020, and August 2021 (Fig. 1).

One of the main contributions of our paper is the proposed method for constructing a disaster-related dataset from tweets posted in Japanese. Most of the disaster tweet datasets represented in CrisisLex [7] and CrisisNLP [8] are in English, and there appear to be insufficient resources available in other languages, although efforts are underway to build datasets for languages such as Spanish and Arabic [9, 10]. A second contribution is the validation of location mention extraction using past disaster tweets posted in Japanese. In their earlier study, Suwaileh [6] et al. sought such validation for English language tweets; in our current study, we show that their approach can be adapted to Japanese heavy rainfall disasters described in tweets composed in Japanese.

Table 1. Disaster-related tweets that include location mentions

	Original Japanese text	Translated English text
Tweet 1	大雨の影響で安芸矢口駅付近の道路が冠水・浸水 現地の様子 <URL>	Roads near Aki Yaguchi Station flooded and submerged due to heavy rains. The situation there is the following. <URL>
Tweet 2	大雨で飯山線止まって北陸新幹線でしか長野に戻れなくなった 🏵 <URL>	Heavy rain stopped the Iiyama line, so I could return to Nagano only by boarding the Hokuriku Shinkansen. 🏵 <URL>.

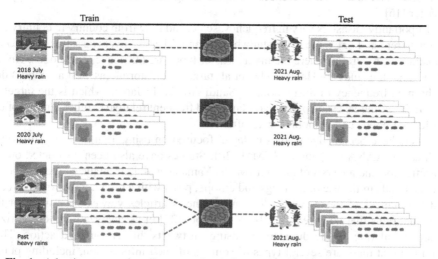

Fig. 1. Adapting to ongoing disasters using inference models learned from past disasters

2 Related Work

2.1 Analysis of Disaster-Related Tweets

In recent years, there have been numerous attempts to facilitate the use of social media to disseminate information and assist early responders in times of disaster. Various researchers have proposed methods to solve the problem of selecting important information from the huge number of tweets posted during a disaster by treating it as a document classification problem. For instance, Kayi [11] et al. developed a method for estimating urgency in order to set disaster response priorities. A method that classifies disaster-related information into four genres ("damage situation," "warning," etc.) as a way to filter the information has also been proposed [12].

Chowdhury [13] et al. offered a method that takes into account the broken writing style of social media users, such as replacing "you" with "u", when extracting situationally important phrases from tweets. Studies are also underway for extracting location mentions from tweets. For example, Al-Olimat et al. proposed a method using open data sources featuring the names of public facilities, tourist attractions, and other landmarks [14]. Such studies are based on the assumption that it is possible to immediately annotate tweets and build machine learning models to make inferences when a disaster occurs. However, Medina [15] et al. argued that such an assumption is not practical in a real catastrophe and discussed the possibility of using tweets posted during previous disasters to help build an accurate model. As noted above, Suwaileh [6] et al. sought to verify various aspects of location mention recognition. For example, they examined the extent to which results differ when inferences are made using tweet data from the same type of disaster and when inferences are made using tweet data from a different type of disaster [16].

Importantly, disasters vary in frequency, scale, and type from country to country and region to region. For example, the study by Olteanu [7] et al. covers disasters in the U.S., Canada, and Australia, where the main disaster types are hurricanes and floods. On the other hand, the study by Hamoui [18] et al. targets sandstorms (as well as floods) due to the high frequency of dust storms in Saudi Arabia. In Japan, which is the target of this study, earthquakes are particularly large and frequent relative to other regions of the world, and floods and typhoons occur often.

There have been active studies in Japan focused on using Twitter during disasters, such as DISAANA [19] and D-SUMM [20]. Studies have also been conducted on the classification and analysis of disaster tweets. Yamada et al. [21] analyzed the number of tweets, trends in the use of hashtags and emojis, posts with a high number of re-tweets, and the number of tweets with URL links to news articles viewed over time for the torrential rains that occurred in 2018. Yamamoto [22] et al. analyzed and categorized tweets circulating during disasters, focusing on tweets that encouraged action. They point out that there are several types of sources of such information, including public outlets and hearsay. However, the main objective of our study is to extract information using past disaster data, which is different from the objectives of most of these other studies.

2.2   Location Mention from Twitter

Filtering information on Twitter according to the situation is especially important during a disaster, where a vast amount of information is typically circulated in a short period. The location information of tweets posted on Twitter is of particular importance. There are three main methods for extracting such location information: The first method is to use geotags, latitude and longitude information that can be added to tweets to identify the location of the poster; however, it has been reported that the number of geotagged tweets tends to be extremely small [23]. The second method is to employ user profiles [24]. This method uses the fact that user profiles (self-introductions) often include the area in which the user lives as well as their various affiliations. However, this approach does not necessarily identify the location from which a particular tweet was sent. The third method focuses on location mentions. This method extracts location references such as landmark names that may be included in a tweet and uses them as hints to infer an address [25–27]. However, identifying a specific location in this way can be difficult since the same name may refer to multiple locations (for example, "Central Park"). Given that each of these methods has its advantages and disadvantages, using some combination of methods may be desirable. For example, if no geotag is attached to a particular tweet, a location mention might be extracted; if there are multiple location candidates, the confusion might be resolved based on the user's profile. In this study, we focus on landmark names in tweets as the primary indicator of tweet location.

3 Problem Definition

Extracting location mentions refers to identifying all location mentions in a tweet. More specifically, it means to identify all words $w_i (i = 1, \cdots, L)$ of a given tweet $t = \{w_1, w_2, \ldots, w_L\}$ that refer to locations. Since location mentions can consist of multiple words, we consider a tweet as a series of words and treat the problem as a series labeling problem that predicts the class of each word. We define the five BILOU classes with reference to Yang [28] et al. Figure 2 gives an overview of the problem setup. Here, label "B" indicates the first word of a location mention; label "L" indicates the last word of the location mention. Label "I" indicates a word between the first and last words of the mention. Words that are not location mentions are assigned the label "O". A location mention consisting of only one word is labeled "U". In this study, we attempt to classify tweets into multiple classes based on this definition.

English translation sentence	Power outage at a local community center in Mabi.						
Token in Japanese (English)	真備 (Mabi)	の (*)	地域 (local)	交流 (community)	センター (center)	が (*)	停電 (power outage)
Label	U	O	B	I	L	O	O

Fig. 2. Problem Definition Overview (*: particle)

4 Tweet Collection

The focus of this study is on three recent heavy rain events in Japan. We annotated tweets that we collected from around the time of these three events using the Twitter Search API. To exclude tweets unrelated to the three rain-related disasters, we conducted preliminary experiments based on the work of Paul et al. [29] and determined the queries to be used for the collection. The details are shown in Table 2.

4.1 Preliminary Experiment

Twitter can be classed as a microblog, characterized by short sentences (as compared to other social media platforms). Because of its length restrictions, subjects and parts of sentences are often omitted. Therefore, a single keyword such as "heavy rain" may not be sufficient to collect tweets referring to disaster-stricken situations such as flooding and landslides. In this study, we collected tweets with a large granularity and analyzed the results to determine keywords to gather more tweets. First, we collected tweets using only the word " 大雨" (which means "heavy rain") and selected 200 tweets that mentioned disaster. We used a morphological analyzer to divide the tweets into words and then aggregated their frequencies. The morphemes with exceptionally high frequency were often associated with lifelines and infrastructure damage and were used to help select tweets referring to the disaster.

4.2 Parameters for Tweet Collection

The information required immediately after a disaster strikes differs from that needed after some time has passed. In this study, which targets the immediate aftermath of a disaster, we collected tweets circulated within the 24-h period beginning at the time the Japan Meteorological Agency issued a heavy rain emergency warning. As shown in Table 2, tweets were collected using queries that were manually selected and extended based on preliminary experiments, with start and end times as parameters.

Table 2. Conditions for tweet collection

Disaster	Starting time	Query
July 2018	July 6, 2018 17:10	大雨(heavy rain) OR冠水(submerged) OR 氾濫(overflow) OR 水没(submergence) OR 増水(high flow) OR 浸水 (inundation) OR 洪水(flood) OR 断水(water failure) OR
July 2020	July 4, 2020 04:50	渋滞(congestion) OR 停電(outage) OR 避難所(shelter) OR 避難場所(salvage place) OR 救助(rescue) OR 通行止 (road closed) OR 通行規制(traffic regulation) OR 通行不 (no road) OR 土砂崩れ(landslip) OR 溢れ(inundate) OR
Aug. 2021	Aug. 13, 2021 08:45	浸かっ(dip) OR 倒木(fallen tree) OR 孤立(isolation) OR 陥没(collapse) OR 落石(rock fall) OR 崖崩れ(landslide) OR がけ崩れ(landslide)

5 Filtering Disaster-Related Tweets

According to a study by Paul et al. [29], very few tweets actually mention disasters, even when they include various disaster-related keywords. In this study, we further narrowed the search to original tweets (tweets other than re-tweets) that satisfied the following conditions:

1. written in Japanese

2. retweeted at least once
3. posted using the official Twitter client
4. contain one or more location mentions

These conditions were set based on the hypothesis that tweets that were re-tweeted at least once contain useful information and that posts from the affected areas do not generally use non-official Twitter clients, unlike BOTs or specific web services.

5.1 Written in Japanese

Since the Japanese language shares characters with Chinese, we could expect that tweets written in Chinese but irrelevant to our study would be included in our search results. To address this problem, we used metadata included in the Twitter Search API responses to filter the tweets and restrict them to those written in Japanese.

5.2 Retweeted at Least Once

We assumed that the reason that a user re-tweets a tweet is that the tweet contains meaningful information that the user wishes to disseminate to a larger audience. (Re-tweeting duplicates an existing tweet and reposts it as the user's own tweet, making it available to the user's followers.) Based on this assumption, tweets that were not re-tweeted were excluded from the annotation since they appeared not to contain useful information. Preliminary experiments showed that tweets such as *"Heavy rain is falling in <LOCATION MENTION>"* or *"Heavy rain is falling, is <LOCATION MENTION> safe?"* are of low importance in disaster response.

5.3 Posted Using the Official Twitter Client

We sought to identify highly immediate information from users who were directly affected the disaster. However, since Twitter includes BOTs that periodically post canned messages and posts from Web services such as news sites that organize information after the fact, we needed a way to exclude such posts as irrelevant to our purpose. Based on the hypothesis that, unlike BOTs and various Web services, users posting from disaster-affected areas do not use unofficial Twitter clients when posting, we selected only tweets posted using official Twitter clients. (Preliminary experiments confirmed that tweets whose client was twittbot.net, a BOT hosting service, and tweets posted by NHK, a Japanese public broadcasting organization, were excluded.) The accepted Twitter clients were:

- Twitter for iPhone
- Twitter for iPad
- Twitter for Android
- Twitter Web Client
- Twitter Web App
- TweetDeck

5.4   Contain One or More Location Mentions

As noted, in order for disaster responders to make important decisions based on tweets, it is necessary to identify the location of the tweets. However, location mentions can range from widely known proper nouns, such as prefecture names, to abbreviations used only in certain regions. In this study, we built a dictionary of location mentions by combining different types of open data, following the work of Al-Olimat [14] et al. The dictionary was used to determine if there is a location mention in a tweet. If there are multiple candidate entries in the dictionary for a mentioned location, the longest candidate is selected as the location. For example, if a tweet contains the sentence "*Yokohama station is flooded*" and the dictionary has as location candidates Yokohama and Yokohama station, Yokohama station would be selected.

To collect a wide range of location mentions, we used three types of open data. First, we used geonames.jp (https://geonames.jp/), an open data source that contains the names of Japanese prefectures and allows us to obtain place name reference expressions with relatively large granularity. Next, we used OpenStreetMapJapan (https://openstreetma p.jp/) to collect specific landmarks, such as hospitals and commercial facilities. Finally, we extended the map data from OpenStreetMapJapan with DBpedia Japanese (https://ja. dbpedia.org/), an open data source that extracts information from Wikipedia and supports not only the official names of various landmarks but also their abbreviations and spelling variants. After integrating these three types of open data, we applied post-processing to format the data and used the formatted data as our place name reference dictionary. In addition, two post-processing steps were applied to the dictionary to avoid matching to unintended substrings and to accommodate more expressions in Twitter shards.

Filtering Location Mention

Due to the nature of editing by an unspecified number of people on the web, open data often contains typographical errors. Therefore, some entries were removed manually. There were also cases where entries in the dictionary matched non-location mentions, e.g., the names of people. These were also removed manually, as necessary. Some entries were removed mechanically using criteria such as character type and number of characters.

Data Augmentation

As noted, we used open data (DBpedia) covering abbreviations and contractions in our study. However, we sought to extend the entries in the location mention dictionary to include an even wider range of expressions. For example, in Japanese, "high school" is formally written as "高等学校," but the abbreviated forms "高校" and "高" are commonly used. Therefore, if there was a dictionary entry for "A 高等学校," "A 高校," and "A 高" were added to the dictionary.

The dictionary created by the above steps was used to exclude tweets that did not contain a location mention.

6 Annotation

The The tweets remaining after applying the filtering methods described above were annotated with location mentions. For the annotation work, we referred to the scheme proposed in the study by Matsuda et al. [25]. Table 3 shows examples of the location mentions annotated in this study. Several types of location mentions were targeted, including "Location," which has a large granularity (e.g., prefecture and municipality), and "Facility," which has a smaller granularity (e.g., station and university). We annotated these place name reference expressions with BILOU tags.

Tweets that did not refer to the disaster-stricken area during the annotation process were excluded. For example, even if a tweet was matched to a dictionary entry for a location mention during the tweet filtering process, the tweet was excluded if the reference was to a specific person rather than, for example, a river. (The name of a river (e.g., 荒川 (Arakawa river)) is also a family name in Japan.) We also removed tweets that did not report damage but only expressed concern over the situation in the affected areas. These processes were repeated until 1,000 tweets were identified for each disaster. As a rule, annotating the results of random sampling without refinement is preferred since it is conceivable that specifying conditions may cause bias. However, as shown in Table 4, a massive number of tweets circulate after a disaster. Thus, we used the conditions mentioned above to filter the tweets.

Table 3. Annotated location types

Type	Original Japanese words	English translation words
Location	岩手県 倉敷市	Iwate prefecture, Kurashiki city
Facility	博多駅 東海大学	Hakata station, Tokai university
Railway	京浜東北線 山手線	Keihinohoku line, Yamanote line
River	球磨川 阿武隈川	Kuma river, Abukuma river
Road	国道4号線 東北道	National Route 4, Tohoku expressway
General	病院 コンビニ	Hospital, Convenience store

Table 4. Aggregate results for each process

Disaster	Collected tweets	Filtered tweets	Annotated tweets
July 2018	1,107,378	26,780	1,000
July 2020	561,311	12,890	1,000
August 2021	441,930	16,186	1,000

7 Experiment

7.1 Experimental Setup

We used tweets from past disasters in the learning and inference phases to test the feasibility of using such tweets. For the learning phase, we used tweet data from either the July 2018 torrential rainstorm, the July 2020 torrential rainstorm, or an equal mix of both. In the inference phase, we used tweets from the August 2021 torrential rainstorm. We did this in order to assess the impact of using either a single disaster or a combination of disasters.

BERT [31] was used to extract location mentions. BERT is widely used as a baseline for the series labeling problem and is known to give good results even with relatively small amounts of data. There are two ways to adapt BERT to a particular language: monolingual models trained on a single language and multilingual models (mBERT) trained on multiple languages. Although mBERT adapts to multiple languages with a single model, models that focus on languages with the same features can produce better results. For example, Xu et al. [32] proposed a model trained only on Japanese and Chinese, using the fact that Japanese and Chinese share certain features, such as identical characters and non-trivial boundaries between words. As a result of validation, Xu et al. [32] reported improved performance in tasks such as translation in Japanese and Chinese. It has also been shown for multiple languages that models trained on only a single language are effective when there is no need for a single model to support multiple languages, as in translation [33, 33]. However, since learning BERT from scratch is very computationally intensive, we decided to fine-tune our approach based on BERT-japanese (https://github.com/cl-tohoku/bert-japanese), a version of BERT specialized for Japanese. BERT-japanese is trained using Japanese Wikipedia and is highly versatile, as it covers a wide variety of fields. In addition, BERT-japanese has been employed in numerous studies targeting the Japanese language [35–37]. Finally, although there are improved models of BERT, such as RoBERTa [38] and ALBERT [39], with enhanced performance and speed, we chose BERT to be consistent with previous studies.

The data were prepared using the following the steps: First, URLs and user names in tweets were replaced with <URL> and <USERNAME>, respectively, as a pre-processing step. The morphological analyzer MeCab (https://taku910.github.io/mecab/) was used for word segmentation. The dictionary used in this study was unidic-lite (https://github.com/polm/unidic-lite). Experiments were conducted with a 0.8/0.1/0.1 ratio for training, development, and testing, respectively. The hyperparameters for training were set based on the original paper [31], and AdamW was selected as the optimizer, with a learning rate of 2e−5 and a batch size of 8, trained in 3 epochs.

7.2 Experimental Results

Table 5 shows the experimental results. Case (1) can be considered the ideal case, where data are available immediately after the occurrence of a disaster. Cases (2) through (4) are cases where data from past disasters are used.

Comparing the results of cases (2) and (3) shows the relative performance when data from a single disaster were used. As can be seen in the table, case (3) shows better results. In case (3), the heavy rain emergency warning was issued at 5 p.m.—a time when many Twitter users would be traveling home or commuting to work. Thus, the available tweets could be expected to include real-time information from the disaster-stricken areas regarding the damage being observed, such as flooding caused be overflowing rivers or road closures due to landslides. In contrast, case (2)'s weather event occurred in the early morning, before 5:00 a.m., which meant that the number of tweets from the affected areas was limited and that there was little variation in content. As a consequence, the model did not produce good generalization results.

Case (4) uses a combination of the data from the two disasters featured in cases (2) and (3). Random sampling was used to produce the combined sample, with half the tweets selected from case (2) and half from case (3). As shown in the table, performance in case (4) is better than in either case (2) or case (3), suggesting that the two cases are complementary. In other words, generalization performance can be expected to improve by combining data from multiple disasters rather than learning from only one.

Finally, by comparing case (1) and case (4), we can assess the extent to which inference results differ between the ideal case, where current data are available immediately, and the case where only past disaster data are available. As shown, there is a gap of nearly 10 points in each of the indices, strongly suggesting that there is still work to be done to achieve performance close to that in the ideal case.

Table 5. Experimental results

	Training Data	Test Data	Precision	Recall	F-Score
(1)	August 2021	August 2021	0.789	0.827	0.808
(2)	July 2021		0.577	0.625	0.600
(3)	July 2018		0.626	0.692	0.657
(4)	(2) + (3)		0.666	0.731	0.697

8 Discussion

Given It seems self-evident that it would be better to use tweets posted during a current disaster for model learning versus tweets from past disasters. However, rapid decision-making and immediate action are critical to ensuring an effective disaster response. On the other hand, there is a need to allow sufficient time to properly prepare potentially crucial data in order to produce accurate inferential results. The conflicting nature of these two considerations means that a trade-off is required. One approach is to use a model learned from past data immediately after the event and to replace it once the current data have been properly prepared. Alternatively, the two models (past and present) can be combined. The point is that conducting research in parallel in order to take advantage of the merits of both is highly desirable.

When using past tweets as the source of data, improving generalization performance is key. In addition to combining data, a number of possible ways to achieve better performance have been suggested. One is to focus on tweets with images and to combine text with image information [40]. Research is also underway to adapt multi-task learning, which attempts to improve generalization performance by allowing a single model to learn to solve multiple tasks, to disaster tweets [41]. Other proposals include improving the BERT models. Wang et al. [42] reported that even naive models such as word2vec [43] are better at representing tweet features when trained on tweets, compared to BERT models trained on Wikipedia. In support of this result, Nguyen et al. [44] proposed BERTweet, which is trained on tweets, and reported improved performance when targeting tweets. Kawintiranon et al. [45] developed PoliBERTweet, which is trained on tweets about politics, and suggested that further performance improvement can be expected by specializing in a particular field. We believe that these variations can be similarly adapted for disaster tweets.

A comparison of the classification performance obtained by Suwaileh et al. [6] with that obtained in this study showed similar results. It is interesting to note that these similar results were produced for Japanese tweets about disasters that occurred in Japan and for English tweets about disasters that occurred overseas. Further study to determine whether the error tendency is the same for Japanese and English tweets due to differences in characters, grammar, etc., appears warranted but is left for future investigation.

9 Conclusion

Identifying the location of relevant disaster-related messages posted on social media is necessary in order to utilize the information contained in those messages to help formulate and implement a proper disaster response. This study examined the recognition of location mentions in tweets posted on Twitter using a model learned from tweets posted during past disasters and verified it using tweet data from three previous heavy rain disasters in Japan. When using past disaster tweets for training, we found that the best performance is obtained when data from multiple cases are combined. As part of our future work, we plan to test whether the same results can be obtained for other heavy rainfall disasters and to examine how performance changes when data from different kinds of disasters, such as earthquakes and typhoons, are combined.

Acknowledgments. This research was supported by JSPS KAKENHI Grant Number 18K11553.

References

1. Saleem, H., Zamal, F., Ruths, D.: Tackling the challenges of situational awareness extraction in twitter with an adaptive approach. Procedia Eng. **107**, 301–311 (2015). https://doi.org/10.1016/j.proeng.2015.06.085
2. Meier, P.: Digital humanitarians: how big data is changing the face of humanitarian response (2015). https://doi.org/10.1201/b18023
3. Uchida, O., Utsu, K.: Utilization of social media at the time of disaster. IEICE ESS Fundam. Rev. **13**, 301–311 (2020). https://doi.org/10.1587/essfr.13.4_301. (inJapanese)

4. Yamada, S., Utsu, K., Uchida, O.: An analysis of tweets during the 2018 Osaka North Earthquake in Japan -a brief report. In: 2018 5th International Conference on Information and Communication Technologies for Disaster Management (ICT-DM), pp. 1–5 (2018). https://doi.org/10.1109/ICT-DM.2018.8636393

5. Villegas, C., Martinez, M., Krause, M.: Lessons from harvey: crisis informatics for urban resilience. Rice University Kinder Institute for Urban Research (2018). https://doi.org/10.25611/np4y-3bil

6. Suwaileh, R., Imran, M., Elsayed, T., Sajjad, H.: Are we ready for this disaster? Towards location mention recognition from crisis tweets. In: Proceedings of the 28th International Conference on Computational Linguistics, Barcelona, Spain, pp. 6252–6263. International Committee on Computational Linguistics (2020)

7. Olteanu, A., Castillo, C., Diaz, F., Vieweg, S.: CrisisLex: a lexicon for collecting and filtering microblogged communications in crises. In: Proceedings of the 8th International Conference on Weblogs and Social Media, ICWSM 2014, pp. 376–385 (2014)

8. Imran, M., Mitra, P., Castillo, C.: Twitter as a lifeline: human-annotated Twitter corpora for NLP of crisis-related messages. In: Proceedings of the Tenth International Conference on Language Resources and Evaluation (LREC 2016), Portorož, Slovenia, pp. 1638–1643. European Language Resources Association (ELRA) (2016)

9. Cobo, A., Parra, D., Navón, J.: Identifying relevant messages in a Twitter-based citizen channel for natural disaster situations. In: Proceedings of the 24th International Conference on World Wide Web, New York, NY, USA, pp. 1189–1194. Association for Computing Machinery (2015). https://doi.org/10.1145/2740908.2741719

10. Alharbi, A., Lee, M.: Kawarith: an Arabic Twitter corpus for crisis events. In: Proceedings of the Sixth Arabic Natural Language Processing Workshop, Kyiv, Ukraine (Virtual), pp. 42–52. Association for Computational Linguistics (2021)

11. Sarioglu Kayi, E., Nan, L., Qu, B., Diab, M., McKeown, K.: Detecting urgency status of crisis tweets: a transfer learning approach for low resource languages. In: Proceedings of the 28th International Conference on Computational Linguistics, Barcelona, Spain, pp. 4693–4703. International Committee on Computational Linguistics (2020)

12. Ray Chowdhury, J., Caragea, C., Caragea, D.: Cross-lingual disaster-related multi-label tweet classification with manifold mixup. In: Proceedings of the 58th Annual Meeting of the Association for Computational Linguistics: Student Research Workshop, pp. 292–298. Association for Computational Linguistics (2020). https://doi.org/10.18653/v1/2020.acl-srw.39

13. Ray Chowdhury, J., Caragea, C., Caragea, D.: Keyphrase extraction from disaster-related tweets. In: The World Wide Web Conference, New York, NY, USA, pp. 1555–1566. Association for Computing Machinery (2019). https://doi.org/10.1145/3308558.3313696

14. Al-Olimat, H., Thirunarayan, K., Shalin, V., Sheth, A.: Location name extraction from targeted text streams using gazetteer-based statistical language models. In: Proceedings of the 27th International Conference on Computational Linguistics, Santa Fe, New Mexico, USA, pp. 1986–1997. Association for Computational Linguistics (2018)

15. Medina Maza, S., Spiliopoulou, E., Hovy, E., Hauptmann, A.: Event-related bias removal for real-time disaster events. In: Findings of the Association for Computational Linguistics: EMNLP 2020, pp. 3858–3868. Association for Computational Linguistics (2020)

16. Suwaileh, R., Elsayed, T., Imran, M., Sajjad, H.: When a disaster happens, we are ready: location mention recognition from crisis tweets. Int. J. Disaster Risk Reduct. **78**, 103107 (2022). https://doi.org/10.1016/j.ijdrr.2022.103107

17. Martínez-García, A., Badia, T., Barnes, J.: Evaluating morphological typology in zero-shot cross-lingual transfer. In: Proceedings of the 59th Annual Meeting of the Association for Computational Linguistics and the 11th International Joint Conference on Natural Language Processing (Volume 1: Long Papers), pp. 3136–3153. Association for Computational Linguistics (2021). https://doi.org/10.18653/v1/2021.acl-long.244

18. Hamoui, B., Mars, M., Almotairi, K.: FloDusTA: Saudi tweets dataset for flood, dust storm, and traffic accident events. In: Proceedings of the 12th Language Resources and Evaluation Conference, Marseille, France, pp. 1391–1396. European Language Resources Association (2020)
19. DISAANA. https://disaana.jp/
20. D-SUMM. https://disaana.jp/d-summ/
21. Yamada, S., Utsu, K., Uchida, O.: An analysis of tweets posted during 2018 Western Japan heavy rain disaster. In: 2019 IEEE International Conference on Big Data and Smart Computing (BigComp), pp. 1–8 (2019). https://doi.org/10.1109/BIGCOMP.2019.8679346
22. Yamamoto, F., Suzuki, Y., Nadamoto, A.: Extraction and analysis of regionally specific behavioral facilitation information in the event of a large-scale disaster. In: IEEE/WIC/ACM International Conference on Web Intelligence and Intelligent Agent Technology, New York, NY, USA, pp. 538–543. Association for Computing Machinery (2021). https://doi.org/10.1145/3486622.3493991
23. Cheng, Z., Caverlee, J., Lee, K.: You are where you tweet: a content-based approach to geo-locating twitter users. In: Proceedings of the 19th ACM international conference on Information and knowledge management, New York, NY, USA, pp. 759–768. Association for Computing Machinery (2010). https://doi.org/10.1145/1871437.1871535
24. Sakaki, T., Matsuno, S., Hino, Y.: Analysis on geographic bias in private graphs on Twitter towards SNS marketing applications. IEICE Technical report, vol. 121, pp. 25–30 (2021). (in Japanese)
25. Gelernter, J., Balaji, S.: An algorithm for local geoparsing of microtext. GeoInformatica 17, 635–667 (2013). https://doi.org/10.1007/s10707-012-0173-8
26. Kumar, A., Singh, J.P.: Deep neural networks for location reference identification from Bilingual disaster-related tweets. IEEE Trans. Comput. Soc. Syst., 1–12 (2022). https://doi.org/10.1109/TCSS.2022.3213702
27. Davari, M., Kosseim, L., Bui, T.: TIMBERT: toponym identifier for the medical domain based on BERT. In: Proceedings of the 28th International Conference on Computational Linguistics, Barcelona, Spain, pp. 662–668. International Committee on Computational Linguistics (2020). https://doi.org/10.18653/v1/2020.coling-main.58
28. Yang, J., Liang, S., Zhang, Y.: Design challenges and misconceptions in neural sequence labeling. In: Proceedings of the 27th International Conference on Computational Linguistics, Santa Fe, New Mexico, USA, pp. 3879–3889. Association for Computational Linguistics (2018)
29. Paul, U., Ermakov, A., Nekrasov, M., Adarsh, V., Belding, E.: #Outage: detecting power and communication outages from social networks. In: Proceedings of The Web Conference 2020, Taipei Taiwan, pp. 1819–1829. ACM (2020). https://doi.org/10.1145/3366423.3380251
30. Matsuda, K., Sasaki, A., Okazaki, N., Inui, K.: Annotating geographical entities on microblog text. In: Proceedings of The 9th Linguistic Annotation Workshop, Denver, Colorado, USA, pp. 85–94. Association for Computational Linguistics (2015). https://doi.org/10.3115/v1/W15-1609
31. Devlin, J., Chang, M.-W., Lee, K., Toutanova, K.: BERT: pre-training of deep bidirectional transformers for language understanding. In: Proceedings of the 2019 Conference of the North American Chapter of the Association for Computational Linguistics: Human Language Technologies, Volume 1 (Long and Short Papers), Minneapolis, Minnesota, pp. 4171–4186. Association for Computational Linguistics (2019). https://doi.org/10.18653/v1/N19-1423
32. Xu, C., Ge, T., Li, C., Wei, F.: UnihanLM: coarse-to-fine Chinese-Japanese language model pretraining with the unihan database. In: Proceedings of the 1st Conference of the Asia-Pacific Chapter of the Association for Computational Linguistics and the 10th International Joint Conference on Natural Language Processing, Suzhou, China, pp. 201–211. Association for Computational Linguistics (2020)

33. Koto, F., Rahimi, A., Lau, J.H., Baldwin, T.: IndoLEM and IndoBERT: a benchmark dataset and pre-trained language model for Indonesian NLP. In: Proceedings of the 28th International Conference on Computational Linguistics, Barcelona, Spain, pp. 757–770. International Committee on Computational Linguistics (2020). https://doi.org/10.18653/v1/2020.coling-main.66

34. Antoun, W., Baly, F., Hajj, H.: AraBERT: transformer-based model for arabic language understanding. In: Proceedings of the 4th Workshop on Open-Source Arabic Corpora and Processing Tools, with a Shared Task on Offensive Language Detection, Marseille, France, pp. 9–15. European Language Resource Association (2020)

35. Kato, T., Miyata, R., Sato, S.: BERT-based simplification of japanese sentence-ending predicates in descriptive text. In: Proceedings of the 13th International Conference on Natural Language Generation, Dublin, Ireland, pp. 242–251. Association for Computational Linguistics (2020)

36. Chen, W.-T., Xia, Y., Shinzato, K.: Extreme multi-label classification with label masking for product attribute value extraction. In: Proceedings of the Fifth Workshop on e-Commerce and NLP (ECNLP 5), Dublin, Ireland, pp. 134–140. Association for Computational Linguistics (2022). https://doi.org/10.18653/v1/2022.ecnlp-1.16

37. Nakayama, Y., Murakami, K., Kumar, G., Bhingardive, S., Hardaway, I.: A large-scale Japanese dataset for aspect-based sentiment analysis. In: Proceedings of the Thirteenth Language Resources and Evaluation Conference, Marseille, France, pp. 7014–7021. European Language Resources Association (2022)

38. Liu, Y., et al.: RoBERTa: a robustly optimized bert pretraining approach (2019). http://arxiv.org/abs/1907.11692. https://doi.org/10.48550/arXiv.1907.11692

39. Lan, Z., Chen, M., Goodman, S., Gimpel, K., Sharma, P., Soricut, R.: ALBERT: a lite BERT for Self-supervised learning of language representations (2020). http://arxiv.org/abs/1909.11942. https://doi.org/10.48550/arXiv.1909.11942

40. Xiao, Z., Blanco, E.: Are people located in the places they mention in their tweets? A multimodal approach. In: Proceedings of the 29th International Conference on Computational Linguistics, Gyeongju, Republic of Korea, pp. 2561–2571. International Committee on Computational Linguistics (2022)

41. Khanal, S., Caragea, D.: Multi-task learning to enable location mention identification in the early hours of a crisis event. In: Findings of the Association for Computational Linguistics: EMNLP 2021, Punta Cana, Dominican Republic, pp. 4051–4056. Association for Computational Linguistics (2021). https://doi.org/10.18653/v1/2021.findings-emnlp.340

42. Wang, L., Gao, C., Wei, J., Ma, W., Liu, R., Vosoughi, S.: An empirical survey of unsupervised text representation methods on Twitter data. In: Proceedings of the Sixth Workshop on Noisy User-Generated Text (W-NUT 2020), pp. 209–214. Association for Computational Linguistics (2020)

43. Mikolov, T., Chen, K., Corrado, G., Dean, J.: Efficient Estimation of Word Representations in Vector Space (2013). http://arxiv.org/abs/1301.3781

44. Nguyen, D.Q., Vu, T., Tuan Nguyen, A.: BERTweet: a pre-trained language model for English Tweets. In: Proceedings of the 2020 Conference on Empirical Methods in Natural Language Processing: System Demonstrations, pp. 9–14. Association for Computational Linguisticse (2020). https://doi.org/10.18653/v1/2020.emnlp-demos.2

45. Kawintiranon, K., Singh, L.: PoliBERTweet: a pre-trained language model for analyzing political content on Twitter. In: Proceedings of the Thirteenth Language Resources and Evaluation Conference, Marseille, France, pp. 7360–7367. European Language Resources Association (2022)

Learning Early Detection of Emergencies from Word Usage Patterns on Social Media

Carlo A. Bono[1]([✉]) [iD], Mehmet Oğuz Mülâyim[2] [iD], and Barbara Pernici[1] [iD]

[1] Politecnico di Milano, DEIB, Piazza Leonardo da Vinci 32, 20133 Milano, Italy
{carlo.bono,barbara.pernici}@polimi.it
[2] Artificial Intelligence Research Institute (IIIA), CSIC, Campus UAB, 08193
Cerdanyola del Vallès, Spain
oguz@iiia.csic.es

Abstract. In the early stages of an emergency, information extracted from social media can support crisis response with evidence-based content. In order to capture this evidence, the events of interest must be first promptly detected. An automated detection system is able to activate other tasks, such as preemptive data processing for extracting event-related information. In this paper, we extend the human-in-the-loop approach in our previous work, TriggerCit, with a machine-learning-based event detection system trained on word count time series and coupled with an automated lexicon building algorithm. We design this framework in a language-agnostic fashion. In this way, the system can be deployed to any language without substantial effort. We evaluate the capacity of the proposed work against authoritative flood data for Nepal recorded over two years.

Keywords: Social Media · Disaster Management · Early Alerting

1 Introduction

The use of social media as a data source during emergencies has been largely investigated in the last decade [6]. Social media are often used to document ongoing events, and can provide real-time information in the form of text and media. As a consequence, social media platforms can deliver situational awareness and support an effective response to large-scale disaster events, helping to mitigate losses. In order to be valuable, data extracted from social media must be as timely and accurate as possible [20]. In our previous work [3], we focused on the automatic derivation of qualified and geolocated evidence to be delivered to responding organizations. In this work, to complement and expand previous results, we focus on the automatic detection of events. A prompt event detection mechanism can be used to trigger or preempt tasks related to emergencies.

The guiding idea of the present work is to build a tool that, with minimal supervision, can detect the onset of emergency events in near-real-time. The

© IFIP International Federation for Information Processing 2023
Published by Springer Nature Switzerland AG 2023
T. Gjøsæter et al. (Eds.): ITDRR 2022, IFIP AICT 672, pp. 308–323, 2023.
https://doi.org/10.1007/978-3-031-34207-3_20

input data for a such tool are word mentions on social media. This objective is achieved through a data-driven approach. A set of keywords linked to the onsets of a certain class of events is retrieved. Then, a predictor making use of the mentions of these keywords over time is built. Both steps are performed automatically and offline, prior to the events. Together with event identification, we also evaluate how to derive an indication of its magnitude, by estimating the number of recent incidents. This approach is meant to be timely, lightweight and general purpose. Multilingual support is achieved by designing a language-based approach, whose construction is both automated and language-independent, so that it can replicated with ease on any language. This approach, as a byproduct, also enhances the recall of the system, since it produces a language-specific lexicon tailored to a class of events. This characteristic is also critical for obtaining representative results in subsequently activated stages, when social media posts are crawled and inspected searching for informative evidence.

The paper is structured as follows. Related work is framed in Sect. 2. The data and methods utilized are documented in Sect. 3, while Sect. 4 presents the experimental results. Discussion is proposed in Sect. 5, and future work is outlined in Sect. 6.

2   Related Work

Emergency event detection can be performed using direct sensor data, remote sensor data or indirect data. Sensor-based approaches are possible for a number of emergency events. In the case of floods, water level data and rainfall intensity are usually measured. While direct-measure approaches can be accurate, their deployment is rather costly, and poses geographical coverage issues. For example, survey data suggests that the majority of river basins are equipped with insufficient gauging stations for observing water level, streamflow and rainfall [16].

Remote observation conducted through satellite imaging and active/passive sensing has been widely adopted for flood monitoring and tracking. Approaches based on remote sensing often exploit machine learning capabilities for task automation [12]. For example, systems like FloodAI [13] utilize Synthetic Aperture Radar (SAR) imagery and machine learning to perform remote flood analysis. Among the main limitations of this type of approaches there is their computational complexity, which requires delimiting the area of interest before their application, and therefore requires some other early detection mechanism in order to be activated.

The use of lexicons in social media emergency management has been investigated in [15]. Multilingual lexicons usually aggregate keywords of interest from a number of supported languages, for example 60 in [5] and 32 in [14].

The use of indirect signals extracted from social media, in particular Twitter, for event detection have been discussed in many scenarios. For example, early warning systems for earthquake events have been extensively studied [2,17]. An interesting solution for flood event detection using exclusively social media data is provided in [4]. The authors leverage the arrival time of flood-related tweets using a fixed dictionary of terms for social media crawling. The viability of a global flood monitoring system with self-activation capabilities has been explored in [11], suggesting recall issues when the approach is purely based on social media data. Additionally, the advantages of combining sensor and social media data for early warning purposes are analyzed in [18], while the potential of integrating remote sensing and social media specifically for early flood detection is explored in [8].

In the present work, we combine a self-building, dictionary-based approach with a machine learning setup, and apply it to flood event detection. Our methodology is agnostic to both the specific kind of event and the language of choice, making it suitable for a multi-language approach and adaptable to other emergency events. It is multi-language in the sense that the approach can be identically applied to any language. Since neither assumption is also made on the kind of ground truth, we speculate that the approach can be replicated on different emergency event data. To the best of our knowledge, such end-to-end approach to event detection is novel. This study complements previous work described in [3], implementing part of the future work envisioned therein towards learning search keywords dictionaries and leveraging machine learning for event detection. Neural network approaches for the supervised learning setups proposed in this paper draw inspiration from the review work in [7] and in particular the fully convolutional network proposed in [21].

3 Data and Methodology

The driving goal for the current work is building a language-centered early alerting system that can detect events using social media data. Two main ingredients are needed to build such a system with a data-driven approach: signal data and a ground truth, which together constitute the training data for our system. The signal data is, in this case, a minimal representation of reality: the count of the usage of specific words over time. As ground truth, we use historical validation data on past events, as described in Sect. 3.1. Once a proper training set is assembled, supervised learning approaches for the automated detection of event onsets can be assessed. We give a description of the approaches we have evaluated in Sect. 3.3.

One of the objectives is to automatically derive a dictionary of words that are significant to events of interest. Since the system has to support multiple languages, and the queries to social media are to be posed as textual queries[1], a sensible solution is to use language-centered word dictionaries. The automatic construction of event-specific queries counterbalances the combined lack of language and domain-specific knowledge. We describe in detail our approach for dictionary derivation in Sect. 3.2 and the relative subsections.

---

[1] Searching on social media is usually done with keywords, in combination with logical and advanced operators.

The overall approach is illustrated in Fig. 1. Starting from a small set of terms, the initial dictionary is expanded using both offline and online methods informed by the ground truth. Once the dictionary is set, the time series corresponding to each keyword count are fed to a supervised learning algorithm, together with the ground truth. The resulting model is able to perform estimations[2] on unseen data and detect an ongoing event.

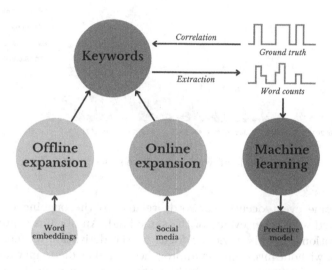

Fig. 1. Overall schematic of our approach to dictionary construction and model fitting.

3.1   Data and Ground Truth

As the signal, we use the occurrences of keywords over time, extracted from Twitter. This approach is grounded on the assumption that some words are remarkably used when a particular event happens. Words that show this behaviour are said to be "correlated" with the event type of interest. Single keywords are a simple feature compared to the complexity of natural languages, yet they are at the core of the queries that can be posed to social media and, for practical purposes, they are frequently exploited.

Utilizing the word count brings about some advantages. First of all, it is a conveniently compact feature consisting in a list of integers, that can be easily computed. Twitter API also exposes a `v2 Tweet counts` endpoint, which directly returns the requested counts. This option makes data interchange and processing negligible. Full archive search required for training is available with the Academic Research access; on the other hand, access to recent data –which

---

[2] Following canonical machine learning terminology, we will henceforth refer to the estimations of an algorithm on real-time data as "predictions".

is suitable for real-time operation– is generally available. Data can be returned at different time granularities depending on application needs. We mainly experimented with counts aggregated at hourly level and windows of 7 days, which coincide with Twitter's "recent search" visibility. An example depiction of the resulting word counts is shown in Fig. 2.

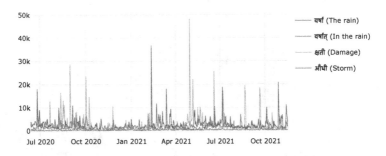

Fig. 2. Example of word count time series from Twitter.

When some event occurs, keywords related to the ongoing event are not always related with other events of the same kind. An obvious example is mentions of locations. In this work, we focus on the derivation of general purpose dictionaries, without investigating approaches aimed at dictionary adaptation to a single, currently ongoing event, such as the one proposed in [1].

Regarding ground truth data, we mainly experimented with data extracted from the *Global Disaster Alert and Coordination System*[3] (GDACS) [19], which is designed to alert the international community during sudden-onset disasters. Since our case study is based on Nepal, we focused on the 12 events reported over the last two years in the country (Fig. 3).[4] As the investigation developed, we also considered the data sources reported in [10]. Some of the listed datasets were not applicable to this study. The comparison with available sources highlighted a data quality and definition issue that is discussed in Sect. 4 and can be observed in Fig. 10. Moreover, we also used incident reports from the Nepal Disaster Risk Reduction Portal[5], both for comparison and training purposes (Fig. 10).

3.2 Automatic Dictionary Building

In the given context, a dictionary building method should have some desirable characteristics. It should be as automatic as possible, in order to be replicable on different languages. It should also rely on widely available resources. Finally, it should leverage accessible ground truth to assess the usefulness of the candidate

---

[3] https://www.gdacs.org.
[4] We did not use previous reports since, ostensibly, the data collection process changed at some point.
[5] http://drrportal.gov.np/.

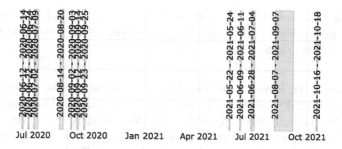

Jul 2020   Oct 2020   Jan 2021   Apr 2021   Jul 2021   Oct 2021

Fig. 3. GDACS time ranges for flood events in Nepal.

keywords. In this section we detail how to achieve such characteristics. The final goal is to obtain a representative set of keywords that can guarantee a high recall, with reasonable specificity, when used to query a social media platform.

Dictionary Expansion. An initial dictionary is created with a small number of "seed" keywords. These keywords are generically related to the event of interest (e.g., "flood" in the desired language). Starting from these few keywords, the first step is to expand the dictionary with candidate keywords that are related to the initial ones. Such relatedness can originate from different sources, such as language models (e.g., bigram models) that are usually available for most languages, or even search engine data such as Google Trends data[6]. We choose to use non-contextual, language-specific word embeddings for the expansion since they roughly capture semantic proximity among words and they are generally available for most languages. For each seed keyword in the initial set, we add the top N most similar words to the set, and then perform the same expansion a second time. A visual representation of the expansion process is given in Fig. 4.

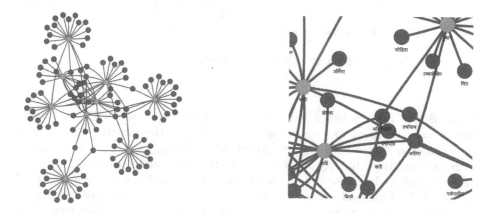

Fig. 4. Offline expansion of the seed dictionary using Nepali word embeddings.

---
[6] https://trends.google.com/.

We also want to filter out obvious outliers. To this end, a simple manual filtering is performed on the candidate keywords, using automatic translation and an interactive dashboard.

Correlation with Event Onsets. Given a set of keywords, we want to retain the most significant candidates. To compute a measure of significance, we combine the Pearson and Kendall coefficients. We compute both the coefficients between time-lagged shifts of each word count vector and the time series of the event onsets. Both these vectors contain all the available data over the same reference period. We take care of shifting the time series in one direction only, in order to avoid measuring inverse causality between events and words. For each word, we take the maximum of each coefficient, and average the two maximums. We then retain only the word candidates that have a positive average, deferring the weighting of the words to the supervised learning stage. Measures of correlation calculated in this way are usually low. There are a number of reasons for this. Some are structural, in the sense that we are looking for keywords correlated with the events onset, while they could instead be correlated with the overall unfolding of the events. Some others are due to the nature of the events, which is variable and unpredictable. An emblematic example is provided in Fig. 5. The keyword "landslide" shows distinctive spikes in correspondence with some of the onsets, while in some others the spike is delayed or missing altogether.

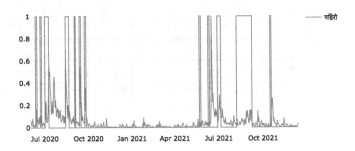

Fig. 5. Normalized hourly count for "landslide" and GDACS flood events.

Data Sampling. Selected keywords, ostensibly correlated with the events onsets, are then used to build a query consisting in the logical OR ($\vee$) of all the keywords. We use this query to download matching posts in correspondence with the onset days, namely *positive* days. In this way, unseen keywords originating from online data now become accessible. However, it would be impractical to get all the historical counts for all the words to compute the correlation as described. A different strategy is then used. We also sample tweets from days that are far from the events by a given interval before and after the event boundaries. We call these days *negative* days. This second query is composed by the

OR of keywords randomly sampled from common terms in the language of interest.[7] The time masking used for positive and negative sampling is illustrated in Fig. 6. All downloaded tweets are then projected to a vector space defined by the keywords witnessed at least K times in the samples coming from the positive days. Then, the χ^2 statistic is used to rank the most significant terms. The top ones are added to the dictionary if they also achieve a significant correlation with the event onsets, as described in the previous step.

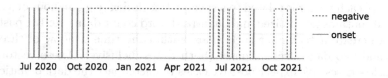

Fig. 6. Event onsets from GDACS, and time windows far from the events.

A validation dashboard, visible in Fig. 7, is finally used to filter out spurious candidates, such as location names, which are event-dependent.

☐ लक्ष्मणपुर (Laxmanpur)	☑ डुबान (Drowning)	☑ बाढी (Flood)	☑ चिरा (Incision)
☑ भूस्खलन (Landslides)	☐ खैरटवा (Khairatwa)	☐ बिग्ही (Bighi)	☑ असिना (Hail)
☑ उच्चजोखिम (High risk)	☑ सुनामी (Tsunami)	☑ आँधी (Storm)	☑ आँधीहुरी (Hurricane)
☑ चक्रवात (Cyclone)	☐ मटेहिया (Matehiya)	☐ भेल (Bhel)	☐ कुच्चौनी (Kuchauni)
☑ वर्षापछि (After rain)	☐ खडेरी (Drought)	☑ वर्षायाम (Rainy season)	☑ हुरीबतास (Hurricane)

Fig. 7. Manual dashboard for keyword filtering.

The whole procedure can be optionally reiterated, since the OR query changes when the dictionary contents change, refining the retrieved terms up to convergence.

3.3 Supervised Learning

Once the dictionary is set, the time series for the selected keywords are used as input data for a supervised classification problem. We first evaluated a classification setup, using GDACS data as a ground truth. We then studied a regression setup using incident data related to our case study.

Features and Preprocessing. For each keyword in the dictionary, we obtained a dense vector of counts at a requested time granularity. We mostly experimented with hourly data. Some machine learning algorithms work better with a proper scaling of the input features. Also, different data preprocessing choices

---

[7] This is mandatory on Twitter since a query consisting of only stopwords is rejected.

could influence the final performance. Different classical feature preprocessing are evaluated, such as min-max scaling, Z-score normalization and median-IQR scaling. For each experiment, the selected scaling is applied individually to each word's time series. Additionally, quantile-based signal quantization is applied to the scaled time series. The choice of the preprocessing is deferred to the experimental stage.

Classification Setup. The first investigated setup is a classification task. In this setup, each vector is related to a specific time index (e.g., an hour of a specific day) and contains normalized and quantized word count data over the past week. First, we create a vector for each index within the time window of three days before and two days after an onset (both dates inclusive). These vectors form the *positive* cases. We expect positive cases to encompass the data of anticipated events (e.g., rains) and early reactions. We do not take into account the remaining dates during the events (i.e., third day after the onset and onwards) since we are interested in alerting. Then, we create vectors belonging to time windows that are "far from the events", as seen in Fig. 6, and these vectors form the *negative* cases.

Vectors indexed by the same time are grouped, so that the resulting input data is a matrix obtained concatenating count vectors of equal length, corresponding to a multivariate time series. Since the relations between the magnitudes of the time series are lost during preprocessing, a vector containing mean, standard deviation, maximum and minimum is computed over the same time range on the raw counts. For each time index, the inputs for the classifier are a $n \times t$ matrix plus a supplementary $n \times 4$ vector, where n is the dictionary cardinality and t is the size of the time window.

We assign class weights inversely proportional to the number of negative and positive instances. Evaluation of the models is based on standard classification metrics, namely, precision, recall, F_1 score and AUC.

The base model for the experiments was the Fully Convolutional Network (FCN) approach proposed by [21]. An exploration of the effect of varying the number of layers, units, kernel size was conducted.[8] Values for learning rate (LR), LR reduction, batch size and early stopping were calibrated during the experiments. Dropout layers were added at the first layer and after the global average pooling layer. Also, the ResNet architecture evaluated by the same authors has been tested. Experiments are performed in a leave-one-event out fashion, repeating each experiment 10 times in order to average stochastic effects. Adam [9] is used for gradient descent optimization, and categorical cross-entropy as a loss function. Validation accuracy is used as a metric for early stopping. The validation loss was computed on a random 33% of the training cases, for each fold.

Regression Setup. Following experimental observations on the classification results, we applied an analogous deep neural network setup to a regression task to estimate the occurrence and impact of flood incidents. Incident count data for the

---

[8] By mixing manual exploration and automatic exploration using KerasTuner.

region of interest are aggregated by day, regardless of the specific location within that region. A multi-headed network setup for predicting life and monetary losses has also been evaluated. In the regression setup, the full data is fed to the network, without masking days. This is motivated by the nature of the ground truth data. As for the classification case, possible anticipation and delay effects between word use and actual events have to be accounted for. Therefore, we chose to replace each data label by a 72-hour arithmetic average, centered in each point, similarly to the classification setup. Mean squared error (MSE) is used as evaluation metric.

Experiments are performed in a 5-fold cross validation fashion, where each fold contains data points that are contiguous in time. Again, each experiment is performed 10 times and the results are averaged. Hyperparameter choices are deferred to experimentation. MSE is used as loss function and evaluation metric. The validation loss is computed on the last 50% of the training cases, for each fold.

4   Experimental Results

We first analyzed the classification setup choosing flood events in Nepal as a case study. This is done in continuity with our previous work, in which a flood event in Nepal was analyzed [3]. We had selected this event since the United Nations Satellite Centre (UNOSAT)[9] was activated to support it. We generalized the validation of our models to all recent flood events in Nepal. Moreover, since Twitter penetration rate is low in Nepal, it also poses a challenging test. Based on the results, we then analyzed the regression setup using the same input data and flood-related incident data reported by the Government of Nepal as ground truth. In both cases, roughly the last two years of data were analyzed.

4.1   Data Gathering

We applied the procedure described in Sect. 3, starting from two flood-related Nepali words (बाढी and बाढि). Publicly available word embeddings for Nepali[10] were used, adding $N = 10$ similar terms per word and performing the expansion two times. After term expansion, manual filtering, and tweet data download-ing[11] in order to get real-world keywords, we conducted the correlation analysis described in Subsect. 3.2 which led to 41 Nepali words that where related to the flood event onsets extracted from GDACS. For each data point, indexed by each round hour in the time series, a one-week count time series was extracted for each word, leading to a $16632 \times 41 \times 168$ input matrix, with each data point consisting in a multivariate time series represented by a 41×168 matrix. The supplementary 41×4 vector containing descriptive statistics was computed for each time window and added to the corresponding multivariate time series.

---

[9] https://unitar.org/sustainable-development-goals/united-nations-satellite-centre-UNOSAT.

[10] https://github.com/rabindralamsal/Word2Vec-Embeddings-for-Nepali-Language.

[11] Approximately 5 million tweets sampled from positive and negative days.

4.2 Preprocessing and Hyperparameter Selection

To select the most suitable configuration for feature preprocessing, we repeated the classification experiments averaging the output probabilities over 10 runs for each configuration. Output probabilities correspond to the softmax probabilities of being a positive case. In Table 1 the Brier score for the average outputs is reported. Based on this analysis, we chose to use MinMax preprocessing and 200 quantization levels.

Table 1. Preprocessing selection with Brier score, average scores over 10 runs.

Normalisation type	Brier avg	Brier stdev
None	0.114	0.003
MinMax	0.069	0.003
MinMax (qcut 100)	0.087	0.002
MinMax (qcut 200)	0.068	0.003
MinMax (qcut 300)	0.070	0.003
Standard	0.083	0.002
Standard (qcut 100)	0.098	0.006
Standard (qcut 200)	0.100	0.005
Standard (qcut 300)	0.083	0.003

Hyperparameter tuning for the classification setup was done through Keras-Tuner and manual testing, focusing on networks with few layers and units since bigger network configurations showed overfitting behaviour. In Fig. 8, an exploration of the number of units per layer and kernel size is reported, focusing on the regression setup. While such exploration is limited by the fact that only a parameter at a time is studied, the analysis shows that the loss is not strongly influenced by the parameter itself, up to some range. This is confirmed by the fact that further random KerasTuner exploration did not lead to models that achieve better performances.

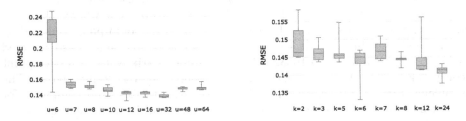

Fig. 8. Response to number of units (u) per layer and kernel size (k) for 1D convolution.

4.3   Results with Classification

Relatively small networks show a reasonable performance in the classification task. For reference, the output probabilities for a 2-layer, 32 units network are reported in Fig. 9. Using 0.2 as a probability threshold for the output layer, this network achieves a 94% precision and a 74% recall. Magnitude-related statistics did not prove to be useful and were discarded from input.

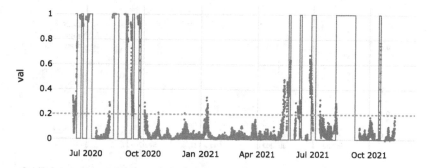

Fig. 9. Probability outputs (red) for event onsets of a 2-layer, 32 units CNN. Blue lines show event days. Dashed line marks the threshold for positive prediction. (Color figure online)

Recall is computed over 1,728 positive cases, evenly distributed over 12 events. Focusing on the ability to intercept the events, such model looks to be able to get all the available event onsets, at the cost of some false positives.

4.4   Reference Issue

However, the output probability is not evenly distributed over the output events. Figure 9 highlights a different prediction behaviour between older and newer events. After evaluating an extensive number of network configurations with no significant enhancement, we conducted a comparative analysis of available ground truths for flood events in Nepal, using accessible datasets listed in [10].[12] In particular, we compared GDACS data with EM-DAT[13] and the Global Active Archive of Large Flood Events[14]. As shown in Fig. 10, the event onsets reported by different data sources are inconsistent.

In an effort to understand the relation between these ground truths, we also compared event data with incident data coming from the Nepal Disaster Risk

---

[12] We did not use Global Flood Monitor data described in [4] since it does not contain certified data, and we were not able to obtain NatCatSERVICE data from Munich Re.

[13] The International Disaster database, https://www.emdat.be/.

[14] https://floodobservatory.colorado.edu/Archives/index.html.

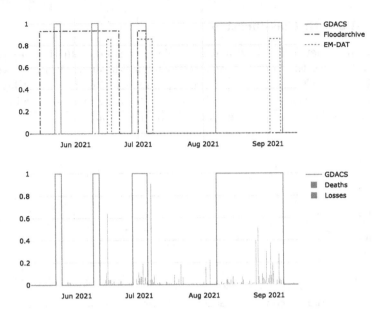

Fig. 10. Comparison between GDACS, EM-DAT, Floodarchive and NDRRP event data.

Reduction Portal (NDRRP). As it can be appreciated in Fig. 11, when the classifier is properly fitting the data it is able to predict days with actual incidents as positive cases, as opposed to days marked as onsets.

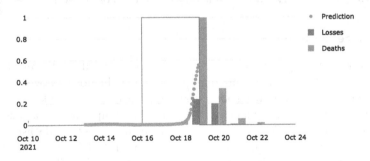

Fig. 11. Classifier generalization on the last flood event reported by GDACS.

4.5   Results with Regression

The previous observations on classification results suggested that incident data could be a reliable target variable. Since incident data is not a binary value, the learning setup was changed to a regression. In Fig. 12 the prediction of the normalized number of events is reported. The predictions are concatenated from a 5-fold cross-validation setup and are performed on unseen data. The corresponding MSE is 0.141.

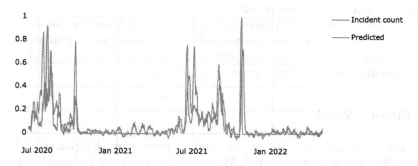

Fig. 12. 5-fold cross-validation results for incident count regression.

The experiments with the ResNet network, configured with a comparable number of units and kernel size, did not enhance the results. Moreover, the ResNet approach was about 20 times slower to train in our experiments. Experiments with supplementary network heads for learning life and monetary losses as additional dependent variables –together with the incident count– did not lead to better performances with respect to the one-headed network.

5 Discussion and Limitations

Both the classification and regression setup showed usable results in terms of generalization capabilities and overall performance metrics. Since the approach is very compact and the computation negligible, the system can be considered ready for an experimental deployment. No particular functional or non-functional constraints are given, apart from the input vectors being related to the last week of data.

While the performances of the classifier setup are fit for event detection, the observations presented about the ground truth make the use of the resulting model less promising. Specifically, even if the events themselves are correctly identified, we observe variation in the probability output of the network depending on the event, partly due to the nature of the ground truth itself. Notwithstanding this limitation, the generalization capability of the model appears to be good.

In the regression setup, under certain circumstances the peaks of the predicted values show a time lag with respect to the reference values. Since the effect only happens for some events, it is more likely to be a real-world tailing effect rather than a byproduct of the chosen preprocessing. This does not invalidate the functionality of the approach since, even if the predicted peaks are possibly shifted, the slope and the absolute value of the prediction are still practicable as a trigger. Given the nature of the results on the negative regions (Fig. 9 and 12), a postprocessing technique to mitigate false positives could be necessary, especially in highly time-sensitive applications. It is also worth noticing that, in the context of emergency alerting, the cost of false positives is usually negligible compared to false negatives.

Moreover, since the dictionary building phase has been consistently tested, we believe that applying this approach to other languages is practicable with no particular effort. However, regarding the regression setup, a suitable ground truth should be obtained for the region of interest.

6   Future Work

We plan to extensively validate our approach on more languages and countries with different characteristics. We also plan to extend the number and the nature of the considered ground truths. Since the ground truth data we used did not show adequate coherence nor completeness, further consideration on how to merge signals –also possibly coming from different domains– has to be put in place. An additional interest is to take into account signals extracted from social media by other automated tools, such as emergency-related classifiers, in order to introduce additional evidence. Also, data fusion techniques could be utilized to evaluate the effect of adding social media data to sensor or forecast data. A natural extension to the proposed network architecture could be to work with separate data sources and concatenate the results before the final dense layer.

Finally, an adaptive extension of the approach to dictionary building described in Sect. 3.2 is foreseen. This approach would be aimed at adaptively updating the dictionary while a newly detected event unfolds, thus enhancing both precision and recall of the subsequent data processing pipeline.

Acknowledgements. The work at Politecnico di Milano and IIIA-CSIC was funded by the European Commission H2020 Project Crowd4SDG, #872944.

References

1. Autelitano, A., Pernici, B., Scalia, G.: Spatio-temporal mining of keywords for social media cross-social crawling of emergency events. GeoInformatica **23**(3), 425–447 (2019)
2. Avvenuti, M., Cimino, M.G.C.A., Cresci, S., Marchetti, A., Tesconi, M.: A framework for detecting unfolding emergencies using humans as sensors. Springerplus **5**, 43 (2016)
3. Bono, C., Pernici, B., Fernandez-Marquez, J.L., Shankar, A.R., Mülâyim, M.O., Nemni, E.: TriggerCit: early flood alerting using twitter and geolocation-a comparison with alternative sources. In: Proceedings of ISCRAM 2022, Tarbes, France (2022)
4. de Bruijn, J.A., de Moel, H., Jongman, B., de Ruiter, M.C., Wagemaker, J., Aerts, J.C.J.H.: A global database of historic and real-time flood events based on social media. Sci. Data **6**(1), 311 (2019)

5. Havas, C., et al.: E2mc: improving emergency management service practice through social media and crowdsourcing analysis in near real time. Sensors **17**(12), 2766 (2017)
6. Imran, M., Castillo, C., Diaz, F., Vieweg, S.: Processing social media messages in mass emergency: survey summary. In: Companion Proceedings of the The Web Conference WWW 2018, Lyon, France, pp. 507–511 (2018)
7. Ismail Fawaz, H., Forestier, G., Weber, J., Idoumghar, L., Muller, P.A.: Deep learning for time series classification: a review. Data Min. Knowl. Discovery **33**(4), 917–963 (2019)
8. Jongman, B., Wagemaker, J., Romero, B.R., De Perez, E.C.: Early flood detection for rapid humanitarian response: harnessing near real-time satellite and twitter signals. ISPRS Int. J. Geo-Inf. **4**(4), 2246–2266 (2015)
9. Kingma, D.P., Ba, J.: Adam: a method for stochastic optimization (2014). arxiv:1412.6980Comment. Published as a conference paper at the 3rd International Conference for Learning Representations, San Diego (2015)
10. Lindersson, S., Brandimarte, L., Mård, J., Di Baldassarre, G.: A review of freely accessible global datasets for the study of floods, droughts and their interactions with human societies. WIREs Water **7**(3), e1424 (2020)
11. Lorini, V., Castillo, C., Nappo, D., Dottori, F., Salamon, P.: Social media alerts can improve, but not replace hydrological models for forecasting floods. In: 2020 IEEE/WIC/ACM International Joint Conference on Web Intelligence and Intelligent Agent Technology (WI-IAT), pp. 351–356. IEEE Computer Society (2020)
12. Munawar, H.S., Hammad, A.W.A., Waller, S.T.: Remote sensing methods for flood prediction: a review. Sensors **22**(3), 960 (2022)
13. Nemni, E., Bullock, J., Belabbes, S., Bromley, L.: Fully convolutional neural network for rapid flood segmentation in synthetic aperture radar imagery. Remote Sens. **12**(16), 2532 (2020)
14. Ofli, F.: A real-time system for detecting landslide reports on social media using artificial intelligence. In: Di Noia, T., Ko, I.Y., Schedl, M., Ardito, C. (eds.) Web Engineering, pp. 49–65. Springer International Publishing, Cham (2022)
15. Olteanu, A., Castillo, C., Diaz, F., Vieweg, S.: Crisislex: a lexicon for collecting and filtering microblogged communications in crises. Proc. Int. AAAI Conf. Web Soc. Media **8**(1), 376–385 (2014)
16. Perera, D., et al.: Flood early warning systems: A review of benefits, challenges and prospects (2019)
17. Sakaki, T., Okazaki, M., Matsuo, Y.: Tweet analysis for real-time event detection and earthquake reporting system development. IEEE Trans. Knowl. Data Eng. **25**(4), 919–931 (2013)
18. Shoyama, K., Cui, Q., Hanashimaa, M., Sano, H., Usuda, Y.: Emergency flood detection using multiple information sources: integrated analysis of natural hazard monitoring and social media data. Sci. Total Environ. **767**(144371), 1–11 (2021)
19. Stollberg, B., De Groeve, T.: The use of social media within the global disaster alert and coordination system (GDACS). In: Proceedings of the 21st International Conference on World Wide Web, pp. 703–706 (2012)
20. United Nations Office for the Coordination of Humanitarian Affairs: Five essentials for the first 72 hours of disaster response. https://www.unocha.org/story/five-essentials-first-72-hours-disaster-response. Accessed 15 Aug 2022
21. Wang, Z., Yan, W., Oates, T.: Time series classification from scratch with deep neural networks: a strong baseline. In: 2017 International Joint Conference on Neural Networks (IJCNN), pp. 1578–1585 (2017)

Community Resilience

Development and Evaluation of a Shelter Simulator Using Gamification

Yutaka Matsuno(✉) and Mei Matsuura

Graduate School of Science and Technology, Nihon University, Tokyo, Japan
matsuno.yutaka@nihon-u.ac.jp, csme22021@g.nihon-u.ac.jp

Abstract. As a part of disaster preparedness, smartphone applications for disaster information sharing is considered as effective. There is a wide range of disaster prevention applications. Among them, we focus on obtaining knowledge of lives in an evacuation shelter, which are difficult to learn in daily lives. In this paper, we develop and evaluate a simulation application for living in an evacuation shelter using the concept of gamification (serious games) to gain knowledge and experience of living in an evacuation shelter. During playing the application, the users answer quizzes related to lives in a shelter, and are expected to learn knowledge on the lives. Two subject experiments are conducted to evaluate the effectiveness of the application by comparing with the results of learning evacuation shelter information by only by documents. Currently, the application is freely available as a Mac or Windows application.

Keywords: Education for Disaster Prevention · Shelter Simulation · Gamification · Serious Games

1 Introduction

It is very important to know about disaster prevention knowledge as a countermeasure against natural disasters such as earthquakes, typhoons, and tsunamis. As an initiative of various local governments, websites and tools summarizing disaster prevention information are being made available on the Internet by the Japanese government [3].

Tokyo Stockpiling Navi [13], one of the contents of the Tokyo Metropolitan Government's disaster prevention website launched in March 2021, provides a web application that displays the type and number of stockpiles needed based on information such as family composition and age, in addition to stockpiling and other preparedness information. This initiative has attracted attention on Twitter and other social media. It has also been reported that the use of the earthquake disaster simulation smartphone applications such as "Moshiyure" [2] have been able to influence people's awareness of earthquakes and earthquake preparedness. These examples suggest that disaster prevention applications for smartphones that provide easy access to information are useful as one of the disaster countermeasures.

© IFIP International Federation for Information Processing 2023
Published by Springer Nature Switzerland AG 2023
T. Gjøsæter et al. (Eds.): ITDRR 2022, IFIP AICT 672, pp. 327–340, 2023.
https://doi.org/10.1007/978-3-031-34207-3_21

Disaster prevention applications cover a wide range of content; as of 2017, applications hit by a search for the keyword "disaster prevention application" could be categorized into 11 types of functions [1]. Specifically, they include those for gathering information during a disaster, tools for interpersonal use such as safety confirmation, and those for preparing knowledge and supplies before a disaster. Among these, we examined the contents to be used before a disaster and focused on lives in an evacuation center, which is a different environment daily lives.

It is desirable to have prior knowledge of how to live in an evacuation center, how to deal with problems, and personal health information that may be needed in an emergency. In this paper, we developed a simulation application for living in an evacuation shelter, using the concept of gamification and serious games, in order to easily experience life in an evacuation shelter and obtain useful knowledge and information. The developed application can be used as a Mac or Windows application, and can be downloaded[1] (currently we are developing smartphone versions).

The structure of the paper is as follows. In Sect. 2, we discuss related work. Section 3 introduces our application for simulating evacuation shelter living experience. Section 4 shows experiments for evaluating the effectiveness of the application. Section 5 states concluding remarks.

2   Related Work

We previously introduced an application that includes an evacuation simulation game in the event of flooding through gamification [9]. The paper [9] evaluated the effectiveness of the application through experiments. The results showed that the application of gamification helped the participants acquire knowledge about the expected flood zone and the location of evacuation facilities, and the participants became more interested in disaster prevention.

Currently, various disaster evacuation support systems have been developed such as [15], but most of them are designed under the assumption that a network is available. However, immediately after a disaster strike, network availability may be severe due to the failure of the communication infrastructure. The paper [15] developed "Akari Map", a system that can be used even when networks are unavailable after a disaster occurs, and that allows users to experience in advance the functions that will be available during a disaster from normal times. However, it is also reported such smartphone applications have not often been used when the users are not home.

There is also a disaster prevention information application for smartphones that allows users to pass disaster prevention information for their current location [11]. The application automatically searches for evacuation centers and shelters in the region and provides route guidance to the facilities and an evacuation compass to support evacuation behavior in the event of a disaster. The main

---

[1] https://onl.la/Rbyxjik.

functions include: disaster risk information on the current location, automatic evacuation center search, hazard map display and area classification and flood depth level display, safety registration and safety confirmation, and area and disaster prevention information registered by the user. Users can know the latest evacuation shelter locations as determined by local governments nationwide.

There is a study that investigated the characteristics of people who use disaster prevention-related smartphone applications [10]. The characteristics of those who own disaster prevention-related applications are "disaster awareness" and have different characteristics among different age groups. Compared to middle-aged and senior citizens, young people (in their 20s and 30s) are less aware of disaster prevention. Furthermore, even among those who are highly aware of disaster prevention, less than half of them own disaster prevention-related applications. A characteristic of the younger generation is that the installation rate of disaster prevention-related applications is higher among young people who have experienced evacuation compared to those who have not.

These related work has shown that young people have low awareness of disaster prevention, with less than half of them owning disaster prevention-related applications. In addition, among disaster prevention-related apps, there are few apps that enable users to acquire knowledge about life in a shelter. Therefore, we referred to recent smartphone applications and examined the elements necessary for disaster prevention applications to be developed:

- Easy and continuous access
- Learn about life in an evacuation center before a disaster
- Implement learning contents mainly for young people who have no experience of evacuation.
- Gamification is utilized so that people can enjoy learning disaster prevention knowledge.

Based on these observations, we have developed a disaster prevention application that specializes in knowledge acquisition about life in an evacuation shelter.

Gamification and serious games have been gaining attention for learning evacuation knowledge, and various applications have been developed such as [12] and [4] using the notion of gamification and serious game. Such applications focus on reality, and sometimes they are developed as 3D applications. Unlike such applications, we aim to develop more friendly, simple, and not too realistic applications. This is because that most of smartphone applications which younger people often use exploit comic book or animation like graphics and characters, and do not use realistic representations. We observe such not too realistic design help users to learn evacuation knowledge easily.

3   Evacuation Shelter Living Experience Application

3.1   Application Overview

The purpose of this application is for users to gain knowledge about disaster prevention by answering quizzes about disaster prevention while experiencing life in an evacuation shelter. Gamification was adopted as the basic policy of the application design in order to encourage continuous and active learning by the user. Gamification is the application of structures used in games in areas other than games [6]. The notion of serious games is also widely used in the literature. One of the definitions of serious games is "any piece of software that merges a non-entertaining purpose (serious) with a video game structure (game)" [5]. In this sense, our application is more like a serious game, rather than an application of gamification. Our intention is to use our application in disaster training workshops of school or company as a gamification. For example, participants of such workshops first play our application, then participate the workshops. In this sense, our application is not only a serious game, but also a part of disaster training workshops.

This application was designed and developed with reference to the structure of simulation games. The reason is that the characteristics of simulation games, in which real-life devices and scenes are simulated and played, were thought to be easily adaptable to the purpose of experiencing a shelter. As a simulation game, the content of this application is "the main character, who cannot live in his/her home due to a disaster, goes to an evacuation center, encounters various events during his/her evacuation, and eventually moves in temporary housing". The screen transition of this application is shown in Fig. 1 as the overall flows of the simulation game.

The top part of Fig. 1 is the basic routine. The game proceeds as follows: answer the quiz on the event selection screen, study the answers and explanations on the event screen, and manage the health of the main character on the selection screen and the meal screen. The main character has the following statuses as elements of health management, and the game will end if the health management is not sufficient.

- Hunger Gauge: Indicates the degree of the main character's hunger on a 10-point scale. It decreases automatically with the passage of days and increases with meals.
- Mental Health Gauge: Indicates the main character's emotional health on a scale of 1 to 10. It decreases with incorrect answers to quizzes and increases with correct answers.
- Water Gauge: Indicates the main character's water intake at 3 levels. It automatically decreases as the time of day changes and increases with rehydration.
- Food and Water Savings: Indicates the amount of savings required for the main character.

The lower part of Fig. 1 shows the sequence of events to finish the game. After living in a shelter for a certain period of time, the user can proceed to a test. Through the test, the user can test how well his/her disaster prevention knowledge has been established. After the confirmation test, an ending scenario is played. There are four different ending scenarios, which change depending on the user's performance in the confirmation test. When the ending scenario

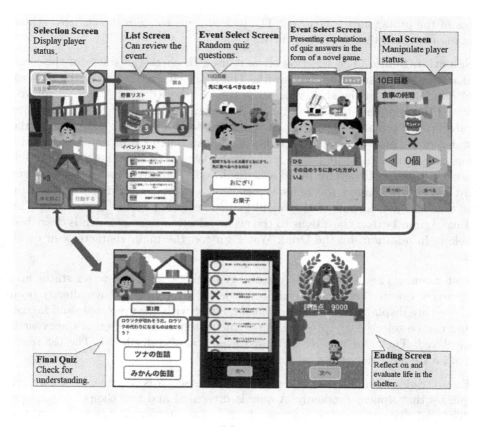

Fig. 1. Application screen transitions

is completed, the user is taken to the ending screen. In the ending screen, the score is calculated and a rank is assigned according to the score. After the rank is displayed, the end roll is played and the game is cleared. When the game ends or the game is cleared, the shelter simulation can be restarted from the beginning. In order to view all 40 types of events, the game must be played repeatedly.

3.2 Functionality of Game Scenes

We explain each scenes of our application as follows.

Title Scene. This is the first scenes that opens when the application is executed. There are two buttons: "Start from the beginning" and "Continue". When the "Start From" button is selected, the game can be started with the main character's status and viewed event data in their initial state. When the "Continue" button is selected, the data in progress can be read and the game can be resumed. This application takes the procedure of loading event data and the status of the main character from a CSV file. Data saving is also performed whenever the status of the protagonist is changed. The procedure is to store the changed status in an array and then overwrite the CSV file.

Selection Scene. The selection scene is used to check the status of the main character and manage his/her health. The main character status, the number of days elapsed in the shelter, and the time of day (day/night) are displayed at the top, and the status of the main character at the center changes into five categories (normal, hungry, lack of water, anxious, and sick) according to the status of the main character. In addition, a menu button, a button to act, and a button to drink water are placed respectively. When the menu button is pressed, a menu panel with several buttons is displayed. The menu panel has an event list button that moves to the list screen, a title button that moves to the title screen, and a help button that displays a description of the application. The Take Action button transitions to the event selection screen, which is described below. In addition, by the Drink Water button the main character can drink water.

List Scene. The list scene has the ability to check food and water status and to review events that have already been viewed. Events that have already been viewed are displayed by the event button, along with the event title and image, and can be selected. By pressing the event button, a description of the event is displayed. The total number of viewed events is also displayed. The list scene can be viewed before the final test.

Event Selection Scene. The event selection scene is a scene for answering quizzes that appear randomly. A quiz is presented and two choice buttons are displayed. By pressing the buttons, the user can answer the question, and the correct or incorrect answer is displayed. After the correct or incorrect answer is displayed, the screen transitions to the event screen, where the scenario changes depending on the answer.

Event Scene. The event scene plays the event scenario. The user can watch the characters conversations about disaster prevention knowledge in a novel game format and view explanations of the quiz in the event selection scene. In addition, the main character's status change value is displayed as the event result at the end.

Meal Scene. The meal scene is for the main character to take meals. The amount of food can be selected, and the hunger gauge increases according to the amount. If the main character's hunger gauge is low, a warning and a panel to encourage eating are displayed.

Final Test Scene. When the user has lived in the shelter for 7 days, a panel that prompts a transition from the selection scene to the final test scene is displayed, and the user can choose whether to continue the shelter experience or proceed to the final test. If the user chooses to proceed to the confirmation test, a panel prompting a transition to the list scene is displayed, allowing the user to review disaster prevention knowledge which the user already viewed. The reason for setting the final test as 7 days is based on the fact that the Disaster Relief Law requires evacuation centers to be open for one week or less. In the final test, 10 quizzes related to disaster prevention are randomly selected. The correct and incorrect answers are displayed each time the quiz is answered, and each question can be reviewed after all quizzes are finished.

Ending Scene. The ending scene has a review function, a score display function, and an end roll function. The review function displays the name of the shelter, the player's name, and the number of days spent in the shelter. The score is calculated based on the number of quizzes answered correctly, the main character's status, and the number of events experienced, and displays the rank associated with the calculation results. The end-roll function displays the developer's name and the references of the game. At the end of the end roll, a button to go to the title scene is displayed. After returning to the title scene, the game can be started from the beginning.

3.3 Creating an Event Scenario

The quiz was based on the literature [7,8,14] related to evacuation and lives in a shelter.

The events and useful knowledge about shelter living described in each literature were summarized, and the question text and two possible answers can be selected by the users are created. The selection of the information found in the literature was done without any particular criteria, but with the goal of covering as much of the literature as possible. After creating the quiz, a scenario was created for each correct answer of the quiz.

Most of the scenarios consisted of the main character being explained to by a character with knowledge about disaster prevention. In addition, animations and diagrams are shown during the conversations to aid in understanding. The conversational content of the scenarios is created by describing the contents of referenced literature in a verbal manner. When information in the literature is insufficient, relevant information is collected from the websites of local governments and other organizations and incorporated into the scenarios.

The incorrect scenarios are mainly modified from the correct scenarios, and explanations of the incorrect answer choices are added.

We show an example of event scenarios. We take the example of disaster prevention information: "By inflating a plastic bag, it can be used as a substitute for a cushion. From this information, the question "Which of the following can be used as a cushion?

The answer choices are then set to "plastic bag" and "plastic bottle". Figure 2 shows the actual event selection scene and event scene. In the event scene, the characters' conversations in the introduction are different for the correct answer and the incorrect answer. In the case of the correct answer, the character says that it is hard to sit in the gymnasium for a long period of time. In the case of incorrect answers, the characters say that they filled a plastic bottle with water and sat down, but the cap fell off because it was difficult to sit for a long time in the gymnasium. After the above introductory part is over, the method of using a plastic bag as a substitute for a cushion is explained in detail, and uses other than cushioning are also introduced.

4   Evaluation by Subject Experiments

4.1   Method

Two subject experiment were conducted to evaluate the degree of knowledge acquisition of disaster prevention by the application. First, participants were asked to answer a pre-learning test and a questionnaire related to disaster prevention, and were divided into groups A and B so that the mean and variance are equal. Group A was then given our simulation application for living in an evacuation shelter, while Group B was given learning document materials.

Finally, the participants were asked to answer a post-learning test and a questionnaire to evaluate the learning effect. The order of the questions in the post-test was changed from that of the pre-test. Both the pre-study test and the post-study test consist of 37 questions.

The document materials were taken from the same literature [7,8,14] and websites of local governments and other organizations as the content of the scenarios implemented in our simulation application, and the documents were summarized and some key points were emphasized.

4.2   Results and Discussion

A subject experiment was conducted with 10 subjects. The subjects were mostly university students studying computer science. The results are shown in Table 1.

In order to verify the validity of the teaming of Group A and Group B based on the results of the pre-study test, F-test and t-test were conducted. The result of the F-test at the 5% significance level yielded a P-value of 0.261. This value does not fall within the rejection range, indicating equal variances. A t-test at the same significance level yielded a t-value of 0.629. The rejection range for the null hypothesis is in the range of less than -2.306 and greater than 2.306. This indicates that there is no significant difference between the two groups and that the teaming of Groups A and B is appropriate.

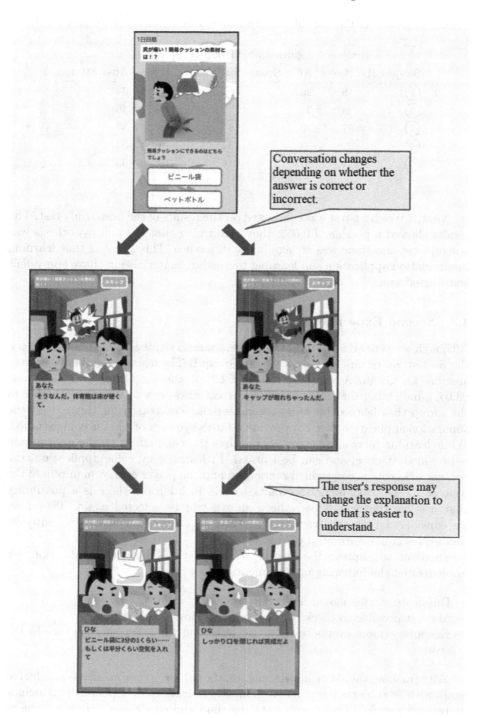

Fig. 2. Specific examples of event scenarios

Table 1. Results of the first subject experimental test (number of correct answers)

Group A (proposed application)			Group B (Materials)		
Subject ID	Before	After Study	Subject ID	Before	After Study
①	18	26	⑥	21	34
②	24	34	⑦	24	36
③	17	28	⑧	18	35
④	22	33	⑨	13	34
⑤	21	31	⑩	19	33

Next, a Welch's t-test was conducted on the results of the post-study test. The results showed a p-value of 0.053, thus confirming that the null hypothesis was not rejected and there was no significant difference. This suggests that learning by simulation application and learning by reading materials may have equivalent learning effects.

4.3   Second Experiment

Although we were able to confirm that there was no significant difference between the post-study results for Group A and Group B The average number of correct answers for Group A was 30.4 (about 82.2%), and for Group B 34.4 (about 93.0%), indicating that the number of correct answers was about 11% higher in the group that learned by using the materials. The reason for this is that the simulation application does not provide a bird's eye view of what is being studied. While learning by reading materials requires time and effort, all the information is provided at once, and can be learned. In learning by game application, the content of events is determined randomly, and the player cannot manipulate the content to see what he or she wants to see. In addition, there is a possibility that a story that has already been shown will be selected again. Therefore, we considered that this was inappropriate in a situation where the subjects themselves could learn at any given time.

In order to improve the learning effect of the simulation application, we implemented the following improvements.

- Duplicate stories should not occur again.
- Make it possible to check the open rate of stories at any time.
- Encourage more events to occur by reflecting the story opening rate in the score.

After making the above improvements, the subject experiment was conducted again with 38 subjects (they were also mostly university students but also include more aged people). The experimental method and conditions were the same as in the previous experiment, but the study time was limited to 25 min or less.

4.4   Results and Discussion of Second Experiment

The results of the subject experiments are shown in Table 2.

Table 2. Results of the second subject experimental test (number of correct answers)

Group A (proposed application)			Group B (Materials)		
Subject ID	Before	After Study	Subject ID	Before	After Study
①	25	34	⑳	29	37
②	21	27	㉑	24	23
③	19	36	㉒	23	32
④	18	34	㉓	22	24
⑤	26	37	㉔	21	34
⑥	25	33	㉕	18	35
⑦	25	29	㉖	18	33
⑧	18	24	㉗	24	29
⑨	25	34	㉘	16	34
⑩	21	31	㉙	21	35
⑪	21	34	㉚	24	30
⑫	25	35	㉛	26	33
⑬	15	34	㉜	22	37
⑭	23	27	㉝	30	35
⑮	24	32	㉞	25	32
⑯	23	34	㉟	28	31
⑰	20	32	㊱	20	33
⑱	19	35	㊲	24	34
⑲	21	29	㊳	21	25

The average number of correct answers for Group A was 32.2 (about 87.0%), and for Group B 31.9 (about 86.2%). In order to verify the validity of the teaming of Group A and Group B according to the results of the pre-study test, F-tests and t-tests were conducted. The result of the F-test at the 5% significance level yielded a P-value of 0.202. This value does not fall within the rejection range, indicating equal variances. A t-test at the same significance level yielded a t-value of 1.114. The rejection range for the null hypothesis is in the range of less than -2.030 and greater than 2.030. This indicates that there is no significant difference between the two groups and that the teaming of Groups A and B is appropriate.

Next, a Welch's t-test was conducted on the results of the post-study test. The results showed a t value of 0.100, thus confirming that the null hypothesis was not rejected and that there was no significant difference between the two groups. Therefore, it is suggested that learning by simulation application and learning by reading materials have equivalent learning effects.

A questionnaire was also administered at the end of the pre- and post-tests. The questions and the number of responses are shown in Tables 3, and 4. Responses are in the order 4,3,2,1 to indicate the strength of affirmation to the questions.

Table 3. Pre-study questionnaire results (number of responses)

Questions	Strength			
	4	3	2	1
Do you usually have the opportunity to play games?	25	9	9	5
Do you think you are well informed about disaster prevention, disaster preparedness, and emergency preparedness and knowledge?	0	4	35	9
Are you confident that you answered correctly the entire content of the Pre-Study Quiz?	0	7	22	19

Table 4. Results of post-study questionnaire (number of responses)

Questions	Strength			
	4	3	2	1
Do you think you have acquired knowledge after completing the study?	29	19	0	0
After completing the study, did you feel ready to prepare specifically for living in a disaster or in an evacuation shelter?	28	18	2	0
Are you confident that you answered the entire content of the Post-Study Quiz correctly?	5	31	10	2

More than 90% of the subjects answered that they "do not know much" or "do not know at all" about disaster preparedness and emergency response methods. However, after the study, more than 60% of the participants answered that they "feel more knowledgeable" and "feel more prepared for disasters. The results also showed that there was little difference in the tendency of responses to the questionnaire between learning by our application and learning by materials. This suggests that this simulation application is expected to be a useful learning tool for young people (in their 20 s and 30 s), who are considered to have relatively low awareness of disaster prevention. If this simulation application can increase learning opportunities more widely, it can be used to raise awareness of disaster prevention and disaster preparedness, as more than half of the participants answered that they usually have many opportunities to play games. In the future, we would like to improve the operation method and visual clarity of the application so that even those who are not familiar with the game can enjoy learning.

Based on the subject experiments and feedback described above, we observe that it would be effective to make the following changes to further enhance the learning effect of the simulation application.

– Encourage experiencing more events for learning by having tests multiple times in a short cycle and gradually increasing the difficulty level.
– By changing the display of scenes according to day and night and the number of days elapsed, manipulate the impression of the passage of time and tension. An example of such direction is decreasing the number of evacuees in the surrounding area.

5   Concluding Remarks

This paper has presented the development and evaluation of a simulation application for living in a shelter. The results of subject experiments suggested that subjects who used the application had at least the same learning effect as those who read the material. Furthermore, the results of pre- and post-learning questionnaires indicated that disaster awareness was improved.

We will consider improvements and additions to the functions of the application based on the results of the subject experiments and feedback on the application. This application will be released to the public after adjustment of its functions.

References

1. Arima, M.: Potential and challenges of disaster prevention apps for soft disaster management. Oukan **11-2**, 145–155 (2017). (in Japanese)
2. Azuma, H.: Effectiveness verification of the disaster prevention application "moshiyure" in making earthquakes a self-goto and promoting countermeasure behaviors. In: Proceedings of 77th National Convention of IPSJ (2015). (in Japanese)
3. Cabinet Office Japan: Disaster Prevention Information Page, Disaster Prevention Information of Each Municipality. https://www.bousai.go.jp/index-e.html
4. de Carvalho, P.V.R., Ranauro, D.O., Mól, A.C.A., Jatobá, A., de Siqueira, A.P.L.: Using serious game in public schools for training fire evacuation procedures. Int. J. Serious Games **9**(3), 125–139 (2022)
5. Felicia, P. (ed.): Handbook of Research on Improving Learning and Motivation Through Educational Games: Multidisciplinary Approaches (Advances in Game-Based Learning). Information Science Reference (2011)
6. Kapp, K.M.: The Gamification of Learning and Instruction: Game-Based Methods and Strategies for Training and Education. Pfeiffer (2012)

7. Kihara, M.: What to do in such a case? Learn by taking a quiz! Natural Disaster Survival. Nihontosho Center Co., Ltd. (2021). (in Japanese)
8. Kuroda, Y., Kanda, H.: Nursing Care in Evacuation Shelters and Temporary Housing through Case Studies Care. Japan Nursing Association Publication Society (2012). (in Japanese)
9. Matsuno, Y., Fukanuma, F., Tsuruoka, S.: Development of flood disaster prevention simulation smartphone application using gamification. Dyn. Disasters **169**, 147–159 (2017)
10. 1st Media Inc.: Disaster prevention information "national evacuation shelter guide" ver. 6.0. https://www.hinanjyo.jp/
11. Mizuno, K.: Characteristics of people who have installed disaster prevention applications to be used on their smartphones. Disaster Inf. **17–2**, 157–167 (2019). (in Japanese)
12. Silva, J.F.M., Almeida, J.E., Rossetti, R.J.F., Coelho, A.L.: A serious game for evacuation training. In: IEEE 2nd International Conference on Serious Games and Applications for Health, SeGAH 2013, Vilamoura, Portugal, 2–3 May 2013, pp. 1–6. IEEE Computer Society (2013)
13. Tokyo Stockpile Navi Office: Tokyo Sotckpile Navi. https://www.bichiku.metro.tokyo.lg.jp/en/
14. Yamamura, T.: Disaster Prevention Encyclopedia for Everyone from Disaster Preparedness to Evacuation Life. PHP Institute, Inc. (2015). (in Japanese)
15. Yoshino, T., Hamamura, A., Fukushima, T., Egusa, N.: Making of disaster-prevention maps by local residents using the AkariMap evacuation support system. J. Inf. Process. **58**, 215–224 (2017). (in Japanese)

Strategic Approach to Food System Resiliency from Community-Based Initiatives During the Covid-19 Pandemic

Juan Camilo Sánchez Gil(✉) ⓘ, Martha Alicia Cadavid Castro ⓘ,
Luis Alirio López Giraldo ⓘ, and Guillermo León Moreno Soto ⓘ

Universidad de Antioquia, Calle 67 #53-108, Medellín, Colombia
`juan.sanchez9@udea.edu.co`

Abstract. Although the Covid-19 pandemic triggered a significant public health challenge to humanity, measures like lockdowns let to cascading effects that impacted the food system to such extent, that its rebuilding became an imminent issue. As part of the food system, "of alternative food networks (AFNs) and emergency food networks (EFNs) did not escape to that change. In fact, because of their predominant community-based background, they highlighted their local capabilities as an asset for the food system to be adaptive from supply chain disruptions during the crisis. Concerned by the exacerbation of food insecurity, which because of the magnitude of crisis could not be exclusively handled by public-private established organizations, these stakeholders supported on social solidarity to keep service levels as stable as possible, not only by struggling to keep their already existing supply and distribution channels running, but also creating new ones. Through a case study approach, this paper characterises and analyses eight community-based initiatives that either rebuilt or started up a food supply chain during the Covid-19 outbreak peaks in Medellín, Colombia. In addition, based on a prospective planning approach, this research identified change factors that had the potential to become a long-term capability to install resiliency in the food system when future threats set on. Finally, a strategic approach is developed as an input to impact local food security risk policies through disaster risk reduction under the frame of preparedness, as well as for the food system resiliency in non-emergency contexts.

Keywords: Food system resiliency · Alternative food networks · Emergency food networks · Prospective planning · Disasters

1 Introduction

Tackling the exacerbation of food insecurity in Colombia during the Covid-19 pan-demic demanded a transdisciplinary view that understood the complexity of the Multiple variables that made the risk of getting the disease not the only concern. In a country where 47,9% of the workforce was employed informally [1] prior to the pandemic and 54% of

© IFIP International Federation for Information Processing 2023
Published by Springer Nature Switzerland AG 2023
T. Gjøsæter et al. (Eds.): ITDRR 2022, IFIP AICT 672, pp. 341–357, 2023.
https://doi.org/10.1007/978-3-031-34207-3_22

households suffered from food insecurity [2], measures such as lockdowns, were effective for flatting the outbreak curve. However, such measures were not considered with regard to guaranteeing the risk of food insecurity for those who ceased working, indeed, would not increase. Despite the efforts of national, regional, and local governments, and the philanthropy from private sector to maintain food accessibility and availability to the demanded levels, food supply chain disruptions remained an added constraint. To contribute to this challenge, the University of Antioquia gathered researchers from the School of Nutrition and Dietetics, the Department of Industrial Engineering, and the Faculty of Nursing, who could provide a systemic vision from food security, supply chain disruptions, and anthropology, to formulate and execute a research project whose objective was to design strategies to impact food sovereignty and safety from the rebuilding of alternative and emergency food networks. Two types of community-based organisations present in Medellín, starting on the changes adopted them by the Covid-19 pandemic and similar potential threats.

Community - Based Food Organisations (CBFOs) play a key role when responding to food security crisis triggered either by political, economic, or ecological threats. CBFOs, as agents of critical food guidance from the bottom-up, provide alternative solutions to food systems' failures and recognising the central role food plays in the life of communities [3]. These organisations arise from the grassroots level with the purpose of building community-based food systems shaped by values of food security, food sovereignty, and food justice [4]. This research characterizes the state of alternative food networks (AFNs) and emergency food networks (EFNs) during the Covid-19 lockdowns periods, as well as the capacities installed, and the changes adopted to deal with the food supply chain disruptions. The research methodology is then introduced prior to presenting the programs and projects that outline the results. Finally, a discussion and concluding remarks highlight the importance of coping with the risk food crisis during slow onset disaster triggered by future threats that not necessarily will have to be biological.

2 Alteration of the Food System During the Covid-19 Pandemic in Colombia

The health crisis caused by Covid-19 pandemic has affected food systems, which are increasingly globalized, risking access to basic foods for people in vulnerable conditions. Not only were food supply chains affected by lockdowns, but further impacts affecting the slow down in economic global scale were evident when referring to a reduction in income of lower socioeconomic groups.

In the city of Medellín, the food crisis revealed that food insecurity manifests itself as the result of profound social inequities and the configuration of precarious sustainable food supply systems in times of pandemic lockdowns. Such a situation came along with actions by civil society that took place independently from state and corporate actions. The strategic objective (prior to the pandemic) of the Food Security Plan of the Municipality of Medellin 2016–2028 was to promote stability, sufficiency, efficiency, and autonomy in the food system. At a local level, the strategies proposed in the plan acquired higher priority in the pandemic context, such as, the improvement of institutional capabilities to food supply within a city-region approach and the development of a food supply system focused on vulnerable populations.

The pandemic revealed and combined hidden needs along with insufficient state responses. The alteration of the food system during the Covid-19 pandemic in Colombia brought with it an increase in food poverty and increasing structural social inequality. For example, the impact on food supply chains generated waste from the loss of perishable products. It was not just this waste of essential foods that came along with the food system disruption. The restrictions on the mobility, the temporary closure of schools, the Venezuelan migration whose workforce participation enlarged even more the informal economy, created the necessary conditions for Colombia to be seen by the FAO as one of the countries in the Latin America region at risk of hunger.

In this context, the responses of civil society to face the health crisis that would come along with the food crisis, took place fundamentally on two fronts: the initiatives of the alternative food networks and the solidarity actions of community-based organizations who exposed new emergency food networks. The arise of these civil society initiatives are justified on the insufficient response from governmental programs and existing emergency food networks to the social challenges caused by the lockdowns and the structural inequality of Colombian society. Hence the importance of describing and analysing these initiatives grounds not only on the response capabilities of civil society during new slow onset disasters, but also to guide it towards redefining public policies.

2.1 Alternative and Emergency Food Networks

Alternative food networks, unlike conventional food systems, operate with short distances between consumers and producers, manage small-scale agriculture with holistic or organic methods, and are committed to social, economic, and environmental dimensions of sustainable food production, distribution, and consumption. Examples of AFN experiences are farmers' markets, local food markets, fair trade markets [5], farm stores, farm sales, box delivery schemes, community garden initiatives [6]. In Colombia, the AFN have been promoted to include farmers in local markets, and consolidate environmental protection strategies, disseminating agroecology as a strategy of food and nutritional sovereignty and security. However, just like it happened all around the world, given the restrictions to contain the Covid-19 pandemic, local urban outdoor markets were forced to close [7]. This triggered crop loss and negative impacts on sales, prices, and income for small producers, as early documented by Harris et al. [8]; This led them to develop new distribution channels and the incursion into digital media with very few resources and capabilities [9].

Similarly, on health crises like the Covid-19 pandemic, CBFOs have evolved to redefine the emergency food system through the uprise of community-based emergency food networks as an add-in to existing organization types, from more formal organizations such as food banks to less informal ones such as food pantries [10].

3   Research Method

This study was conducted throughout 3 stages. Stage 1 carried out to characterize the state of the AFN and the EFN under study, during the initial periods of the Covid-19 lockdowns in Medellín, Colombia. Following a qualitative perspective analysed 8 case studies; four of which operated as AFN and four as EFN. In addition, the division of public policies for food security and nutrition of Medellín's municipality was also interviewed in relation to their role in the AFN. The selection criteria of the AFN were driven by three conditions: that they had run operations (minimum five years) prior to and during the pandemic, that they had presence in Medellin and its metropolitan area, and that they had carried out food production and distribution involving fresh food diversity, either produced through agroecological practices or in the process of achieving so and setting short food supply chains. Likewise, EFN chosen had to comply with either of the two following conditions even if they were led by individuals, groups, or organizations, both public and private: that they had emerged spontaneously from a community-based approach as a response to the pandemic's food crisis, or from a non-philanthropic established organization whose purpose was not to carry out food aid actions prior to the pandemic.

The selection of the initiatives under study was carried out using the stakeholder mapping technique. People and civil society organizations who were considered to have a key role in developing initiatives to address food requirements during the pandemic's lockdowns were identified. This facilitated the identification of key informants who led the initiatives analysed, as well as their purposes, interests, and actions. As a result of this technique, it was possible to ensure the representativeness of the cases chosen for the study, basing on the understanding of the phenomenon studied from a descriptive and comparative approach rather than ensuring statistical representativeness. By using the constant comparison method, categories and indicators were identified according to the type of stakeholder chosen as key informant, which led to inquire about similarities and differences among the initiatives analysed and introduced as follows.

(1) Solidarity barter: One EFN case where people within the same neighborhood delivered food donations to a table located in a public space. These donations are available to those in need, under the premise of "if you have spare food, donate it, if you lack of it, take it." (2) Food aid kits delivery: Two EFN cases, one of them civilian oriented and the other one set up by a public organization that received monetary or in-kind donations to configure food packages and deliver it to prioritized beneficiaries. (3) Food stamps: One EFN case that used its resources to offer stamps redeemable for food in supermarkets close to the homes of the beneficiaries. (4) Farmers' organizations: Three AFN cases that grouped farmers. They were chosen to contrast experiences during the Covid-19 pandemic, one just born prior to the pandemic, another one struggling to stay on the market, and a third one reattempting to emerge during the pandemic. (5) Community garden: An AFN case of community gardens, supported by the Food and Nutritional Security team of the Municipality, which was also interviewed to understand the policies and initiatives developed by the local government during COVID-19 pandemic.

Based on the stakeholder mapping technique and the previous representativeness criteria, a decision was made on the number of key informants required, using the data saturation point. The saturation is based on the continuous review of the information provided by the key informants in the interviews until establishing that the new interviews tend to repeat (saturate) the data of the information previously obtained. By returning the information to the stakeholders and their participation in the next stage of the research, possible interpretation biases were eliminated and the data to be used in the prospective analysis was validated.

On stage 2, the strategies, initiatives, and the necessary interventions to run operations in both, AFN and EFN in the context of the Covid-19 lockdowns, were identified. The scope of this stage was to identify change factors, which are the main facts or phenomena that determined the evolution or transformation of both kinds of network, which aim at driving future scenarios. Finally, stage 3 projects the redefinition of AFN and EFN so that they permanently appropriate some of the characteristics and capabilities developed during the crisis, to make them more resilient in the future. Thus, prospective planning techniques were used: Regnier abacus principle, structural analysis, and stakeholders mapping, which together, allowed to envision interventions that would contribute to closing the gap between the current and an ideal scenario.

3.1 Semi-structured Interviews and Open Coding

Two interview guides were designed, one for the AFN and for the EFN, considering eight categories of analysis that were identified as a result of documented analysis carried out by the transcapillary research team and their expertise. These categories, presented in Table 1, outlines the structure of the nine semi-structured interviews that were conducted, reaching 231 transcribed pages among all.

Table 1. Driving categories to the characterization process

Category of analysis	Characterization
Governance	Complex set of relationships resulting from the mutual exchange of rules, ideas, and knowledge, which, in turn, serve a set of interests
Stability	Refers to physical, economic, and social access to food in a timely and permanent manner
Normativity	Norms that define, or should define, authorities or organizations for the functioning of the food system
Information	Production, transfer and transformation of data and knowledge
Technology	New digital technologies as an important resource in the information flow and communication in the food system
Logistics	Stakeholders, processes, and resources necessary to materialize the flow of food in the supply chain
Quality and safety	Guarantees offered so that food does not cause harm
Sustainability	Environmental, social, and cultural dimensions of supply and distribution in food systems

The open coding took place by first selecting the units of analysis for each interview transcription, and then, defining categories and codes that best represented the concept or fact in it. Next, analytical memos were developed for each unit of analysis, from which were identified the change factors that had the capability of installing resiliency in the food system under study. Thus, for both AFN and EFN distinct change factors were identified, which will be introduced in the results section.

3.2 Prospective Planning

The aim of this methodological moment was to design future scenarios for the re-building of alternative and emergency food networks based on the changes adopted with the Covid - 19 pandemic, through a prospective relational analysis from the change factors identified, supported by a participatory approach with the stakeholders involved in the object of study. Three moments were addressed to achieve so: 1) prioritization of change factors, 2) future scenarios and 3) strategic design.

Gaston Berger [11] defined prospective as "the science that studies the future in order to understand it and being able to influence it". When carrying out a prospective approach, it is recognized as a systematic, participatory process that builds a long-term vision for current decision-making and the mobilization of joint actions. As for this, Medina [12] states that in prospective approaches, there are "social dialogue methods to better channel civilian participation and social power in the territory", promoting the social construction of future from the various territorial dynamics contextualized and located in daily life. Indeed, the alternative and emergency food networks were addressed in this research pursuing the interaction at various scales that "supposes a structured and systematic reflection about the future alternatives of a country, territory, sector or institution, through organized interaction with experts, networks and communities, based on a dialogue based on facts and data" [12].

With respect to the first moment, identification and prioritization of factors of change, 35 factors of change were identified for the alternative food supply and distribution system and 19 for the solidarity system, which arise from the diagnostic process explaining the current situation, but also the analysis of future issues that may have a favourable or unfavourable impact on the object of study in the medium or long term, depending on the decisions taken in the present.

The prioritization process included the analysis of key factors, which aims to identify the phenomena that have the capacity to structurally influence the future of the alternative and solidarity systems, by any action taken in response to them; but without ignoring that they belong to a system where all the variables or phenomena are dynamically related; because of these characteristics, they are considered strategic variables.

For the prioritizing process, two techniques were implemented. Firstly, structural analysis, as presented by Godet [13], which allows a collective structuring and thinking of a system, offering the possibility to outlining the alternative and emergency networks, supporting on a matrix that relates all the constituent elements of such system. The second technique used was Regnier Abacus, which allowed the consultation of stakeholders and experts using a colour code (red, yellow, and green) [13, 14] collect their opinions on the change factors that contribute the most to the rebuilding of alternative and emergency food networks. As a result of triangulation from both techniques, three strategic lines, and one line, were achieved for the alternative and emergency food networks, respectively. These results drive the guidelines to defining both the future scenario and the strategic design.

The second moment was the design of scenarios, according to Godet [13], "a future scenario is a set formed by the description of a future situation and a path of events that allow moving from an original situation to a future one". A scenario simultaneously meets five conditions: relevance, coherence, plausibility, importance, and transparency" [13]. This moment of construction of the scenario is based on the results obtained by the interviews carried out, the characterization of case studies, the prioritization of change factors, and the reading and analysis of future trends.

The third moment was the strategic deployment, defined as the set of actions expressed in programs and projects that seek to consciously close the gap between the future scenario and the current one. From the prospective planning, it was possible to identify possible scenarios and their feasibility based on the stakeholders' interests and from the needed mechanisms to reach them.

4 Research Results

The three phases through which the research method was carried out allowed to reach specific outcomes not only for each phase but for each of the two types of initiatives under study. Subsection 4.1 characterizes how the community-based initiatives belonging to AFN adapted themselves to keep their operations on running. Thus, change factors identified through the open coding are summarized to highlight the impact that these factors could have on installing resiliency capabilities in AFN. This then leads to the outcomes of the prospective planning approach by outlining a future narrative scenario that, although written in present tense, implies how AFN should be in the future if change factors managed to install resiliency capabilities. Finally, the strategic design outlines strategic lines of action, which are deepened by programs and projects. Subsection 4.2 presents the same content structure as to Subsect. 4.1, outlining the results for the community-based case studies that belong to the EFNs.

4.1 The Adaptation of Alternative Food Networks

Despite the difficulties in connectivity and access to digital technology, and the fact that some knowledge transfer processes were interrupted by the pandemic, a highlighting new production and transfer of information and knowledge in agroecology, logistics processes and waste management was identified. Likewise, the flow of information and communication were identified as an important resource, which along with logistics, caused a redirection of the food supply chain through new consolidation points and an increase in last mile deliveries. In such a situation, to guarantee the quality and safety of food, non-certified new biosafety protocols were adopted, applied to all phases of the supply chain. Regarding stability, it was found an increase in crops for self-consumption, the substitution of certified seeds and agrochemicals for other inputs available on farms such as native seeds and composting, alongside changes in eating habits. From environmental, social, and cultural dimensions of sustainability, the characterization of AFN revealed critical issues in the process of urbanization of rural areas that put the proximity of food supply chains at risk, as well as problems with the excessive use of plastic bags and other materials during the pandemic. Finally, from the governance perspective, the purpose of linking organizational capabilities and strengthening cooperation between producers, distributors and consumers was identified as a result of the articulation with solidarity economy sectors, making producers and food distributors not feeling included in the regulations defined by governmental institutions, as is the case of farmers markets. In addition, the fact that regulations on public food purchases have not turned into opportunities, triggered a setback in their application during the pandemic.

Change Factors. For codification purposes, the change factors identified throughout the interviews' open coding analysis are the following: (1) Networking strengthening among producers, distributors, and consumers. (2) Changes in food markets structures. (3) Inclusion of the initiatives of alternative producers and distributors in new markets and public food purchasing. (4) Local articulation for a diverse, stable, and accessible food availability. (5) Governmental and community-networks support to producers and distributors for the development of markets. (6) Production for self-consumption and local supply. (7) Interinstitutional and intersectoral coordination. (8) Consolidation of family and community-based peasant agriculture. (9) Adaptation and expansion of farmers markets in the metropolitan area. (10) Education for responsible and conscious consumption. (11) Logistics changes. (12) Access to resources for food production and marketing. (13) Knowledge transfer and exchange of experiences. (14) Adequate transportation of food produced by agroecological, family and community farming. (15) Changes in income and poverty. (16) Participation and incidence in public policy. (17) Regulation for the protection of food production. (18) Contextualized application of tax and health regulations. (19) Transformations in food practices. (20) Institutional and community networks capabilities. (21) Food loss and waste management. (22) Adequacy of farmers markets regulation. (23) Food traceability and access to certifications. (24) New digital technologies with connectivity, access, and proper use. (25) Changes in dietary diversity. (26) Dynamics of road accessibility and connectivity in the metropolitan area. (27) Transition to agroecological production. (28) Changes in the basic food basket costs. (29) Territorial inequalities (30) Agroecological education. (31) Use of biodegradable and sustainable packaging. (32) Change in the proportions and severity of food insecurity. (33) Changes in population and demographic dynamics. (34) Transformations in lifestyles. (35) Environmental sustainability.

Future Scenario Narrative. Alternative food networks have been contributing increasingly to the nutrition and food safety (NFS) of Medellín. This is the result of a strengthening process that has consolidated it into a feasible, resilient, and sustainable food system, even in emergency situations that cause disruptions in the system's supply chain. This process was made possible due to both the governmental and non-governmental institutions, and society in general, who have understood the importance of having community-based capabilities for the food supply system in the territory, which has led to greater institutional and civilian support. The participation of the stakeholders of alternative food networks in the design and implementation of public policies related to food has resulted in a greater incidence of these, which has expanded the opportunities and improved the deployment capabilities of lower socioeconomic communities, small producers, and alternative dealers. Overall, this has enhanced progress in guaranteeing the human right to adequate food for the population, based on the food sovereignty of the territory.

One of the most key results of this process is the strengthening of the alternative markets, which are now more feasible in social, economic, and environmental terms. This has contributed to a better functioning of the food supply chain. Thus, healthy eating is now understood by society and governmental institutions as a fundamental right, which is guaranteed based on the food sovereignty of the territory. Consequently, with the increase in the contribution of the alternative networks in the subregion, the assurance of health eating has been reinforced in relation to the nutritional quality, safety and cultural suitability of the food consumed.

Similarly, with a greater emphasis on food sovereignty, progress was made in reducing the inequality gaps between rural and urban communities in the territory, through the implementation of public policies that prioritize peasant agriculture and agroecology. These policies made possible a greater connection to small agroecological producers and local peasant communities with individual, collective, and institutional consumers in the metropolitan area, which has contributed to reducing food insecurity in the urban population, mainly with lower income and purchasing power.

Strategic Design. Three strategic lines were identified, each of these has the following structure: aim, programs, and projects.

Line 1: Development of Alternative Food Markets. The aim of this line is to strengthen alternative food markets to ensure its operations in emergency contexts while reaching economic, social, and environmental benefits. Line 1 programs and projects are listed in Table 2.

Table 2. Line 1 programs and projects to development of alternative food markets

Program	Projects
Expanding the participation of the alternative networks in food markets	Capabilities to contributing to the quality of state food assistance services
	Farmers, green and agroecological markets throughout the metropolitan area
	Farmers, family, and community agriculture and agroecology supplying conventional food markets
Accessing resources to strengthen food production and distribution	More urban spaces for small-scale and low-volume subsistence horticulture
	Access to resources to improve the marketing of crops
	Community banks of supplies, tools and equipment
	Adequate advice and technical assistance
Adapting the regulation to strengthen alternative food networks	Permanence of transitory norms
	New regulatory developments to institutional support
Educating for healthy, conscious, and responsible consumption	Strengthening traditional educational strategies on alternative food networks
	Alliances with the cooperative and solidarity sector
	Keeping and transforming food practices

Line 2: Changes in the Supply Chain.   The aim of this line is to better operate the supply chain of alternative food networks in the metropolitan area, by improving its resilience in emergency situations and contribute to its economic and environmental sustainability in non-emergency contexts. Line 2 programs and projects are listed in Table 3.

Table 3. Line 2 programs and projects to changes in the supply chain

Program	Project
Adapting the logistics process for the direct connection between producers and consumers	Institutionalization of small networks to trade aggregated supply of crops obtained by small and medium producers from farmers, family, and community agriculture
	Development of supply chain models customized according to consumers' preference
Minimizing food loss and waste	Characterising and tackling food loss and waste in alternative networks
	Subsistence crops and short distribution circuits to reduce food losses and waste
	Alliances with food banks and other philanthropic stakeholders
	Partnerships to prevent food loss and waste during crisis
Adapting transportation of farmers, family, and community agriculture towards agroecology practices	Last mile delivery model safe and sustainable
	Community participation in last mile deliveries
	Alliances with the transport cluster of the traditional food networks
Food traceability and access to certifications for food safety and quality	Promotion and facilitation of traceability and certifications
	Promotion and protection of participatory guarantee systems
New digital technologies with connectivity, accessibility, and proper use	Diagnosing and finding solutions
	Developing capacities with ICT
	Youth promoting the adoption of new technologies for producer-consumer direct food trading

Line 3: Development of Territorial Capacities.   The aim of this line is to develop the necessary territorial capabilities, to improve the resilience of the alternative food networks in emergency situations and its contribution to guaranteeing the human right to adequate food Medellín. Line 3 programs and projects are listed in Table 4.

Table 4. Programs and projects of the line development of territorial capacities

Program	Project
Strengthened networks of producers, distributors, and consumers	Aggregating the supply of logistics resources
	Aggregating the food offer
	Fair trade alliances
	Interaction with other stakeholders of the alternative networks and social movements
Interinstitutional and intersectoral articulation for a healthy and sustainable diet	Coordinating food supply between institutions and clusters
	Alliances and agreements to enhance research on alternative food supply
Participation and incidence in food public policies	Participation of stakeholders from civil society and alternative networks in the diagnosis and planning of public policies for a healthy and sustainable diet
	Ensuring instances and mechanisms for direct participation of civil society and alternative networks in defying public food policies
Strengthening farmers, family, and community agriculture	Inclusion in local and regional food and nutrition security plans
	Continuity of food production and distribution in emergency situations
	Reaching the autonomy of farmers, family, and community agriculture
	Access to irrigation resources for agricultural production
Knowledge transfer and dialogue of knowledge in the alternative food networks	Deepening the dialogue of knowledge and the exchange of experiences
	Research and social appropriation of knowledge
Development of governmental institutional capabilities to achieve a healthy and sustainable food supply	Improving government's understanding of the alternative food networks
	Development of public-private partnerships for the trading of healthy foods
	Establishment of a food supply observatory
Transition towards agroecological production	Networks of agroecological producers and distributors
	Encouraging the transition to agroecology

(*continued*)

Table 4. (*continued*)

Program	Project
Organization and consolidation of rural territories	Implementation of public policy instruments for healthy and sustainable food supply
	Incentives for the protection and development of environmental conservation areas and food production
	Coverage and quality in the supply of utility services in the rural areas
	Adequate infrastructure to potentiate capabilities of rural areas
Territorial articulation for a diverse, stable, and accessible food availability	Strengthen relations of regional and domestic interdependence
	Food supply commercial alliances

4.2   The Arise of New Emergency Food Networks

As to governance, the EFN under study rose spontaneously driven by the social consciousness and mechanical solidarity from structural social capital in response to the social and economic phenomena that had a direct impact on food security of a distinct community. Its management is based on relational capabilities and the linking of different stakeholders in the form of synergistic alliances that strengthen social capital or organizational partners. Outsourcing practices were recurrent on organizational/community-based initiatives, which allowed successful outcomes to reaching a much larger geographic coverage than established emergency food assistance programs. As to stability, different mechanisms for receiving donations such as wire transfers, in kind donations, volunteering, and logistics infrastructure such as equipment, utensils and transportation. Although the overall donations were abundant at the beginning of the lockdowns, they decreased over time despite the worsening of the outbreak, which affected the food supply rate. Regarding normativity, it was identified a structured set of internal operating rules when it comes to organizational/community-based emergency food networks, whereas new norms were created jointly in civil society community-based emergency food networks. Regarding external regulations, mobility, and transit restrictions affected the performance of all both EFN.

In relation to information, the data for selecting beneficiaries came from multiple sources such as community leaders and databases that were set mainly through phone calls. There was evidence of access to technologies for communication between leaders such as phone calls, virtual meeting platforms, email, social networks, as well as initiatives to store beneficiaries' information and photographic records to verify the delivery of donations as evidence to donors. Regarding logistics, inventories were empirically managed given the available human and infrastructure resources, which had no logistics background indeed. Primary and secondary transportation was carried out using own or borrowed private vehicles as well as vehicles made available as in-kind donation. Conversely, the necessary actions to guarantee food quality and safety were conditioned by accessibility to re-sources such as physical infrastructure, adequate transportation, and qualified human resources. However, volunteers did implement inventory control strategies such as the application of the first in, first out technique (FIFO) as well as inventory turnover of perishable food to prevent loss and waste. From a cultural sustainability point of view, most EFN under study sought to supply and distribute food according to the food culture of territories. Finally, although environmental sustainability was not considered a priority, the use of plastics for packaging of donations was avoided, preferring recycling packaging materials as a strategy to reduce environmental impact.

Change Factors. The open coding carried out to the transcriptions of the four semi-structured interviews revealed findings that, according to the interviewees, had the potential to make changes, either because they stated it explicitly or because they outlined particular facts proving so. (1). Alliances for supply and distribution of material convergence. (2) Assistance to population not prioritized by governmental response. (3) Local food purchasing. (4) Unification of logistics information systems. (5) Strengthening physical infrastructure for managing material convergence. (6) Training on disaster management. (7) Income and poverty changes. (8) Strengthening internal relationship management. (9) Donated food safety insurance. (10) Strengthening social awareness and solidarity. (11) Affordability of commodities in the food market. (12) Traceability and transparency in the donation process. (13) Social networks to promote donations. (14) Measures for ensuring supply from urban and rural vegetable gardens. (15) Encouragement of tax regulations for individual donors. (16) Environmental sustainability during supply and distribution of donations. (17) De-regulation of last mile restrictions for food donations. (18) Volunteering regulation for emergency food supply and distribution. (19) Changes in social vulnerability from economic protection.

Future Scenario Narrative. Medellín and its metropolitan area have been contributing to guarantee adequate, safe, and sustainable food to its population during emergencies. This is the outcome from understanding how emergency food networks are capable of orchestrating supply and distribution thanks to the interdependent work of social, community, governmental, institutional, and corporate stakeholders, who consolidated alliances to minimize risks and address vulnerability in food security.

Closing the gaps in access to food during supply chain disruptions in the food system in Medellín was possible due to the development of capabilities for emergency response based on what was learned from the Covid-19 pandemic. The development of response capabilities was greatly benefited from the enhancement of the disaster preparedness stage, which encouraged and ensured the integration of response capabilities from structural social capital by aggregating resources and actions with the remaining stakeholders of the National Unit for Disaster Risk Management.

The consolidation of information systems set as an optimal tool for the collecting, storing, and processing key information for decision making. In this sense, local food purchasing by community-based emergency food networks gained special relevance, which was reached due to the inclusion of small local producers, individuals or associated, as food suppliers during the emergency response. The relaxation of tax regulations encouraged civilian donors to join community-based food emergency networks, including access to certificates for tax discount purposes.

Alliances with local food suppliers allowed an increase in the delivery of highly perishable fresh food, for which it was necessary to take actions to guarantee quality and safety. Some of these actions were the creation and implementation of a traceability system, supported by the information system described above, as well as for monitoring and control of contaminants present in food.

This is how capabilities were developed based on a collective purpose to combine actions and resources for supplying emergency food to vulnerable populations during disaster scenarios, focusing on the population not prioritized in governmental food assistance programs. In emergency food networks, the capacity for internal relationships, the consolidation of an information system and reciprocity in data management are the foundation to generate rapid and effective responses.

Strategic Design. A single strategic line was identified, which has the following structure.

Line: Development of Response Capabilities to Food Crisis Such as the Covid-19 Pandemic. The aim of this line is to develop capabilities to respond to health, environmental and anthropic threats in Medellín, to guarantee the human right to adequate food. Line programs and projects are listed in Table 5.

Table 5. Programs and projects of the line Development of response capabilities to food crisis such as the Covid-19 pandemic.

Program	Project
Food supply and distribution capabilities of emergency food networks	Developing humanitarian logistics competences for emergency food networks
Supply and distribution information systems	Identification of beneficiaries
	Fast and efficient communication channels
Strengthening social capital response capabilities to supply and distribute emergency food	Live together to serve
	Cooperation agreements to strengthen solidarity action
	Tax benefits to encourage donations to community-based emergency food networks
Local purchases during slow on-set disasters	Strategies for safe last mile delivery of local food
Material convergence safe handling	Physical infrastructure for food storage

(*continued*)

Table 5. (*continued*)

Program	Project
	Strengthening the quality and safety guarantee of food donations
Donations with environmental sustainability	Sustainable packaging
	Reducing food loss and waste
	Waste management and disposal

5 Discussion

The transdisciplinary approach required by the response to the Covid-19 pandemic and its consequent lockdown constituted not only a research challenge but also a propositional challenge. The initiatives of Colombian civil society described and analysed above contemplate concrete responses to intervene food crisis, emergency situations, or the convergence of both. The AFN studied adapted their production and distribution system during the lockdown to maintain their operations. In this context, change factors were identified exposing their potential to develop resiliency, which range from the inclusion of initiatives in new markets, public food purchasing, production for self-consumption and local supply, to participation and influence in public policies. Likewise, the organizational and community-based emergency food networks studied created a supply and distribution system almost from scratch yet proving remarkable capabilities to developing resiliency to the food system during crisis, which range from transferring humanitarian logistics knowledge to civil society, to strengthening the internal relations frame to avoid conflicts among volunteers.

The future scenario narrative and the strategic design of both AFN and organizational/community based EFN matched the need for programs and transversal projects to appropriate, access and use ICT to timely close the gap between producer and consumer and between donors and beneficiaries, respectively. Indeed, some programs and projects identified in this study expose the relationship between ICT and society as in alternative food networks they seek the promotion of ICT for trading products, the characterization of current state of ICTs' appropriation, and identifying the digital tools that represent opportunities for new trading channels for alternative markets. Likewise, programs and projects that seek the creation of information systems represent opportunities to collect, store and process information necessary for decision making within emergency food initiatives. Also, government's support in the creation of digital platforms and strategies for information management that favours the updating, dissemination, and transfer of data within emergency food networks arises a strong capability to installing resiliency in the food system.

The use of the prospective planning approach made it possible to suggest a future narrative scenario about how AFN and community-based EFN should be. This scenario indicates that the consolidation of a feasible, resilient, and sustainable food system requires a continuous supply chain, even in emergency situations. To achieve this, it is necessary to undertake an articulated work process in the territory between governmental institutions and non-governmental organizations, and civil society in general. A process in this direction must encompass democratic participation in the design and implementation of public policies related to food risk policies.

6 Conclusions

The necessary actions to give resilience to the food system aimed at developing and strengthening capacities in humanitarian logistics; the creation of alliances for the supply of local and healthy food and the optimization of own and shared resources; the strengthening of physical infrastructure for the safe collection and storage of donations; and finally, the creation of information systems that strengthen communication between the stakeholders involved, collect information on processes and resources (necessary and available) and facilitate operational decision-making and selection of beneficiaries. These strategic actions require the interdependent work of social, community, governmental, institutional, and corporate stakeholders to guarantee their effectiveness. Studying the food system of the city of Medellín during the Covid-19 pandemic using the strategic-prospective approach by a transdisciplinary team of researchers allowed the generation of public policy guidelines for programs and projects related to food supply at a local scale. These guidelines also seek to significantly reduce the risks of disasters triggered by future threats that would restrict access to food. The change factors and the future narrative scenarios identified through the combination of qualitative and quantitative methodological strategies must be consolidated in the design of public policies and, for this, the strengthening of the democratic participation of community stakeholders is required, in a dialogue of knowledge with government and academic stakeholders.

References

1. DANE. https://www.andi.com.co/Home/Noticia/17140-la-camara-de-alimentos-de-la-andi-y-aba. Accessed 29 November 2022
2. ANDI. https://www.andi.com.co/Home/Noticia/17140-la-camara-de-alimentos-de-la-andi-y-aba. Accessed 29 November 2022
3. Manganelli, A., Esteron F.: "Good healthy food for all": examining FoodShare Toronto's approach to critical food guidance through a reflexivity lens. Can. Food Stud. **9**(1), 217–241 (2022)
4. Holt Giménez, E.: Food security, food justice or food sovereignty? Crises, food movements and regime change. In: Alkon, A.H., Agyeman, J. (eds.) Cultivating Food Justice, Oakland (2011)
5. De Rezende, D.: Alternative agri-food networks: convergences and differences in the evolution of the markets. Agroalimentaria **19**(37) (2013)
6. Jarosz, L.: The city in the country: growing alternative food networks in Metropolitan areas. J. Rural Stud. **24**(3) (2008)
7. Béné, C.: Resilience of local food systems and links to food security – a review of some important concepts in the context of COVID-19 and other shocks. Food Secur. **12** (2020)
8. Harris, J., Depenbusch, L., Pal, A.A., Nair, R.M., Ramasamy, S.: Food system disruption: initial livelihood and dietary effects of COVID-19 on vegetable producers in India. Food Secur. **12**(4) (2020)

9. Butu, A., Brumă, I.S., Tanasă, L., Rodino, S., Vasiliu, C.D., Doboş, S.: The impact of COVID-19 crisis upon the consumer buying behavior of fresh vegetables directly from local producers. Case study: the quarantined area of Suceava County, Romania. Int. J. Environ. Res. Public Health **17**(15) (2020)

10. Helmick, M.: Determining the adoption and implementation of nutrition policies at food pantries across the united states. University of Nebraska Medical Center (2018)

11. Berger, G.: Etapes de la prospective. PUF, París (1967)

12. Medina Vásquez, J., Becerra, S., Castaño, P.: Prospectiva y política pública para el cambio estructural en América Latina y el Caribe. CEPAL, Santiago de Chile (2014)

13. Godet, M.: De la Anticipación a la Acción. Editorial Marcombo, Barcelona (1995)

14. Mojica, F.: La Prospectiva: Técnicas para Visualizar el Futuro. Legis Editores, Bogotá (1991)

Web-Based Tool to Facilitate Resilience-Related Information Management

Hoang Long Nguyen[1], Salvatore Antonio Marchese[2],
Valentino Gandolfo[2], Leonardo Luca Trombetta[2], Massimo Cristaldi[2],
Uberto Delprato[2], and Rajendra Akerkar[1]($\boxtimes$)

[1] Big Data Research Group, Western Norway Research Institute, Sogndal, Norway
{hln,rak}@vestforsk.no
[2] IES Solutions, Catania, Italy
{s.marchese,v.gandolfo,l.trombetta,m.cristaldi,u.delprato}@i4es.it

Abstract. This paper provides a comprehensive design of an inventory to gather and manage resilience-related information. A conceptual architecture is introduced followed by an Agile approach by breaking the development task into four sprints, which involves constant collaboration with community users, offering continuous improvement, and getting approval from stakeholders at every stage. By facilitating an agile implementation process, we ensure that the inventory development is highly dynamic, flexible, and collaborative.

Keywords: Community resilience · Resilience-related inventory · AGILE development

1 Introduction

The concept of community resilience [15] is now used widely in often quite different contexts [2]. This speaks to a shift from traditional risk management and purely technical approaches towards a more positive concept of resilience as a strategic approach to be integrated with developmental goals representing a pro-active and essentially positive societal response [5] to adversity. A number of prominent policies, strategies and initiatives exist, but it is the Sendai Framework for Disaster Risk Reduction 2015–2030 that represents a transition from understanding the interactions between hazard, exposure and vulnerability [10] to a greater concern with how to act upon these risk factors [13] through prospective, corrective and compensatory measures [29].

The aim of this paper is to support local communities to increase their resilience by developing a web-based tool to help them gather and organise their resilience-related information. Compared to a desktop application, a web-based tool can provide a whole range of advantages by *i*) allowing access from any computer as long as there is the internet and *ii*), supporting different individuals to

© IFIP International Federation for Information Processing 2023
Published by Springer Nature Switzerland AG 2023
T. Gjøsæter et al. (Eds.): ITDRR 2022, IFIP AICT 672, pp. 358–373, 2023.
https://doi.org/10.1007/978-3-031-34207-3_23

collaborate effectively and efficiently. It is seen predominantly as a strategic tool for assessment and planning [11], with the aim of increasing resilience in local communities [6], and focus on supporting the mitigation and preparedness phases of Disaster Risk Management [27]. As a result, the web-based tool should not be limited by pre-determined weights or data combinations but should instead be adapted to the specific context of local communities and different hazards [7]. For the sake of convenience, we name our Web-based tool as the RESILOC Inventory.

The RESILOC Inventory responds to the need to have a useful tool that allows to collect a large amount of structured and functional data [9] that is necessary in order to perform resilience study. The innovation inherent in the tool is to give all actors the opportunity to identify and assess the validity of actions to increase resilience in their communities; in particular, local managers, citizens and resilience experts have been targeted as end users. The inventory will also have a value in itself for all researchers and commercial companies (e.g., insurance and reinsurance companies) who may be interested in the RESILOC Inventory as a stand-alone tool.

The RESILOC Inventory is a functional digital container that defines and classifies basic information about communities (including the level of risk perception by citizens) and stores all that information through a living data structure that represents the relevant traits of a local community. Based on the literature review [15] about resilience and the need to help local communities increase their resilience, our database design [16], our developers' experience and end-users' recommendations, the inventory is developed targeting the following goals.

- To support local managers and resilience experts of a specific community to collect and consult a large amount of data about the community, it will be useful to get the community basic info related to resilience assessment represented by the values of a predefined set of Proxies identified during the local community definition. Every community will be defined by a simple set of basic attributes (i.e., textual metadata) and a set of Proxies that will be relevant to describe the community in relation to resilience.
- To provide the data structure allowing the creation (by end users defined below) of relationships between Scenarios, Proxies, Indicators and Dimensions.
- To allow policy makers (public administrations of cities and regions, civil protection organisations, etc.), first responders, civil society (citizens, volunteers, NGOs...) and technical services (consultants, urban planners, experts etc.) to access a large amount of useful information to draw inspiration from it including resilience assessment and dimensions, using it to create local projects increasing resilience and contribute with local insights and success stories.
- To be used in all phases of Disaster Risk Reduction (DRR), being the "Mitigation" and "Preparedness" activities where it will bring the most added value.

From our definition, Proxy is an indirect data source contributing to the assessment of an Indicator. Respectively, Indicator is a variable which provides an operational representation of a characteristic of a community and Dimension is a synthetic representation of resilience under a specific topic. The RESILOC Inventory will, thus, store all the information needed to assess resilience, considering social [19], economic [21], governance [18], environment [14], infrastructure [20], and DRR dimensions.

Through validation meetings with end-users (i.e., local civil protection department members), they have also brought valuable contribution to the RESILOC Inventory core architecture design which delivers performance and user-tailored functionalities. Several European projects and products (i.e., SmartResilience [12], DRIVER+ [24], EmerGent [25], EPISECC [26]) have been analysed and, although a ready solution for the task at hand was not found, these studies have been proven effective as source of inspiration to forge the core aspects of the RESILOC Inventory.

The collection of the requirements followed a Spring-based method. The requirements have been collected during the various spring meeting and end-user workshops and the contributions gathered through/by interaction paved the way and the direction for the next sprint until the end of the project. A Sprint pays a lot of attention to the definition of a plan for the implementation of each iteration of the products; it consists in organising a discussion between all involved actors, from the analyst to the developer, from the testers to the product owner. The objective of the sprint is to check if users' needs and expectations have been met or it is desirable/recommended to adopt some changes; gathering and translating these comments as new requirements for developers. Each Sprint has been taken as an opportunity to remind the users about the RESILOC scientific timeline, the sprint series, the RESILOC vision, and what RESILOC will make available relevant to the subsequent Sprints.

In this section, our target is to introduce the problem and emphasize our motivation to conduct this resilience-related database. The rest of the paper is organized as follows. Next, Sect. 2 provides a comprehensive summary of the existing research on community resilience inventories. In Sect. 3, we mention important scopes of the inventory for the sake of simplicity in further sections. Further, Sect. 4 proposes a conceptual design of the database. Then, we come up with the AGILE approach to develop the inventory in Sect. 5. Finally, we mention user validation in Sect. 6 and conclude this work and state some future work in Sect. 7.

2   Literature Review

Community resilience is critical in determining how well communities can withstand, adapt, and recover from disasters and crises. This section examines the development and use of community resilience inventories, highlighting their importance in strengthening communities' abilities to cope with adversities.

In [17], the authors provided a comprehensive framework to understand community resilience and emphasize the importance of social capital, information and communication. Particularly, they argued that these factors can be harnessed by developing community resilience inventories to inform and empower local decision-makers. Besides, Cutter et al. [8] provided the basis for developing resilience inventories, which local governments and organizations can use to evaluate and improve their communities' capacity to withstand and recover from disasters. Recognizing the importance of a community resilience platform, the authors in [23] presented a method for assessing community resilience, allowing communities to identify vulnerabilities and prioritize actions. This research included a resilience inventory with both quantitative and qualitative data, serving as a helpful resource for not only local governments and organizations but also researchers. Nonetheless, there are challenges in developing and implementing community resilience inventories. In [3], the authors emphasized the challenges of data quality and availability in the growth of community resilience inventories, such as the requirement for precise, trustworthy, and up-to-date data to guarantee the effectiveness of these tools in informing resilience-building efforts. Interdisciplinary collaboration could also be another challenge. Aldrich [1] mentioned that interdisciplinary collaboration is necessary for developing and implementing community resilience inventories successfully. He emphasized the need for experts from various fields, such as social sciences, engineering, and urban planning, to collaborate in designing and developing these inventories.

Hence, it is essential to integrate emerging technologies, such as machine learning and big data analytics, to enhance the capabilities of community resilience inventories [4]. These technologies could help enhance data quality, identify trends and patterns, and facilitate more efficient and effective decision-making. Moreover, the United Nations Office for Disaster Risk Reduction (UNDRR) also mentioned the importance of developing community resilience inventories used to support global resilience efforts [28]. By constructing inventories adaptable to different contexts and accessible to communities worldwide, researchers and practitioners can contribute to the broader goal of reducing disaster risk and increasing resilience. Community resilience inventories have the potential to play a crucial role in enhancing communities' capacity to withstand and recover from disasters and crises.

3   Scope of the Inventory

The RESILOC Inventory will store data related to disasters. Analysing them and then making them available to the main stakeholders after the event, it will be possible to learn from the experience: this part of the recovery phase will be another important aspect of the data stored in the RESILOC Inventory. In this way, local communities will be able to use the relevant information to assess local resilience dimensions and the best approaches to improve it through a combination of institutional and technological solutions.

The inventory will be able to support the community definition operations by providing specific features to import Proxies already defined for other local communities that, by a local manager point of view, matches with the target one.

The inventory will be populated by the local managers, resilience experts and local communities' citizens across Europe using data on specific characteristics of the area (e.g., environment, natural hazards, infrastructure, man-made or industrial hazards, etc.), social aspects of the community (e.g., age and census population distribution, social cohesion, risk awareness, institutional trust, local knowledge) and human factors, such as risk perception and awareness, coordination and leadership. It will also accommodate raw (or refined data) data acquired through sensors and/or information collected from Social Media and Crowdsourcing. The data in the RESILOC Inventory will be always available as open data.

The users of the RESILOC Inventory will have different permissions and abilities in accordance with the role they are given for a particular community. The roles currently defined in the platform are listed below:

– RESILOC admin: users who come from the RESILOC consortium responsible for the management and configuration of the RESILOC entities mentioned above and guarantee the inventory's performance, integrity, and security.
– Community side: Below are defined roles for community users. There are five different roles:
  • Community admin: the users who are responsible for managing and assigning roles for other community users. Community admins are set by RESILOC admins to generate a working environment for different communities.
  • Local manager: the users who have control over community settings (such as community description, metadata, or privacy settings) and can create, view, edit, and remove community entities, i.e., community Proxies, Indicators, and Scenarios.
  • Resilience expert: the users who own in-depth knowledge about resilience. They can assist local managers in organising community entities for resilience assessment.
  • Local Resilience Team (LRT): the members of LRTs that have full access to view all the community configurations that resilience assessment results.
  • Citizen: this is the lowest-level role that is automatically given to a user when he/she starts following a community. This user will have the ability to view public community configuration and resilience assessment information only.

Defining the scope is an essential step in developing an inventory, as it helps to ensure that the inventory is comprehensive, relevant, and well-organized, which meets the needs of target audience and supports overall objectives.

4 Conceptual Architecture

All the data in the RESILOC Inventory, which will be filled in by users manually, must belong to particular communities pre-defined by stakeholders. As in Fig. 1, each area contains "Community Metadata", along with other information such as Scenario, which is shown in Fig. 2, and Timelines.

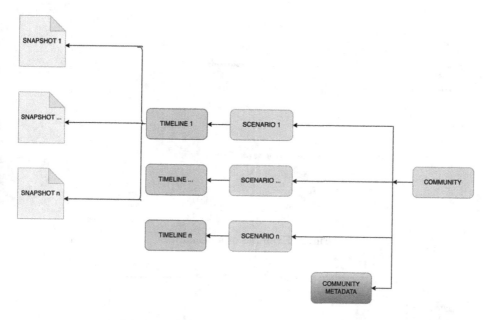

Fig. 1. Overview of the RESILOC Inventory.

Each Timeline related to a specific Scenario, as shown in Fig. 3, contains one or more Snapshot Datasets added at a specific point in time, each of which is organised as Indicators and Proxies.

These Proxies come with important attributes with different scales for a defined Community as shown in Fig. 4; therefore, the use of some attributes is crucial to ensure that all the necessary information is adequate for calculating Indicators as shown in Fig. 5.

Then, professionals and experts can leverage the stored data to conduct various resilience assessments based on their experience. Each assessment needs a list of relevant Proxies (coming from a specific Snapshot Dataset) along with their attributes. These assessments give the first insights and ideas into practical strategies for making communities resilient; however, they have the possibility to submit an undefined number of Snapshot. Regarding the Dataset, the RESILOC users will need to populate the section with past/present/future hazards and capacities.

Fig. 2. Example of a Scenario.

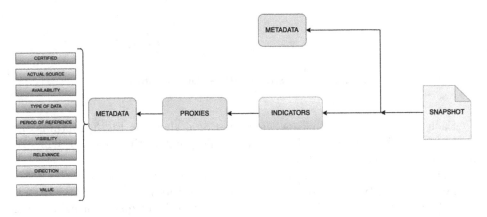

Fig. 3. Snapshot of a Scenario.

Users with the appropriate capabilities are allowed to access the RESILOC proxy, indicator and scenario lists, so that these can be imported into their community lists; in this way proxies, indicators and scenarios can be easily retrieved and used to conduct a community resilience assessment. An editing feature is also available to allow the customisation of proxies, indicators and scenarios imported from RESILOC lists, facilitating their adaptation to suit the community context in which they are used. Professional and experts can make use of

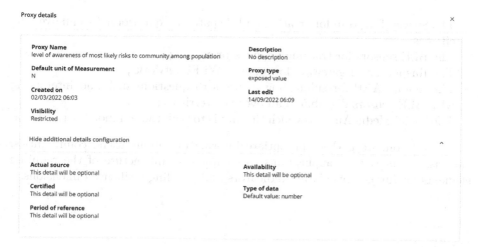

Fig. 4. Examples of a Proxy.

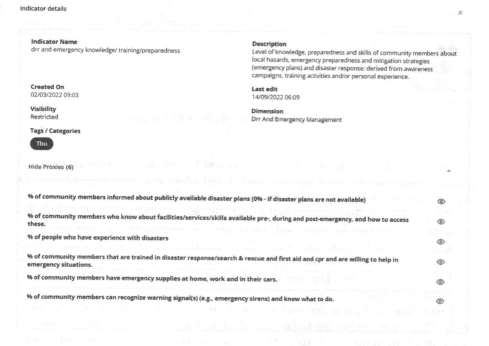

Fig. 5. Examples of an Indicator and its Proxies.

other sources, as depicted in Fig. 6, for conducting the study of the resilience, and then the RESILOC project provides a number of tools that they can involve in their job:

- The Survey Platform for creating and dispatching questionnaires all over the citizens;
- The BLE sensors for tracking people's proximity;
- The Raspberry PI gateways for analyse Wi-Fi networks,
- The mobile APP for submitting answers to questionnaires and interacting with BLE sensors distributed all over the territory;
- The Social Media Analysis which the aim is to scan the common Social Media.

In addition, we gather appropriate information about users, communities, and risks from various applications to complete a full picture of the required elements for further calculating Indicators and building resilience dimensions.

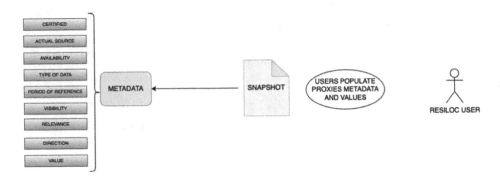

Fig. 6. The use of designed RESILOC Inventory.

For a specific community it will be needed to define and store at least one Scenario configuration that will be used to calculate resilience assessments, for one or more resilience dimensions, using Snapshot Datasets.

Each resilience dimension, together with its mandatory information (i.e., relevant Indicators and Proxies), will be stored as Snapshots for later recall and retrieval as well. By selecting a specific Scenario, it will be possible to make several resilience assessments and analyse them (i.e., comparing outcomes after adding a new Snapshot Dataset triggered by a hypothetical action defined by the resilience expert).

Regarding the Indicators, each one will be defined through the identification of the Proxies participating in the calculation. Each Proxy will also be assigned two crucial attributes that state the impact in the resilience calculation for a specific Indicator, which are the relevance and the direction. The relevance and direction of each Proxy in the calculation of an Indicator will depend on the characteristics of the community involved and the specific Scenario considered. This conceptual architecture has been designed keeping in mind the following requirements:

1. The ability to receive a large and heterogeneous amount of data provided from different communities, and to collect it in a functional structure and with a homogeneous format, easing the sharing and comparing of the RESILOC Inventory's data by end users.
2. The level of performance and reliability needed to make the cloud platform able to perform complex queries and fetch well-structured data in order to elaborate the resilience assessment operations.

5 AGILE Implementation of the RESILOC Inventory

This section describes the usage of Agile software development [22] to develop the RESILOC Inventory. It is open to changing requirements over time and encourages regular feedback from the end-users. The Agile implementation guarantees that the inventory is iterative, incremental, evolutionary, and adaptive through continuous delivery, integration, and collaboration. The agile methodology aims to shorten the time between the decision-making process and the feedback gained from the community users. This is a software development model used to build complex software and product development with iterations that are of definite duration, known as "sprints".

During the development process, we always categorise the tasks into different groups based on their complexity for the purpose of better management and a more organised workflow. We prioritise to develop baseline features or the ones having strong associations with other services (i.e., open data service, semantic layer, or survey tool) in the initial versions, while more complicated ones are implemented in subsequent releases.

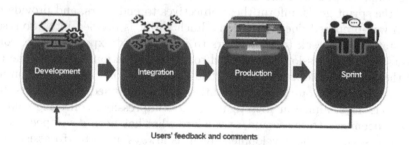

Fig. 7. The RESILOC Inventory development process.

To make the inventory development effective, some essential stages need to be taken into account as in Fig. 7 including development, integration, and production stages. As sketched already, the general idea in the development of the inventory is to follow a circle of very small via the communication among members in our team and verification steps through different sprints with all community users. This enables the desired feedback loop, in which inputs from the community users lead to new functionality and changes of existing features or the implementation of new functionalities according to users' needs.

- **Development:** the team organised meetings at the beginning to identify, discuss, and analyse overall requirements of users to make adjustments and to ensure that system functions appropriately at the end. At this stage, the development teams also set standards and stick to it to avoid possible flaws later on. After guaranteeing that all components and functionalities were considered, developers begin the actual implementation process thoroughly. The backend in this stage uses WM3 as the development environment.
- **Integration:** the objective of the stage is to perform integration of the RESILOC Inventory frontend and backend. Before starting the integration, our team must ensure that both the frontend and backend are error-free and fit the designs. Each function on the UI is mapped precisely to developed endpoints given by the inventory backend. Communications between frontend and backend will be done using Hypertext Transfer Protocol (HTTP) using a REST architectural style. A number of assessments including security, accessibility, performance, stress, and compatibility tests are conducted to make sure that systems meet all the technical requirements with the components integrated.
- **Production:** this is where the community end-users access and actually use the latest version of the inventory after all of the updates and testing from the integration stage. The time to release the inventory to production is several weeks before each sprint. This is to help our team having adequate time for final checks and verification to certify that the system is up and running and all functionalities operate fine with this latest and updated version before giving it to users during the sprints.
- **Sprint:** this stage aims at removing any gaps between community users and our team. To plan and execute sprints productively and correctly, we articulate the sprint goals, inform these objectives to end-users, and provide them with well-prepared documentations. Each sprint is divided into two sessions separated by a week to allow users to interact and experience new components. The first session is dedicated to the presentation and real-time usage of the latest developed features while the second one includes an in-depth exchange of ideas on the functionalities shown and tried by the users during previous days, aimed at investigating their impression, collecting comments and judgements to revise and/or validate what has been developed. Between the two sessions, the development team is always available to assist users if requested.

During all phases of the development lifecycle, API documentation and observability are developed to turn the lights on, see, and understand details and states of components of the inventory.

6   User Validation and Discussion

The development of the RESILOC Inventory was characterised by an AGILE implementation process including interaction phases with the other consortium partners as well as with the end-user representative communities. Sprint aims to update users on the implementation progress, presenting the solutions and discussing its usability through the developed user interface (UI); the users have the opportunity of real-time interaction (when scheduled) and provide feedback and suggestions for the improvement. Last but not least, get approval by users to continue the implementation of the solutions proposed. In addition to that, the directions for the resilience assessment Framework, the connections with the trials, and the inclusion of the LRTs in various Sprints are additional topics included as well. These RESILOC Sprints are usually carried out in two separate sessions; realise a 2-day Sprint helping to provide an overall picture, giving time to assimilate and metabolise the information transmitted and provide sufficient time to return more thoughtful feedback and suggestions. Day 1 usually focuses on the contents scheduled for the Sprint. On the other hand, Day 2 aims to receive and discuss user feedback as well as side topics and next Sprint preparation.

Specifically, the RESILOC Inventory was presented during the 1st Sprint (December 4, 2020), introducing a first mock-up and describing its earliest functionalities. From it the RESILOC Inventory was further developed and represented the main focus of the 2nd Sprint (April 26–27, 2021), and partially reintroduced in the 3rd Sprint (September 10 and September 17, 2021). During these Sprints, the inventory was presented, users were updated on the progress of the implementation and its usability was discussed in detail via the developed user interface. In addition, the users were allowed to interact with the inventory in real time (interactive session between developers, researchers, and users), in order to give feedback and suggestions on the functionalities offered and exchange thoughts on their use and effectiveness; such information was useful for improvement but above all to obtain the users' approval to continue the implementation. Lastly, the end-users have been invited to evaluate some additional inventory's functionalities including sorting and filtering features, as well as the duplication function during the 4th Sprint (November 26 and December 3, 2021).

During Sprints, community representatives have raised questions or comments and to share their experience on the inventory usage; the highlights and key points for the improvement of the RESILOC Inventory, grouped by topics, are presented below.

- **Usability:** researchers and community representatives gave a positive response, expressing appreciation for the current version, reporting a simple and user-friendly environment to enter the data required. However, they reserve the opportunity to raise some remarks once intensive use of the system begins, so that some features could be identified to be optimised in order to improve usability. The usability of the application on mobile devices was another topic raised by the representatives of the communities; however, the layouts used are responsive (i.e., the contents are automatically organised and modelled) so all pages can be used on mobile devices as they are automatically adapted (some specific pages may be more difficult to use due to their higher complexity).

- **Accessibility:** role management and role assignment were discussed extensively; in particular, the conversations involved the way in which roles are managed and assigned to inventory users, focusing on the possibility of having multiple roles assignable to each user and the minimum number of roles required to have a community capable of operating the inventory comprehensively. The accepted solution envisages that each user has a unique account, whereby he/she can login to the inventory and have access to different communities; in each community, a user may have different roles properly assigned according to his/her expertise and responsibilities, wherein each role provides different capabilities to interact with the system. In addition, every community needs to have users holding the role of local manager, resilience expert and community admin, even if assigned to the same person and thus to a single user. It was also strongly suggested to make visible on the screen the roles played by the user for the community selected; the development team proposed a possible solution, consisting in displaying the roles played by the user next to the name of the community he/she is operating into.
- **Possible corrections/changes to be done:** users pointed out a very short autosave time delay (introduced to avoid data loss in case of connection drop) when entering certain values, e.g., min and max target, causing trouble in filling in the form. In reply, the delay time of the autosave function has already been modified, extending it by an appropriate amount of time to make the required operation easier and more fluent. Regarding the roles management and assignment, it was suggested to make the users' roles management layout as compact as possible, aiming to facilitate the users' identification in case there are several registered.

The execution of the Sprints allowed not only the collection of productive feedback and suggestions for the inventory improvement, but also stimulated the users to identify beneficial/useful features. During the interactive phase, the users came up with a requirement to include a filter feature in the Proxy, Indicator, and Scenario lists layout; so that they could be easily retrieved by typing their names into a search box. Likewise, introducing the import and management functionalities for Proxies, Indicators and Scenarios, some users expressed the interest in having a feature that allows the duplication of these elements. In addition to what has already been stated, users manifested the necessity of a widespread use of tooltips, transversal to all the sections composing the inventory; their implementation is aimed at favouring an exhaustive understanding of the items and terminologies presented on screen.

In addition to what has already been stated, users manifested the necessity of a widespread use of tooltips, transversal to all the sections composing the inventory; their implementation is aimed at favouring an exhaustive understanding of the items and terminologies presented on screen. The implementation of a notification system within the inventory was also suggested, in order to notify designated users on the execution of certain operations involving their community (e.g., if a user follows his community).

The requests and suggestions collected have been evaluated and prioritised; some of the previously mentioned functionalities have already been developed and are currently available in the inventory, such as some tooltips and the filtering and duplication features, while the implementation of the notification system has not been released yet.

During the presentation of the latest implementations, which included the language settings component, the new sorting and searching functionalities, and the duplication functionality; the users showed appreciation for the accomplishment of their previous requests, stating also that the tooltips integrated and deployed are easy to understand. The users provided comments on the utility to have a what-if tool, suggesting some functionality in this respect, like a sort of versioning tool for the Proxies.

According to the discussions on the inventory emerged during the sprints, users appreciated and approved what has been developed in the inventory so far, states that the inventory does not have components that needs to be redone or replaced and says that the system is flexible for further small adaptations.

7 Conclusions

The RESILOC Inventory is developed as a web-based set of interfaces, services, and datastores, providing end-users and researchers the possibility to populate and make use of the RESILOC Inventory SaaS. The tool is developed on top of Open Source based technologies (e.g., JavaScript, PostgreSQL, and MongoDB) and run on a Cloud infrastructure to be easily scaled and maintained. The approach to follow is distributed, and the inventory itself is highly customisable for future evolution and future-proof capabilities.

In general, the inventory provides an effective UI to help users manage their data. The RESILOC Inventory UI also offers the user varied features for collecting and organising data through numerous functions at hand such as template inheritance, data duplication, event notification, and searching, sorting & filtering options. Running in parallel and handling requests from the UI is the inventory backend that aims at processing all heavy tasks in the background. It ensures performing all the required actions in the most efficient and logical manner, spending as little time and resources as possible.

In our future work, we will continue expanding Inventory features to better adapt to different users' requirements. For instance, a semantic layer will be implemented to suggest proxies and indicators already used by existing communities to newcomers (new communities) or to be able to provide a list of "similar" communities. Moreover, it will be connected with other tools (e.g., social media analysis and survey tools) to gather more information from various sources.

Acknowledgements. This work has been supported by the RESILOC project. RESILOC has received funding from the European Union's Horizon 2020 research and innovation program under grant agreement No 833671.

References

1. Aldrich, D.P.: Building Resilience: Social Capital in Post-Disaster Recovery. University of Chicago Press (2012)
2. Bodin, P., Wiman, B.: Resilience and other stability concepts in ecology: notes on their origin, validity, and usefulness. ESS Bull. **2**(2), 33–43 (2004)
3. Chandra, A., et al.: Building community resilience to disasters: a way forward to enhance national health security. Rand Health Q. **1**(1) (2011)
4. Cimellaro, G.P., Renschler, C., Reinhorn, A.M., Arendt, L.: Peoples: a framework for evaluating resilience. J. Struct. Eng. **142**(10), 04016063 (2016)
5. Coles, E., Buckle, P.: Developing community resilience as a foundation for effective disaster recovery. Aust. J. Emerg. Manag. **19**(4), 6–15 (2004)
6. Crowe, P.R., Foley, K., Collier, M.J.: Operationalizing urban resilience through a framework for adaptive co-management and design: five experiments in urban planning practice and policy. Environ. Sci. Policy **62**, 112–119 (2016)
7. Cutter, S., et al.: Community and regional resilience: perspectives from hazards, disasters, and emergency management. Geography **1**(7), 2301–2306 (2008)
8. Cutter, S.L., Burton, C.G., Emrich, C.T.: Disaster resilience indicators for benchmarking baseline conditions. J. Homeland Secur. Emerg. Manag. **7**(1) (2010)
9. Garvin, S., Hunter, K., McNally, D., Barnett, D., Dakin, R.: Property flood resilience database: an innovative response for the insurance market. In: E3S Web of Conferences, vol. 7, p. 22002. EDP Sciences (2016)
10. Hosseini, S., Barker, K., Ramirez-Marquez, J.E.: A review of definitions and measures of system resilience. Reliab. Eng. Syst. Saf. **145**, 47–61 (2016)
11. Jabareen, Y.: Planning the resilient city: concepts and strategies for coping with climate change and environmental risk. Cities **31**, 220–229 (2013)
12. Jovanović, A., Auerkari, P.: EU project smartresilience: the concept and its application on critical energy infrastructure in Finland. In: BALTICA X - International Conference on Life Management and Maintenance for Power Plants (June 07–09, 2016)
13. Kuhlicke, C.: Embracing community resilience in ecosystem management and research. In: Schröter, M., Bonn, A., Klotz, S., Seppelt, R., Baessler, C. (eds.) Atlas Ecosyst. Serv., pp. 17–20. Springer, Cham, Switzerland (2019)
14. Longstaff, P.H.: Security, resilience, and communication in unpredictable environments such as terrorism, natural disasters, and complex technology. Harvard University, Center for Information Policy Research (2005)
15. Nguyen, H.L., Akerkar, R.: Modelling, measuring, and visualising community resilience: a systematic review. Sustainability **12**(19), 7896 (2020)
16. Nguyen, H.L., Senarath, Y., Purohit, H., Akerkar, R.: Towards a design of resilience data repository for community resilience. In: Proceedings of the 18th International Conference on Information Systems for Crisis Response and Management (ISCRAM 2021), Blacksburg, Virginia, USA, 23–26 May 2021, pp. 271–281 (2021)
17. Norris, F.H., Stevens, S.P., Pfefferbaum, B., Wyche, K.F., Pfefferbaum, R.L.: Community resilience as a metaphor, theory, set of capacities, and strategy for disaster readiness. Am. J. Community Psychol. **41**, 127–150 (2008)
18. Osman, L.H., et al.: Cobra framework to evaluate e-government services: a citizen-centric perspective. Gov. Inf. Q. **31**(2), 243–256 (2014)
19. Rahman, M.S., Kausel, T.: Coastal community resilience to tsunami: a study on planning capacity and social capacity, dichato, chile. IOSR J. Hum. Soc. Sci. **12**(6), 55–63 (2013)

20. Reiner, M., McElvaney, L.: Foundational infrastructure framework for city resilience. Sustain. Resilient Infrastruct. **2**(1), 1–7 (2017)
21. Rose, A.: Defining and measuring economic resilience to disasters. Disaster Prev Manag **13**(4), 307–314 (2004)
22. Schwaber, K., Beedle, M.: Agile Software Development with Scrum. Series in Agile Software Development, vol. 1. Prentice Hall Upper Saddle River (2002)
23. Sherrieb, K., Norris, F.H., Galea, S.: Measuring capacities for community resilience. Soc. Indic. Res. **99**, 227–247 (2010)
24. The DRIVER+ project for crisis management: www.driver-project.eu/. Accessed 10 Nov 2022
25. The EmerGent project: www.fp7-emergent.eu/. Accessed 10 Nov 2022
26. The EPISECC project: www.episecc.eu/. Accessed 10. Nov 2022
27. United Nations Office for Disaster Risk Reduction (UNDRR): Disaster resilience scorecard for cities. www.unisdr.org/campaign/resilientcities/toolkit/article/disaster-resilience-scorecard-for-cities. Accessed 16 Nov 2022
28. United Nations Office for Disaster Risk Reduction (UNDRR): Sendai framework for disaster risk reduction 2015–2030, www.undrr.org/publication/sendai-framework-disaster-risk-reduction-2015-2030. Accessed 10 Nov 2022
29. Yoon, D.K., Kang, J.E., Brody, S.D.: A measurement of community disaster resilience in korea. J. Environ. Planning Manage. **59**(3), 436–460 (2016)

Author Index

A

Abdullah, Atje Setiawan   276
Agray, Abir   170
Akerkar, Rajendra   358
Andreassen, Jarl   230
Anugrahwaty, Rina   261
Argyrakis, Panagiotis   185

B

Basu, Saurabh   101
Behera, Suvam Suvabrata   101
Ben Amara, Oussema   197
Benaben, Frederick   197
Bertelli, Virginia   244
Biron, Bettina   136
Bono, Carlo A.   308
Borges, Marcos R. S.   69
Bu Daher, Julie   39

C

Castro, Martha Alicia Cadavid   341
Charalabidou, Stavroula   185
Chouvardas, Konstantinos   185
Christoforou, Sofia   185
Cristaldi, Massimo   358

D

Dalela, Pankaj Kumar   101
Delprato, Uberto   358
Dias, Angélica F. S.   69
Dithisari, Indri   261
Dokas, Ioannis M.   185

E

Eden, Colin   3
Eileraas, Martin   230

F

Fijalkow, Ygal   197
França, Juliana B. S.   69
Fujita, Shono   118

G

Gandolfo, Valentino   358
Gil, Juan Camilo Sánchez   341
Giraldo, Luis Alirio López   341
Gjøsæter, Terje   55
Gonzalez, Jose J.   3

H

Hatayama, Michinori   118
Helen, Afrida   276
Hernandez, Nathalie   39
Herrera, Lucia Castro   230
Huygue, Tom   39

J

Jha, Sumit Kumar   101

K

Kamissoko, Daouda   197
Kumar, Anugandula Naveen   101
Kushwaha, Niraj Kant   101

L

Ley, Tobias   23

M

Majumdar, Sabyasachi   101
Manik, M. Rikwan E. S.   261
Marchese, Salvatore Antonio   358
Mardi, Rina Walmiaty   261
Matsuno, Yutaka   327
Matsuura, Mei   327
Meesters, Kenny   170, 215
Monika, Putri   276

© IFIP International Federation for Information Processing 2023
Published by Springer Nature Switzerland AG 2023
T. Gjøsæter et al. (Eds.): ITDRR 2022, IFIP AICT 672, pp. 375–376, 2023.
https://doi.org/10.1007/978-3-031-34207-3

Mülâyim, Mehmet Oğuz   308
Munandar, Devi   276
Munkvold, Bjørn Erik   153

N
Nasution, Benny Benyamin   261
Newton, Natasha   244
Nguyen, Hoang Long   358
Noori, Nadia Saad   230

O
Ogbonna, Uchenna   55

P
Paschalidou, Anastasia K.   185
Paupini, Cristina   55
Pernici, Barbara   308
Petersen, Laura   244
Petrou, Ilias   185
Pilemalm, Sofie   153
Pirannejad, Ali   215
Polikarpus, Stella   23
Pospisil, Bettina   136
Psistaki, Kyriaki   185

R
Radianti, Jaziar   153
Rahman, Abdul   261
Rokuse, Toshihiro   293
Ruchjana, Budi Nurani   276

S
Salsabila, Ajeng Berliana   276
Sari, Marliana   261
Sarmiento-Márquez, Edna Milena   23
Seböck, Walter   136
Sembiring, Rahmat Widia   261
Seri, Ermyna   261
Sharma, Sandeep   101
Siregar, Indra   261
Soshino, Yasuhiro   89
Sotiris, Valkaniotis   185
Soto, Guillermo León Moreno   341
Stassen, Joshua   215
Stolf, Patricia   39

T
Tarigan, Liwat   261
Tavares, Jacimar F.   69
Trombetta, Leonardo Luca   358

U
Uchida, Osamu   293

V
Vasileiou, Apostolos   185

Y
Yadav, Arun   101

Z
Zamorano, Mariano Martín   244
Zeleskidis, Apostolos   185

Printed in the United States
by Baker & Taylor Publisher Services